And So to Bath

BY CECIL ROBERTS

NEW YORK

THE MACMILLAN COMPANY

1940

PRINTED IN THE UNITED STATES OF AMERICA
AMERICAN BOOK–STRATFORD PRESS, INC., NEW YORK

AND SO TO BATH

To

HARRIET AND LOUIS PAGET

Contents

AND SO TO BATH

CHAPTER I

Concerning Rudolf and Richardson

ON A SOUTHERN SPUR OF THE CHILTERNS, where the chalk hills, crowned with beechwoods, sweep down to the Thames valley, I have a country retreat. It is, to be exact, thirty-seven and a half miles from Hyde Park Corner. From one of my three dormer windows that look southwards on to the road I can see the yellow and red motor-coach slip by, London or Oxford bound. Near by, from the old bay window of *The Golden Ball,* mine host, one hundred years ago, watched the Oxford *Defiance,* the Birmingham *Tantivy,* or the Worcester *Comet* come down the Oxford Road. A new road lies a hundred yards north of the old leafy highway and hums with traffic as we of the twentieth century "go the pace" at seventy miles an hour, just as our great-grandfathers thought they went the pace at twelve miles an hour.

But in 1838 the Western Rail Road, with a frightening disregard of life—it was declared passengers were suffocated by the speed with which they rushed through the air—had begun to kill the coach traffic. Trains were running at the terrible speed of forty miles an hour on the main lines.

The coach is once again running down the highway past my cottage, but no guard blows the tin horn as the horses go by with a clatter, after having cleared the toll-gate up at Bix. The new coach, of forty horse-power, measured by millimetres in compression cylinders, requiring not oats, but "gas," to use the American term, rarely sounds its horn, electrically operated by the chauffeur. When I want to stop the coach, I merely step forth a little into the main road, and by thus risking death, intimate that I wish to board the London motor-coach. The old horse coach achieved a maximum of twelve miles an hour; the motor-coach is permitted a maximum of thirty, which, however, is always its minimum.

Frequently I go to London by car. A moderate driver would say he could "make" the journey in one hour and a quarter, from my snug Elizabethan cottage by the tall poplars to a slim London house almost in the shadow of Buckingham Palace. Many say they can "do it" in one hour. A friend I am not very proud of, "automobilly speaking," proudly declares he "does it" in three-quarters of an hour. He is a road-hog, a horn-blaring blackguard who does all the outrageous things on the highway for which he should be sentenced to a term of hard labour. But he never has an accident, never kills or injures anyone or breaks anything, whereas my old friend Miss Whissitt, who in her wildest moments has never exceeded forty miles an hour, has had three accidents in her first nine months. None of them was serious. She killed a goat on the Henley Fairmile, one of a herd of twenty led to their roadside pasture by an old soldier on a bicycle. A week passed before she could go out again, after an experience that was *tellement tragique* as she declared, lapsing into French. Then, finding courage again, she went forth, this time with a piece of red cotton pasted on the face of the speedometer at the 30 m.p.h. mark to warn her of excessive daring.

For a fortnight all was well, but coming out of the Marlow Road into the Oxford highway, a corner deliberately narrowed and made dangerous by the authorities in order to make it "safe," Miss Whissitt caught, amidships, a local milk cart, a flimsy affair on pneumatic tyres, hand propelled. She capsized the whole freight of fifty milk bottles, a resounding performance that brought the world and its wives to the windows, and whitened the King's Highway from kerb to kerb. Like a sportsman, Miss Whissitt paid four pounds damages, and had to buy a new headlamp. But it took her a month to recover her nerve and go forth again in her rampant Austin Seven, a three-year-old of unblemished reputation heretofore. Only to me did she convey her deep conviction. "That milkman was waiting for me—*vraiment!* He knows I won't buy his cow manure for my garden because he will drive his cows past my gate, and leave the road in such a state—*c'est dégoûtant!*"

Miss Whissitt will never "do" the Henley-London journey in three-quarters of an hour, or in an hour, or in an hour and a half. My road-hog friend, by deserts, should have knocked every milk cart off the road, and have been thrice charged with manslaughter. When I protest against his hooliganism he merely smiles and says, "You see, I'm a good driver." And when I retort, "But the other fool on the road?" he shrugs his shoulders and replies, "Oh, they can't catch me." He is incorrigible.

I belong to the Whissitt school of motorists. I am over-cautious, preoccupied by the business of driving, aware of strain, glad when I am home and it is over. I close my garage doors with a sense of having escaped the clutches of Fate. I am only some thirty-seven miles from door to door, but I am relieved when I arrive. In the United States my friends gaily motor four hundred miles a day. They go to dinner-parties and picnics a hundred miles away as though it were next door. In a continent of such vast distances the proportions are all changed. I have breakfasted in Florida, lunched in Georgia and dined in Louisiana.

One thing I have in common with hardened motorists. I am so anxious to arrive that I am impatient of delay. The motorist's Euclidean axiom runs, "A journey is the shortest time between two given points." Who patronizes the innumerable inns along the wayside? Surely not the motorist, who has the greatest objection to stopping en route. I suspect that these inns are stages of delay in the dreary lives of lorry drivers.

This passion to arrive, the common affliction of motorists, has produced a curious anomaly. Never were the means of general investigation easier. We can stop where we will, for as long as we will. But do we? No. We are bound for Exeter, perhaps. We know the distance to Exeter, which means at an average of forty miles an hour we shall be there at four o'clock. And if it happens that we arrive at a quarter to four—"That's an excellent run," we exclaim, proudly.

The aviator is entitled to talk like this. He has little to see, and therefore nothing to halt him. The earth three thousand feet up is a patchwork bore. You can fly across three European countries and scarcely notice the fact; there is no noticeable change of costume, accent, or architecture. The Thames, the Seine, the Rhine and the Danube are alike, shining serpents winding through the quilted landscape.

But the motorist, had he the eyes and ears, could see and hear so much that is new and interesting. Occasionally he makes a deliberate tour, and, guide-book in hand, does the "sights" *en route*. But how many of us journey with eyes unseeing along the familiar route, timed from point to point by clock and speedometer? "Six o'clock," I say, leaving my London home, "I'll be at the cottage in nice time for dinner." And if I step into my low, flower-laden dining-room as the clock strikes half-past seven, "That was a good run," I observe to the guest I have switched out of London down the Bath Road towards my Chiltern retreat.

II

We are easily irritated by those who repeat themselves, but reiteration is not confined to old people. I began to be annoyed by a series of signposts. Once a week, sometimes two or three times a week, I make the journey from Hyde Park Corner to Henley-on-Thames. I go by the obvious route, which for a motorist means the quickest, in other words, the straightest, widest road with the best surface. So up and down the Great West Road and the Bath Road as far as Maidenhead Thicket, where I turn north for Henley and home, I have journeyed for several years. And ever on that road I saw the sign *To Bath.* I had seen it so often that I decided to go there one day, to break my natural inclination to turn off that famous road at Maidenhead Thicket.

I went for a cure, not of the waters, but of mingled irritation and curiosity. I was doing nothing singular, I was following a road as old, in part, as the Roman occupation of Britain, but there was this much of the unusual in my progress to that ancient city—I did not travel to arrive. I was determined to miss as little as possible on the way, to plunder the riches our old highways offer if only we have the patience to stop, look, listen and question.

I could have motored from London to Bath in three hours and have got out of the car at the end, preening myself on "a good run," by which we mean a long sitting. Instead of three hours I took three months, and I do not feel I wasted a minute of the time. For more than six years the first twenty miles of that road had bored me. Nay, I had grown to hate that hideous road, with its grim suburbs, fantastic factories, cheap villas, and dreary stretches of ground that looked like London's backyard. For an hour out of London I drove unconsciously, merely keeping my eyes fixed on the traffic signals and the speedometer. At Maidenhead Thicket I always turned off into the woodlands, a paradise of trees after a journey through a hell of bricks.

The manner in which my firm determination to turn off was at last broken arose from a curious incident. To explain it we must go, temporarily, to Salzburg, in Austria, at Festival Time, before the Nazi invasion destroyed that *rendez-vous* of the musical.

III

I had motored one summer from Venice to Salzburg over the stupendous mountain highway which climbs out of the Venetian plain, up beyond the torrential Piave, into the Friulian Alps and thence through the peaks of the Dolomites, via Cortina nestling in the valley under the rosy wall of the giant Monte Cristallo. A little farther north, on the frontier of Austria, one was frustrated of old by the tremendous Grossglockner range, and from lovely Heiligenblut the daring alpinist ascended through eternal snowfields to the northern side of this natural fortress wall. From the crest and its glaciers he then made a swift descent to the valley of the Salzach, to Ferleiten, Zell-am-See, and, eventually, Salzburg. Now one can make the whole journey from Venice to Salzburg by car, in two days, and Europe has nothing finer to offer in grandeur, and variety of climate and scenery than this route via the Grossglocknerstrasse.

One evening, on my arrival in Salzburg, I was sitting in the café by the river, where the Festival enthusiasts pack themselves towards sundown, and found myself jammed at a table amid a babel of English and American voices. Despite the voices the scene was overwhelmingly Tyrolean. The city, for this month of August, was given over to the worship of Toscanini, Reinhardt and Mozart, and the worshippers had one and all assumed the gay attire of the Tyrol. The *Café Bazaar* had become a scene out of *White Horse Inn,* and the stage was filled with supers in leather shorts, embroidered jackets, feathered hats, tasselled stockings, short-sleeved bodices, flowered skirts and coloured shoes. Everybody generously exhibited legs and arms of a correct sunburnt hue. It was all exhilaratingly native, except that there were no natives, and the conversation, far from being rustic or musical, followed the familiar cocktail pattern of, "She said . . ." and "I said," and "My dear, it was very funny," followed by a mirthful explosion.

A young man at our table of strangers annexed my drink. It

was an honest mistake, though an advantageous one for him. I
made no protest, but when he honourably tried to pay for my
drink I pointed out the error. He was very apologetic, and
something in his English made me suspicious. He then spoke in
fluent German to a very pretty girl at his side. "Is it possible
you aren't English or American?" I asked, in astonishment.

He laughed gaily. "No—I'm an Austrian, and I feel very
strange here," he replied.

"You are improperly dressed," I said, reprovingly, for he
wore trousers and a plain coat. There was not even a feather in
his hat. For a moment I feared he would not see the intended
humour. But he laughed again.

"Please, if I go to London may I wear a kilt—it would give
me much excitement," he asked.

"It might give us much more," I retorted. "We should like to
see a café at Stratford-on-Avon filled with Austrians all in kilts,
attending the Shakespeare Festival."

The pretty young lady clapped her hands excitedly. "Oh,
wunderbar!" she exclaimed.

At this point the young Austrian made formal introductions
of himself and his sister. They were Rudolf and Mitzi, from
Vienna, on holiday in Salzburg. I learned he was a student,
with a passion to visit London.

"Why?" I asked. "Not to wear a kilt?"

"Oh, no. Because of Richardson."

I looked a little astonished.

"Richardson?" I repeated.

"Your great writer which I read fervently."

His enthusiasm could not be doubted, despite the fact that
the name was obviously wrong. Wells, Conrad, Shaw, Gals-
worthy, Dickens, Thackeray, Shelley, Wordsworth, Shakespeare. Not one of these names could be made to sound like
Richardson.

To say that no such writer existed, at least of any considerable reputation, might hurt his feelings, so tactfully I in-

quired, "Which books of his do you like?" thinking this might give me a clue.

"Oh, *Clarissa*—it is wonderful, even more than *Pamela*."

The lad had caught me out. The forgotten, unread father of the English novel was disinterred from the eighteenth century by this Austrian student.

"Oh, Samuel Richardson!" I exclaimed, wondering by what freakish path of study this youngster had been led to an author so forgotten, so buried beneath the avalanche he provoked.

It transpired that Samuel Richardson was part of his course of English studies at the Theresianum in Vienna. When I inquired about the English poets, prepared for the usual Continental enthusiasm for Byron, I learned that he had studied Thomson's *The Seasons*. Obviously our eighteenth century was his province.

At this moment the charming young lady revealed her taste in English literature. "I most enjoy Edgar Wallace and Longfellow," she said, nervously.

Well, that was honest if simple fare, I thought, though I was no more at home with these authors than with Samuel.

We parted cordially, with a rendezvous fixed for the morrow. Later, in Vienna, I saw much of them. London, I learned from Rudolf, was his Mecca. He wished to visit the home of *Clarissa's* creator.

"But does his home exist?" I asked.

"Yes, certainly. I know of it. A moment, it is here," said Rudolf, pulling out a notebook, as we sat at the Café Schwarzenberg.

"The Grange, 111 North End Road, Hammerschmidt, London," he cried out.

"Goodness gracious! Then you must visit me and take me to see it," I said.

And thus it was Rudolf came to London. I went to North End Road, and so to Bath.

IV

Rudolf's visit had started the idea. Here I was, two or three times a week, going up and down a highway that was crammed with historical associations of which I knew nothing. I motored from Hyde Park Corner, down Kensington High Street, through Hammersmith and Chiswick, and on to the Great West Road and the Bath Road, and all it offered to me was irritation at the delays caused by traffic congestion.

Musing upon Rudolf's curious passion I became aware of the blindness which habit induces. The visit to North End Road gave me a shock of delight. I had been only dimly aware of the existence of this road. On my way out of London, in the first part of the Hammersmith Road, just after passing Olympia, I had often been checked by a policeman, holding up the main-stream of traffic, while a contributory trickle emerged from North End Road. Rudolf, as we approached his Mecca, was curious about Olympia. He looked at the grim concrete build-ing, with window slits that suggested machine-gun emplace-ments, and said: "But why do you call it Olympia—it is not Greek?"

Anything more unlike the architecture of Greece has never been devised than this concrete fortress devoted to trade exhi-bitions. But somehow I managed to make a plea for the name, if not the place, by explaining that Olympia was the ancient name of a valley in Elis, Peloponnesus, where the famous games in honour of the Olympian Zeus were held.

"And is this a valley?" asked Rudolf, with that Teutonic passion for exactitude which later made my rôle of cicerone somewhat trying.

I agreed that the Hammersmith Road might be a valley, since it ran towards the Thames.

"And you hold your Olympic Games here?" pursued Rudolf.

"Oh, no," I said, hurriedly. "It's not exactly a sports ground."

He looked puzzled, and I made a desperate wriggle to justify the name by explaining further that at ancient Olympia the Greeks had erected a building called the Altis, which had contained, besides the temple of Zeus, a stadium with baths and gymnasia. Thus it had come about that a large building in which sporting events and spectacles were presented was often called Olympia.

"But should it not be called the Altis?" asked Rudolf, very serious as he gazed at Olympia.

"Perhaps it should," I said, unable to battle with the matter any longer. "And here's your North End Road."

The policeman on point duty checked the traffic, then allowed us to turn left into the road.

"I am in great excitement to make the acquaintance of Mr. Richardson. I will take a photograph, please?" asked Rudolf.

I almost groaned. It was barely half an hour since he had arrived in London, with three suitcases now stacked up in the back of the car. When I had asked him whether he would like to see a little of London, or go down to my cottage, he eagerly decided for the cottage. "I am much tired now and not happy," he said.

"Not happy?" I queried, surprised, for his face was radiant as he stepped from the train and greeted me boisterously with "Cheerio, how do you do?" He put his hand on his stomach and looked at me, and I remembered that this was his first experience of the sea. The Channel had been choppy.

But as soon as we were speeding out of London he had asked, "Do we see Richardson's house?" I replied that we passed the road where it stood. Then he would like to see it. "The first of many excitements," he said, in his charming way.

Now, as we turned into North End Road I warned him that the house had probably been pulled down long ago. Richardson had lived there in the age of Dr. Johnson, Goldsmith, Fielding and Sterne. It was up this same road that henpecked Addison, after he had married the Dowager Countess of Warwick and taken up his abode in magnificent Holland House, had fled for a brief respite to congenial company at *The Bull and Bush*.

Certainly the beginning of the road offered no vestige of romance. Mechanical dredgers were clearing a vast site for new buildings. There was a block of new flats, some shabby shops, and, at the end of a long hoarding masking the excavations, a house, No. 111. On the face of the house there was a blue and white plaque. To my complete surprise it was the "country" home of Samuel Richardson. The plaque announced that he had written *Clarissa* there.

We got out of the car. Rudolf was jubilant. He had never doubted for a moment but that we should find the house. And what we had found was a perfect if melancholy piece of early Georgian architecture. It stood there, behind a high railing, with massive brick piers supporting decorative urns, in the most astonishing contrast with its new and vulgar neighbours. In Richardson's day it had been called "Selby Lodge." Later occupants had named it "The Grange." The name fitted it perfectly. It was a highly suitable lodging for a respectable family ghost, though none has ever been attributed to it.

The building has been divided into two houses, and one half has a sad, derelict air, as though the muses had long deserted their temple and the bats had made it their lair. But even so, what a lovely old-world countenance it presents to the blatant London that has swallowed it up! By those tall piers one can imagine the young Georgian buck waiting, with a carriage and postilions, to carry off his lady to Gretna Green, while the old squire dozes in the study. At night the linkmen arrive and the sedan chairs are set down for delicate ladies in brocade, with mountainous coiffures and patched cheeks, to alight and enter rooms soft with lit candles and the glint of silver. It may be that Mr. Richardson himself, the writer of the age, beloved of fashionable ladies as the creator of *Pamela* and *Clarissa*, is giving a dinner-party.

But it is in summer that he loves most to receive visitors in the grounds decorated with one of those grottoes which Pope made fashionable. Here, under a chestnut tree, he reads to an admiring circle a new chapter of the interminable *Clarissa*, for he is not only the first of the novelists, and the foremost, he is the most prolix. Our modern novelists who want a thousand pages in which to do themselves justice are not so original, so much masters of the garrulous manner, as they imagine. It takes Richardson the whole seven volumes of *Clarissa* to cover only eleven months in the life of his heroine, a slow-motion picture compared with the cradle-to-grave gallops of our moderns. Moreover, he struck a fashionable up-to-date note by proving that virtue is not rewarded, but suffers outrage and contumely, a view Fielding was to elaborate a little later in *Tom Jones*, destined to be *Clarissa's* rival.

Richardson wrote part of *Clarissa* at The Grange and part at his house in Salisbury Court, off Fleet Street. He had risen from being a printer's apprentice, to the ownership of a large printing establishment. He became Law-Printer to the King, and printer of the *Journals* of the House of Commons. He provided the necessitous Goldsmith with work as a printer's reader, but we know of him because when he shut the door of his shop he sat down and wrote *Pamela* and *Clarissa*. His work drew upon him the feminine adulation which now visits the film star. When his heroine Pamela triumphed, the people of Slough along the Bath Road rang their bells for joy and relief.

It was a fussy, famous little man, then, that went in and out of these imposing gates of his country retreat. In keeping with the times he was careful not to be too far out in the country, which was still regarded as a place for barbarians. The fashion liked to journey down to Kew, to my Lord Burlington at Chiswick, to Mr. Pope's famous villa at Twickenham, but no farther. Friends dropped in on a summer's day, as they now drop in on friends in Surrey, Kent, Bucks and Berks, whose retreats are a convenient call for tea after a pleasant run in the car.

Discreetly we examined the old house. Rudolf in his "excitements" would have rung the bell and trusted to his enthusiasm, but I forbade this. From sad experience I know what it is to be treated like a caretaker in a museum. So without ringing the bell we made a study of the old place.

The ruinous half was as entrancing as the preserved half. We learned from the plaque that Sir Edward Burne-Jones had lived in the house, and I wondered if it contained one of those staircases up and down which passed his wan-faced, drop-wristed damozels whose glandular throats and consumptive faces were so fashionable in the Victorian era. But Rudolf was not interested in the Pre-Raphaelite painter destined to marry the aunt of Rudyard Kipling and Stanley Baldwin, nor was he impressed when I informed him that Ruskin was a frequent visitor to the Burne-Joneses when they lived at The Grange. He was only interested in the connection with *Clarissa*, which he and twenty fellow students had read in the English course at his school. Strange that Samuel Richardson, almost forgotten in the land of his birth, should be representing English literature in an Austrian academy! Not even William Shakespeare was held in higher honour, according to Rudolf.

The ruinous half of The Grange, significantly No. 113, was occupied by someone who conducted there the most appropriate business. It was the store of a house-breaker. His stock in trade, dumped about the front garden, and in a side court which had once been an imposing carriage-way to the main entrance, consisted of leaden cherubs, cisterns, broken columns of marble, urns, classical seats and other spoils of some far-off Italian grand tour. All this paraphernalia, dusty and weather-stained, converted what might have been a dismal London backyard into the semblance of one of those *settecento* villas of Italy, whose gardens were so profusely decorated with grotesques, figurines and terminal busts. Had a gentleman in a toga come out of the house and walked across it to the Forum seat by the garden wall, I should not have felt it incongruous.

It was while we were gazing entrancedly at these old decora-

tions, noticing the ornamental urns on each corner of The
Grange, that our eyes fell upon a sundial still intact upon the
southern side. Under it was the date, 1732.

When I pointed this out Rudolf visibly jumped. Its significance was apparent. Richardson left the house in 1754 and
moved to another a few miles away, where he died in 1761. The
sundial, therefore, was there when the author of *Clarissa* was
living at The Grange. How often, arriving at his retreat, he
must have looked up at that sundial to see if he had had a
"good run" in his chaise from the City! And Mr. Pope, or Mr.
Hogarth, after some pleasant gossip with the ladies taking
coffee at Mr. Richardson's table, had glanced up on departing,
alarmed to find the summer's afternoon so rapidly gone.

Rudolf stared at the sundial, and since the sun was shining
this April morning, it told him the hour. *"Wunderbar*—my
eyes see what Mr. Richardson saw," he exclaimed, excitedly.

But as he was looking intently at Mr. Richardson's sundial
my eyes had seen something that was even more astonishing.
At the back of the courtyard there was an old coach-house with
a wide carriage entrance. Through this entrance, in all the
splendour of its spring green, stretched a long lawn and leafy
garden, shaded with trees.

It was such an astonishing sight lying there, between great
blocks of buildings, excavations, and rows of drab Victorian
villas, that I could scarcely credit the existence of this ancient
garden. Here, where one could hear the roar of traffic along the
Hammersmith Road, while automatic shovels clattered, and
great cranes whined, lay an Elysian retreat, the same in which
Samuel had escorted his adoring ladies, on whose green turf
and in whose green shade he had read the latest progress of
Clarissa. And all this only three minutes away from that press
of traffic! By what miracle had it escaped the destructive hand
of man through two centuries of building, road-making and
slumification of a London suburb?

We tore ourselves away at last, and while Rudolf excitedly

chattered about this adventure—he must write to his friends at once, perhaps a postcard or a photograph could be obtained? —I was thinking, as I threaded my car through the maze of traffic towards Hammersmith Broadway, how blind and neg- lectful swift transport had made us, through what treasures of history we rushed, anxious that the car behind us should not pass, the omnibus in front of us should not block our way, the green traffic lights not flicker over to the arresting yellow. Here had I been for more than six years, motoring up and down this road, blind to the ghosts that haunted it, to the panorama stretching across the centuries. Scarcely a minute's journey down a by-street, I had been made to discover, through the curiosity of a visiting foreigner, a perfect vignette of the age of Dr. Johnson, set between Victorian villas, a car park, a block of flats and a bus route!

Supposing, starting from Hyde Park Corner, I examined every mile of this monotonous highway down which I fled with such impatience to reach the garden peace of my cottage in its Chiltern valley? Supposing I learned all I could of this hideous main route from London? Might it not offer even more surpris- ing rewards than that we had just discovered?

The idea lingered in my mind all the way home. Preoccupied, I said little to my companion until he asked me a question as we ran down the Great West Road, mile on mile, and then along the Colnbrook by-pass.

"Why have you so many swim-places?" he said.

"Swim-places—do you mean swimming-pools? We've only passed one, at a road-house on the Great West Road," I an- swered.

"I have counted six."

"No—you're mistaken," I said.

A quarter of an hour later he suddenly exclaimed, "There— it is another swim-place."

I looked and laughed. "To Bath" ran a sign. I explained that Bath was a city not a swim-place.

"We go there?"

"Not now."

"Some day?"

"Some day," I replied.

It occurred to me, then, that I had been going to Bath "some day" for the last six years, but I had always turned off the Bath Road, anxious to get home "in good time." I would break this tyranny of custom. I really would go to Bath, very soon, and very slowly.

So, in a manner, it was Rudolf and Richardson who created this book.

CHAPTER II

The Way Out

IT IS A MOOT QUESTION whether Bath was founded by the Romans or the pigs. If we accord the honour to the latter we accept the pleasant legend that gives Prince Bladud, the father of King Lear, and of a family destined to misfortune, the honour of having discovered the place.

The prince, heir to the sceptre of Britain centuries and centuries ago, was beloved by his father, King Hudibras. Alas, this darling of the court contracted the dread disease of leprosy and he had to suffer banishment. Amid the tears of his parents, and the mourning of the courtiers who loved the bright youth, he departed, keeping only a ring given to him by his Queen Mother, as a mark of royal blood, in the event that, cured, he should return to human society.

At Keynsham, near Bath, he obtained work as a swineherd, and forthwith contaminated the herd. Alarmed by this development, and afraid to return to his master, he drove his herd across the river Avon to an opposite meadow, giving as his reason that the acorns were more plentiful there. From this place, since called Swineford, he gradually ascended the surrounding hills, in the hollows of which sprang secret springs. The swine soon discovered the water and proceeded to indulge their love of filth. The distracted prince finally succeeded in dislodging them from their quagmire, but when, that evening, he came to wash them down, he discovered they were rid of their leprosy.

Since the swine were cured the young prince thought there must be virtues in these springs, and straightway went and wallowed himself. He emerged, cured of leprosy, drove back his pigs in joy to his master, procured his release, and set forth for his father's court where he was received with great joy. In honour of the place that had cured him he uncovered the springs, made baths and founded a royal city, where he reigned happily for many years.

Here the legend might well end, but, alas, it goes on to a disastrous finale. King Bladud lived on until he suffered from senile decay, for this can be the only reason for his sudden passion to fly like a bird. One day he leapt from the pinnacle of a temple to Minerva, which he had erected at Bath, confident of his power to fly. He crashed, and that was the end of King Bladud, founder of Bath.

The legend that Bath water cured leprosy seems to have persisted down the centuries, for there is the carved testimony of "William Berry, of Galthorp, near Melton Mowbray, County of Leicester, cured of a dry leprosy by the help of God and Bath, 1737."

In 1699 the inhabitants of Bath had little doubt about King Bladud and dates, for they put up a statue to him which boldly declared he was the eighth king of the Britons descended from "Brute, a great philosopher and mathematician bred at Athens" and that he had founded the baths in 863 B.C.

This declaration firmly wipes out all Roman claims to have founded the city. But there is visible evidence that the Romans established elaborate baths there. They called the place Aquae Solis, and the first London to Bath Road became thronged with the chariots of officers and officials on leave, who went there to take the waters, and to hibernate in one of the warmest spots in Britain. Part of that Roman road has never been lost, and the traveller to Bath to-day proceeds over its course. It is a curious fact that the standard gauge of our first railways was determined by the Romans. For they made roads to correspond with the width of the Roman wagons, these in turn seemed to have determined the width of our stage coaches and wagons, and they in turn that of our first railways.

The Roman road from London to Bath was part of a great thoroughfare running from the east coast to the west; from Camulodunum (Colchester), ancient capital of King Cymbeline, through Londinium (London), straight on to Pontes (Staines), thence to Calleva (Silchester), through Spinae (Speen), Cunetio (Marlborough), on to Aquae Solis (Bath), and the port of Abona (Bristol). The road, therefore, may be said to have run from the ancient kingdom of King Cymbeline to that of King Lear. We can complete the evocation of Shakespeare's name by observing that Stratford-on-Avon was connected with a great Roman highroad, the Foss Way, which still runs through Warwickshire down through Bath.

We are apt to forget how long the Romans were with us, how settled was their civilization on this island. They ruled longer than any dynasty of Saxon kings, for they were here, well established, from A.D. 43 to A.D. 410. I cannot leave my garden gate without walking upon a road they cut through from the Thames to their camp at Dorcina (Dorchester) in the Oxfordshire plain. In the lovely Hambleden valley, by the Thameside, near to me, they have left the remains of their villas, and in the village museum you may see their domestic utensils, the stiluses with which they wrote to Rome, probably informing cousin Caius Plautus that the summer in Britain was the worst they had ever known.

A Roman living in Britain might be descended from ten generations of British-born Romans, and at school he would learn about the distant and glorious reign of Claudius Caesar in Britain, or of the Emperor Hadrian and the building of the great north wall, just as to-day we are taught the history of Queen Elizabeth's reign, and the defeat of the Armada. There was a long period when the Brito-Roman must have felt that the hundreds of years of peace and good government behind him were a sure guarantee of their continuance for his descendants. Alas, what a long night of horror descended when Rome weakened and withdrew. The fine temples, baths and villas disappeared into the darkness of the fifth century.

The roads were not so easily destroyed; some parts were quarried, but they were too long and too solid to suffer complete extinction. When the Londoner drives down Holborn and Oxford Street, along Hyde Park and through Notting Hill he is following the old Roman road. It goes on through Shepherd's Bush, is lost for a time and is again encountered at Chiswick, where it skirts the Thames, passes through Brentford and Hounslow and drives straight on to Staines, the ancient Pontes. Thence it crossed the Thames, and ran west to Silchester. We shall find it again at Newbury and Marlborough, and pick it up from time to time as we near Bath.

How did these Romans contrive to carry their roads so straight across dense forests and wildernesses, across country they could not see distantly? On the whole the straightness of their roads is remarkable, though they were not stubborn, and veered to avoid nasty obstacles. They had a most comprehensive understanding of the problems to be faced, the characteristics of the country to be traversed. Where possible they did not deviate more than a quarter of a mile in a thirty-mile track. Try to dig a straight rut across an acre field and you will appreciate their skill. When the motorist lets himself go "all out" on that straight road to Staines he should remember that a long-dead Roman engineer planned his track.

How was it done? A favourite method was the smoke-signal, which, for instance, from Staines could be picked up at Notting Hill. They also worked from extreme points to intermediate points, bringing the visible intermediate points into line. Their roads are still the wonder of the world, and again and again, going to Bath, we shall have cause to recall their achievement.

II

The era of travel in England may be said to have opened with the stage-coach. It was the wonder of the age. It provoked a road problem and a speed problem, it gave birth to countless inns and highwaymen. Journeys which had taken a week on horseback were now accomplished with the comparative comfort of the stage-coach in three days. But the coachman took your life in his hands. If you escaped the highwayman you probably fell into the ditch or the bog, or were buried in the snowdrift or lost in the fog. The coaches were often dubbed "God-permits," for you arrived God-willing. Rain, sleet, and snow beat down upon the passengers. Innkeepers lied about the perils ahead to detain customers in their beds; drunken drivers took the wrong turning, a frost brought down the horses, the mud engulfed the coach up to its axles. The bright stage-coach of the merry Christmas card was almost a thing of fiction. It existed only on fine days and jolly days when the spanking team flew along the King's highway to the tootling of the guard on his yard-long horn. Inside, passengers almost died of stenches; outside, passengers sometimes died of cold. Until the Turnpike Acts did something to improve the roads, coaches often capsized, or lost the road, or sank into it. To travel was to embark on an adventure.

It is hard to realize that through fifteen centuries, beginning with the Roman era, travellers in Britain had only one means of transport. It is true the Elizabethans, if very rich, had coaches, but even the great Eliza complained bitterly that she could not sit down after a coach journey. She therefore preferred her horse, and by horseback the world and his wife travelled about England, except the very few who could afford and were prepared to take the risks of a private coach.

And with the private coach often went a guide to show the road. Pepys, on his way back from Bath in 1668, hired such a guide, yet nevertheless got lost between Newbury and Reading. Nor, given even a fair road and good conditions, was progress rapid. If the coachman drove too fast he was in danger of fire. The wheels created a perilous friction on the axles. Just as in the early days of motoring one had to let the radiator cool off, so also the coach-driver had to let his axles cool down. One driver of a wagon, laden with the scenery of the Bath Theatre, ignored the warnings shouted to him as he crossed the Salisbury Plain in 1759. He merely laughed, for had he not come twelve miles with his wheels smoking all the way? But ere he reached Salisbury the wagon burst into flames and two thousand pounds worth of scenery and costumes were consumed.

The public coach opened a new era of travel. Later it was referred to as a "slow coach," a term that, applied subsequently to human beings, is considered uncomplimentary. But a time soon came when the slow coach was speeded up. So great became its speed it took on the name "flying machine," and, accordingly, we find one announced to "fly" from London to Bath in the astounding time of three days.

"All those desirous to pass from London to Bath, or any other place on their Road, let them repair to the *Bell Savage* on Ludgate Hill in London, and the *White Lion* at Bath, at both of which places they may be received in a Stage Coach every Monday, Wednesday, and Friday, which performs the Whole Journey in Three Days (if God permits) and sets forth at five o'clock in the morning."

The cost of this miraculous flight through space was twenty-five shillings, the equivalent of a hundred shillings to-day. Fourteen pounds weight of luggage was allowed.

The fashionable flight to Bath had not set in, in 1667, when this announcement appeared. Fifty years later the Bath Road was crammed with stage-coaches, and the élite of the kingdom were speeding to the City of Springs, either in the public coach or in their own private equipages. And on a fine summer's morning what a dashing spectacle these coaches must have made, gaily painted, fantastically named—the *Regulator,* the *York House,* the *Beaufort Hunt*—with the jingle of harness, the clop-clop of the well-groomed horses, the red-faced driver high on the box, with a flower in his buttonhole, the guard blowing cheerily on his horn as they approached the roadside inn.

The "quality" went in their own coaches. A dashing blade, who cared little for the cost, went down in a pair-horsed post, with a yellow-jacketed, high-gaitered post-boy driving it hell-for-leather and trying to make it keep pace with the stage-coach's ten miles per hour. As for the man who wished to travel cheap, there was the stage-wagon that lumbered along at four miles an hour, a kind of carrier's cart that stopped anywhere along the route.

The grand era of the Bath Road coincided with Beau Nash, who brought the traffic along it, an era of prodigiously rich and intolerant aristocrats, of swaggering gallants in wigs, embroidered waistcoats, knee-breeches, buckled shoes and sword on thigh, of ladies with powder and patches, and periodic attacks of the "vapours," of wild gamblers, pimps, and those nondescript, handsome gentry, ever with us, whose stock-in-trade is a broken accent, sex-appeal, and a background of romantic misfortune.

At the opening of the eighteenth century, at the very time when impecunious young Mr. Richard Nash travelled by stage-coach to the City of Infinite Opportunities, the turnpike system was rapidly changing the face of England. In the first seventy years of the century over five hundred turnpike trusts had been created. The erection of toll-bars, to levy a tax for using the roads, aroused a storm of protest, and there was a powerful opposition, from politicians, economists, and the general public, against the monstrous taxation for the making of roads. Who wanted roads, sir? Only a lot of wild, young road-hogs.

Is there merit to gallop dead drunk in the dark
On a plain turnpike road, as plain as Hyde Park,
Where Londoners fine may tittup along,
And coaches may pass and repass in a throng?
No, sir, though a blockhead, I won't be a knave;
Good roads are the glory of Papist and slave.

These lines reveal a good mixture of bigotry and old fogey-ism, but the jingle voiced public feeling. Hyde Park had had tolls even before the erection of the highway toll-gate, for Evelyn in his *Diary*, dated April 11, 1653, complained, "I went to take the aire in Hyde Park, where every coach was made to pay a shilling, and horse sixpence, by the sordid fellow who had purchased it of the State." Later, when a regular toll-gate was established at Hyde Park Corner, it was leased for seven thousand pounds. These gates were changed from time to time, until at last they were esteemed to be truly elegant, ac-cording to the *Examiner*, in 1813.

"Near Hyde Park Corner on the south side of the road, stands St. George's Hospital. The Grand Western entrance here into the Me-tropolis is marked by an ascent from Knightsbridge to the Turnpike at Hyde Park Corner, and the enchanting view which in every quar-ter attracts the eye forms such an assemblage of picturesque beauty as is seldom to be met with at the entrance of a vast and populous city. The toll houses and their multiplicity of lamps add also to the variety of the scene, which at night exhibits an uncommon degree of lustre from the several lamps, at once useful and ornamental."

But Cobbett, who had a nose for grievances, did not look with admiration on the toll-gate. He pointed out that there was a way into Hyde Park on one side of the gate, and a way out of Hyde Park on the other side of the gate, and that those who kept a carriage were allowed to go in at one gate and out at the other and thus evade the toll.

It is over a hundred years since Cobbett made his complaint, but I think of him whenever I drive up to Hyde Park Corner,

for coming up Grosvenor Place by St. George's Hospital I do a
little traffic-dodging, as the carriage folk did a little toll-dodg-
ing, by going straight across and in at one gate of Hyde Park,
and then coming out of another lower down on the Kensington
Road.

There is still a hill down to Knightsbridge, though to-day we
scarcely notice small inclines in London. Once it led down into
the village of Knightsbridge, but this western side of the turnpike was a perilous place, for the road was in an execrable state
and many a coach became stuck in the mud. Gradually an improvement was effected, and Sloane Street became such a civ-
ilized area that the Commissioners of the Hyde Park Toll Trust
held their monthly court of jurisdiction at *The Feathers Tavern*
there. These monthly courts were followed by a prodigious
feast and the critics of turnpikes asserted that gluttony and
rapacity were well matched.

Hyde Park Corner was not the first of the toll-gate entrances
to London. It was moved there in 1721 from Piccadilly, near
Berkeley Street and the present Ritz Hotel. The Hyde Park
Corner site was used until 1825, when London was all country
beyond, with Kensington Palace two miles away, to which the
Court went when it wanted quiet and country air. Up till the
beginning of the nineteenth century Knightsbridge and Kensington were dangerous domains, the passenger having to encounter mud, footpads and mounted desperadoes with horse-
pistols. Prince of Wales Gate is near the site of an old inn,
Halfway House, where the highwaymen's spies had their headquarters. Even the *Bristol and Bath Mail* was raided, and, as
late as 1750, a highwayman was caught here, red-handed, and
hanged at Tyburn. The fashionable houses of this Kensington
highway look on a former scene of murder and highway robbery.

But we must hurry on out of London. Kensington itself lies
ahead. We may glance wonderingly at the site of *Halfway*

House, which, between the demolition of the inn in 1848 and
the erection of a block of flats in 1937, grew in value from
£6,000 to £204,000, a good turnover in less than a century.

I halt occasionally at the home of a fellow novelist down Victoria Road, just before one enters Kensington High Street. He
lives in a house that is buried behind cherry and almond blossom in springtime. In a villa that might well stand on a cliff
overlooking the Mediterranean, he writes frightening crime
stories that have a great vogue with a law-abiding public. It
was just by Victoria Road, between 1856 and 1864, that the
first of the toll-gates out of London was encountered by the
traveller to Bath. It demanded a halfpenny toll, which resulted
in the gate being known as the Halfpenny Hatch. Beyond this
lay the pleasant village of Kensington and the wide, open
spaces towards Hammersmith and Chiswick.

Before coming to the place of this old toll-gate, and my
friend's retreat, we have passed the Albert Hall, whose site,
prior to 1857, was occupied by Gore House. Let us halt the car
and meditate, not on the engaging proposal that the Albert
Memorial should have been placed on the top of the Albert
Hall, but on the astonishing and pathetic history of Gore
House's beautiful inhabitant. We are on our way to Bath, the
haunt of Beau Nash and the dandies; we are now passing the
home of the last of those dandies, Count d'Orsay.

CHAPTER III

The Ghosts of Kensington

It was to Gore House, in March 1836, that the Countess of Blessington and her *ami*, Count d'Orsay, came from Seamore Place. The world had no doubt about the relationship of one of the most beautiful women of the age with one of its handsomest men. Almost a century had to pass before Mr. Michael Sadler cleared their characters, with a solution that is as sad as it is singular. The Blessington story surpasses fiction in every chapter of its sad progress. Lovely Sally Power was sold by her father into marriage at the age of fifteen. Her husband, Mr. Farmer, was a sadistic brute. He beat her and drove her back to her home after three months of married life. Three years later her drunken father was charged with murder, following a raid on rebel Irish peasantry, and a kindly young officer succeeded in inducing the frightened girl to join his household.

For five years young Mrs. Farmer lived with this Captain Jenkin and his relatives. It was in his house that she met Lord Mountjoy, then in his early thirties, and enjoying an income of thirty thousand pounds a year. Volatile, a dilettante, restless but energetic, he pursued a career of complete futility. A liaison with a Mrs. Browne had made him the father of two children. In a desire to make his relationship with the lady more regular he married her, only to see her first husband, Major Browne, walk into their house a few weeks later! Very sympathetically Browne again vanished, to avoid embarrassing the pair. Mount-

joy, uneasy in his conscience, again married Mrs. Browne, only
to receive news soon after the wedding that Major Browne had
at last but too tardily died! The lady bore Mountjoy two more
children, legitimate this time, and then died. Mountjoy gave her
a four-thousand pound funeral, forgot her, and went to visit
Captain Jenkin, where he encountered and fell in love with
Jenkin's Mrs. Farmer, whose husband still lived somewhere!
No French comedy could provide a better "situation" than this.

In 1816 Mountjoy became the Earl of Blessington. He then
proposed to "buy" Mrs. Farmer from Jenkin for ten thousand
pounds, and to instal her in a suitable establishment until such
time as the long lost Mr. Farmer could be found and settled
with. The bargain was struck, the farce proceeded to its next
act. Mrs. Farmer was housed in Manchester Square, but the
Earl's attentions throughout were strictly honourable. The search
for Mr. Farmer began, and the matter was scarcely afoot when
that drunken gentleman obligingly fell from an upper window
and killed himself. The way was now clear for witty, beautiful
Margaret Farmer to become Countess of Blessington, in 1818,
after a splendid wedding.

But this was only the opening act of an incredible drama.
The happy couple moved to a town house in St. James's Square.
Her wit and beauty and her great natural gift as a hostess,
allied with her husband's rank and wealth, served to conquer
London—almost. Their dinners and soirées became famous.
Politicians and authors thronged the Blessington *salon*. Then
one day the Duc de Guiche brought to St. James's Square his
brother-in-law, a youth of incredible beauty and elegance. He
was Alfred, Comte d'Orsay, a wit, a fine horseman, a dandy of
surpassing manners. He became a favourite in the household.
A little later the Blessingtons left for the Continent, with Count
d'Orsay in attendance.

Thus it began. Blessington, wealthy, volatile, half-crazy; the
Countess, lovely, witty, kind, but overshadowed by her dreadful early experience; d'Orsay, handsome, vain, extravagant,

idle and clever, the noble lord's fancy and protégé as well as milady's exquisite page—they set forth, with heavy scandal among their luggage. The world reached an easy verdict. D'Orsay was Lady Blessington's paramour, the Earl a blind cuckold whose wealth made the going good; but the obvious verdict was incorrect, for d'Orsay was impotent. All Lady Blessington's instincts were maternal, and the Earl was vaguely perverse. He was a connoisseur of beauty and cherished both objects in his domestic collection.

The Continent could not ignore this trio. Such beauty, wealth, wit and elegance commanded attention. They made a triumphal progress. They travelled with an immense cavalcade of carriages, servants, furniture, plate and glass. The Blessington Circus it was called. D'Orsay had resigned his commission, to be aide-de-camp to the Blessington household. It was like an army marching; to Paris, Geneva and Grenoble they journeyed, and then to Avignon for a halt of three months. After Avignon they gravitated towards Genoa, and Byron. He was then a lodestar to travelling constellations, particularly if a similar mist of scandal clouded their brilliance. Moreover, Lady Blessington was writing. She kept a copious Journal.

She found Byron tawdry and vulgar, but fascinating. They came to appreciate each other. Wrote Byron: "Miladi is the Miladi of whom Lawrence made a picture that set all London raving." Exactly twenty-six years later, to a day, that Lawrence portrait was knocked down to a bid of £336 at the Gore House sale of the lady's furniture. The buyer was Lord Hertford, and via him it went into the Wallace Collection and thus now lives in that Manchester Square where Lord Blessington "stored" the original sitter for a time.

Byron was then living with the Contessa Guiccioli. The result of this visit was a lively book called *Conversations of Lord Byron with the Countess of Blessington*. It reveals Lady Blessington's literary skill, as well as her singular personality and her great tact as a hostess. There now followed another

strange act in the drama. Blessington's only legitimate son by
his first wife died. He proceeded to settle his vast Irish estate
and revenue on Count d'Orsay, who had completely fascinated
him. The reason of this amazing act was based on the fact that
an "engagement" had been made between d'Orsay and either of
Blessington's two daughters, neither of whom he had ever seen,
and who were respectively eleven and twelve years old! Out of
this monstrous settlement Lady Blessington received an annual
charge of three thousand pounds. There was a useless stipulation that d'Orsay's marriage should not be consummated for
four years.

This fantastic arrangement had only one interpretation for
the world. When d'Orsay married the daughter it seemed a
clear case that Lady Blessington and d'Orsay had conspired to
seize Blessington's fortune and make the daughter a mask for
their base liaison. Actually Lady Blessington did nothing but
dutifully accept her husband's scheme.

The Blessington circus now moved to Naples and took the
palace of Prince Belvedere on the Vomero. In this paradise,
Lady Blessington, in the zenith of her beauty and good fortune,
began to entertain. Blessington had returned from Ireland with
a handsome young architect, the son of Charles Mathews the
actor, and with these two youths in her court Lady Blessington
made her excursions, but the two cockatoos soon set each
other's feathers flying.

Four years passed, then d'Orsay took his bride, and she was
brought over to the Blessington circus. The marriage was a fail-
ure from the beginning. One morning, in May 1829, the Earl of
Blessington lay dead. Immediately afterwards scandal was
loose, and a garbage sheet printed its comment:

"This young gentleman (d'Orsay), Lady Blessington, and the
virgin bride of twenty-six, all live together. You must surely remember a lady who, some fifteen years ago, was acting wife to a Captain J."

This effusion of a blackmailing journalist helped on the ruin of Lady Blessington's public character. She challenged the scandal boldly by coming to London. She rented a house in Seamore Place and made a costly bid for the leadership of social and artistic London. She challenged at once an enemy in the same world, Lady Holland, whose *salon* was well established.

Lady Blessington's wit, beauty and tact soon made her a formidable rival. The house was perfectly equipped. Statesmen, diplomats, soldiers, men of letters, artists, all the lions of London flocked to her brilliant dinners.

Meanwhile, d'Orsay, premier dandy, was squandering his new fortune. His marriage came unstuck in 1831. His wife joined the enemy's camp. An attack was made on Blessington's will, with no definite benefit for either party, but it gave fuel to the scandal now blazing. D'Orsay was piling up debts, Lady Blessington was overspending her modest income. By 1832 she was merely acting a rôle which previously had made no tax on her great natural gifts. A friend wrote, "After a lapse of two or three years my acquaintance with her was renewed at Gore House. There was no happiness in the circles of Gore House comparable to that of the Palazzo Belvedere in Naples . . . the conversation generally was no longer of that peculiarly gay, enlivening and cheerful character, which made the great charm of the Palazzo Belvedere and, in a minor degree, of Seamore Place."

She had now to find means of augmenting her income. She turned to authorship. The receptions and dinners went on, but she wrote assiduously. Now in the early forties, she was still a very beautiful woman, with natural grace of manner added to her bright mind. Her memoirs of Byron began to appear. She then wrote a three-volume novel. She made levies on her friends. "Wherever a man of note was to be found the enterprising Irish lady was sure to press him into her service," wrote Grantley Berkeley, who lived farther along the road to Bath. But work and entertaining were wearing her down. In 1836 she moved to

Gore House. She reduced her social activities and sat longer at her desk.

Gore House was then almost in the country. It had been, from 1808 to 1821, the home of anti-slavery Wilberforce, which resulted in a wag writing:

Mild Wilberforce, by all beloved,
Once owned this brilliant spot
Whose zealous eloquence improved
The fetter'd negro's lot.

Yet here still slavery attacks
When Blessington invites:
The chains from which he freed the blacks
She rivets on the whites.

The house was a small palace, standing back behind its high wall with the double entrance gates. It had three acres of gardens on the south side, and the large rooms ran the whole width of the house, from north to south. There was a library, a long gallery, two studies, and a suite of entertaining rooms.

Count d'Orsay, true to his *genre,* proved an admirable interior decorator. He established himself in a small house adjoining the grounds, and had a large studio for his artistic work in a half basement on the south side of Gore House. One new note in the decoration set a fashion that has endured. The book shelves were enamelled white. The doors were panelled with mirrors, the sofas and chairs were covered in apple-green damask, the drawing-room was crimson and gold, the long gallery and library were green, and Lady Blessington's own bedroom was blue and gold, with blue damask hangings to the large Malmaison bed. The note of luxury predominated, and there was nothing to indicate an owner feeling the financial strain.

The garden on to which these pleasant rooms looked possessed noble trees, and was enclosed in old red-brick walls. The south terrace was ablaze with lilacs. In this garden there was a menagerie of pets, gold and silver pheasants, pigeons, a poodle, a parrot, a greyhound and a well-stocked aviary. All London soon flocked to Gore House, where the entertaining was on the old lavish style. The Duke of Wellington, Bulwer Lytton, Walter Savage Landor, the young Dickens, the faltering Contessa Guiccioli, and Prince Louis Napoleon Bonaparte were among her visitors.

There was one other, an adventurous young Jew, a dandy and crony of d'Orsay's, who came when he could—Mr. Benjamin Disraeli. But in 1836 he was in sore financial straits, following upon the pace d'Orsay had set him, and he dared not venture afield "for fear of my being nabbed" for debt. He had even to decline the chance of proposing a toast of "the House of Lords" at a Conservative banquet because the writ-servers were dogging him. So he kept himself immured down at Bradenham and busily wrote *Venetia* for a publisher's cheque.

In February, 1837, he ventured forth to Gore House on a visit of several weeks, during which he revised the proofs of *Venetia,* with Lady Blessington's help. Landor also came up from Bath, where he had settled after the breaking up of his family life. She gave a party for the irascible lion. He loved Gore House, came often, and had a favourite seat on the terrace amid the lilac trees, where he talked brilliantly with his hostess, d'Orsay and Disraeli.

All seemed well on the surface; the parties were as thronged, the dinners as lavish, the wit as bright, but Lady Blessington was tiring. Her health began to break under the strain of much writing. The spendthrift d'Orsay turned artist and became the rage as a society portraitist. Lady Blessington worked harder than ever. Her unfailing kindness of heart responded to every appeal, and they were many, made by unfortunate relatives and friends.

And then, suddenly, a crack was seen in the bright façade of Gore House. In 1841 it became public knowledge that d'Orsay was insolvent. He had to remain behind walls, except on Sundays and after sunset, to escape writ-servers and the debtor's prison. Lady Blessington tried to keep a cheerful face throughout. But sorrows fell fast upon her now. Some she loved deeply died. Then, in 1846, following the potato blight and the famine in Ireland, the trustees informed her that the Blessington estates had no revenue with which to pay her jointure. In the same year her publisher went bankrupt.

She was ill, tired, written out. For another year she battled on while the bailiffs prowled outside, but the doors were shut to everyone between sunrise and sunset. A grim siege followed. At the very hour when Gore House was about to crash, one who had enjoyed its safety in his days of exile, Prince Louis Napoleon, was about to regain his country.

Meanwhile a crisis approached for the irresponsible, vain d'Orsay. From 1832–1841 he had lived in prodigal splendour. He dazzled the age with his horsemanship, his clothes, his wit, his imperturbable calm and good nature in all circumstances. He cheerfully ignored the scandal attached to his name, to the shady circumstances of his marriage with Blessington's daughter, and the conditions by which he inherited part of the Blessington fortune. He pranced gaily through life, intoxicatingly handsome, consistently selfish. But the curtain fell in 1841. He fled from his own little house, on a threat of arrest for debt, and took shelter within the walls of Gore House.

A curious law established the fact that a debtor could not be served with a writ or arrested for debt between sundown and sunrise on weekdays, nor at any hour on Sundays. This immunity resulted in much hide and seek among debtors. So on Sundays d'Orsay boldly emerged from the gates of Gore House and went riding with his friends. On weekdays he tried to make a little money by portraiture. His sitters had to knock at the gates, and prove their identity before admittance. The guard satisfied, they were conducted past two great mastiffs to the studio door in the garden. Even the great Duke of Wellington, of whom he made an equestrian statuette, visited him under these conditions.

But there came a fatal day when the enemy invaded the citadel. Late one afternoon, in April, 1849, a pastry-cook's errand boy knocked at the back door of Gore House. He was admitted to the kitchen and delivered his goods, but instead of walking out, he went upstairs to the Count's dressing-room. He knocked, and on being challenged by the dandy, who was dressing, the young man walked into the room, and showed the astonished occupant the badge of a sheriff's officer.

Even then d'Orsay proved imperturbable. He asked the officer to sit down while he finished his toilet. For well over an hour the famous dandy fascinated the law's representative by an elaborate ritual of dress. Throughout this performance d'Orsay was watching the sun sinking in the west. As soon as it was set he very courteously informed his dupe that the writ no longer ran. The outwitted fellow was shown to the gates by a servant.

D'Orsay had won, for the moment, but alarm spread through the house. Lady Blessington herself had just received a summons for debt from one of the tradesmen. Plainly the siege could not be fought off. Unlike d'Orsay, she was not insolvent and not, therefore, in fear of prison. But her mind was made up. She made plans for the Count's escape, and at three o'clock one Sunday morning, accompanied by a valet, bearing a portmanteau and a jewelled umbrella, the mirror of fashion fled from Gore House and was safe in France by that evening.

The Countess now faced her creditors and obtained their permission to sell the entire contents of Gore House. She wrote letters of farewell to Landor, Lytton and Disraeli, packed a few personal belongings and left England. On May 4, 1849, a curious crowd swarmed through Gore House, and three days later a twelve-days' sale began of the "costly and elegant effects of the Rt. Honble the Countess of Blessington, retiring to the Continent."

Her enemies triumphantly marched through the rooms, turning over her things. Virtue had triumphed over vice. Yet a kinder, less selfish woman, nor one of more wit and beauty, the century had not produced. "The armchair in which the lady of the mansion was wont to sit was occupied by a stout, coarse gentleman of the Jewish persuasion, engaged in examining a marble hand," wrote a friend, sadly. "It was the most signal ruin of an establishment I ever witnessed. Here was a total smash, a crash on a grand scale of ruin."

One acquaintance of better days was there, Thackeray, deeply moved by the sad scene. "I have just come away from a dismal sight—Gore House full of snobs looking at the furniture. Foul Jews, odious bombazine women; brutes keeping their hats on in the kind old drawing-room—I longed to knock some of them off and say: Sir, be civil in a lady's room! Ah, it was a strange, sad picture of Vanity Fair!"

A few old friends bought in some of her effects. Bulwer Lytton bought a set of Byron's works bound with her arms, and sent them to her in Paris, where d'Orsay had received tardy recognition of his consistent support of Prince Louis Napoleon, now President of France.

The Gore House sale was a success in that it more than covered the Countess's debts. Many of her old friends flocked to her when she arrived in Paris, but her valiant spirit was broken. Within twenty-four hours of entering her new apartment, she was dead, scarcely a month after the Gore House sale. She had still a respectable income, but she was worn out with overwork, anxieties, and the knowledge that the bubble of social success had burst. She had begun with a wretched childhood in Ireland, known fame for her rank, wit and beauty, and had died, with all illusions shattered, in a foreign land.

Years later, old Walter Savage Landor, recalling the lilac trees on the terrace at Gore House, in whose shade he had so often enjoyed the feast of wit and beauty, wrote:

White and dim purple breathed my favourite pair
Under thy terrace, hospitable heart,
Whom twenty summers more and more endeared;
Part on the Arno, part where every clime
Sent its most graceful sons to kiss thy hand,
To make the humble proud, the proud submiss,
Wiser the wisest, and the brave more brave.

II

When, to-day, I motor past the Albert Hall, on my way to the Great West Road, it is not of the rotunda that I think, but of Gore House that stood in pleasant grounds where the terra-cotta concert hall now rises. I wonder at what spot in the van-ished garden wall the sham pastry-cook gained entrance and proved to the Countess and the dandy that the siege was near-ing its end.

One evening while sitting in a stall in the vast arena of the Albert Hall and listening to Paderewski, a young dandy in front of me, fidgeting with his tie, suddenly switched my mind from Liszt's *Rapsodie Hongroise* to Count d'Orsay. Was it on this very spot that Count d'Orsay had tied his bow so elaborately to defeat the sheriff's officer? An absurd but not wholly irrelevant thought; perhaps the fidgety young beau in front of me was disturbed by the *genius loci*. And I no longer saw Paderewski at the long piano, playing a Liszt *Rapsodie Hongroise* to an en-thralled audience, but another pianist of genius, who on the evening of September 12, 1843, had sat perhaps in that very spot, in the *salon* of Lady Blessington.

"Dined with Lady B., where, after dinner, Liszt played and Rubini sang," recorded a guest, Baron Philipp von Neumann. Closing my eyes, it was not difficult to imagine I was hearing Liszt, sitting with other guests on that long-forgotten evening. Fame has remembered the Abbé, and Lady Blessington is a faint legend, but who remembers the great Rubini, the tenor who invented the "sob" and the "vibrato"?

I have one slight link with the drama played out on this spot. When a very small boy I was sent once a week to a dowdy little villa in a provincial town to have a painting lesson, for it was an era when small boys and girls had to learn two "genteel" things, to play the piano and to paint. Few of them ever achieved any proficiency in either, but progress was considered to be praiseworthy when the small pupils could play a tremulous monstrosity called *The Maiden's Prayer* or they could paint a spray of roses on a white porcelain plaque, later framed in plush.

I achieved, at the age of ten, both *The Maiden's Prayer* and the plaque, but the most vivid memories of my painstaking teacher are singular and ludicrous. One of these is of the music mistress's dentures, the first I had ever seen, which sat grinning at me from the piano top where, poor soul, she must have placed them in a moment of irritation. The other memory, associated with the painting mistress, a pinched little spinster with a kind, tired voice, is of a singular clock under a glass dome, which fascinated me because the whole of its works were visible to the eye. On its white porcelain dial was an inscription that seemed the epitome of romance. In a fine black script in the centre of the dial ran the words *Pierre Louvain fecit. Paris 1792.*

To think that I looked at a clock made in Paris, more than a hundred years ago! And yet the real wonder of this thing, which I did not realize then, and whose significance came to me twenty years later, had little to do with its maker or its age. My painting mistress, very proudly lifting down the clock and removing the dome before an admiring group of pupils, always made the same little speech.

"When you press this little stud it strikes the hours, quarters and minutes," she said. "It was the bedside clock of the beautiful Lady Blessington and was given to my great-aunt, who was her housekeeper, when her home was broken up in London."

Caring little for the great-aunt or the beautiful Lady Blessington, how excitedly we pressed the stud and, waiting in an
awed silence, heard the wonderful clock strike the hours, quarters and minutes. *Ting-ting-ting.* Then *ting-ting,* and then, after
another pause, *ting-ting.* And it was exactly twenty-eight minutes to four.

Did the handsome Count d'Orsay give Lady Blessington the
clock as a present, and in those sleepless nights through the last
sad years of life at Gore House did her finger press that stud in
the darkness? Vain speculations, but they still arise as I motor
down Kensington Gore and pass the site of the vanished house.

III

It was possible until very recently to know what Gore House
looked like, for near by, just beyond Ennismore Gardens, stood,
until the summer of 1937, Kingston House, built in 1757, and
once owned by a woman whose history was even more astonishing than that of Lady Blessington's. Its dingy but impressive
façade looked out over a high protecting wall, towards Hyde
Park, and on the south side it possessed a very large garden,
like Gore House. It was the last of the private palaces that
once lined the Kensington Road. Its melancholy verandahed
façade had always fascinated me, and on the very day that I
was carrying my Austrian visitor towards his Mecca in North
End Road a breach had been made by the house-breaker in its
defensive walls. The temptation was too much. I went in by it.

The spectacle before us was disheartening. The noble old
house, in all its outward decay, retained some vestiges of its
former ducal dignity. Summer had come back to the neglected
garden that stretched behind it. Here, once upon a time, had
walked the amazing Duchess of Kingston, who privately married the third Earl of Bristol in 1744, but kept the fact secret
in order to retain her position as maid-of-honour to the Princess

of Wales. She early distinguished herself as a nudist, by going to a ball with nothing on but a pair of shoes and a spray of ivy. While Countess of Bristol, she became the mistress of the Duke of Kingston. To get rid of her husband she began a "suit of jactitation" and the Courts made her a spinster.

It is a pity that we have let the word "jactitation" die out— it is so much more descriptive of a state of conjugal misery than "incompatibility of temperament," for it means, according to the dictionary, a "restless tossing of the body in illness, a twitching of limb or muscle." One does not wonder that Lord Bristol got the twitches living with such a woman.

After her successful suit of jactitation she married the Duke of Kingston, who died four years later, leaving her all his property on condition that she remained a widow. She led the most boisterous element in society and Kingston House was the scene of wild revels. When a widow, she went to Rome and was honoured by Pope Clement XIV, but had to come hurrying home on a charge of bigamy, which the House of Lords upheld. She then fled the country and died in exile in 1788.

A man with a pick-axe was heartily attacking the stout garden wall as we entered the breach. I engaged him in conversation and found him swollen with indignation. "Fair makes me heart ache!" he exclaimed, as he paused and gazed over the garden. For the moment I ignored his remark, while I shared his indignation. The garden on the south side of the house was one of those surprising things that are disappearing from London. It must have been quite three acres in area, with noble trees in full leaf, guarding a long emerald lawn. Away behind the house one could just hear the murmur of traffic along the Kensington Road. The housebreaker, on inquiry, informed me that the house and trees were all coming down. The old garden was to be excavated and blocks of flats were to rise from this green oasis. A syndicate was "exploiting" the site, said the wielder of the pick-axe.

He then regaled us with surprising news. The old Duchess
had only just died, " 'er as went naked to a ball when she was
young. She used to sit on that terrace a-sunning 'erself." He
dolefully smashed down another line of bricks, and the old
mortar crumbled. He was a little muddled about the Duchess,
for he had confused her with the Dowager Countess of Listo-
wel, who had died that spring at the age of ninety-two, the old
house's last tenant. But I shared his honest indignation. The
adenoidal voice of the radio will bellow from steel casements
above a courtyard where once the thrushes sang in the trees at
evening, or, at daybreak, on the level lawns, searched for the
early worm.

CHAPTER IV

By Way of Chiswick

THIS KENSINGTON ROAD out of London offers endless enticement but we must push on. Kensington Palace seems safe for all time, since without it Kensington Gardens would lose its chief ornament, but nervously I glanced at the high iron gates that shut off Holland House from the rout of traffic pouring westwards. For how long I wonder will this Tudor house in its own park defy the pressure of taxation and the devouring eye of the speculative builder? It was here that Lady Holland, a rival *salon* keeper, waged war on that *demi-monde* Lady Blessington, higher up the Kensington Road. She had begun the battle by studied rudeness to Count d'Orsay. She was arrogant, formidable, and staunch to those she liked. As, perhaps, the leading hostess of London she had to be placated, but there was always a furtive landslide from Holland House to Gore House, where wit, beauty and a certain air of adventure surrounded the lovely countess, the dandy, and the men of genius who flocked there.

But as I glance at the iron gates and the great wall so gallantly keeping the speculative builder at bay, it is not of formidable Lady Holland, but of Addison I think. He married an earlier owner of that famous house, the Dowager Countess of Warwick. The Grand Cham of the Augustan age, the Coffee House dictator who so successfully combined literature with political pickings, appears to have been hen-pecked, and he survived only three years after his marriage, but it was more

42

likely that wine rather than women brought him to his end at forty-nine. Tom Moore, who was in and out of Holland House in Lady Holland's era, narrates that, while composing, Addison used to walk up and down the famous long gallery, where a bottle of wine stood on the table at each end.

Addison had an inn of refuge outside the grounds. It was then known as *The White Horse Inn* and is now called *The Holland Arms,* and stands where the Hammersmith turnpike had a gate. Addison also journeyed as far as the North End Road, to *The Bull and Bush,* so it was difficult for my lady's footman to run him to ground.

Only a few read Addison's works to-day. He was the shining figure of the age, and statesmen were as nervous of his prose as they were of Pope's verse. With Steele he made *The Spectator* a force, and his very bad play "Cato" was a great public event. The fame of journalists is apt to be as transitory as that of ballerinas. My young Austrian guest was eager to pay homage to Richardson in the North End Road, I could awaken no interest for Addison in Holland Park.

It is the irony of Fate that Addison's last sentence seems to be his most famous one. As he neared his end he sent for his rather profligate son-in-law, Lord Warwick, and told him, "I have sent for you that you may see how a Christian can die," whereupon in Dr. Johnson's delightful phrase "he prepared to die comfortably to his own precepts and professions."

We have tarried on the road, our journey scarcely begun, detained by a few of the social and literary ghosts on the famous highway. When shall we reach Bath? Candidly I have no idea, for I am willing to be buttonholed by people and places that reveal the course of history along the partly obliterated track. The hideous new roads that we create, lined with standardized villas, road-houses and garages, have one virtue, they often leave stranded an ancient road or village that preserves its historic landmarks, its beauty of leafy trees, crumbling walls, old roofs and green hedgerows. My sympathy for the village that is suddenly cut off from life by a new by-pass road that leaves it marooned on a church-centred isle of green peace is mitigated by the knowledge it will no longer be menaced by road-widening plans, and a general erasion of its old houses. The local motor-bus will come in and collect the Robinson Crusoes who pine for the shops and cinemas in the nearest large town. Then the village will go to sleep again, which is what it has done happily for centuries. The innkeeper will depend on local customers, which means that mine host will not suddenly find himself set back thirty feet in a pseudo-Tudor inn, too large, too ostentatious, where the ploughman fears to slake his thirst and the brewery company only seeks to bury its profits.

We have reached Hammersmith at last, and after success-fully crossing the maelstrom of traffic at the Broadway we proceed along Chiswick High Road until we come to St. Peter's Square, sheltering behind a large cinema, and Eyot Gardens. At the end of the Gardens we turn right into Chiswick Mall and gain a surprising view of the river with some waterside gardens fronting a row of noble old houses. When I first found Chiswick Mall spring daffodils bloomed in the slips of gardens that divide the Mall from the Thames, and cherry trees carried their snowy burdens of blossom. The first house to command the eye, so majestic with its white classical portico, and generous windows is Walpole House. Thackeray was at school at this house on the Mall, and when he penned the opening chapter of *Vanity Fair* his mind returned to this scene. He could not resist making Walpole House the academy where Becky Sharp threw a lexicon at Miss Pinkerton, though another house in Chiswick Square also lays claim to this distinction. The house we look at so enviously was once inhabited by Sir Herbert Beerbohm Tree, and through its fine iron gates and up its magnificent staircase the famous actor went to bed, arriving home late from one of his gorgeous entertainments at His Majesty's Theatre. His superb instinct for the theatrical must have been stimulated by this fine "property." It was once occupied by that indefatigable gossip and letter writer, Horace Walpole, and was largely rebuilt by Charles II for his notorious mistress, Barbara Villiers, Duchess of Cleveland.

This lovely but loose lady contrived to have for lovers Charles II, John Churchill and Wycherley the dramatist, and to marry Beau Feilding whose wife was still living! She bore five children to Charles and a daughter to Churchill. She helped to found the fortunes of the latter when he was an impecunious adventurer and had not become a general of genius. Surprised one day in the Duchess's bedroom by the King, Churchill saved the situation by jumping from a high window into the courtyard below. It was a well-rewarded jump, for the Duchess gave him five thousand pounds as the measure of her relief, and he had the good sense to purchase from Lord Halifax a life annuity of five hundred pounds. He lived to enjoy it for nearly fifty years, and, turning from bed to battle, he exchanged Venus's favours for those of Mars.

Historians are severe on lovely Barbara Villiers, and she merited their censure. "She was a woman of great beauty, but most enormously vicious and ravenous; foolish but imperious, very uneasy to the King, and always carrying on intrigues with other men, while yet pretending she was jealous of him," wrote Barnet. She did not, however, come to a bad end, as is so often the story. Her fortune seemed to grow as her beauty diminished, and she retained a large circle of friends. She died at this Chiswick house in 1709, and was buried in the churchyard at the end of the Mall. She was the mother of three dukes, and her daughter Barbara, by Churchill, inherited the family flightiness, for although she entered a nunnery she contrived to bear the Duke of Hamilton an illegitimate son.

No one knows exactly where the lovely loose Duchess mingled her dust in the Chiswick churchyard. All that remains is the legend of her naughtiness, and her last vain cry as she lay dying, "Give me back my lost beauty." She lies in distinguished company in that churchyard by the river, the view of which is obstructed by a monstrous factory.

I know of no capital in the world which has more foully desecrated a noble river flowing through its heart. Wharves, refuse tilts, generating stations, coal yards and gas works crowd the banks of the Thames, and make us sadly compare its treatment with that of the Tiber in Rome, the Danube in Budapest, the Arno in Florence, the Seine in Paris, the Neva in Petrograd, and the Hudson in New York. Once upon a time Chiswick churchyard must have enjoyed a river prospect as fine as that of Bisham churchyard by Marlow, or a dozen others one might name, where the stripling Thames glides by the green banks of God's acre. Here at Chiswick we see what a sordid, mercenary age has made of a scene that must have been lovely. The churchyard deserved a better fate than to look on broken factory windows and tumbledown walls.

It is strange that in death a King's mistress should meet a Protector's daughters, for here lie two of Cromwell's daughters, both in nameless, forgotten tombs. Visible to the eye rises the monumental urn that marks the resting-place of Hogarth, with Garrick's epitaph inscribed. And here too lies that splendid Earl of Burlington, who spent and built magnificently; his landscape gardener-painter-architect-sculptor, William Kent; and Cary, the translator of Dante; while, some distance along the boundary wall of the new cemetery, lies the bronze altar tomb of J. M. Whistler.

Once, when in Lowell, Massachusetts, I made my way one dark winter's afternoon to the squat wooden house in which Whistler was born in 1834, now turned into a museum-gallery for some of his works. And here in a Chiswick churchyard, not far from that river he painted with such wistfulness, he lies after a wayward pilgrimage. Should he sleep in American soil? One recalls his brilliant jibe when he failed to be re-elected President of the Royal Society of British Artists, "The artists had come out and the British had remained." Yes, it is fitting he should sleep here, in the land where he had his great triumphs, despite his unique gift for creating and provoking enemies.

"Does anyone come to visit Whistler's grave?" I asked the sexton.

"Oh, yes, he's a lot of visitors, Americans and others, in the summer, but there's one fat old lady comes every Wednesday, summer and winter, and has a good cry."

I asked for more about the fat old lady, but he could tell me nothing. Whistler died in 1903 aged sixty-nine. Did she once love him, or was she once his charwoman or—but the dates rule out mere conjectures. I had to leave the churchyard with the mystery unsolved, nor does it seem worth while waiting on a Wednesday for a fat and tearful old lady!

II

The narrow street that runs from the church and the end of the Mall takes us past an old inn, founded in the fifteenth century, which was *The Burlington Arms*, but is now a private dwelling. With its Tudor overhanging storey and ancient tiles it is made more curious by the fact that it cowers beneath a cliff face of brickwork belonging to a yeast factory. This tiny street is in imminent danger of being crushed out of existence, but a serene face is shown by Latimer House opposite, and the nautical touch is supplied by a building called The Guardship, which carries on its front wall a ship's figurehead and a ship's wheel. Gazing up at these strange objects on this little building I discovered on the upper floor, behind a window shrouded in greenery, a canary lustily singing and a typist making tea. But what I was really looking for was an old salt who would emerge hitching his trousers and singing a sea chanty. The Guardship is, I am afraid, not nautical in origin at all, but an artist's little bit of nonsense.

And now, across a wide road and down a mean street we

come to Hogarth's House. It was built in 1700 and the famous painter of his age passed the summer months in it from 1749 until his death in 1764. Here also lived Cary, the translator of Dante, from 1814 to 1826.

To-day, despite a laudable effort to preserve this memorial to Hogarth, the place is a depressing spectacle bearing witness to the march of commerce. Slummy streets crowd up to the garden wall, and the green retreat where Hogarth loved to sit with his pet dog Trump, whose portrait with his master hangs in the National Gallery, and his bullfinch "Dick," is no longer a place for the evening thrush to sing in. Something else sings in it, filling the air with its incessant whine, the machinery of a large boot polish factory whose walls and chimneys tower over the ancient mulberry trees, beneath which, on a fine evening, Hogarth took a pinch of snuff with Mr. Garrick the actor and Mr. Fielding the novelist.

The boot polish factory has also absorbed the seventeenth-century houses in Chiswick Square, but the noblest of these, Boston House, has been saved, as a canteen and work-girl's club. One room of this house has an authentic Adam ceiling and fire-place, and as is so often the case with these old houses with their long brick walls there is a secret garden containing some noble cedar trees.

A wide road now takes the place of the old Burlington Lane, and we have wandered thus far from the Bath Road for the purpose of finding the real *pièce de résistance,* a perfect Italian villa set down in an English Park. For presently, in the Burlington Lane, we come to a pair of massive gates and a vista that takes one's breath in pleasant surprise.

At the time when it was the fashion for the young aristocrat to make the grand tour, the lure of Italy was quite irresistible. Our national life has been greatly enriched by those works of art and classical objects which were then to be found in the baggage of the returned tourist. But there were more ambitious travellers who coveted whole buildings which they discovered in Italy and, greatly daring, some of them began to build in England's sunless landscape the classically inspired villas of Palladio, whose designs catered for the blinding sunshine. The result was a number of beautiful but somewhat uninhabitable Italian villas set in the English scene.

The great Lord Burlington, born in 1695, was enchanted by the appearance of the Villa Rotonda at Vicenza, as countless English tourists have been since. Living in an age when the boundless resources of Englishmen created across Europe a legend of fabulous wealth, Lord Burlington proved worthy of his race. Two adapted copies of La Rotonda were built in England by Clive Campbell, one of Burlington's trio of Architects, the villa called Mereworth Castle in Kent, and the villa now standing in the heart of Chiswick known as Chiswick House, which confronts us at the end of a stately avenue with terminal figures and green lawns.

Palladio, since he built summer villas for the merchant princes of Venice, had not to consider heating problems—they were often ignored in the Venetian palaces—but the English architect could not ignore that very heart of the Englishman's home, the fire-place. This necessitated the Palladian villa's putting forth chimneys. The Mereworth Castle copy ingeniously overcame the difficulty by having flues that ended in the cupola crowning the central dome. Chiswick House sprouts chimneys, but they are kept discreetly low and they do not obtrude upon a building of classical beauty.

The Earl of Burlington had embellished London with his Piccadilly house, now the home of the Royal Academy, but this enthusiastic patron of the fine arts suddenly conceived the idea of a Palladian villa just outside of London in which he could entertain his friends. The site he chose had belonged to the Earl of Somerset, the favourite of James I: and his notorious countess had resided there in a Jacobean house. Burlington pulled down this house. We know that one of its handsome fire-places went to the Assembly Rooms at York, of which the Earl

was a patron, and where it may now be seen. The old house
cleared away, Campbell set to work to reproduce the Villa Rotonda. The result was one of the wonders of Society, which
flocked there to these lavish entertainments given by the owner.
Here came Gay, Pope and Horace Walpole.

In Burlington's day it lacked the wings added some thirty
years later by his descendant, the Duke of Devonshire. In an
age when the *folie de grandeur* made men build houses with
forty bedrooms and consider them modest, the villa at Chiswick seemed almost a toy place. One guest described it as "too
small to live in and too large to hang on a watch-chain." Walpole thought too much had been sacrificed to symmetry; it had
"chimneys between windows and, which is worse, windows between chimneys," but the consensus of opinion was that the
villa was noble to look at, from which few will dissent to-day.
The double flight of steps leading to the columned portico is a
departure from the Villa Rotonda, but it is a successful departure, and true to the spirit of the age which insisted on the
aristocratic dilemma presented by an alternative flight of steps.

The gardens, too, were worthy of the noble façade, and kept
the Italian spirit. The Palladian mode required a formal garden, and for a century Lord Burlington and his friends set a
fashion for avenues bordered with terminal figures, for hemi-
cycles with stone seats and the statues of Roman emperors,
senators and writers. A formal stretch of water generally re-
flected at one end the garden-house in the form of a Roman
temple. The Italian cypresses and the Lebanon cedar spread
their shadows over the green English lawns. All these things
may be seen to-day in the grounds of Chiswick House.

Lord Burlington married a cousin of the great Lord Chesterfield. They were a gifted couple and took a foremost part in the
life of the eighteenth century, when Society reached the zenith
of its extravagance, licentiousness and artificiality. Burlington
was an outstanding figure, not only as a handsome, rich nobleman in an age of *grands seigneurs,* but also because he made a

serious contribution to the age. He moved, a resplendent figure, with the diamond star of the Order of the Garter blazing on his coat. His equipage was princely, but with all the ostentation then so fashionable, he combined a passion for the arts. He was not only a Knight of the Garter, Lord High Treasurer of Ireland, Captain of the Yeomen of the Guard, and Governor of Greenwich Hospital; he was also an early member of the Dilettanti Society, composed of young noblemen who had returned from the Grand Tour, for the purpose of encouraging the arts. Now that all the grandeur with which Burlington lived has passed into oblivion, it is his contributions to architecture and art which keep his name alive.

We may smile at this Palladian passion. It often imposed upon England highly unsuitable forms, and sacrificed much to the grand façade, yet who has ever looked upon Stowe or Castle Howard without feeling the essential nobility of such building? In a minor degree Chiswick House has its majesty. One treasures it for what it is, as well as for the associations it evokes.

This house forms an essential sight in our progress to Bath; from here the splendid Earl and his lady often set out for Nassau House, at Bath, where they spent the season. Their coach with its postilions, and the accompanying cavalcade of retainers with which a nobleman always travelled, must have made a dazzling spectacle as it swept out through the massive iron gates. These gates had been designed by Inigo Jones for Beaufort House, Chelsea, in 1621, and were presented a hundred years later to Lord Burlington by Sir Hans Sloane. Had we stood by them one evening, we should have seen the fashion arrive for a reception, some in coaches, some in sedan-chairs with linkmen carrying flambeaux. The house inside blazed with candlelight falling on the bright brocade dresses of the ladies, the embroidered coats of the gentlemen, the resplendent liveries of the footmen. The ladies' hair was piled up over their heads, built on a frame and augmented with pads. The whole of this edifice was greased with pomatum and dusted with powder, white for choice, but black if a widow. This expensive hair-dressing often had to last for three weeks, and to accommodate it the tops of sedan-chairs were made to open, until the lady sat down.

The gentlemen, too, wore elaborate periwigs. They had their faces polished, while the ladies had theirs painted. The scent of musk pervaded all their clothing and mitigated the odour of unwashed bodies. An elegant young gentleman of fashion minced and giggled, ejaculated "Demme," "Egad" or "Stap me vitals" as he fanned the air with a perfumed handkerchief, while the ladies at the approach of any crisis had the vapours. But some of the gallants fought nobly in the wars, despite face-creams, stays and scent-bottles. It was an age in which ludi-crous refinement was mixed with gross brutality.

The aristocratic guests seen in the *salons* of Chiswick House, this particular night of our watch, include the Duke of Nor-folk, the Duke and Duchess of Rutland, the Duke and Duchess of Grafton, the Duke and Duchess of Hamilton. They have all come on from their town houses, for the Bath season has not yet opened. And here comes an ever-welcome guest, the famous Mr. David Garrick. He and his lady have just greeted their host's daughter, the Lady Charlotte Boyle, who is to marry the fourth Duke of Devonshire and thus become the ancestress of our present Queen Elizabeth. Garrick is a great favourite of Lord Burlington, his wife is her Ladyship's protégée. She is a dancer from Vienna, and having become the rage, married her beloved David. Lord Burlington gave her six thousand pounds for a wedding present. Lady Burlington, who had planned a society match for her adored "Violette," reluctantly consented to the marriage, which was a lifelong success.

Mr. Pope has now arrived and scans the assembly with a satiric leer. The *salon* is thronged and the guests admire the lofty rooms with their mantelpieces, ceilings and exquisite mouldings of doors and windows. Under a lustre, hanging from a central dome, stands the Earl, welcoming his guests, a magnificent figure, wearing the Order of the Garter, his fine face beaming affably beneath its white periwig. You may stand to-day in that circular entrance-hall under the high dome, and see, though faded with time, the gilded mouldings, the patined marble, the frescoes of flying cupids, the walls covered with silk brocade. Wandering through the rooms to-day one experiences a melancholy which all faded beauty induces. We know on what a seething foundation of social injustice arose buildings such as these, yet we must mourn to-day that men can no longer find the means or opportunity to create a loveliness that is not strictly utilitarian.

What ghosts this old villa knows! The Dukes of Devonshire, who followed the Earl, entertained here foreign Kings and Emperors. Here lived and died two famous statesmen, Charles James Fox in 1806, and George Canning in 1827. Within a year of the latter's death there came a quick-eyed visitor, Sir Walter Scott, by name, who wrote in his diary of May 17, 1828:

"A numerous and gay party were assembled to walk and enjoy the beauties of that Palladian dome. The park and highly ornamented gardens belonging to it resemble a picture of Watteau. There is some affectation, but in the *ensemble* the original looked very well. The Duke of Devonshire received everyone with the best possible manners. The scene was dignified by the presence of an immense elephant, who, under the charge of a groom, wandered up and down, giving an air of Asiatic pageantry to the entertainment."

An elephant at a garden-party is a nice touch. There was once a vogue for the private elephant, so essential to the retinue of a wealthy rajah. I recall a relative of mine who greatly astonished me, when a little boy, by telling me that he had just come back from a garden-party at Warwick Castle where the Countess of Warwick and King Edward VII had fed an elephant on the lawn. The combination of a king, a castle, a countess and an elephant made an impression on me that has never faded, but I often wondered if my relative was romancing. Thirty years later, when writing the life of Sir Alfred

Fripp, the King's surgeon, I came across a photograph of the Countess feeding that elephant on the lawn at Warwick Castle!

The private elephant supplies the right note of eccentricity. One recalls that Rossetti wanted to buy an elephant. When asked the reason he replied that he wanted it taught to wash the windows of his Chelsea house. Then everyone would stare and say, "That elephant is washing the windows of the house in which lives Dante Gabriel Rossetti, the famous artist."

There is no elephant now at Chiswick House, but there is a tea-room in which one can buy buns. I was a little perplexed by the religious frescoes that decorated the tea-room and was informed that it had originally been the chapel of the house.

The fifth Duke of Devonshire married Georgiana, Earl Spencer's daughter, a famous beauty, who kissed the butcher for a vote, and sat to Reynolds and Gainsborough. The Duke added wings to the house, and built the beautiful stone bridge which still spans the lake. His successor, the sixth Duke, entertained on the grand scale, and dwelling there briefly, when not at Chatsworth or Devonshire House, he gave it its last hours of social glory. Garibaldi came here, and was cheered by a crowd below the colonnade, and in 1844 Queen Victoria and the Emperor Alexander were guests of the Duke.

After that the house suffered a sharp decline. The Duke forsook it, and one pair of magnificent gates were transported to the Green Park, where they stand to-day, opposite Half Moon Street, commanding the Broad Walk, never used, which leads from Piccadilly to Buckingham Palace. From Chiswick House also came a young gardener who, under the patronage of the Duke, climbed the ladder of fame and became Sir Joseph Paxton, the hero of the Great Exhibition. The large conservatory he built at Chatsworth House was blown up, and his vast Crystal Palace was burnt down, so nothing remains but the memory of his achievement.

There was a brief revival of the glory of Chiswick House when it was occupied by King Edward VII, then Prince of

Wales. He took the house chiefly for the benefit of his children, who could play there in its sixty acres of wooded gardens. George V and his brother ran free there, and the place where they worked with buckets and spades still carries the name of "The Princes' Gardens." The house was occupied by the Royal family from 1866 to 1879, and after a succession of occupants it finally became a private asylum.

So here, beneath the painted ceilings, the flying cherubs, the carved cornices, the domes, arches and architraves of the great Earl of Burlington's Italian Villa a sad company of half-wits mumbled and laughed. The villa began to fade and crumble, the lawns grew ragged under the cedars and beeches, the ivy smothered the terminal figures and urns. The gilded *salons* which had once echoed with the voices of Royalties, of the great social leaders of the eighteenth century, of the wits, the men of letters, the arbiters of fashion, now in their faded grandeur, heard only the senseless chatter of the living dead.

What a mockery of human vanity, wealth and ambition was here! The great earl, so splendid, had built his Palladian villa, had filled his grounds with fashion and his rooms with treasures, and now the walls threw back the sudden harsh cries of the mentally deranged, while in the untidy grounds where my lady, stepping from her sedan-chair, had once coquetted with milord, the watchful keeper herded his witless flock.

The watchful keeper is still present, but in happier circumstances. He is there to stop small boys breaking the shrubs, and to keep the public in order. For happily Chiswick has awakened to consciousness of the jewel in its midst, and the house and park have been public property since 1928. Once more the villa has a well-kept air, though wisely it is preserved rather than "done up," and in the neatly kept grounds, with its sweeping cedars, its avenues bordered with statues, its delightful vistas of villa, garden temple, bridge and lake, something of that dream translated from Italy to England by the splendid Earl of Burlington has been preserved.

Such decay as rests upon its noble façade and its garden avenues gives it that wistfulness, that patina of ancient memories which invoke so much of the charm of Italy's own famed villas, from whom the great lords and ladies have gone, and where the plaster crumbles in a silence broken only by the feet of tourists and the listless patter of the shabby custodian.

III

We return to Chiswick High Street by way of Turnham Green, a triangle of green grass with a church in its centre which cuts off the traffic roaring along its north side from the quieter residential streets of Chiswick. Nine out of ten persons rushing up and down the High Road towards Bath and the West could not tell you whether they had passed Turnham Green. It is just a small open space on which, rather gallantly, Chiswickians still insist on playing cricket on a Saturday afternoon. On one occasion as I passed a sensation had been created by a lusty batsman who had succeeded in sending a ball through the window of a London omnibus. But Turnham Green has a place in history. It was the spot chosen for the attempted assassination of William III, by the Jacobites, on his return from a day's hunting in Richmond Park. The plan was to hold up his coach as it floundered through the quagmire. Forty gentlemen were in the conspiracy, but when the day approached the conspirators' hearts failed them; someone betrayed the plot and the ringleaders were captured and hanged.

Turnham Green has more stirring memories going back to the time of the Civil War. For it was here that dashing Prince Rupert's plan for the capture of London was smashed. It was not his fault, but that of his overcautious generals, and of a king who hesitated to attack the city which he hoped in vain would be faithful to him. The Gallant Prince, or the Devil Prince, as he was variously viewed, saw at a glance the Royalist Army's opportunity when Edgehill had been fought. It mattered little who claimed the victory. A Parliamentary cavalry officer had ridden hastily into London, shouting that Rupert was on their heels. London was stunned. They had heard of the Civil War. Was it possible they were now to see it?

Panic had to be checked. Parliament passed a vote declaring the Battle of Edgehill a victory, gave the Earl of Essex five thousand pounds for a battle he had not won, and appointed a day of thanksgiving to God. A vote, a bonus and a prayer should have settled the matter since *vox populi vox dei*. Then came the news that the wicked Prince had seized Reading. No sooner did the citizens begin to shiver than London heard that Rupert was at Maidenhead. Like the plague he travelled on the wind and soon had smitten Kingston-on-Thames. It was now no use calling down curses on this villainous nephew of the wicked King. He was coming to London to satisfy his appetite for atrocities.

In fever heat all the apprentice lads were armed and drilled, and all the older citizens scurried around on war work. When the brave lads marched westwards along the Kensington Road, all London cheered them, harder because of the fear sitting in the pit of their stomachs.

Prince Rupert was now at Colnbrook, swearing to smash down all the London ramparts, burn all the houses, hang all the members of Parliament. The tall young Prince in the scarlet coat became the personification of the devil. Had he not declared no human power could kill him, did not bullets splash in vain upon him and his black charger as he rode impetuously down upon the train bands?

But Rupert had lost London before they knew it. Weak counsels, jealous generals, and a King without the will to inflict defeat on his capital, had wrecked the Prince's bold design. He pushed on and took Brentford, captured its guns and ammunition, but he had been held in check too long. Essex had come up with twenty thousand men and stood barring the way at Turnham Green.

The opposing army at Turnham Green was too large even for Rupert, weakened by wavering counsels behind him. Coolly he drew off his men, relinquished Brentford, and saw the tide of victory turn. The blow at the capital had not been struck, and, although they knew it not, the Royalist cause was lost.

CHAPTER V

Caesar in Brentford

AND NOW, HASTY PILGRIM, you must make a choice. You have arrived at last at the beginning of the Great West Road. A traffic roundabout will beguile you into taking the wide, speedy concrete track that leads through factory-land and villadom, in varying hues and shapes, for twenty more miles. I call it the Great Middle West, and those who are familiar with the highways of Illinois or Ohio will know what I mean. Here is industrial America transplanted on the perimeter of London. To our left lies Brentford, hideously symbolized by its gasometers; before us lies the new age of advertisement, symbolized by petrol pumps, garages and factories, framed by night in neon lighting. For the next straight four miles big business, eating up the apple orchards that I once saw blooming across this plain, proclaims the triumph of big dividends. A cosmetic factory that transforms the faces of our women lies not far distant from a razor-blade factory that keeps smooth the faces of our men, while near by, a fountain of neon lights proclaims the toothpaste factory that keeps bright our teeth. From potato chips in bags, to cleaning by suction, we proceed through such various activities as the manufacture of screen-wipers, golf balls, swimming costumes, motor-cars, tyres and throat-gargles, all housed in buildings that suggest the pursuit of the fine arts rather than the elusive shekel. This stretch of the West Road is the exhibition ground of a new spirit in industrial architecture.

One concedes that it is wonderful, but one wonders whether it does not indicate a cowardly retreat from the industrial north, with its half dead towns, depressed areas, and semi-derelict factories and workshops. The result is not only disastrous for the Midlands and the north of England, but also for London, already terribly congested. Too late in the day an attempt has been made to preserve for the capital a green belt. For twenty-five miles along the Bath Road, from Hyde Park to Maidenhead, there is an unbroken succession of factories, garages and small houses that seem to have been pressed out of moulds. A greater part of the land thus gripped in the tentacles of London was some of the richest market gardening soil in the country. Here and there a patch has escaped the speculative builder and the factory squatter, but it cannot be for long. Thus London's stomach grows more pendulous, its larder more distant and precarious.

One is aware, of course, that Jeremiahs have been writing in this strain for the last two hundred years. They will be writing so until the factories and houses stretch in an unbroken line from London to Manchester and Newcastle, unless the check of a disastrous war brings our top-heavy economic edifice crashing into ruins. The garrulous Horace Walpole was lamenting, as far back as 1776, that "rows of houses shoot out of every ray like a polypus; and so great is the rage for building everywhere, that if I stay here a fortnight without going to town, I look about to see if no new house is built since I went last." Cobbett observed that London was "spreading like a pestilence over the home counties," yet in his day the country was only half an hour's walk from the centre of London. St. George's Hospital at Hyde Park Corner was almost the first building encountered by the western traveller into London. Lord Burlington entertained Handel both at Chiswick and in his London house in Piccadilly. From the windows of both he could look out over green fields.

Our road to Bath sometimes leaves the old highway, with a clear gain for those who are willing to follow the ancient track, for it is in these quiet backwaters that something remains from another age. At the end of the Chiswick High Road we have our first choice. We can let the traffic-roundabout switch us on to the grand factory avenue which calls itself the Great West Road, or, keeping straight on, leaving Kew Bridge on our left, continue on the old Bath Road which takes us through Brentford and Hounslow.

At the outset let us be truthful. The entrance to Brentford is like the gate of Hell; already the gas-works and the coal yards are there for stoking the punishing fires. The monstrous things that Londoners in the last two hundred years have done to the banks of its once noble river are unutterable. Industrial depravity, reaching its apex in the mid-Victorian era, has left London with an incurable cancer. At Kew, on the right bank of the river, man created a garden of Eden, at Brentford on the left he created a Hell.

By the irony of fate Brentford almost escaped its Satanic rôle and became the New Jerusalem. Certain Jews leading a Zionist movement approached Lord Godolphin, of the King's Ministry, and made an offer of five hundred thousand pounds. They would have made it "a million if the Government would allow them to purchase the whole town of Brentford, with leave of settling there entirely, with full privileges of trade." They declared "the affair was already concerted with the chief of their brethren abroad, that it would bring the richest of their merchants hither, and some twenty millions of money to circulate in the town."

Godolphin was afraid that the proposal would provoke the clergy and the merchants, and no more came of the scheme. So instead of a new Jerusalem there is a gas-works commanding the river front, and shutting off the highway user from any view.

Brentford has always had an unenviable reputation for dirt. Dr. Johnson could not resist a jibe when Adam Smith was extolling the beauties of Glasgow. "Pray, sir, have you ever seen Brentford?" he asked. The two miles of brick misery that comprises Brentford made a joke for wits and dramatists.

> Brentford, tedious town,
> For dirty streets and white-legged chickens known.

wrote Gay, at a time when the place was surrounded by gardens, and the river wharves offered plenty of local colour. It was a standing joke against George I that he enjoyed driving through Brentford on his way to Windsor Castle because its filth reminded him of his beloved Hanover. Since the King's day Hanover has improved beyond recognition. Brentford has slipped back into deeper gloom, although it no longer takes a whole day to reach it from London, as in 1727. It was considered a good highway then, although George II and Queen Caroline were pitched out of their coach into the mud. Twenty years earlier, Prince George of Denmark, having made the journey to Brentford, the Court Circular recorded "His Highness made no stop during the journey except when overturned or stuck in the mud."

And yet so many things can be said on behalf of Brentford that it is worth while resisting the temptation of the new Great West Road, despite the gas-works and the narrow high street. William Shakespeare knew of the place, and it finds a mention in *The Merry Wives of Windsor*. Falstaff disguises himself as "my maid's aunt, the fat woman of Brentford." In the sixteenth and seventeenth centuries it was a favourite resort of the Londoner, as well as the gateway to the West. One of Shakespeare's company came here as the landlord of *The Three Pigeons*. The Globe Theatre had been suppressed by the Puritans, and in his old age he moved out of town and died at his hostelry about 1659, "very old, for he was an actor of note in the reign of James the First." It was this old fellow who

probably drew Jonson and his satellites to the inn, whose fame
was already established, for Jonson had alluded to it in one of
his plays:

> *We will turn our course*
> *To Brainford, Westward, if thou sayst the word . . .*
> *My bird o' the night. We'll tickle it at* The Pigeons.

The old inn disappeared about 1850. It stood near the
Market Square. But a town mentioned by Shakespeare and
Jonson has something to counterbalance the ill odour of its gas-
works and mean streets. Brentford can claim one staggering
historical fact. If you have any interest in the place where the
great Julius Caesar crossed the Thames and drove the Britons
before him it is in Brentford you will find it.

Few of the millions who rush along the Brentford High
Street can be aware of the odd sights that lie down the narrow
alleys leading to the Thames. Curious, I stopped my car by
the fire station, and, resisting the appeal of Goat Wharf,
plunged down Ferry Lane. The name seemed to promise a
ferry at least. In the first hundred yards the scene became
nautical. Two men in fishing jerseys came out of an inn called
The Waterman's Arms. They were not old salts but one wore
sea-boots and smoked a clay pipe. My curiosity grew. The
lane became only a passage-way. Presently a Georgian house,
built of dark grey bricks, revealed a rural past. It had once
stood in a large garden. An outdoor clock with gilt numerals
still kept the time on one of the walls. The old house was now
the offices of a timber merchant. The alley narrowed to a few
feet. Then suddenly I came to the River Thames.

It was low tide, a pebbly beach below me was reached by a
flight of steps. Across the river lay the green, tree-bordered
expanse of Kew Gardens. On the broad silver stream a rowing
club "eight" went swiftly by. What a transformation of scene
a few yards had effected! A hoarding provoked my curiosity.
Beyond a high wall I could see a mountain of coal slack. It was

on a wharf where coal barges unloaded, hidden from view. I
peered over the barricade on the edge of the stone jetty and my
heart jumped. A massive wall had cracked under the pressure
of the coal slack, bringing down the coping stone and some
masonry. A granite column standing in a triangular space was
already in peril of being overthrown. The purpose of the
'wooden barricade was now clear—to keep the public away
from the collapsing wall. Why the heap of coal slack was not
removed I do not know, and when I saw what it threatened to
overturn I marvelled still more.

There were inscriptions on this round pillar of granite, about
ten feet high, and to read them, at peril of my life, I went over
the barricade. This is what I found.

54 B.C. At this ancient fortified ford the British tribesmen under
Cassivelaunus bravely opposed Julius Caesar on his march to Veru-
lamium.

I paused in my reading and took a deep breath. So here, in
the very shadow of this heap of coal slack cracking the
boundary wall, the great Caesar had crossed the Thames,
driving before him the wild natives. Local patriotism had
erected this granite memorial, local industry seemed likely to
push it down.

The first excitement subsiding, I read on:

A.D. 780–1. Near by Offa, King of Mercia, with his Queen, the
Bishops and principal officers held a council of the Church.
A.D. 1016. Here Edmund Ironside, King of England, drove Cnut
and his defeated Danes across the Thames.
A.D. 1642. Close by was fought the Battle of Brentford between the
forces of King Charles I and the Parliament.

I was absorbed in my discovery, oblivious of the menacing
coal slack, when a voice fell on my startled ears.

"Hey, you! What are you doing in there?" it cried, threaten-
ingly.

I looked up quickly to find a policeman's helmet and face visible over the hoarding.

"I am raising the ghosts of Julius Caesar, the King of Mercia, King Canute and Charles I," I replied, solemnly.

"And what if that wall cracks over you," demanded the Law, young and fresh-complexioned.

"I shall feel I have perished in noble company," I retorted.

"Don't you feel ashamed?"

"Ashamed? Me?" asked Robert, now really astonished by my madness.

"Mussolini would raise a temple here. We raise a coal heap. King Canute tried to push back the sea, can't Brentford try to push back a coal heap? I'm ashamed of you!" I said, severely.

"You'd better come out of there," said Robert, but this time with a note of entreaty.

"Have you read what is on this pillar?"

"I can't say as I have, sir."

"Then I will read it to you. You should feel proud that your beat leads down Ferry Lane."

"It doesn't—I'm looking for a lost kid."

Resisting the temptation to tell him to go to Goat Wharf, I read out one of the inscriptions while he listened, solemnly.

"Well, it does surprise me. Nobody around here ever told me that," said Robert. "It's a pity that wall's knocking it over."

"Perhaps you'll report the matter," I said, climbing over the barricade. "I feel it's just as important as a lost kid."

"More!" said the policeman, feelingly. "Kids are lost every day, their mothers don't bother about 'em until bedtime, but a thing like this you can't find every day. And nowhere else but in Brentford, I'll warrant!"

The fellow was visibly swelling with local pride. "And where will you find a lovely picture like this, sir?" he asked, turning to survey the Thames, now reflecting the crimson upper sky.

I agreed that it was lovely. There was beauty before us— and horror behind. Together we walked back up Ferry Lane in the friendliest fashion. Robert began to be very indignant about the column threatened by the coal. I paused by *The Waterman's Arms* and looked at him.

"Thank you very much, sir, but I'm on duty."

"Oh, of course. Well, I hope you find the kid."

"He'll turn up all right," said Robert. "Well, good evening, sir. Something ought to be done about that column."

"You might report that wall—for disorderly conduct."

He grinned and we parted.

One day I shall go back and see what happened to the column. Like Robert I feel no curiosity about the kid.

But I was not to leave Ferry Lane without a further adventure. The door of *The Waterman's Arms* swung open to reveal a jolly waterman. He was a curly headed young "tough" in a blue sweater, blue trousers and sea-boots. Not more than twenty-two, his snub-nosed face beamed with rosy goodwill.

"—evening!" he said, grinning.

"—evening!" I replied, grinning, and added: "Do you mind telling me what you are doing in those sea-boots? Are you a bit of local colour for *The Waterman's Arms*, or are you the real thing?"

He considered this for a moment and looked at me with his clear blue eyes, suspicious of "leg-pulling." "I'm the captain of that boat," he answered at length, nodding his head in the direction of the high wall.

I turned and saw the mast-head of a boat, with a pennant fluttering there, above the high wall hiding the timber wharf.

"The Captain!" I exclaimed, duly impressed. "But you're very young for such a position."

"Twenty—but I've worked my way up," he answered. "And now I'm sailing that boat all over England," he said, proudly.

I expressed my interest, and showed that I was deeply impressed by the contact with a captain. On my invitation we adjourned to *The Waterman's Arms*.

The phrase "all over England" had puzzled me a little, but it transpired he was captain of a sailing barge. There was not a canal in any part of England he had not sailed on. He had just come from Colchester with a cargo. He was picking up another and taking it to Bristol. He never knew where he would be sent. Sometimes he left the inland canals and went coastwise.

"In your barge?" I asked, astonished, and saw I had made a bad slip.

"It ain't a barge—it's a sailing boat. Barges get pulled or pushed. We sail," he declared, proudly. "Would you like to see her?"

I accepted the invitation at once. We finished our drinks and went out. The captain led the way through a small door in the opposite wall. Alongside the wharf lay the ship, with its great russet sail furled. The bow was brightly painted with green and blue bands. Her name was *Annie Laurie*. A terrier jumped up on to the hatch and barked at us. There was no one visible.

"The crew's ashore?" I asked, as we picked our way towards her.

"No—he's there, cooking supper," answered the captain.

I smothered my surprise. We clambered on board, and the captain, looking down the hatchway, from which emerged a strong smell of kippers, bellowed, "Bert!"

The crew emerged, a freckled, red-haired imp wearing nothing but a pair of khaki shorts. His eyebrows rose at the outer corners, giving him a clownish smirk. He was a lad of fifteen or so, with a shock of red hair and a sturdy body tanned with the sun.

"This is Bert," said the captain.

The crew grinned at me.

"Supper ready?" asked the captain.

"In 'alf a mo'," replied Bert, and disappeared again.

"Ain't she fine?" asked the captain, surveying his ship with pride. "You know, some blokes ask me if I ain't lonely, allus on the move. Why, it's grand! I've been all over England, and I've allus got me 'ome with me. How many fellows can say that—and I'm me own boss in a way."

"And you sail this—just you and the boy?"

"Yes—me and the kid. He's not on the log really," added the captain, "the Company won't pay him anything—so I keep him."

"But surely, if the boy's working——"

"Well, you see—he's a what-do-you-call-it?" said the captain, picking up the terrier and pulling its ears.

I looked puzzled, and then the word came to me.

"A stowaway?" I asked.

"That's it—'im and his dog. I came on board one night—been to the pictures at Grantham—and there he was, with the dog, both of 'em asleep in a crate of straw. I yanked them out of it. They both looked pinched to death, so I gave 'em a meal. They been here ever since, that's over a year ago."

"But his people—they know he's here?" I asked.

"His folk—says he ain't got none. And I'm asking no questions. He's a good kid," said the captain.

He sniffed the kippery odour whirling up out of the cabin, and then his blue eyes twinkled.

"Funny, you know," he said, pushing up the mongrel's head, "he gets a shilling a week, and he——" nodding in the direction of the cabin—"gets nowt! You see the dog's on the rating as a rat-killer and the kid don't exist; he's my pigeon. But he'll get a boat one day—he's a spry kid," added the captain, proudly.

"And good with the frying-pan?"

"He can cook, work, sew, paint—and find a rabbit or a bird

now and then, when it don't really matter," said the captain, grinning.

It was time to go. I thanked the captain. I left him, spitting over the bow of the *Annie Laurie*, a reek of kippers filling the evening air, and after this singular and pleasant interlude regained my car and the road to Bath.

II

Farther along the Brentford High Street, over the bridge that spans the River Brent, and its cluster of barges, and under the railway bridge that marks the disorderly end of Brentford proper we come to a wider stretch of road, and find ourselves crossing historic ground. In the dim past this was a primeval swamp and when, a little to the north, they were excavating to make the new Great West Road, the skeleton of a hippopotamus was dug out; and for those who remain doubtful, it can be seen carefully preserved in the Brentford Museum.

We are on ground now known to Prince Rupert, where he defeated the Parliamentarians, and pressed on to Turnham Green. Brentford has seen various kings fighting for their realms. As the stone column at the ferry reminds us, long after Caesar pressed back the Britons on the Brentford bank, where the oaken stakes of their defences have been found in the present century, there was Edmund Ironside pursuing King Canute over the river. It was a long, ding-dong affair, fifty years before William the Conqueror appeared on the scene, and the battle swayed backwards and forwards over this part of the country, seven times in the space of seven months, until the people became sick of it, and the two kings decided to divide the territory. A popular saying had reference to these two kings, who fought so vainly and were at last reconciled— "Like the two Kings of Brentford smelling at one nosegay." This allusion to Brentford history was made in a seventeenth-century play by the Duke of Buckingham, and the actors, to heighten the absurdity, used to make their entrances smelling at one nosegay.

Prince Rupert's successful affair at Brentford, calling for a desperate stand by the Parliamentarians at Turnham Green, had a by-product in literature. It caused Milton, in a state of apprehension at Prince Rupert's threat, to write a sonnet, for pinning to the door of his house in Aldersgate. He hoped by the aid of the Muse, and the establishing of notable precedents in history, to avert a dire fate.

> *Captain or Colonel, or Knight in Arms,*
> *Whose chance on these defenceless doors may seize,*
> *If ever deed of honour did thee please,*
> *Guard them, and him within protect from harms.*
> *He can requite thee, for he knows the charms*
> *That call Fame on such gentle acts as these,*
> *And he can spread thy Name o'er Lands and Seas,*
> *What ever clime the Sun's bright circle warms.*
> *Lift not thy spear against the Muses Bower,*
> *The great Emathian Conqueror bid spare*
> · *The house of Pindarus, where Temple and Tower*
> *Went to the ground: And the repeated air*
> *Of sad Electra's Poet had the power*
> *To save th' Athenian Walls from ruin bare.*

This sonnet surely exhibits one of the earliest bribes of favourable publicity, but no Knight in Arms knocked at Milton's door, and the offer to endow the turbulent visitor with immortality went unaccepted. But to-day our thoughts are turned, not to battles, but ducal magnificence. We are arrested by the sight of a screen and a gateway, but before we linger in front of this impressive entrance to the Duke of Northumberland's suburban seat, let us linger on the roadway outside the great gates, our attention attracted by a gazebo opposite the high walls. We must look at it at once, for I have a feeling that it will not long be left there, commanding the broad highway. It has a sad air as it rots, perched upon an old brick wall, beneath an immense chestnut tree. Behind it, in what doubtless was once a beautiful garden, stands a substantial brick Georgian mansion, of the same kind as that we have seen at The Grange, in North End Road. It is now a sad ruin, yet it has still a genteel air, with its dignified central door, its symmetrical sash windows, its parapet roof.

Men and women lived here once in spacious style. In that gazebo overlooking the Bath Road the owner and his wife must have passed many a pleasant hour, watching the post-chaises and coaches carrying the Fashion to Bath. And they must have been very familiar with every coming and going of His Grace the Duke, their neighbour, and all his famous guests. One wonders if the scrutiny from that gazebo irritated the ducal family, so blatantly does it command the approach to this great house. What fun it must have been to own a gazebo. It is one of a trio of names which has always excited me. A gazebo, a zareba, and a ha-ha, happy the country house that possesses all these. But if I may only have one of these, give me a gazebo, a quizzing-box hung on my garden wall whence I can see the world go past.

Syon Park House, and its gazebo overlooking the highway, cannot exist much longer. The gazebo is falling to pieces, the garden is a wilderness, there are cracks in the walls of the noble old house, and its floors have fallen in with dry-rot. A transport company, installed in a new building behind the old house, takes its lorries in and out over a carriage-drive long since disappeared. Surely this old house had a history? What Georgian buck pulled the handle of the door-bell, what children played in the great garden, who sat in the gazebo and looked down on the world and his wife coming and going from London Town, the dread ordeal of Hounslow Heath before or behind them?

My first inquiries found no reward. The house was old, it would soon come down. No one seemed to know what a gazebo meant. "Oh, that!" exclaimed a lorry-driver, contemptuously,

"I thought it was a summer-house." But he had heard that the old house had once been a school, long ago. The lorry-driver was correct, it was a school, and in a sense a famous school. It was the scene of Dr. Greenlaw's Academy for Young Gentlemen, and it could claim to have had at least one immortal pupil. For it was to Syon Academy that the young Shelley was sent. Dowden, in his *Life* of the poet, tells us how Shelley entered the Academy at Brentford End as a new pupil in 1802. He had for school-fellows, John Rennie, destined to fame as an engineer and the builder of London Bridge, and Medwin, who became one of the poet's biographers. Dowden could never find the school, but a local historian was able to identify the Academy beyond all doubt. Shelley's school-fellow, Sir John Rennie, has left a description of the place, as well as of the young Shelley.

It is the successor to a large house formerly belonging to Dr. King, a Bishop of London. To the house were attached excellent gardens and a playground. The situation, moreover, was open and healthy, and the total number of boys was about fifty, ranging from eight to sixteen years of age. They were well fed and taken care of by the doctor's wife and his sister-in-law, Miss Hodgkins. The doctor's eldest daughter, Miss Greenlaw, taught the youngest boys their letters, whilst the doctor and his assistants devoted themselves to the education of the others, which education consisted chiefly of classics, writing, arithmetic, French and occasional geography, and the elements of astronomy. The Bishop who owned the previous house is said to have entertained there the celebrated Princess Pocahontas, the American Indian princess brought back by Captain John Smith, the founder of Virginia, who again met her under the Bishop's roof.

Medwin, unlike Rennie, had no kind memories of the place. He called it "a perfect Hell" and his account differs so widely from Rennie's that it is clear that personal prejudice has guided his pen.

"The school, though not a Dotheboys Hall, was conducted with the greatest regard to economy. A slice of bread with an iota of butter smeared on the surface, and thrice-skimmed milk, sky-blue, to use an expression of Bloomfield, was called a breakfast, the supper a repetition of the same frugal meal, and dinner, at which it was never allowed to send up the plate twice without it eliciting an observation from the distributor that effectually prevented a repetition of the offence, was made up generally of ingredients that were anonymous. The lady of the house was by no means a Mrs. Squeers . . . she was too firm to have anything to do with all the dirty details of the household; she was, or was said to be, connected with the Duke of Argyle . . . Dr. Greenlaw, a Scotch doctor of law and a divine, was a choleric man of sanguinary complexion, in a green old age; not wanting in good qualities but very capricious in his temper, which, good or bad, was influenced by the daily occurrences of a domestic life not the most harmonious."

Medwin, whose picture of the place is etched in acid, declared that Shelley's "pure and virgin" mind was shocked by the language and manner of his new companions; but though forced to be with them, he was not of them. "So odious was the place to both of us that we never made it the subject of conversation in after life."

Nevertheless, despite Shelley's sojourn among the barbarians —did they shoot their catapults from the gazebo at the occupants of the Bath and Exeter coaches, one wonders?—he spoke of his headmaster as "a man of rather liberal opinions" and, despite the misery described by Medwin, there was a touch of romance to light the gloomy hell, for, in later years, Shelley recalled "an attachment at school at the age of eleven or twelve. The object was a boy about my own age, of a character eminently generous, brave and gentle. It has never been my fortune to meet him since my schooldays." There is a portrait of the child Shelley, as seen by his contemporary Rennie, which shows that Dr. Greenlaw must have suffered provocation, and was not the only inhabitant of Syon Academy with a capricious temper.

"During the time that I was there the most remarkable scholar was the celebrated poet, who was then about twelve or thirteen and even at that early age exhibited considerable poetic talent, accompanied by a violent and extremely exciteable temper which manifested itself in all kinds of eccentricities. His figure was of the middle size, although slight, but well made. His head was well proportioned, and covered with a profusion of brown locks; his features regular, but rather small; his eyes hazel, restless, and brilliant; his complexion fair and transparent; and his countenance rather effeminate, but exceedingly animated. The least circumstance that thwarted him produced the most violent paroxysms of rage; and when irritated by other boys, which they, knowing his infirmity, frequently did, by way of teasing him, he would take up anything to throw at his tormentors."

We can see poor Dr. Greenlaw, confronted by this enraged infant, in fear of his windows if not of his life. As for Miss Greenlaw, she must have thought him a little terror, and have dreaded the lesson hour.

"His imagination was always roving upon something romantic and extraordinary—such as spirits, fairies, fighting, volcanoes, etc.—and he not infrequently astonished his schoolfellows by blowing up the boundary palings of the playground with gunpowder, also the lid of his desk in the middle of school-time, to the great astonishment of Dr. Greenlaw himself and the whole school. In fact, at times he was considered to be on the border of insanity; yet with all this, when treated with kindness, he was very amiable, noble, high-spirited and generous; he used to write verse, English and Latin, with considerable facility, and attained a high position in the school before he left for Eton, where, I understand, he was equally, if not more, extraordinary and eccentric."

If the Doctor's daughter lived long enough to learn of Shelley's subsequent fame she may have wondered whether all the trouble was worth an immortal ode to a Skylark and the West Wind, and have felt confirmed in her certainty that this frightful child would come to a violent end. Or did she proudly claim to have taught him his letters, and thereby have played no small part in the creation of some of the greatest passages in

English poetry, the tantrums, and the explosions softened by
Time? "And did you once see Shelley plain, Miss Greenlaw?"
we might ask with Browning. The Greenlaws have long gone
from the scene, but the ghosts seem all around this sad old
house falling into ruin. The broken windows of the decaying
gazebo give it the appearance of a skull, staring with empty
sockets on the old Bath Road. There still remains, in the garden once the playground, a part of the old Bell Tree "so called
from its having suspended in its branches the odious bell whose
din," said Medwin, "when I think of it, yet jars in my ears."

It is only a few years since the old house was deserted, but
the hand of ruin is already heavy upon it. The passing lorries
shake its walls, the garden is a wilderness of rubbish, the
gazebo is threatened with imminent collapse, the ghost of Dr.
Greenlaw, if he haunts the domain over which he ruled with
such terror, must be feeling damp and depressed. One more
gunpowder exploit of that *enfant terrible* would bring the
whole place down in a shower of powdered brick. Before we
grow too depressed, let us cross the road and pause by the
impressive gateway where a duke gallantly defies the hand of
time and the toll of death-duties.

CHAPTER VI

Syon, a Ducal House

SYON HOUSE IS ONE OF THOSE DUCAL HOUSES, planned on a lordly scale, which no one to-day will ever build, and few could afford to live in. A few years ago it seemed as if this old mansion, now engulfed in a suburb of London, a dormitory where the city worker comes to sleep, would fall to the vandals who, enticed by the pleasant park that faces the Thames and Kew Gardens on the opposite bank, thought it eminently suitable for a sewage works! Happily the public outcry nipped this offensive scheme in its bud, and Syon House was reprieved. For how long, one cannot help wondering, for it is an oasis of aristocratic seclusion in a wilderness of democratic vulgarity. The massive wall surrounding the estate on three sides, which fronts the River Thames at Isleworth, holds off the jerry builder like a dam. Across the old Bath Road, housing settlements have sprung up, and not far off there is the ominous roar of the traffic on the new Great West Road. But so far the outer defences, keeping the world at bay, are certainly sound and of a dignity that makes one pause before the high gates, its lovely screen, and the proud lion above this arch, who holds a stiff tail and a menacing head towards the threats of the twentieth century.

This superb entrance to the park has been called the Lacework Gateway, from a jibe of the egregious Horace Walpole, who wrote from the Gothic horror of Strawberry Hill: "It is all lace and embroidery . . . consequently most improper to be exposed in the high road to Brentford. From Kent's mahogany we are dwindled to Adam's filigree."

We can ignore the sneer of the ineffable Horace, and applaud Robert Adam's superb gate, worthy of the Palladian influence that inspired it. The screen consists of four Corinthian columns on either side of the arch, joined with iron grilles. The pilasters have panels carved after Italian cinquecento models, and, surmounting the arch, which has a Roman grandeur, stands the Percy Lion, a copy of the one brought from the demolished Northumberland House in the Strand, in 1874, now on the front of the house. The large pilasters are based on lions' claws, a subtle tribute to the heraldic lion of the Percys.

Robert Adam was not only inspired by his instinct for beauty but also by kindliness in the creation of this superb screen. "The colonnade and iron rail beneath," he tells us, "not only gives an air of magnificence to this building, but were also intended by his Grace to gratify the curiosity of the public by giving to travellers an opportunity of viewing from the road, the park, lawn, bridge and house itself at a little distance, closing the beautiful scene." So to-day, pausing on the old highway to Bath, we can be grateful to Adam's Duke, who in the eighteenth century did not reflect the usual arrogance towards the curiosity of the mob.

But we can inspect the house and the park at closer range, for a public pathway is kept open across the grounds, from the Brentford side to the Isleworth side. The gazebo of Shelley's old school looks directly down the lane that leads us to the park. As we approach the house we look over a greensward between twin gate-houses, symmetrically placed but oddly isolated in relation to the house. In fact the gate-houses are placed in position for a drive which does not and could not exist since they are connected by the wall of a ha-ha.

No one could say that Syon House, built squarely, surrounding an inner court, is a beautiful building, not even on the riverside, where the magnificent Long Gallery is carried over piazza arches. The whole edifice is castellated, with a turret at each corner, and the yellowish facing of Bath stone is not conducive to cheerfulness or lightness of design. It still carries, architecturally, the disadvantage inherited from its early design, based on its initial use, that of a monastery. Its history goes back to the reign of Henry V, who gave leave to the St. Augustinian monks for the building of Syon. Shakespeare has an allusion to this, and its twin institution across the river at Sheen, when, in Henry V's prayer before the battle of Agincourt, he says:

> *And I have built*
> *Two Chantries where the sad and solemn priests*
> *—Sing still for Richard's soul.*

Henry laid the foundation stone of Syon in 1415, but he did not live to see the monastery completed. The first occupants in 1420 were thirty-five in number, but this sum grew to over eighty, consisting of sixty nuns, thirteen priests, four deacons and eight lay brethren. It was a strict order, a house of silence, and all communications were made by signs. In 1431, Henry VI gave permission for this monastery to be moved a little distance to its present site, and, as, in 1492, its endowment exceeded £1,700, it was one of the richest in the land, a grave disadvantage when Henry VIII, in the course of looting the monasteries and displacing the Pope, cast eyes upon Syon. It was one of the first large monasteries to suffer suppression. All its inmates had acknowledged Henry as supreme head of the Church, save Richard Reynolds, the Confessor, who, along with the Vicar of Isleworth, opposed the King, and were executed at Tyburn.

The monastery now passed to the King, who soon made it a prison for his Queen, Katherine Howard. She was meanly confined here from November 14th, 1541, until February 10th, 1542, while the charge of treason was pressed against her. The unhappy Queen was then taken by barge from Syon to the Tower for execution. Five years later, Henry VIII died, and the great funeral procession from Westminster to Windsor halted here for the night on the first stage of its journey. It is a gruesome fact that the swollen body of the dead king burst in the chapel while a service was being celebrated.

Henry's successor, the boy king, Edward VI, gave Syon Monastery to the ill-starred Duke of Seymour, the Lord Protector of the Realm. He was the founder of the present house. He pulled down much of the old monastery and built a new house for his occupation, and created a garden that was long famous. But the Duke held the property for only six years, being executed in 1552. His estates, including Syon, were confiscated, and went to the new Lord Protector, John Dudley, Duke of Northumberland. He was an ambitious man, and aware that the King was dying, married his son, Lord Dudley, to the King's cousin, Lady Jane Grey, persuading the King to pass over the princesses Mary and Elizabeth and leave the crown to her.

The King died, and the scheme went forward. Lady Jane Grey came to Syon House, and met there the assembled Council, who offered her the crown. With grave foreboding she reluctantly accepted it. The night of July 9th, 1553, was spent at Syon, and the next day she left by river, in great state, to take up her residence in the Tower of London as Queen of England. She reigned for nine days. The scheme failed and Northumberland and Lady Jane Grey were executed. Syon became crown property again. The nuns who had formerly owned it were given it back by Queen Mary. They returned from Termond, in Flanders, where they had spent their exile since Henry VIII evicted them, but they were sent on their wanderings again when Elizabeth succeeded Mary in 1558, and finally settled in Lisbon in 1594. Centuries after, a later Duke of Northumberland visited the convent in Lisbon and presented the nuns with a silver model of Syon. "We still hold the keys," said the Abbess. "Yes, but we've altered all the locks now," responded the Duke, jokingly.

James I gave Syon to Henry Percy, the ninth Earl of Northumberland. He was suspected of being connected with the Gunpowder Plot, and although the charge seems to have been groundless, he was brought before the Court of Star Chamber, fined £30,000, stripped of his offices and sent to the Tower for life. On payment of £11,000 he was released after fifteen years' imprisonment, and he spent his last years in his riverside home. The tenth Earl called in Inigo Jones to make many improvements to the house. It was this Earl, a Parliamentarian during the Civil War, who became, at the Parliament's request, the custodian of Charles I's children, after the surrender of the King. The Royal children were the Duke of York, aged fourteen, the Princess Elizabeth, aged twelve, and the Duke of Gloucester, seven years old. While a prisoner at Hampden Court the King was permitted to go over and visit them, and to have them visit him in turn, and it was from Syon that they went to Whitehall to take that last farewell of their father before he went to the scaffold. One of these children, then the Duke of York, returned to Syon years later, where, as Charles II, he held a Council during the Great Plague, in 1665. Evelyn, the diarist, has recorded this Council. "Went to Sion, where His Majesty sat at Council during the Contagion; when business was over I viewed the seate belonging to the Earl of Northumberland, built out of an old Nunnerie, of stone, and fair enough, but more celebrated for the garden than it deserves; yet there is excellent wall fruit and a pretty fountain, nothing else extraordinarie." Another famous diarist, Pepys, was there in the same year. He visited a friend who "walked with me to Syon, and there I took water to London."

The real splendour, its history apart, came to Syon when in the middle of the eighteenth century Sir Hugh Smithson married a Percy heiress, and thus took control of the property. He

was afterwards created the first Duke of Northumberland of
the new order, and took the name of Percy. A contemporary
recorded that "he had been one of the handsomest men in the
kingdom, he possessed great talents; a mind highly cultivated,
and more knowledge than is generally found among the nobility. Born of genteel though not illustrious parents, he had
been raised by his marriage with the heiress of the name and
wealth of the House of Percy, and he showed that he was
worthy of them. By the wisdom of his economy he improved
the immense estates of that family and so increased its revenue
that this now amounted to £50,000 a year. He restored the
ancient splendour of the Percys by his taste and magnificence.
Alnwick Castle, formerly the residence of the Earl of Northumberland, had entirely fallen to decay; he completely rebuilt it,
and out of complaisance to the Duchess, his lady, ornamented
it in Gothic style, which he did not himself like, but he did it
with so much taste that he made it one of the most superb
buildings of that kind in Europe. . . . He embellished Syon
House, a country seat not far from London, and exhausted the
resources of art at an immense expense to embellish these two
houses with masterpieces of taste, and render them worthy of
their possessors."

This Duke was a great builder. Horace Walpole recorded in
1752: "They are building at Northumberland House, Strand,
at Alnwick and Warkworth Castles. They live by the etiquette
of the old peerage, have Swiss porters, the Countess has pipers,
in short, they will very soon have no estate," and the waspish
Walpole could not forbear to add, regarding the Strand mansion, "it might have been in better taste."

Nevertheless, there was little wrong in the taste of this magnificent duke. He employed a master, Robert Adam, who was
just fresh from the creation of Shardeloes. He was not stinted
in any way. In 1762 the Duke decided to fit up the house entirely in the antique style, that is, the Roman style then being
made famous by Adam. "The idea was to me a favourite one,

the subject great, the expense unlimited, and the Duke himself
a person of extensive knowledge and correct taste in architecture," wrote Adam. He applied himself with zest to his task,
and the result is one of the most magnificently ornamented
houses in England.

Syon House is very seldom on view and the Northumberlands are little in residence there. London scarcely knows what
an astonishing house is hidden behind that drab quadrangle
of bath stone. An American friend of mine once laid siege to it
for a month before he got in. I think he went the wrong way
about it. He was connected with the famous Smithsonian Institution in Washington. This institute was founded by James
Macie Smithson, who was a natural son of our splendid Duke.
Smithson, who was born in Paris, a great chemist and min-
eralogist, left a large fortune to a nephew, with the stipulation
that, should the nephew die without issue, the whole estate
should go "to the United States of America to found at Washington, under the name of the Smithsonian Institution, an
establishment for the increase and diffusion of knowledge
among men." The nephew died without issue and, in September 1838, the clipper *Mediator* sailed to Philadelphia with
£104,960 gold sovereigns on board. Strange as it may seem
this legacy, a huge fortune in those days, aroused much opposition in the United States. A bigoted section, still recalling
the revolution, wanted no favours from Englishmen, particularly a duke's illegitimate son, who had the double offense of
being an aristocrat and a bastard. They bitterly opposed ac-
ceptance of the gift, affirming that Congress had no power under the Constitution to accept it, but through the strenuous
efforts of John Quincy Adams, after ten years of debate, Congress accepted the trust, and the U.S. Treasury made a bad
bargain by agreeing to pay perpetually six per cent on the
fortune that was loaned to them. We are so often indebted to
American generosity for gifts to our public buildings and in-
stitutions that it is pleasant to record Smithson's legacy to the

United States. To-day the Smithsonian Institution is a prosperous and highly important factor in the scientific life of the American nation, and, extended by subsequent legacies, its influence has expanded far beyond the dreams of the original donor.

I have often found that life has a perverse trick of opening doors to those who have no deep desire to pass through them. Within a few months of the difficult entry of my friend, I found myself inside the house, a guest, almost without knowing it. I was a member of a dinner-party whose hostess had been asked to take on her guests to a dance given by the Northumberlands.

"Where?" I asked, as we went downstairs to the car.

"At Syon House—they've opened it specially for the occasion," replied my hostess.

I sat back in the car meditating on the perversity of Fate. Six months ago I had never heard of Syon House, and only my American friend's importunity had brought it to my notice. Even now, as we journeyed through the late summer evening and turned in at the great Lion Gate, I had no idea of the astonishing revelation that awaited me. For when eventually we entered the Great Hall, and proceeded by the ante-room to the Long Gallery, the magnificence of these rooms created for a time the impression that, clad in the toga instead of the "tails," we were being entertained by one of the Roman Emperors, and that the river, glimpsed from the windows, was the Tiber and not the Thames.

It is a house like this at Syon that gives us some measure of the power and the wealth of dominant English families in the eighteenth century, whose equipages, crossing Europe, established a legend of the English Lord, not yet wholly demolished by our ignominious foreign policy in recent years. The social student is aware of the glaring inequalities and the harsh labour conditions on which this great personal wealth of the eighteenth-century aristocracy was based. It was quite indefensible, but with its elimination and a wider prosperity spread over the masses, we may be grateful for such legacies as Syon House, which bears witness to the genius of Robert Adam, as much as to the taste of the Duke who gave him his opportunity. For these state-rooms are his masterwork. The note of classic grandeur is struck at once on entering the Great Hall. It maintains the classic ideal of pure form and simple ornament with its creamy white tone, its black and white marble floor, its upper tier of windows from which the western sun pours golden shafts of light, and the great ceiling with its cross beams and deep borders of ornamented stucco. The Doric order is used with the greatest skill, the fluted columns of wood being painted white. The main floor is reached by marble steps from a lower hall faced with a screen of columns surmounted by an entablature. Statues of Roman Emperors, the Apollo Belvedere, and a large bronze of the Dying Gladiator, strike the classic note. One curious relic, preserved in a glass case, links this room with the Roman era, a stake used in the British stockade at Brentford, to resist Caesar when he crossed the Thames.

The ante-room is Rome, in its most luxurious phase. The cold simplicity of the Great Hall changes here to a symphony of coloured marbles. The ornate ceiling is supported by twelve superb columns of *verd antique*. It is reported that they were recovered from the bed of the Tiber where they had lain since the destruction of Rome. They have square bases of marble, in white and gold, and the columns have been capped with Ionic capitals of solid gilt, carrying an entablature designed by Adam, with a gold frieze of honeysuckle on a blue ground. Walls of pale green have doors of mahogany and gold. The fire-place has a beautiful bas-relief of deep green-bronze, a note that is repeated in the niche opposite with its statue of Hector. The few pieces of furniture in the room belong to an Empire-suite in blue and gold which was in Northumberland House, and originally came from the Tuileries.

The floor is perhaps the most remarkable exhibit in this

splendid room. It is related in pattern to the ceiling, scagliola work, very highly polished, with blended colours of chocolate, blue and greenish grey, which time has reduced to a harmonious softness. Above the entablature the height of the ceiling is emphasized by famous antique statues supported by the *verd antique* columns. This ante-room, with its exquisite Adam fire-place, was used as a waiting-room for servants out of livery, and in the Great Hall itself stood the servants in livery in attendance. The tops of the tables in the recesses are said to be made of marble slabs found in the Roman baths of Titus. It is odd to reflect that many a corpulent Roman senator may have sat sweating on these slabs, and that they echoed the gossip of the proud capital of the ancient world.

The State dining-room reverts to simplicity in tone and design, but it is majestic in size, an oblong balanced by fluted columns at each end carrying an entablature with an apse. The marble mantelpiece has an overmantel, formed in columns, with a panel of the Three Graces. Three niches on either side, with dark grounds, throw into relief six antique statues. There are deep windows to the room, revealing the thickness of the walls, and they have richly panelled shutters. Adam, always of a practical mind, preferred to ornament his dining-room with stucco and statues rather than tapestries and paintings that "they might not retain the smell of victuals," and in the immense dining-room at Syon he has strictly adhered to this plan. The less ornate private dining-room holds some of the treasured works of art, Turner's "Temple of Jupiter," a full-length study of Sir Hugh Smithson, the first Duke of the present creation, a portrait of his Duchess by Reynolds, and a number of works of Hoppner and Kneller.

The drawing-room which follows immediately after the dining-room was originally intended as an ante-room leading to the Long Gallery, which was planned to be the real withdrawing-room. Robert Adam had his own ideas about allowing the diners to burst directly in upon the ladies. He liked to interpose a room between so that the ladies who had withdrawn should not be disturbed by the notorious uproar of gentlemen over their bottles in the eighteenth century. One recalls the snub which Hannah More administered to the hilarious Boswell on his unseemly entrance into a drawing-room. But Adam's good intention was not observed and the tremendous Long Gallery was kept for great social events, more as a show-piece than a retiring-room.

The State drawing-room reflects warmth and colour. Its walls are hung with the first damask made in England, a Spitalfields silk with a rich plum-red ground in which shimmers a profuse floral pattern. This great rectangular room has an elaborate coved ceiling with a pattern of octagons and diamonds, painted with figures by Angelica Kauffmann, and picked out in blue and crimson. One looks and wonders. It is immensely striking but too busy, and gives the eye no repose. The two doorways are of Italian Renaissance design, and the furniture, in crimson damask and gold, is Regency, again brought from Northumberland House.

We now come to the most striking feature of Adam's masterpiece, the Long Gallery, on the south side facing the river, with Kew Gardens filling the vista on the opposite bank. It is 136 feet long, and 14 feet broad. It propounded a problem for Adam which he ingeniously solved. Here is the long gallery of Elizabethan and Jacobean architecture dealt with on the lines of Palladio, a triumph of the adaptation of inner decoration to a fixed form. It is an astonishing room, and the effect is quite breath-taking in the majesty of its design and the note it strikes of luxurious but not opulent decoration. The problem was to get rid of the impression of narrowness, to convert a long corridor, with eleven deeply recessed south windows and three doors and two fire-places on the opposite side, into a visibly proportionate room.

The successful result is so neatly achieved that one must look carefully to find how the eye has been decoyed and the mind satisfied. Between the doors and fire-places Adam grouped units of four pilasters. In between these pilasters, within frames of secondary Ionic pilasters, he placed bookshelves, and this made the Long Gallery a library also. The books, therefore, face the light, as they should and seldom do in libraries, architects having a passion for black spaces between windows. The window side is relieved with mirrors or delightful panels in relief, worked in *stucco duro* which, polished, has the effect of marble. But it is the ceiling that tricks the eye into believing that this long corridor has a breadth it does not possess. It is coloured stucco, designed in a series of circles repeated down the room, each circle held in an octagonal tied with intermittent squares. This pattern, together with a deep cornice decorated with landscapes and portrait panels, and circular recesses containing vases and busts, combined with an exaggerated width of doors, is surely one of the most beautiful and ingenious triumphs of a great genius.

The two towers, part of the four turrets of this quadrilateral mansion, have been cleverly utilized as separate closets at either end of the gallery. One of them might be called a "conceit" for the delight of the ladies. It is a circular boudoir with a dome held up by columns decorated with arabesque stuccoes. Between the columns there are niches, and the two half doors giving admission complete the circular design. From the centre of the dome, beautifully decorated, hangs a golden bird-cage, with a stuffed bird that sings when wound up, and the visible bottom of the cage is a porcelain clock face. But I doubt whether the ladies would be content to be shut up in this circular box, for all its beautiful decoration, its mechanical birdsong and its enchanting view of the smooth Thames. Adam made these terminal closets with the purpose of reducing the great length of the gallery.

The general effect of the decoration is one of faded pink and green, of toned leather on the bindings, of rich mahogany on the doors, and of white marble encasing the fire-places. It is a

ducal dignity of an era when men of great wealth had the
power, if they had the taste, to command the labour of men of
genius, and in this superb home the proud owners set furniture,
pictures, and statues ravished from the treasuries of Italy and
France. The furniture of the Long Gallery belongs in part to a
set of crimson damask and to a set, in pale green and carved
gilt, of Louis XV *petit point*. Each chair is an *objet d'art* with
its convent-worked needlework covers. No wonder the envious
Walpole exclaimed, "I have been this evening to Sion, which
is becoming another Mount Palatine. Adam had displayed great
taste and the Earl matches it with magnificence. His Gallery
is converting into a museum . . ."

One might linger, sustaining a connoisseur's delight, over
the series of rooms, and the pictures they contain, including a
room of Albrecht Dürers and one of the few genuine Holbeins
in England, a portrait of Edward VI as a boy. These are note-
worthy and impressive, but I confess my interest was equally
held by two singular objects. One was a crucifix which belonged to Henry IX, as he was self-styled, otherwise that last
representative of the ill-fated Stuarts, Henry, Cardinal York,
the second son of the Old Pretender. However harsh may be
the criticism of the unlovely Georges who occupied the Stuart
throne, let it be known to his credit that George III, hearing
the rival claimant was in distress and poverty during the
French Revolution, magnanimously made him a grant of £4,000
a year. Gratitude was duly expressed when the Cardinal, dying
at 82, left to King George's son the Crown jewels his grandfather, James II, had run off with from England in 1688.

The other object, a little gruesome, was the death-mask of
Henry VII, a vivid and impressive piece of work. It shows us
Henry VII, the trickster and rapacious miser, who beat Richard III into the dust of Bosworth Field, thus giving England
the great Tudor line of Henry VIII and Queen Elizabeth. This
mask is an authentic work, made by that Torrigiano whose
tomb for the monarch can be seen in Westminster Abbey.

There is an unfulfilled part of Adam's design for Syon House. It was originally intended to place, in the interior of the open court formed by the house, a great rotunda. Had it been built it would have made a central hall "for general rendezvous and for public entertainments with illuminations, dancing and music," in Adam's words, and have been the connecting *salon* with all the surrounding apartments. The nearest approach to this intention was when, in September 1768, the Duke gave a great gala and reception for the King of Denmark. A temporary pantheon was erected in the court, illuminated with four hundred decorative lamps. The building bore the King's cypher on its walls, and with its three hundred guests, its plush-breeched, powdered lackeys, and its royal table where twenty of the more illustrious persons in the land were honoured by dining with the King, it must have been a spectacle of regal splendour. Certainly the King expressed his delight and admiration at this entertainment, but horrible Horace Walpole, true to form, kept at home by an attack of gout, could not forbear to sneer at entertainment and guest. "I was to have gone to the great ball at Sion on Friday, for which a new road, paddock and bridge were made, as other folks made a dessert . . . I believe he is a silly lad, but the mob adore him, though he has neither done nor said anything worth repeating."

Syon House has gardens worthy of its splendour, but the most attractive feature of all is the charming riverside pavilion designed by Robert Adam and beautifully situated against a background of trees, at the Isleworth corner of the estate. It probably gives more pleasure to those on the river than to those walking in the grounds. It has a ribbed dome, and three large French windows with fanlights. The alcoves hold statuary, and the walls have a delicately painted theme of bulrushes, embodying the trident of Father Thames. The windows command a wide prospect of the river, up and down, with the level gardens of Kew on the opposite bank. One legend connected with this boat-house cannot be killed. It kindles the imagination of the local inhabitants, who repeat it with irrepressible certainty. The old boat-house, a part of the pavilion, does contain a state barge, but it is not, as all, except the local owner, avow, the original barge in which Lady Jane Grey was conveyed from Syon to the Tower on that historic day.

One other legend has some foundation in fact. The fifth Duke, a practical joker, liked to stand in the road pointing at the horizontal tail of the Percy Lion when it occupied its original position at Northumberland House. "Look, it moves!" he would declare, and sure of the incredulity of the mob, he won his bet that he could collect a crowd of a hundred in half an hour, many of whom believed they saw the tail wag. There is no truth, however, in the story of a much greater movement on the part of the second lion on the Brentford gateway, which was reported to have been turned about, with its rump towards London, thus expressing the Duke's disgust over a costly financial transaction he had had in the City.

II

It is a morning in April, 1939, there is a crowd gathered before the screen gateway on the old Bath Road at Brentford. Syon House is open again, for the reception of one thousand five hundred guests at the wedding of a Percy to an Egerton. Lady Diana, the sister of the Duke of Northumberland, is being married this day to Viscount Brackley, the only son of the Earl and Countess of Ellesmere. They are young, the bridegroom, Viscount Brackley, being a handsome lad of twenty-four, the bride a charming girl of twenty-two. The world and his wife have crowded Westminster Abbey to see the marriage ceremony performed by the Archbishop of Canterbury. The great families of England are there; together with some humble ones, for near the chancel Industry and Bellona sends its representatives in the persons of twelve girls, chosen by ballot, from the Vickers-Armstrong munition works at Elswick-on-Tyne, in the Percy domain.

In a side chapel, near the tomb of the Unknown Warrior, two tiny pages, Simon Scrope aged five, and David Gordon-Lennox aged six, in white satin trousers, with shirts of white chiffon, frilled at the neck and wrists, wait with a diminutive bridesmaid between them. "He would tickle me," she complained later of one of her young grooms. But just now they are very grave, prompted by four little girls just their seniors, who, in turn, are in charge of a bevy of lovely grown-up bridesmaids.

The bride's mother, the widowed Duchess of Northumberland, in a costume of pale blue, with a wide straw hat of the same soft shade, and satin slippers, stands with her eldest daughter, the Marchioness of Douglas and Clydesdale, and her youngest son, in an Eton suit, Lord Geoffrey Percy. The organ now breaks into the Bridal March from *Lohengrin,* there is a noise of cheering from London outside, the wide doors are flung open, and, silhouetted against the light, stands the bride, on the arm of her young brother, the Duke of Northumberland. She wears an exquisite dress of pale silver and ivory, shrouded in clouds of white tulle. Her wedding veil is of priceless old lace falling on to the corsage of her gown, which is cut heart-shaped in its decolletage. The sleeves are long and tight-fitting and almost cover her fragile hands as they hold a sheaf of lilies tied with a great bow of silver ribbon. The skirt of her gown swells out in classic folds over the floors.

The bride's hair is red-gold, it balances a pearl coronet which holds the veil in place. She smiles as the Archbishop gives her a reassuring word. The choir begin the wedding hymn, the pure treble voices of the choir-boys go soaring up into the tracery of the Abbey transept. The procession moves forward, with all the gold, crimson and green of ecclesiastical vestments; the bride in silver, two little pages, five small bridesmaids, eight grown-ups following, with great bouquets of bright red carnations pressed against their white tulle dresses, whose bouffant skirts are embroidered over the hips with mother-o'-pearl sequins.

The procession has reached the choir, the hushed chancel waits, the Archbishop of Canterbury, the Dean of Westminster, and the Archdeacon of far away Lindisfarne, proceed with the marriage ceremony. The choir and congregation sing, the bride and bridegroom retreat to sign the register, and later, to the strains of Mendelssohn's *Wedding March*, the pageant of youth and beauty moves down the aisle towards the white light beyond the Abbey doors. A babel breaks forth. All London is going on to Syon House, half an hour's car ride away.

The crowd waiting by the Lion Gate is rewarded at last by the sight of the bride and bridegroom, as their car turns in and proceeds up the drive to the house. For the next three-quarters of an hour there is an uninterrupted line of cars and guests. One thinks of other festive occasions in the history of this house, when the long drive was crowded with coaches, chaises, the glitter of harnessed horses, the cries of linkmen, postilions, grooms and running footmen.

The guests have gathered first in Robert Adam's noble atrium, with its black and white marble floor, its apse with the Apollo Belvedere. They wait in this lovely entrance hall while in the ante-room beyond the wedding party is photographed. So, amid the gay company, they look at the statuary and examine the stake in a glass case, that relic of the river palisades built by the early Britons to prevent the Romans crossing the river here. I cannot help thinking of the unknown Briton who shaped that stake, and wondering what he would make of this throng of fashionable guests gathered by the banks of the Thames nearly two thousand years later. And the invading Roman would find a reminder of home in those twelve *verd antique* marble columns brought from the bed of the Tiber, standing now in the ante-room, framing the lovely group of bride, bridegroom and bridesmaids. For we are going forward now, up the marble steps into that exquisite room with its gilt-capped Ionic capitals.

The Duchess of Northumberland has taken her stand by the door, and looks as graceful and beautiful as any duchess in the fiction of the high-life novelist, as she greets her guests. Now there is a handshake from the bride and bridegroom, a hurried word, a glance at the bridesmaids, human flowers in that setting of classic marble, with the deep windows opening on England's April greenery in the park beyond.

We move on into the State dining-room. But we cannot linger, the crowd swells behind and, coming to the State drawing-room, with its silk damask hangings, we should be inclined to halt before the great fire blazing in the superb Adam grate on this cold April day, except for the excitement of passing on into the breath-taking Long Gallery. It seems longer each time one sees it, with its noble vista towards that closet where hangs the singing-bird clock. How many guests in this room now—four hundred? Yet it does not seem crowded. And it would be nice to linger, to scrutinize these walls yard by yard, to sit in the deep embrasure of the windows and gaze towards distant Kew Gardens beyond the silver Thames, or to begin the dizzy task of examining the skilful design of the ceiling, planned to diminish the great length of the gallery. But the hustling dowagers push us on. A lean and hungry vicar has somehow scented the distant buffet. The world and his wife crowd down a narrow back-staircase, and hesitate briefly, as between Scylla and Charybdis. "Presents on the right, refreshments in the loggia below. Kindly move on, ladies and gentlemen!" cries a footman.

Shades of Horace Walpole and the dear, dull King of Denmark! A great orange awning has covered in the quadrangle formed by the four sides of the house. It was here that Adam had planned his general rendezvous for "public entertainments, with Illuminations, Dancing and Music," and here that the

Duke, in 1768, had erected a temporary pantheon for the reception of the young King of Denmark, whom Walpole sniffed at for a silly lad. To-day Robert Adam's plan seems fulfilled. Under the orange canopy rows and rows of tables display the wedding-presents.

There is a more intimate buffet in the immense drawing-room. Here the young Duke is passing sandwiches while his ancestors look down upon him from the walls. He is so happy and hospitable that I utter a little prayer on his behalf to the Commissioners of Inland Revenue, pleading that he may live in enjoyment of his Syon House.

But away all menacing shadows. Young Lord Geoffrey, in the widest of Eton collars, is busy at the buffet, and at a round table, carefully watched by their nannies, the two little pages, Simon Scrope and David Gordon-Lennox have somehow kept their satin suits and shirts of frilled chiffon unspotted. At a safe distance sits the tiny bridesmaid who complained of being tickled at a solemn moment.

It is four o'clock, and soon the bride and bridegroom will be leaving. Out in the great park a crowd of chauffeurs wait by their cars. But few guests seem to be departing. The magnificent house, the lavish hospitality, the beauty and gaiety of so many young people, so many lovely women, the famous, the rich, the high-born, and a general concourse of those whose lives are in some way linked with the fate of the Percys, all make a scene which cannot but be rare now in this changing England.

III

The public footpath through the Park from the east to the west side is said to have had its origin in the fact that Henry VIII's body lay at Syon on its way to Windsor. . . . It was often held that the passage of a dead body created a public right of way. Whether that be true or not we can enjoy the walk to-day, across the park, and out into the roadway beyond the wall, where a surprise awaits us. For there, hidden by a bend in the road, lies Isleworth, on its reach of the Thames, almost forgotten by the world. There is a raised promenade in front of the church, and on this "beach" of the Thames a few stranded boats give a nautical air to the scene. The first time I turned this corner and found Isleworth, I could hardly believe what I saw. The old church is not particularly beautiful, though derived in part from Wren's plans. The churchwardens had asked Sir Christopher to design them a church, but on seeing the plans they thought they could do better themselves, and they proceeded to alter them. Whatever one may think of the result, and I like its old tower, its flagged approach to the great door, its general lazy air of creeper-covered neglect, it has a superb position, facing Kew Gardens and the Observatory meadows at the end of Syon reach. There is a wide open space from which the church can be viewed, and seen from the river it fits the picture perfectly. Its companion in this composition is equally notable. It is an inn as picturesque as its name. *The London Apprentice* was plainly built to catch the river traffic, and at one end of it there is a gazebo whose windows command the Thames, and the long island of osiers that divides the river, where some barge or sailing boat, in the process of unloading, creates the illusion of an old seaport. When the tide is out and the seagulls hover about these barges, with their rudders lying exposed above the wet mud, the illusion is complete. Few artists have been able to resist *The London Apprentice*. It recalls the eighteenth century when the young apprentices of the London Guild came here by boat to celebrate their feast days and holidays.

I was fortunate in the hour of my visit. The door of the saloon bar was open. In I went, and, as should be the case, I found what appeared to be a brace of apprentices drinking with a quartette of old salts. But the apprentices, very smart in their flannel trousers and sports jackets, manfully puffing at their pipes, had aroused the ire of the old salts, whose only

claim to seamanship was established by blue jerseys, sea-boots
and lurid language. They were off lighters whose longest voy-
ages were between Gravesend and some local mills. One of
them had some claim as a local historian. He retailed with
much detail how "Bloody" Mary, who had had her head
chopped off by Henry VIII (he kept his "sweeties" at Syon
House), had been taken to the Tower in a barge that was still
in the Duke's boathouse.

Here was a hoary legend, slightly redressed in regard to the
chief actresses. But one of the apprentices, removing his pipe,
created a scene by a blank contradiction.

"It wasn't 'Bloody' Mary at all—it was Lady Jane Grey,
and it wasn't Henry VIII who chopped off her head, it was
Queen Elizabeth," said the London apprentice.

"And what's more—it's all nonsense about it being the same
barge—it rotted away long ago," added the second apprentice.

There was a menacing silence for a few moments. The four
salts shuffled their feet, moved their beer-cans, and looked at
each other. Then the spokesman of the party turned to the
London apprentice and his companion.

"I know what you are," he said, scornfully, "you're one of
those young know-alls from London. When you've been un-
pinned from your napkins a bit longer you'll be wiser!"

The old salt turned to me with a hurt expression.

"Can't tell these Cockney sparrows anything, Guvnor. All
chirp and cheek! I was born here, so I ought to know."

"Then you ought to know better," replied the second apprentice, unabashed.

The outlook became stormy. I asked the landlord to fill up
our cans.

"I'm sure you know a lot of interesting things about this
place," I said, addressing the glowering man in the jersey.

"I'm saying nothing. Ask them know-alls," he replied,
truculently.

"Very well!" exclaimed the bright youth in the spotted

sports jacket. "Did you know, sir, that the American expression 'O Gee!' came from the church here?"

I confessed I did not, and expressed my surprise that something so hundred-per-cent American should have originated in Isleworth.

"Well, sir, believe it or not," replied the bright youth, after puffing hard at his pipe, and looking with a merry eye at his companion, "in a way America started from here. Lord Baltimore, James I's Secretary of State, lived here, and, as you know, he founded the colony of Baltimore. And then, in 1764, one of the Earls of Northumberland, living at Syon House, was appointed Vice-Admiral of all America."

The four companions in jerseys began to stare at the London apprentice. It was too much for their spokesman.

"An' I suppose, my friend, you'll tell us next that George Washington 'isself's buried in the churchyard!" he exclaimed, spitting in emphasis of his disbelief.

The bright youth laughed, in no way disconcerted by the scornful comment.

"No—but O Gee is!" he replied.

I looked at him. He had a merry eye and was a born legpuller, obviously.

"It's true," asserted his companion, through a cloud of pipesmoke. "I didn't believe it myself until he showed me."

"I don't understand," I said.

"Well, it's like this, sir," replied the youth. "If you go inside the church you'll find a bust there. It's a memorial to Sir Orlando Gee, who died in 1705. He must have known Samuel Pepys, for he was Registrar of the Admiralty, and acted as Steward to the Earl of Northumberland. It's sober fact, sir; you can go and see it for yourself."

"But we couldn't find any memorial to Mr. O. Kay," added his companion, facetiously.

"Now I'll tell you something—and it's solemn truth," cried the man in the jersey, banging down his empty can, his good humour returned. "Have you seen the sun-dial on the wall facing the river? It tells the time at Moscow, Jamaica, Jerusalem and London."

"Yes—I've seen it," said the bright youth. "Why does it give the time in those places?"

"Oh, that's something you don't know, then," chuckled the old salt. "Well, I'll tell you. The man who put it up, he was a sailor, like me, an' he 'ad four wives, all at the same time."

"Like you?" asked the younger apprentice, facetiously.

The old salt gave him a withering look.

"I'm a respectable married man, with five kids," he retorted, "an' no girls looking for me with a maintenance order, young feller! As I was saying, he 'ad four wives all at the same time. One was a Russian, and she lived in Moscow, and one was a Negress, and she lived in Jamaica, and one was a Jewess, and she lived in Jerusalem, and one was an English girl, and she lived in London. He put up that sundial so as he could think of 'em all at the same time!"

"O Gee, that's a good one," cried the bright youth. "The drinks are on me!"

The London apprentice, I found, was actually an articled pupil in the office of the architect who was doing some work on the church, hence his knowledge. I went with him and his friend across to the church, where he showed me the memorial to O Gee. Sir Orlando is a cheerful-looking old gentleman in a flowing wig, and he must have been a good four-bottle man, despite the fact that he lived to the ripe age of eighty-five. And here we can find the baptismal registration of a child who, in her teens, filled a poet with romantic passion, and inspired one of the loveliest lyrics in the English tongue. Lady Dorothy Sidney, the daughter of the Earl of Leicester, was baptized here in 1617, and lived in Isleworth during her widowhood. She was born at Syon House while the Earl of Northumberland, her grandfather, was confined to the Tower on the suspicion of being connected with the Gunpowder Plot. We only remember her now because Edmund Waller, seeing this maiden in 1635, conferred immortality on himself and her with his poem *Sacharissa*, the name he gave to the lady. His lyric *Go, Lovely Rose* keeps fresh their memories.

> *Small is the worth*
> *Of beauty from the light retired:*
> *Bid her come forth,*
> *Suffer herself to be desired,*
> *And not blush so to be admired.*
> *Then die—that she*
> *The common fate of all things rare*
> *May read in thee;*
> *How small a part of time they share*
> *That are so wondrous sweet and fair!*

These old registers, dating from 1566, record the marriage in 1679 of another fair one, the Lady Elizabeth Percy, to a gentleman with the singular title of Earl of Ogle.

Lady Elizabeth was the daughter of the last Earl of Northumberland, of the first creation, and on her father's death she was an heiress at the age of four, to great wealth and six of the oldest baronies. She was, therefore, a good "catch," and every ambitious man in the land sought for her hand in marriage. Her grandmother had refused the hand of Charles II's son, the Duke of Richmond, by his mistress, Louise de Kéroualle, Duchess of Portsmouth. At the age of thirteen, Lady Elizabeth was married to the Duke of Newcastle's heir, the Earl of Ogle, a sickly boy of fifteen—"the ugliest and saddest creature," said her great-aunt, the lady of Waller's muse. The boy-husband died within a year, whereupon, aged fourteen, the child-widow was married, in 1681, to Thomas Thynne, a battered rake known in all the gaming *salons* of London. The marriage was never consummated. The child-wife took refuge with a relation abroad, and Thynne laid claim to her fortune, which he obtained, whereupon she returned to live with him. But he was soon to be the victim of a crime of jealousy. Count Königsmark, who had unsuccessfully wooed the heiress, challenged Thynne to a duel. Failing to obtain satisfaction he hired two assassins, who held up Thynne's coach in Pall Mall and killed him with a blunderbuss. The Count and his hirelings were tried for murder. Königsmark was acquitted through bribery, but his two associates were hanged on the scene of the crime.

Widowed Mrs. Thynne was married again, within three months, and still only fifteen, to Charles, Duke of Somerset. He was both vain and arrogant, but without ability. He had a passion for funerals, and lived to attend those of Charles II, Queen Mary, William III, Queen Anne and George I. He never stirred abroad without having the roads cleared by outriders to protect him from the gaze of the vulgar. He would not speak to servants, who received his orders by signs, and because his daughter once presumed to sit in his presence he took from her £20,000 of her inheritance. But the measure of his vanity lives in the story of his rebuke to his second wife who, to attract his attention, had tapped him with her fan. "Madam," he said, freezingly, "my first wife was a Percy, and she never took such a liberty." It was this peacock who entertained Queen Anne at Syon House.

Despite the fact that the churchwardens adhered to their own plans, in preference to those of Wren, the church inside is extremely pleasing. It has a very fine barrel roof supported by pillars from a wide upper gallery on each side. This formation gives it light and spaciousness, and the monuments in the church are both interesting and well preserved. Sir Orlando Gee occupies a prominent space on the wall of the belfry tower.

On the opposite wall it would seem fitting to find Mr. O. Kay, as the London apprentice suggested. But there is a memorial opposite to someone who really proved herself quite right, and in every respect worthy of tribute. It celebrates one, Ann Tolson, and tells its own story.

"In the last State of her Widowhood She was reduced to narrow and confined circumstances and supported herself keeping School for the Education of Young Ladies, for which She was Qualified by a Natural Ingenuity, a strict regular Education, a Mild and gentle Disposition. By the loss of sight She became unfit for her Employment, and a proper Object to receive that Charity she was Solicitous to Distribute."

Fate was kind to thrice-widowed Ann Tolson. She inherited a fortune, and in gratitude left instructions for her benefactors to be remembered. So here they are, in medallions on either side of her. Dr. and Mrs. Susannah Cotesworth. "By long and successful Practice and great Economy he became possessed of a Fortune to the amount of One Hundred and Fifty Thousand Pounds and Upwards." This leaves one wondering how remarkable must have been the practice, or how rigid the economy. The doctor's wife on her death left this fortune among three next-of-kin, and thus it was Ann Tolson, in penury and blindness, was raised to wealth. She remembered her days of want, and in gratitude endowed an almshouse, which exists to-day, a double row of quaint cottages running down to the river, a little behind *The London Apprentice*. Moreover, she instructed a descendant to erect a memorial to the good Cotesworths and herself, at a cost of five hundred pounds. It seems very dear at the price, and is significantly by a sculptor named Halfpenny. Since Ann died, aged eighty-nine, in 1759, it was possible for her to have been at the funeral of her *vis-à-vis*, Sir Orlando Gee.

There is a long list of the vicars, dating from the fourteenth century, among them the unfortunate Rev. John Hall, vicar for fourteen years, who was hanged by Henry VIII at Tyburn in 1535. Some of the vicars would seem to have been less troubled by conscience. Isleworth played its part in the smuggling days, and it was declared that barrels were smuggled into the vaults of the church at high tide, and thence transported for disposal, by subterranean passage, to *The London*

Apprentice, with the connivance of the vicar. But in the course of my investigations in various parts of England, I find these underground passages as persistent as the hiding holes of Dick Turpin, and the sleeping places of Queen Elizabeth. One wonders whether air-raid shelters in this present century will raise another crop of legendary passages for the next.

Before we leave Isleworth, let us recall a strange visitor here, Vincent Van Gogh, the mentally deranged man of genius, famous as a Dutch post-impressionist painter. In the spring of 1876, at the age of twenty-four, he accepted a post as teacher of languages and came to Isleworth shortly afterwards as a kind of assistant preacher in a Methodist school, kept by a Mr. Jones, for whom he served in the role of curate. He had come to London as assistant at the Goupil Gallery at £70 a year, and the first things he did were to buy a silk hat and fall in love. "It is impossible to go out in London without a top hat," he wrote to his brother. In about a year he returned to Holland to study theology, his religious mania increasing. A strange tortured creature—he once cut off the lobe of his ear and presented it in an envelope to a café waitress. He worked in intervals of inspired sanity, and finally shot himself at the age of thirty-seven.

CHAPTER VII

Osterley Park, Exterior

SYON PARK is not the only large house and estate on this outskirt of London, adjacent to the Old Bath Road. It has a worthy and remarkable neighbour in Osterley Park. The road leading up from Isleworth Church, the river front, and along Syon Park wall, crosses the Old Bath Road leading into Hounslow and, as Syon Lane, intersects the new Great West Road and takes us to the lodge gates of Osterley Park.

Hundreds of motor-cars pass daily within a few yards of this great park without being aware of its existence, for the broad straight surface of this factory and villa-hemmed highway is too tempting to the lover of speed. On roar the cars, at forty, fifty and sixty miles an hour. From Syon Park we may have seen a tower incongruously obtruding on the northern horizon. It bears a massive clock, and is a landmark for the motorist. It belongs neither to a cathedral nor a town hall, but commemorates the prosperous industry of shaving male chins with the safety-razor invented and given world-wide fame by Mr. Gillette of U.S.A.

We shall look in vain for a house once on that site. Mr. Archibald Robertson, journeying along the Bath Road in 1792, remarked on "an elegant little villa belonging to the Duke of Marlborough. It serves as a pleasant retreat for His Grace and his noble family. The land here is rich and valuable." It is indeed, and being ripe for development the site of the ducal villa has produced a crop of factories and semi-detached villadom.

There is one respect in which this new Great West Road is something of a world's industrial fair, and the owners of the businesses who have built their factories here have vied with each other in architectural originality. The classical, the modern and the ultra-modern styles all compete for attention. The result is a praiseworthy gaiety which has completely banished the hideousness and the prison-like gloom of the nineteenth-century factories. Here are Greek temples, Egyptian and Roman halls, stone, glass, steel and concrete edifices housing employees who make scent, tyres, golf balls, potato chips, razor blades, motorcar bodies, screen-wipers, air-conditioning shafts, toothpastes, swimming-costumes, and the innumerable articles of a twentieth-century civilization. Can these be factories, or have the children of modern industry learned to play in Elysian fields of union labour? This long façade of palaces devoted to business, where once the flat plain was clad in a white drift of apple blossom at springtime, is as astonishing a feature on the road to Bath as any we shall encounter. Let us not hurry too much; earth has many prospects more enchanting but few more provocative of thought than the spirit of a new age expressed in the buildings of those industrial demi-gods, Messrs. Coty (scents), Firestone (tyres), Gillette (razor blades), Smith (potato crisps) and Maclean (tooth-paste).

Over the Great West Road, in the shadow of Mr. Gillette's tower, let us pass on towards the gates of Osterley Park. Here survives a peer with a park six miles in circumference, and a vast mansion, less than ten miles from the heart of London. Within this park, whose wall holds at bay a besieging army of villas, thronged with city-commuting clerks, the ghost of the *grand seigneur* of the eighteenth century still walks in a house with a fine Ionic portico, four turrets, and stables that reach back to the era of Queen Elizabeth.

If its history is not so closely related to England's long story as is that of Syon, Osterley Park is no parvenu. An Abbess of Syon once owned it, but it is a great merchant adventurer who

made Osterley Park notable. Sir Thomas Gresham began business as Henry VIII's agent in the Low Counties, and he seems
to have been the first of currency manipulators, for he succeeded
in raising the value of the pound sterling on the Antwerp
bourse, and in getting rid of Edward VI's debt. He was a
shrewd business man, like his father, and he built at his own
expense a bourse or exchange in London, begging the site from
the city aldermen, and letting out the upper part as shops.
Thus began the Royal Exchange, and when we look at the
statue of Sir Thomas on the east face of the campanile, let us
not overlook the gilded vane in the form of a grasshopper,
which was Gresham's crest. In Osterley Park to-day you can
encounter grasshoppers and marigolds, which is significant, for
on the Royal Exchange is the grasshopper, the crest of one
owner of Osterley, and on a cheque drawn on Child's Bank, the
watermark is a marigold, the crest of another owner.

Shrewd Sir Thomas was given Osterley Park by Queen
Elizabeth, and he proceeded to build himself a vast mansion.
He also enclosed a large part of Hounslow Heath to create a
park, which did not make him popular in the district. His magnificent mansion was completed in 1577, and Queen Elizabeth
came to look at it, and, undoubtedly this time, slept in it. She
had only one criticism to make. The courtyard was so vast
that she thought it would look better divided by a wall; whereupon she went to bed. "What doeth Sir Thomas but in the
night-time sends for workmen to London who so speedily and
silently applied their business that the next morning that court
was double which the night before was single." Surely this
sounds like the origin of that mathematical absurdity whereby
if ten men can build a wall in one hour, therefore six hundred
and forty men can build it in less than a minute. In any case
Elizabeth must have been a sound sleeper.

Certainly she spent more than one night there. Gresham entertained her sumptuously and had a play performed for her.
The tranquillity of the visit was marred by some local inhab-

itants who, resenting the heath enclosure, set fire to the park palings, which so offended the Queen that she had four men put into prison.

Gresham was involved by another form of his Queen's displeasure. Her cousin, Lady Mary Grey, a sister of the ill-fated Lady Jane of Syon House, had secretly married Thomas Keyes, the Royal sergeant-porter, in his room at the Westminster Water Gate. The infuriated Queen considered this a shocking *mésalliance*. She had them separated at once. Keyes was locked up in the Fleet, and Lady Mary was sent to Chequers, the present country house of our Prime Minister. Later she passed into the charge of Gresham, much against his will. He kept her in custody at Osterley and pleaded again and again to be relieved of his unpleasant duty. His request was met only when the husband died in prison after seven years of captivity. The unhappy Lady Mary was then permitted to leave Osterley Park, but did not long survive her husband.

Gresham died in 1578, having suffered the loss of his only son Richard. This loss had ended his ambition to found a great house. The building of the Exchange, the founding of Gresham College, and various charitable enterprises, absorbed his final years. Osterley Park passed successively to a stepson, to the Countess of Desmond, and then by purchase to Sir William Waller, the Parliamentary General. In 1683 it came into the hands of a singular person who called himself Dr. Nicholas Barbon, the son of the famous Praise-God Barebones of Cromwell's Parliament, a noisy Baptist politician. The son, with no relish for his father's views, dropped the "e's" and became plain Barbon. He had an extraordinary career as a speculative builder, though he had been trained as a doctor of physic. The destruction of London by the Great Fire in 1666 gave him his opportunity, and he made a large fortune rebuilding in the City, the Temple, Lincoln's Inn, and St. James' Square. He was notable also for having been the first to do business as an insurer of property against fire.

About twelve years after Barbon's death, Osterley was purchased by Sir Francis Child, a man quite as remarkable as the first owner. He was one of seven sons of a Wiltshire man. At the age of fourteen he was apprenticed to a London goldsmith. In 1664 he went into partnership with a goldsmith named Wheeler who carried on a business as goldsmith and banker at the Sign of the Marigold by Temple Bar, where Child and his partner kept "running cashes." Thus the bank began, where it exists to this day, with the marigold watermark on its cheques. In 1671 young Child had married Miss Wheeler, and eventually two fortunes passed into his hands. Shrewdly capable, he became Lord Mayor, and was knighted, and his bank subsequently numbered among its clients Charles II, Nell Gwynn, Prince Rupert, Pepys and Dryden.

Sir Francis, who never occupied Osterley Park, left his fortune to ten sons and three daughters. Robert and Francis, the eldest and fourth sons, carried on the banking business, and were both knighted. Sir Robert died and Osterley Park passed to Sir Francis, who died in 1740, leaving it to Samuel, the youngest of the ten brothers, all his seniors having died without male descendants. It was Samuel's elder surviving son, Francis, who succeeded to the property and, in 1761, called in Robert Adam to create the magnificent house we now see.

Adam had scarcely begun his task of changing an Elizabethan house into a Georgian one when his client died. Poor young man, he was cut off while preparing a home for a young lady to whom he had been engaged only two months. The watchful Horace Walpole had something to say, of course. Nothing in his district, or in England for that matter, escaped the shrew of Strawberry Hill. His note is acid as usual. He had been inspecting Osterley in 1763, and wrote to a companion on that visit:

". . . Now suddenly the prospect of joy at Osterley was dashed after our seeing it. However, the young lover died handsomely. £50,000 will dry tears that at most would be but two months old.

His brother, I heard, has behaved still more handsomely, and confirmed the legacy, and added from himself the diamonds that had been prepared for her—here is a charming wife ready for anybody that likes a sentimental situation, a pretty woman and a large fortune."

The caustic prophecy was soon fulfilled, for a year later the bereaved Miss Hampden became the Countess of Suffolk.

Robert now became the head of the bank and the family. He left the Child house in London, and completed Osterley Park. He brought from its position on the staircase ceiling in the London house the great Rubens canvas of the Apotheosis of William I of Orange, which the first Sir Francis had bought in the Low Countries in 1697 for £400, the same price as he had paid for another Rubens of "The Duke of Buckingham on Horseback," which also was now brought to Osterley, the Apotheosis being placed, as in London, on the staircase ceiling, the Buckingham at the end of the gallery, where they have been ever since Robert Adam placed them there.

Walpole who had visited the completed house, except for three rooms on the south-east side, in the summer of 1773, was this time enthusiastic, except for a derogatory comparison with Strawberry Hill, his own gimcrack Gothic mansion.

"On Friday we went to see—oh, the palace of palaces!—and yet a palace *sans* crown, *sans* coronet, but such expense! such taste! such profusion! and yet half an acre produces all the rents that furnish such magnificence." This was an allusion to Child's Bank by Temple Bar. He continued, "The old house I have often seen, which was built by Sir Thomas Gresham; but it is so improved and enriched, that all the Percies and Seymours of Syon must die of envy. There is a double portico that fills the space between the towers of the front, and is as noble as the Propyleum of Athens. There is a hall, library, breakfast-room, eating-room, all *chefs d'œuvre* of Adam, a gallery 130 feet long and a drawing-room worthy of Eve before the Fall. Mrs. Child's dressing-room is full of pictures, gold filigree, china and japan. So is all the house; the chairs are taken from antique lyres, and make charming harmony; there are Salvators, Poussins, and, to a beautiful staircase, a ceiling by Rubens. There is a kitchen garden that costs £1,400 a year, a menagerie full of birds . . . and in the drawing-room are door-cases and a crimson and gold frieze, that I believe was borrowed from the Palace of the Sun; and then the park is the ugliest spot in the universe, and so I returned comforted to Strawberry."

Robert Child, like Sir Thomas Gresham, craved a male heir in vain, and his only daughter Sarah gave him a shock and became the heroine of a runaway match that kept to the full romantic tradition. Sarah Child was a great catch, being young, pretty and an heiress. The Marquess of Graham sought her hand, and the Duchess of Marlborough produced her son, Lord Blandford, as a candidate. But Mr. Child had other views. He had no son to succeed. He wanted, therefore, an untitled son-in-law who would take the name of Child, and provide a grandson for the eventual headship of the bank.

There was a dashing young man upon whom Sarah looked with favour. Unhappily he was a peer of the realm, the tenth Earl of Westmorland. So often the rich business man is anxious to marry his children into the Peerage that Mr. Child's opposition must have appeared both unique and fantastic. Moreover, he was almost to blame for what happened. The young Earl, handsome and intelligent, was very much in love, and Sarah returned his attachment. At dinner one night at Mr. Child's he asked his host, "If you were in love with a girl, and her father refused his consent to the union, what would you do?" "Why, run away with her, to be sure!" replied the resolute Mr. Child.

The Earl took his advice. It was the era of Gretna Green, and what followed is faithful in every detail to the novelette manner of romantic elopement. The young couple set off by coach for Gretna Green, and were pursued by the irate father. *The Morning Herald*, May 21st, 1782, tells the sequel.

"Mr. Child, the banker, and his attendants returned yesterday morning to town, after a vain pursuit of the Earl of Westmorland, who carried off that gentleman's daughter early on Friday morning last; two of Mr. Child's pursuers came up with the amorous fugitives a little on the other side of Baldock, one of whose horses was instantly shot under him by Lord Westmorland's people, to prevent his getting ahead of them, the man's intent being to retain all the carriages at the next stage and thus stop the lovers' progress; the other servants instantly turned tail, and from that moment the pursuit was abandoned, so that there is not the smallest doubt but the young spirited heroine has before this time been hailed the lovely Countess of Westmorland."

Mr. Child could do nothing but accept the marriage. He consented to a licence for a church ceremony a month later, but absented himself. Two months afterwards Mr. Child died. He passed over his defiant daughter in his will, and over the first-born son of the marriage, who would be the heir to the earldom, and bequeathed his fortune to the second son of Sarah, or failing him, the eldest daughter. As only one son was born, the future eleventh Earl of Westmorland, the fortune went to the daughter, Lady Sarah Sophia Child Fanes, Mr. Child's granddaughter. His widow married Lord Ducie, and died two years later, in 1793. Meanwhile, her daughter Sarah was Vicereine of Ireland, where she had followed her husband, the Viceroy, from 1789–1795. In the same year as Mrs. Child's death the Countess succumbed to fever at Phœnix Park, and the Countess's daughter, Sarah, inherited Mr. Child's wealth, which had been estimated at £30,000 a year from the banking business, and £15,000 from the estates, not including the magnificent Osterley Park. Lady Sarah was only eight years old at this time when she lost both mother and grandmother. At nineteen she married Lord Villiers, soon to succeed as the fifth Earl of Jersey. Thus again Mr. Child's plan was defeated; there was no male child to succeed, except a titled one. The young Countess of Jersey thus brought Osterley Park to the Jersey family. She assumed the headship of Child's Bank, and outlived both her husband and her eldest son, the sixth Earl of Jersey, who only survived his father by three weeks. The Dowager Countess, a great figure in Society, died in 1867, aged eighty-two. Her grandson, the seventh Earl, inherited Osterley. There was a short interval, during which the house was let to Caroline, Duchess of Cleveland, and it was her to whom August Hare alluded "June 1877 Lady Manners drove me to Osterley. The great wide park looked dark and dull under a leaden sky, the house as gloomy and ghostly as Bleak House, the old Duchess, stumping about with her ebony stick, seemed part of the place."

Elopement was in the Child blood, and it was a case later of, like grandmother, like granddaughter, for Lady Adele Villiers also eloped to Gretna Green with a gallant captain, who was not considered of the first rank. Lady Adele was forgiven, and when the Countess finally consented to receive the husband, she observed that she had no idea the middle classes were so clean!

Osterley Park witnessed some gay scenes in the Regency days when it was reigned over by the "victorious" Countess of Jersey. The beautiful and renowned Lady was the daughter of the Bishop of Raphoe, and another Countess of Jersey, in her reminiscences, tells us that the Bishop combined the calling of highwayman on the adjacent Hounslow Heath with that of the Church.

"Visitors who dined with him at Osterley were often attacked on their homeward way, and if they shot in self-defence found their weapons missed fire. One night a guest was warned that his charges had been drawn. He reloaded, and on being accosted by a masked man, fired, and his assailant made off. The Bishop was for some weeks unable to perform his episcopal functions."

The menagerie which Walpole saw has gone, so we shall look in vain for a sight that excited Mr. Archibald Robertson in 1792, who remarked on "an elegant menagerie, containing a large collection of exotic and curious birds, and a rookery, the numerous tricks of which seemed to have been in a superior degree directed by instinct to make choice of this, as an asylum, and secure place of abode, as it is for the rest of the feathered creation; and through their hoarse-sounding throats proclaim the happiness and liberty they enjoy in common with the more beautiful inhabitants of this protected spot."

It is still a protected spot, with the great park gallantly defying the engulfing sea of London all around it. The glory of the park, the house with its stately façade, the Orangery, the Aviary, and other buildings, all the work of Robert Adam, together with the splendid Tudor stables, are still there for us to marvel at. And still intact is the lovely upper lake framed in noble trees, and the lower lake in a dense bluebell-carpeted wood that might be a thousand miles from civilization, in its utter solitude. And yet all this is but a mile distant from the unceasing rumble of traffic on the Great West Road, and little more than seven from Hyde Park Corner.

As with Syon House, one wonders how long it can survive the double pressure of high taxation and encroaching bricks and mortar. For both these great houses with their parks are gripped by the tentacles of the great City, oases of green beauty in a wilderness of houses.

II

Having been endowed from birth with an insatiable curiosity, I could not leave Osterley Park without having completely encircled the grounds. It is a good two hours' walk, but on a May day, with the apple orchards in full blossom, the thrushes singing madly, the calves standing knee-deep in lush meadows, and all the trees in their maiden green leaf, I had no mercy on Rudolf, my Austrian guest, still with me.

It must be said for Rudolf, eighteen, and with a tremendous zest for going everywhere and seeing everything, that I always found him ready to aid my excursions. A little bolder, perhaps conscious of the charm of his smile and the attraction of his broken accent, he had shown himself adept at pushing open doors, trespassing in gardens, and penetrating into many places where I hesitated. If the guardian of the place happened to be a lady, and a young one, then all doors flew open.

"You English are kind; you so much like Austrians," said Rudolf one day, after a particularly agreeable encounter with a vicar's pretty daughter. "Some Austrians," I felt it my duty to say. "Young ones and good-looking ones?" asked the shameless Rudolf. I looked disapprovingly, but a peal of laughter marked the enjoyment of his childlike conceit.

He agreed at once that we must walk all round Osterley Park, even if it took all day and night. The Schloss, as he called it, enchanted him. So off we started, and the encircling Osterley Lane brought us eventually past kitchen-gardens and fields out on to Norwood Green, a triangle of turf and trees set round with houses that might have been in the heart of Shropshire. Then we retraced our steps a little and struck a path leading past an old farm-house. It was there Rudolf saw a church-tower. I realized that it was Heston Church, and at once he decided it must be viewed before we resumed the circuit of Osterley Park.

So across open fields, some ploughed, some converted into market-gardens, and some, alas, showing the encroachment of the builder, to Heston Church we went. The church was disappointing, but two things rewarded us, one an old lich-gate, the other a tombstone with a tragic story behind it.

Heston has for centuries been famous for the quality of its land. All around this district of Hounslow, Heston and Isleworth, the rich soil has furnished the larder of London, until the Great West Road ran through the endless orchards and plantations and produced a crop of factories in the place of apples, potatoes, onions, tomatoes, cabbages, lettuces, and wheat. A few of these rich market-gardens still exist to emphasize the devastation that out-growing London spreads over the countryside.

It is difficult now to realize that Heston was once a great
granary. "A more fertyle place of wheate, yet not so much to
be commended for the quantitie, as for the qualitie, for the
wheate is most pure, accompted the purest in mannie shires.
And therefore Queen Elizabeth hath the most part of her pro-
vision from that place for manchet for her Highnes owne diet,
as is reported," wrote a chronicler in 1593.

Fruit gardens were once upon a time particularly plentiful
around here. "First the ground is stocked with apples, pears,
cherries, plums, walnuts, etc., like a complete orchard which
they call the upper crop. It is secondly fully planted with rasp-
berries, gooseberries, currants, strawberries, and all such fruits,
and herbs as we know sustain the shade and drip from the trees
above them with the least injury. This they term the under
crop. Some of these gardens have walls, which are completely
clothed with wall fruits; such as nectarines, peaches, apricots,
plums, and various others, all properly adapted to the aspect of
the wall."

Gone are most of the orchards and fruit gardens, but Osterley Park kitchen-gardens and orchards, in their extent and cul-
tivation, still retain the former aspect of this rich soil. Even until 1930 the motorist made his way along the new Great West
Road through six consecutive miles of apple and cherry orchards, for which one now looks in vain, seeing only factories,
and houses that seem cast out of a mould, like the jellied horror
that accompanies the prunes of Sunday evening supper in suburban England.

In such market-gardens and farm-lands as have survived, one
may still witness a certain custom lingering on from the former
centuries. This is the annual invasion of women from Shropshire, fruit-pickers and harvesters, who formerly made the journey by canal. Like the Kent hop-pickers, they live in the local
barns or their own tents, in much the fashion of their ancestors
who came here each year as long ago as 1700. Many of them
carried the fruit into London, and in the old days there were

wooden posts, some four or five feet high, placed along the road to London, so that the women, who carried their baskets on their heads, could rest them without having to raise them from the ground when they restarted.

All these posts have disappeared, but I did find another relic of the old days, and one that sent my mind back to a familiar sight that greets the rider across the great Hungarian plains. This was a water-raiser, a device formerly used in these gardens. Water was always found some eight or ten feet below the surface. A shallow well was dug and a post was set in the ground a little way off. At the top of this post a beam of about twelve feet turned on a pin. The bucket and rope hung from one end of the beam, and a weight was fastened as a counterpoise to the other end. The beam was pulled down until the bucket was immersed, and, helped by the weight, a small lift brought it full to the surface. Evening after evening, while the wide-winged sunset burned over the Hungarian Puszta, I have watched the peasants water their cattle and horses, and it was a singular experience to see a Heston market-gardener water his garden with the same primitive but effective device. Rudolf immediately offered his services, and took the greatest delight in swinging the bucket. "In Tyrol all water goes down. Here it goes up. Upla!" he shouted, gleefully.

Lovers of England have so much to lament to-day in the reckless and appalling changes in the English landscape that almost every new book on the countryside is filled, in wearisome reiteration, with unavailing protests against the vandalism and vulgarity of the age. But have we changed really; shall we ever change? As far back as 1793 a correspondent of the Board of Agriculture, writing of this same district, lamented that "to the astonishment of every foreigner who visits us it still contains many thousands of acres, still in a state of nature; and, though within a few miles of the capital, as little improved by the labour of man, as if they belonged to the Cherokees, or any other tribe of American savages."

But let us never again refer to this, let us pass over, in sad silence, the spectacle of a ruined countryside, a vanishing art of husbandry, and tens of thousands of able-bodied men standing in queues at Labour Exchanges while the land clamours in vain for labour. It will take a century yet before the last of England's countryside has been buried in bricks or ravaged by a scab of villas. It will last us out, we hope.

Having tarried by the farm, the market-gardens, and the well, Rudolf and I arrived at last at Heston Church. It did not reward us except for the lich-gate. It is the real thing, and as fine a specimen as any in the country. It has one wide door which revolves on a central pivot, ingeniously contrived so that it is self-closing by means of a large pulley-wheel under the roof, the leverage of the opened gate being counterpoised by a large iron-framed stone. For nearly four hundred years it has swung thus. The old oak gate creaks and wheezes, and has been strengthened by kindly hands, but it is still a thing of beauty. Rudolf was so enchanted with its simple but clever mechanism, that he had to be pulled away.

"Lich-gate—what means lich-gate?" he demanded. "It was for carriages?"

"No, for coffins," I answered. "It comes from Old English, like the German word, *leiche,* meaning funeral corpse. The coffin used to rest under this long roof while the clergyman pronounced the initial words of the burial service when he came to meet the funeral party."

"But you have a lich-gate at your cottage—and there's no body?" asked Rudolf.

I had not realized the fact and felt startled. I hurriedly explained that these gates were very popular as garden entrances, and doubtless had been copied because they were picturesque. But Rudolf's question always now provokes an imaginary corpse whenever I pass under my "lich-gate."

We went into the well-kept cemetery surrounding the church. I examined the tombstones closely.

"You look for a friend?" asked Rudolf.

I made no answer. Suddenly, on the north side, I found what I sought. It was a well-kept grave with a clear headstone.

Frederick John White, Pte. in the 7th Hussars, who died 11 July, 1846, aged 27 years. This stone was erected by his comrades in their sympathy for his fate, and their respect for his memory.

Re-erected by the Officers and Men of the 7th Hussars, May, 1866.

"What was his fate?" asked Rudolf. "He was a very brave soldier who was killed?"

"No, he was a very unfortunate one, but his fate changed a tradition in the British Army," I said, and told Rudolf the story behind the simple inscription.

It is difficult to realize within how short a time human nature has improved in the treatment of its own species. Public hangings, tortures, floggings, the chain-gang, the galley, transportation, and frightful penal settlements, many of these horrors have vanished from human society since more than two hundred, though some only since one hundred years. Men in the Army and Navy, as well as the criminal classes, were mercilessly flogged. Some of them died under the lash. The most enlightened figureheads of the two services, including Nelson and the Duke of Wellington, did not believe it was possible to maintain discipline without the threat of the cat-o'-nine-tails. Men were flogged round the Fleet, five hundred, eight hundred, and a thousand lashes being no unusual sentence. Some of the victims died under this barbarous punishment.

In the year 1846 a young man, Frederick John White, who had left his home in Nottingham a few years previously and had joined the 7th Hussars, was stationed with his regiment at Hounslow Barracks. It transpired later that this young soldier from birth had been the victim of brain-storms. One evening, annoyed by some taunting remark of the corporal, he struck him. For this he was given a drumhead court-martial, and sentenced to one hundred and fifty lashes. The sentence was con-

firmed by the War Office, and on June 15th, in the presence of
Colonel Whyte, the commanding officer, and the regiment's doctor, the young soldier was stripped to the waist, and pinioned to
a ladder fastened on the walls of the riding school.

It was the custom in infantry regiments for the drummer-
boys to flog, in cavalry regiments this odious task fell to the
farriers, chosen because of their strength. Accordingly, with
three hundred soldiers of the regiment lined up to witness the
flogging, two farriers, under the command of a sergeant, began
their task in relays of twenty-five lashes each. It was a punishment that soon drew blood, and ten privates, four of them old
soldiers, fainted before the sickening spectacle. When the victim had been taken down from the ladder, the doctor never
once having examined the condition of the soldier, Colonel
Whyte then addressed the whole regiment, calling White a
brutish fellow, and threatening similar punishment on every
occasion that reports of insubordination were made.

White went straight into the military hospital, but received
no attention from the doctor, until, on the fourth day, the fes-
tering condition of the man's back drew attention. White improved sufficiently after a time to get up for mild exercise, but
after a few days complained of a pain in his side, took to his
bed again, and died in less than a month from the date of the
flogging.

Normally this would have been the end of the matter. Thousands of men were flogged, and many of them died, but it was
never considered a matter for protest. In due course application
was made to the Vicar of Heston for a burial certificate for the
young soldier, whose death had been certified as from natural
causes, by the regiment's doctor.

In Hounslow Barracks White's death had so enraged his
comrades that their ball cartridges had to be taken away from
them lest they resorted to violence against their superior officers. The ugliest rumours began to circulate in the surrounding
district. These had already reached the Vicar of Heston, who

expressed himself dissatisfied with the statement on the death certificate. He refused to give an order until an inquest had been held on the young man, and the rumours, if false, effectively scotched.

The vicar's action created a sensation, and the inquest opened in a crowded court at *The George IV* inn at Hounslow. There were appalling revelations. In the interim, between White's death and the coroner's inquiry, he had been buried, but such was the evidence that the coroner made an order for the exhumation of the body. The War Office strenuously opposed this order, but in vain. During the exhumation two military surgeons arrived at the churchyard, determined to obstruct the Court's officers, but the coroner, who had foreseen the possibility of some such attempt, forestalled their action by strictly forbidding anyone but the authorized surgeons to be admitted to the churchyard. Baffled, the War Office's representatives retired. They had already completely exonerated the regimental doctor, and before burial they had actually taken some twelve square inches of skin from White's back, with the obvious intention of removing all evidence of the fearful result of the flogging. Following the post-mortem a battle ensued between the surgeons of the War Office and the specialists called in by the coroner. The opinion of the latter was that White had died as the sole result of excessive punishment.

By this time the whole country, nauseated by the details that came to light in the coroner's court, was seething with indignation. During the evidence further brutalities came to light. A seven weeks' recruit named Mathewson, who had been bullied by a sergeant, and whose only offence had been to retort with a reasonable question when told to go on his knees, had been court-martialled for insubordination and sentenced to one hundred lashes. So loud were the screams of some of the victims during their flogging that soldiers were sent outside the barracks to keep pedestrians out of hearing. Hounslow Barracks was not the only scene of these floggings. Every barracks in the country, every ship in the Navy had its flogging ladder or triangle, and sentences of one hundred up to a thousand lashes were all too common.

The Times, in those days "The Thunderer," voiced the general indignation which grew in volume as the inquest progressed. At the close of these proceedings the jury, in its verdict, expressed itself in language that called for action. It found "that the deceased soldier, Frederick John White, died on 4th July, 1846, from the mortal effects of a severe and cruel flogging of one hundred and fifty lashes, which he received on the 15th June, 1846, at the Cavalry Barracks on Hounslow Heath at Heston; that the said flogging was inflicted on the back and neck, under the sentence of a district court-martial composed of officers of the 7th Regiment of Hussars, held on the 10th of June previous, duly constituted for his trial; that the said court-martial was authorized by the law to pass the said severe and cruel sentence; that the flogging was inflicted upon him by two farriers in the presence of John James Whyte, the Lieutenant-Colonel, and James Low Warren, the surgeon of the regiment; and that so and by means of this flogging the death of the said Frederick John White was caused. In returning this verdict the jury cannot refrain from expressing their horror and disgust at the existence of any law among the statutes or the regulations of this realm which permits the revolting punishment of flogging to be inflicted upon British soldiers; and at the same time the jury implore every man in this kingdom to give hand and heart in forwarding petitions to the legislature, praying in the most urgent terms for the abolition of every law, order and regulation which permits the disgraceful practice of flogging to remain one moment longer a slur upon the humanity and fair name of the people of this country."

By now public opinion had expressed itself in a great volume of protest. Such was the pressure that the Government was compelled to bow to the storm. It devoted a whole day's debate

to the subject of Army and Navy floggings, and a series of letters to *The Times* gave such a revelation of merciless and often
fatal lashings, in barracks, penal colonies and aboard ship, that
the public was deeply shocked by the barbarism it had tolerated
so long.

But there were strong reactionary forces in the more conservative circles. An attempt was made by testimony in the
House to prove that Colonel Whyte was all that a soldier and
gentleman should be, and of a most kindly disposition! The War
Office surgeons, who had plainly connived at the attempt to get
the unfortunate soldier buried without an inquest, came in for
scathing comment. It was an era when almost all public crises
were referred to the Duke of Wellington. Ex-military and naval
big-wigs, sitting in the House, made eloquent appeals for the
wholesome discipline and the maintenance of law and order
which flogging ensured. It would seem, according to their testimony, that the greatness of England, that Waterloo and Trafalgar, had depended on the right of summary courts-martial to
tear the skin off the backs of lads and young men for the slightest infraction of discipline. Finally, as a great concession, following the advice of the Duke, the War Office altered its regulations, making fifty lashes the maximum punishment. With
this concession, public opinion was somewhat soothed, but the
reactionaries sadly shook their heads. What was the country
coming to when a man could not take a flogging without whim-
pering—though he was often insensible in the last stages.

The wretched Colonel Whyte by this time was the theme of
ballads sold and sung in the public streets, in which it was not
safe for him to show his face. After a time he was quietly moved
to the command of a native cavalry regiment in India, and so
passes out of history.

Private White was re-interred, after the post-mortem and,
later, the officers and men of the 7th Hussars subscribed for a
memorial tablet, and offered to maintain the grave in decent

order, which the regiment does to this day. So poor young White sleeps peacefully in the shade of neighbouring trees in Heston churchyard. His death was not altogether in vain, since it served to move the public conscience against the barbarity of flogging. But it is impressive to observe that the Navy still went without reform for some years, and only in 1939 was flogging officially abolished in the senior services, though it had long fallen into abeyance.

While standing in the churchyard at Heston, my companion was excited by the frequent flight of aeroplanes overhead, and when I told him that an adjacent aerodrome was rapidly eating up ancient Heston, he immediately suggested a visit to it. But I was obdurate. We would complete our circuit of Osterley Park, I affirmed, and then, regaining the car, added that we might have tea at the club-house of the airport.

Alas, for the irreverent spirit of youth. Osterley Park, he declared, would make a marvellous aerodrome—why, even hydroplanes could descend on the lake! And the Schloss would be a marvellous club-house.

Indignantly I denounced his proposal. Everybody was wanting to turn everything into something else. Let Osterley Park at least continue to exist in its splendour and seclusion.

"But have not you hoped much to go inside the Schloss to see it? I too would much like that. If we knock on the door to go inside what do they do?" demanded Rudolf.

"Quite naturally shut it in our faces again—after all it is a private house."

"We can try by the kitchen door."

"No—one can't do that sort of thing."

"But you want to go in—to see things?"

"I should like to see it, but——"

Rudolf gave a triumphant shout.

"Then why don't you ask the Herr Graf?" he cried.

"I don't know him. Just because the Earl of Jersey is kind enough to let us walk over his park it doesn't entitle us to walk about his house."

"But at Pilgrim Cottage, they knock and ask and you——" said Rudolf.

"That's different," I retorted.

"Warum?"

"Ich weiss nicht—now if you want to have tea at the airport you must step out," I said. "I'm not going to knock on any doors."

The prospect of seeing the airport silenced any further proposal to push our way into Schloss Osterley. Half-way through tea my guest jumped up from the table, stared through the window and then rushed out and embraced a pretty girl standing on the terrace. A few minutes later, from a spate of excited talk in a language I could not understand, this strange behaviour was explained.

"But it is my cousin Ilonka from Budapest," he said, introducing the lovely young lady, who could not speak a word of English. "She has just come in that aeroplane. She left Budapest at nine this morning and she is here! *Wunderbar!"*

I asked why Ilonka had made this sudden descent upon England from the clouds. She spoke Magyar with Rudolf, who, it transpired, had a Hungarian mother. She had come to study English in a family in London, she told me in German. Unfortunately she could not join us at tea, the air company's coach was taking the passengers on to London. We accompanied her to the coach and saw her off. Rudolf was quite overwhelmed by this meeting.

"It is—what you say—*das Zusammentreffen!"*

"A coincidence, yes. You know I can't do this sort of thing when I write novels," I said.

"Why?" he asked.

"Because none of my readers would believe it."

III

The morning after Rudolf's *"Zusammentreffen"* there was a card among my morning letters bearing the inscription, "The Earl and Countess of Jersey request the honour of the company of Mr. Cecil Roberts and lady at Osterley Park, Isleworth, at 3.30 P.M., on Thursday, May 25th." The occasion was the opening to the public of the house and grounds. The inaugural ceremony was to be performed by the High Commissioner for Australia.

So I was to penetrate Schloss Osterley with all due decorum and not to take it by storm via the kitchen door, as Rudolf urged on me. The Earl of Jersey had decided to throw open to the public on three days a week this superb mansion and its grounds, and I had been invited to the opening ceremony.

Casting around for the accompanying lady, I decided there could be no better companion than my friend, Miss Whissitt. Highly intelligent, inquisitive, with a zest for public functions, I felt certain the opportunity would delight her. I also knew that out of her inexhaustible fund of curious knowledge she would produce surprising information.

Her response over the telephone was ecstatic.

"How nice of you. *Mais oui, c'est formidable!*" she cried, breaking into the inevitable French which any excitement provoked. "How very kind of you! What shall I wear?"

I suggested a hat trimmed with eucalyptus and a Koala stole, in honour of the High Commissioner.

"The stole would be doubly appropriate—the right ecclesiastical note," retorted Miss Whissitt.

"Why ecclesiastical?"

"Well, Osterley once belonged to the Abbess of Syon."

"Did it?" I asked, astonished. So she knew all about it!

"*Vraiment.* At the beginning of the sixteenth century it belonged to Syon Monastery. At the Dissolution Henry VIII gave it to the Marquis of Exeter, and Edward VI to the Duke of

Somerset. They were both beheaded, you know, and it was acquired later from Queen Elizabeth by Sir Thomas Gresham, who built the house. He founded the Exchange, you know—there's a grasshopper on the top of it now, that was his crest, and——"

"Yes, yes," I murmured, overwhelmed. "You've never seen the house?"

"*Mais oui*—a long time ago. I went to make a copy of a ceiling decoration by Angelica Kauffmann, and some other pictures. You know she married Zucchi. She was the first woman R.A. There's a lot of their work there, and at Syon House. The Adam brothers employed them and they became the rage."

I did not know. It would not have been surprising if Miss Whissitt knew exactly what Angelica Kauffmann had been paid for that ceiling. And I did not know until then that Miss Whissitt could paint. I knew she could make plants grow magically, had built a loggia, created an Italian garden at Filldyke Cottage, and was an astonishing mixture of gossip, archæologist, antiquarian, ubiquitous spinster, philanthropist and parish worker.

We discussed the time of the meeting and method of transport.

"In your car or mine?" she asked, innocently.

"Oh, mine," I replied, firmly, knowing her prowess as a motorist.

"*A bientôt*," she said, and rang off.

CHAPTER VIII

Osterley Park, Interior

WE SET OFF on a bright May afternoon, and at Osterley went to the nearest gate from the Great West Road. We were sent on a circumnavigation of the park before we could find the long avenue that led us to the Elizabethan stables in whose courtyard the cars were parked. On a lawn in front of the house there was a band playing, composed of young boys in red coats, from an orphanage. A cordon had been stretched across the foot of the broad flight of stone steps leading up to the double-colonnaded portico. Here Lord and Lady Jersey were receiving the guests.

We mounted the steps, were greeted by our host and hostess, and then, standing under the great portico, looked down across the lawns, to the lake and the surrounding park.

"How gay and lovely! *C'est ravissant*," murmured Miss Whissitt.

"But look," I said, pointing to a table with three chairs and the microphone of a loud-speaker. "Speeches!"

"How many. do you think—before we go into the house— and tea?"

"Three, perhaps five," I answered, looking at the small crowd of guests who had assembled in the courtyard made by the three sides of the house, and the colonnade on the fourth.

"Have you noticed something?" asked Miss Whissitt. "The ground floor of the house has been buried."

"Buried? What do you mean?"

"Well, look at the floor of this courtyard—it's been filled in to the level of the first floor. All the first floor of the house has been turned into a basement. When Robert Adam arrived back from his Italian tour in 1758, he was impressed with the idea of living on the first floor, making it a *piano nobile,* as in the Italian *palazzi,* particularly if the house looked out over a flat pastureland as here. So you see what he did—quite wonderful, don't you think? He lowered the floor of the first floor, taking it out of the ground floor, whose windows he shortened, lengthened the windows of his new floor, and, to keep balance, shortened the windows of the top floor. Then to get on to his new first floor, he built up this great flight of steps, filled in the quadrangle and gave us this stage between the wings. What fun it must have been, because, you see, when you get through the house on to the south part, you go down a flight of steps again to the lawns. It's not only great fun to play about like this—Adam did much the same thing at Syon—it's psychologically impressive, *n'est-ce pas?*"

"How do you mean?" I queried, out of my depth.

"You mount up here, like going to a Greek temple to greet your god. It gives you a feeling of pageantry. But it also makes you feel insignificant, which humbles you, like having to walk down a very long room to greet your host—the same sort of trick Mussolini plays at the Palazzo Venezia when he receives you——"

"Were you received by him there?" I asked, never knowing what Miss Whissitt had achieved.

"No—but a friend of mine was, and he says that that long marble approach across his *salon* makes you feel a worm. It undoes you, and then he can do what he likes with you. But what I want to say is—you get the reverse feeling when you're in the house and go out of it, down the steps, on the other side. The other side always has a double flight, winding down—it has here, and it does make you feel royal," said Miss Whissitt. "Why, there's Lord Esher taking the chair."

We grouped ourselves on the steps around Lord Esher, Lord and Lady Jersey, and the High Commissioner for Australia, who was to declare Osterley House open to the public. There were three speeches, mercifully short. A cold wind with a threat of rain blew upon us to rebuke our folly for thinking to-day would be like the glorious summer day of yesterday. The ceremony was soon over, with a graceful little final speech from young Lord Jersey. The guests trooped into the house for tea, served in the large vestibule.

"Oh!" I said, as we entered, overwhelmed by it. Miss Whissitt gave a chuckle of delight, as though she had contrived this surprise for me.

It was the Wedgwood Hall, so called because of its plaster decorations and colour scheme. At either end of the room was an apse with a fire-place in it. The walls were decorated with "The Trophies of War" in plaster relief. There were giant marble urns, and long stools with cabriole legs. One looked around on the lovely fire-places, the superb mahogany doors, the framed dial of the stucco ceiling, but most of all at the double vista, for the wide open doors of the Picture Gallery commanded a view of the lawns on the south side. The entrance door, framed by the great colonnaded portico on the north, looked on the lake and park.

We decided not to scramble for tea at the immense buffet. We would return later.

"He's doing it very well—and isn't she pretty," said Miss Whissitt, watching the Countess among her guests.

We passed on into the Picture Gallery. The long stately room with its high south-west windows, its magnificent pictures, furniture and carpets, robbed me of words.

"Well?" asked Miss Whissitt, with a proud smile, "this is where I worked for six months."

"Worked—you worked here—what at?" I stammered.

"Copying these pictures—I had a commission from an American lady."

"But I never knew you were an artist—you could do work like that. You've never told me that before."

I did remember now some water-colours at Filldyke Cottage which looked as if they had been out in the rain, and, of course, she had created her amazing Italian garden almost out of nothing.

"I started life as an art student—I was full of hope then. I——" she stopped her autobiographical flight. "It is a wonderful room, isn't it? May I tell you about the pictures, or don't you care much about——?"

"Oh, please—why, they're——" I began, and failed for words.

"Yes, they're like that," said Miss Whissitt. "I always think of what Henry James wrote about this gallery. He used to stay here frequently, and he put the house in his novel *The Lesson of the Master*. He said 'it went together and spoke in one voice —a rich English voice of the early part of the eighteenth century,' and he called this gallery 'a cheerful upholstered avenue into the other century.' "

"That's just what it is," I commented, looking at the nine high windows with wall spaces lit by gilt Adam mirrors. Each end of the long gallery was dominated by an immense canvas. We approached the one on our right.

"Can you bear stories about pictures?" asked Miss Whissitt.

"Tell me everything—I've a thirst for anecdotes with art, they're the soda-water with the whisky. 'The Apotheosis of the Duke of Buckingham, by Rubens,' " I read, from the catalogue.

"That's the picture Francis Child bought in Amsterdam in 1697 for £400."

"But how did it get to Amsterdam?"

"The portrait's of the first Duke—the dashing young man whom Felton assassinated at Portsmouth in 1628. Do you see that cherub up in the right-hand corner blowing out a flame— that signifies Life being puffed out by Fate. Rubens painted this picture after the Duke's death, probably as a tribute to a splendid patron. He has shown him as the Lord High Admiral, on horseback, which is odd."

"Admirals were always soldiers in those days—naval strategy was a side-line," I explained.

"Oh, that is it! Well, there's the Fleet in the background, with Neptune and a nymph under the charger's feet, with Envy and Malice being pushed aside. Buckingham's son, the second Duke, known as a wit, inherited the family pictures, but he fled the Continent after the Civil War until the return of Charles II. His valet succeeded in smuggling the pictures to Amsterdam, and the Duke, being penniless, sold them. That's how Mr. Child bought this Apotheosis."

" 'Lady Ponsonby, by Opie, posing as Rebecca at the Well,' " I read, turning to the next picture.

"Deaf after measles, poor child—daughter of the fourth Lady Jersey, lovely. But look at this Reynolds—here's Robert Child, the last male of the line, who finished this house. He was father of the girl who eloped to Gretna Green with Lord West-morland."

Robert Child wore a red coat, carried a gun and had a spaniel at his feet. It was a magnificent specimen of Sir Joshua at his best. Two pictures by Claude Lorraine followed, and there was a Poussin over the marble mantelpiece, one of a pair in the long room. The next picture held us entranced. It was a Van Dyck of the Duchess of Buckingham with her children, Lady Mary Villiers, successively in after life, the Countess of Montgomery, the Duchess of Richmond and the Countess of Carlisle; George, the second and last Duke, Charles II's witty minister, who could not resist adding on a solemn Court occasion when Charles was being addressed as Defender of the Faith, and the Father of his people—"or quite a lot of them" —for which *lèse majesté* he was banished from Court for a time; and Francis, the youngest son, killed in a Civil War skirmish. The eldest boy in this picture was the second and last Duke. His mother, Kitty Manners, was a daughter of the Earl of Rutland.

"Very singular this," commented Miss Whissitt, when she had given me the history of the picture. "It belonged to the Jersey Villiers, and when Robert Child's granddaughter and heiress married the fifth Lord Jersey, she brought the Rubens of the Duke to join this Van Dyck of the Duke's wife and children, owned by her husband. The Duchess was very much in love with the Duke, despite his flirtatious disposition. They said, you know, he was the father of the Man in the Iron Mask, by Anne of Austria, when he went on that famous visit to the Court of France—do you think they'll ever clear up that mystery?" But Miss Whissitt was not interested in my view of the Man in the Iron Mask, and was already in front of a pair of portraits of Queen Charlotte and George III.

"I always think she looks like a performing seal—but she was a good wife," said my companion.

I began to read from the catalogue.

"Oh, yes, I know the story," rambled on Miss Whissitt. "The King gave the pictures to Lord Harcourt, and Harcourt settled a gaming debt to Lord Jersey with them, because he'd had a quarrel with the King and didn't want them on his walls at Nuneham. Then, having made it up, he wanted them back when he knew the King was coming to visit him, and Jersey would only let Harcourt have copies of them. As the King didn't know the difference, all was well. Now here's the gem of the lot, to my mind, a superb Reynolds of the Bedford family."

"Also with a story?" I asked, by this time quite reconciled to Miss Whissitt's insistence that every picture should tell a story.

We looked at it in silence, after Miss Whissitt, looking up and down the gallery, had observed, "Aren't we lucky to get a private view before the public comes flooding in? I hate being trailed round by a housekeeper in a black dress and being kept out of the private apartments."

The picture was certainly one of Reynolds' loveliest and freshest works, the colours as vivid as the day it was painted. The boy, Lord John Russell, later fifth Duke of Bedford, was dressed as St. George, with a dragon at his feet. His relation, Miss Vernon, was the rescued Princess, and two boys loomed out of the background, one of them, kneeling, being Lord William Russell, murdered later by his valet at the age of twenty-two.

"You know, of course," said Miss Whissitt, "that he shouldn't have been in the picture, but he was so anxious to know what was going on in the studio, that Reynolds caught him and put him in also."

"Lucky boy—except it's not lucky to be murdered at twenty-two. And yet Reynolds immortalized him here—we'd never have known of him otherwise."

"Is that any good to him?" chirped Miss Whissitt.

"I'm not going to argue with you about the merits of immortality," I retorted.

She moved on, past a pair of Lawrence portraits of the fifth Lord Jersey and his Countess.

"Byron's friend," she observed, "the one who gave the party at which he was so severely 'cut' that he fled the country in a few days, and here's a Gainsborough landscape, and a Ruysdael, and——"

Miss Whissitt was silent. We had come to the immense canvas of Charles I and his Master of the Horse, by Van Dyck, which covered the end wall of the Gallery, *vis-à-vis* to the great Marlborough of Rubens.

"Not exclusive," said Miss Whissitt, "Van Dyck did several versions, and the Cromwellians actually substituted Cromwell's head for Charles's in contemporary engravings. Having themselves severed poor Charles's head, they might have replaced something as beautiful," sniffed my companion, always a fierce Royalist.

I was studying a head of Wellington by Lawrence, not finished, in the corner of the Gallery.

"Lawrence died before he could finish it, and Lady Jersey wouldn't let anyone else touch it. She was a great friend of Wellington's—you know the story?"

"I don't know any of the stories," I replied.

"Well, this shall be the last."

"I like stories with pictures—I know it's considered the wrong thing," I said, "but I'm one of those people who can't help being thrilled at finding that Giotto painted a portrait of Dante in one of his crowds. What's the Wellington story?"

"There are hundreds of them—but this proves that the grim old man could be quite skittish, so I like it," prefaced Miss Whissitt. "Lady Jersey gave a birthday party and expected a present from every guest. Wellington forgot his, but seeing a nice china piece in the hall, he picked it up and solemnly presented it to her. She was enchanted, particularly as it made a perfect pair to the one in the hall. She went off to put them together, but when she got into the hall, well——"

"Wherever did you get all these stories from?" I asked, astonished at Miss Whissitt's repertoire.

"Out of the private catalogue when I was copying here," she replied, with disarming candour. "You didn't think I'd invented them? Well, we've finished the Gallery, now for the drawing-room."

When Robert Adam undertook to design you a house he was prepared to design the furniture and the carpets for it. The art of interior decoration in his hands has never been practised with greater taste and genius. These rooms at Osterley reveal him at his best. One is apt to overlook the wealth of his detail. While gazing at the ceiling one neglects the carpet, which repeats the design, or the mantelpiece and the carved door cases. In the Tapestry Room he has covered the walls with rose-coloured tapestry, woven at Beauvais, and he employed Angelica Kauffmann to paint the ceiling panels. Armchairs and sofas are covered with the same tapestry after his design.

But before Miss Whissitt had led me into the Tapestry Room I had been held by the brilliant portrait of a handsome young soldier in a scarlet coat. If the young man was half as dashing and handsome as Romney had made him, it is easy to understand why, defying her father, Sarah Child galloped off to Gretna Green with the young Earl of Westmorland.

On the opposite wall Romney's brush has given us the lively Sarah, and a splendid pair they make, so splendid that one wonders how Robert Child could remain so obdurate. He died within a few months of the marriage, at the age of forty-three, which supports the suggestion of a broken heart. In the library one still finds Sarah's harpsichord, and the violin she played. Did she ever regret her runaway marriage, one wonders?

In the drawing-room there is an earlier portrait of the spirited Sarah, this time as a little girl aged nine, with some pet doves, the work of Sir Joshua Reynolds, for which Mr. Child paid £100 in 1773. Mr. Child did not exactly suffer from *folie de grandeur*, but he certainly did things handsomely, as his employment of Robert Adam proves. In nothing was he more lavish than in the stupendous state bed that dominates Mrs. Child's bedroom. What he paid for it no one knows, for he was so shocked by the size of the bill that he tore it up when he had settled it, saying no one must ever know its cost. It is a *chef d'œuvre* of Robert Adam, with its posts of painted laurel leaves, its embroidered velvet with the device of the Child marigold, its immense coronet-like canopy. Let us hope Mrs. Child slept well in her splendour, undisturbed by the size of the bill. It is a superb symbol of an age of magnificence, in vivid contrast with our own era of divans, single beds, and collapsible shake-me-downs, generally shake-me-ups, clipped of all splendour and size owing to the exigencies of space. The fashionable fancy of the age can be seen again in the Etruscan

dressing-room. What fun it must have been for Robert Adam
to design this room! Pompeii had just been excavated, and an
illustrated book of the astonishing discoveries of Etruscan and
Pompeian art had just been published by Sir William Hamilton, husband of Nelson's Emma. The Etruscan vases and the
wall paintings, uncovered after centuries, inspired Adam; his
Grand Tour of Italy had converted him to the Roman classical
style, sustained in the engravings of Piranesi and the architecture of Palladio. One can hear him saying to Mr. Child,
"What about a Pompeian room—with designs taken from
Etruscan vases?" If Mr. Child felt doubtful he must have been
pleased with the novelty of this room. It strikes a note unlike
any other in this house.

We had reached the dining-room at last, having traversed
the South passage, with a portrait of the highwayman Bishop,
and the North passage, with portraits of the Child family.
Here is the shrewd Sir Francis, who journeyed to London,
married his employer's daughter, and became the Father of
Banking. He is in his robes as the Lord Mayor, in 1699, carrying the Sword of State presented by Queen Elizabeth to the
City of London. It is singular to note that every Lord Mayor
offers this Sword to his sovereign when he formally visits the
City, and the offering is made where Temple Bar once stood,
and in front of Child's Bank, No. 1 Fleet Street; which still
keeps open its door, and hangs out the sign of the marigold,
with the motto *ainsi mon âme* painted beneath it.

Sir Francis had twelve sons, two of them knights. One of
them was a Lord Mayor in 1721. In the yellow sitting-room,
we find a charming portrait of young Francis Child, grand-
child of the first Sir Francis, painted by Allan Ramsay. It was
this ill-starred young man who left his fiancée £50,000 when
he died, and Osterley and the banking business passed to his
brother Robert.

On our way to the dining-room Miss Whissitt stood entranced by the main staircase and looked up at the ceiling,

where hung Rubens' great canvas of the Apotheosis of William
of Orange, which Sir Francis had bought in Amsterdam in
1702 for his town house.

"I suppose no one will ever paint an Apotheosis again?"
commented Miss Whissitt. "We've given up deifying people.
We've too much sense of the ridiculous to send our great men
riding the heavens on clouds of glory dripping with cherubs,
and fat-limbed goddesses."

"Someone may attempt an Apotheosis of Hitler or Mussolini," I suggested.

"In trousers or top-boots?" mocked Miss Whissitt, as we
entered the dining-room.

We examined the room in silence. Zucchi and his wife,
Angelica Kauffmann, had been at work in the pictures and
panels, Wedgwood in the black vases on the white marble mantelpiece. The lyre-backed chairs, the gilt sideboards, the ormolu-
mounted candlesticks, all revealed the most exquisite crafts-
manship. I found myself wondering whether such a lovely
room would increase the appetite or take it away. As if in
answer to my thoughts, Miss Whissitt exclaimed at that moment, "I'm dying for a cup of tea and something to eat—how
wise of us to end the tour with the dining-room. *En avant,
mon cher!*"

The crowd at the buffet in the Wedgwood Hall had thinned.
I got Miss Whissitt her tea, and she sat triumphantly under
a "trophy" gazing out across the court to the green lawns and
silver lake beyond the colonnaded portico. Half a dozen figures
stood by the great columns, silhouetted against the sky.

"Look at them—ghosts," exclaimed Miss Whissitt.

"Ghosts?" I repeated, bewildered.

"*Vraiment*—Mr. Balfour, Henry James, King Edward VII,
the Countess of Jersey, Queen Alexandra, General Botha,
James Russell Lowell—they all stood there once, they used to
come here. I remember seeing two powdered footmen standing
by that door."

"Do you like powdered footmen?" I asked.

"Not particularly—but now they're becoming rarer than Chippendale it's something to have seen them *sans* cinema!"

Miss Whissitt had had her second cup. She stood up. I knew by the expression on her face she was preparing for action.

"And now for the lakes, the orangery, the Elizabethan stables, and the cedars on the front lawn. After that we can——"

"But I can't walk another yard," I pleaded.

Miss Whissitt looked at me scornfully.

"I've come to do it all—I'm going to do it all. Wait for me in the car," she said, determinedly.

"Oh, no, I'll come with you," I replied, ashamed of my masculine weakness.

The sunlight was slanting through the cedars and the elms when we drove down the avenue to the gates.

"*C'est tout ravissant!*" exclaimed Miss Whissitt. "Thank you very much!"

She gave a little laugh as we turned towards the Bath Road, and I looked at her questioningly. She looked so animated and pretty that I realized what that poor young soldier, dead in France these twenty-five years, had missed when a German bullet made her a spinster for life.

"I'm laughing," she said, "because I'm wondering when you will get to Bath at this rate. You'll never finish that book."

"The whole purpose of the book is to demonstrate how difficult it is to get to Bath, if you are prepared to see everything on the way. And you're not going home yet," I said, as I came to the Great West Road and crossed it southwards at Osterley Road, going again towards Syon Park.

"Where are you taking me?"

"To Spring Grove, to show you something which is just off the Old Bath Road before you come to Hounslow High Street —then we'll go home."

II

There is little at Spring Grove now, except a large mansion built by a soap millionaire which has been turned into a Council School. And yet it should be hallowed ground for visiting Australians, for at Spring Grove, in the early part of the nineteenth century, dwelt a most remarkable man. This was Sir Joseph Banks, whose name is commemorated there by a short avenue called Banksian Way. He lived at Spring Grove until his death in 1820, when he was buried at Heston. He was a most remarkable and gifted man who has been almost forgotten, though every garden that possesses a Banksia rose-tree owes something to him. It was at Spring Grove that this famous rose was cultivated. But perhaps the most remarkable fact is that without his aid Australia would never have been discovered and made an English colony by Captain Cook, for it was Banks who, in his passion for botanical and scientific investigation, fitted out H.M.S. *Endeavour* and sailed in it with Captain Cook on his momentous journey round the world in 1768–9. When they first sighted Australia, and landed at a bay whose variety of plants and flowers filled the explorers with amazement, it was Banks who named it Botany Bay. It must be admitted also that it was his fertile brain that wrote the memorandum suggesting that it was a most suitable place for a settlement of transported prisoners.

Previous to equipping H.M.S. *Endeavour* he had fitted out, for another scientific exploration, H.M.S. *Bounty*, destined to acquire such ill-fame because of the mutiny on board in 1787. His whole life and his wealth were devoted to scientific investigation, and he owed the trend of his interests to a small incident when a boy at Eton. He had been a young harum-scarum, but one evening, after bathing in the Thames, he lingered behind until all his schoolfellows had left him. Walking back along a lane, rich with spring flowers, he was suddenly aware of their extraordinary beauty. A few days later, in a lumber-room at home, he chanced upon Gerard's *Herbal*, and a new world opened before the eyes of the boy of fourteen. From now on he pursued his passion of botany with singleness of mind, and using his considerable wealth to further all kinds of scientific exploration, to which he also gave his own energies, he soon became a notable figure in the nation.

He was elected President of the Royal Society in 1777, a position he held through many stormy assaults upon his autocratic rule for the next forty years. He was a staunch friend and believer in Captain Cook, and sailed with him from Plymouth in August, 1768, for the purpose of observing the transit of Venus at Tahiti, which they reached in April, 1769. The great Barrier Reef off Australia was nearly their grave. The ship struck a submerged rock, and would have foundered but for the ingenious idea of a midshipman who suggested "fothering" the ship. This process consisted of sewing oakum and wool on to a sail and drawing it under the hull. The suction caused by the leak kept the sail firmly fixed over the cavity. The plan worked admirably, assisted greatly, as they discovered later, by a large rock which had also been drawn in and had plugged the hole.

Banks was the first man to see a kangaroo, and one cannot help wondering how long it was before he could believe his own eyes, when that strange animal leapt across the landscape around Botany Bay.

The great sheep-farming and wool industry of Australia to-day owes much to the interest of Banks. He was a tireless experimenter at Spring Grove, and all his neighbours were always wondering what he was "up to" now. "On the right, before we enter Hounslow," records an 1818 Guide, "is the seat of Sir Joseph Banks, a neat mansion with considerable gardens, where curious plants are reared with care and assiduity."

At the end of the eighteenth century, not a field was allowed to lie fallow around Hounslow. The various enclosure Acts had begun to operate locally, and there was such an improvement

in the breeding of sheep that they increased in weight from
an average of 48 lbs. to 80 lbs. Banks began numerous experiments in breeding. In 1782 he brought over the Channel a ram
and a ewe of Merino breed. By 1798 he had demonstrated that
wool could be produced in England as good as any that was
imported. "Upon the whole the cloth you send me, which is
made from your Spanish sheep reared upon Hounslow Heath,
may be ranked with the best superfine cloth manufactured in
England," wrote a woollen merchant, in response to a request
from Banks for a report upon his wool.

His enthusiasm often led him to strange habits. He possessed
an eccentric sister who lived with him, and they were to be seen
journeying abroad in a strange attire made of rough wools.
Miss Banks had three riding habits made of them, all woolly
and washable. She called them Hightum, Tightum, and Scrub,
being for best, second-best, and everyday wear.

Miss Banks was one of the "sights." She wore a Barcelona
quilted petticoat with a hole on either side for rummaging in
the two pockets filled with books and oddments. Over her petticoat she wore a long stomachered gown. Whenever she went
out, she was followed by a man-servant, six feet tall, who carried a wand of the same height. She collected coins and broad-
sheets, and was such an extraordinary sight that she was often
taken for a ballad-singer in the streets. To the end of her life
she kept house for her brother, and at one time had been quite
a fashionable whip, driving a four-in-hand through the Park.

Sir Joseph himself developed into a character. He could be
obstinate and was a bonny fighter, as an obstreperous Bishop,
who tried to oust him from the Presidency of the Royal Society,
discovered. He went about the countryside gathering specimens, dressed like a footpad, and there was an occasion when,
in mistake, he was arrested by some Bow Street Runners on
Hounslow Heath and taken before a magistrate, an incident
which delighted the wags and inspired the popular rhymester,
"Peter Pindar."

"Sirs, what d'ye take me for?" the Knight exclaimed.
"A thief," replied the Runners, with a curse;
"And now, Sir, let us search you and be damned"—
And then they searched his pockets, fobs and purse,

But 'stead of pistol dire, and death-like crêpe,
A pocket handkerchief they cast their eye on,
Containing frogs and toads of various shape,
Dock, daisy, nettle-top and dandelion.

Sir Joseph entertained at Spring Grove all the notable men of the day. Pitt, Nelson, Cook and Wellington were among his guests, and, being a very celebrated figure in the neighbourhood, he must often have been observed by Shelley, at school near by, who no doubt looked with wonder at the celebrated man who had sailed round the world with Captain Cook.

There was a living link with Sir Joseph Banks long after his time. This was a tortoise in the zoo at Sydney, which was presented to a chief of Tonga when H.M.S. *Endeavour* called at that island. Cook's ship carried another animal that lived in an aura of fame, a goat, which, after going round the world, ended its days at Mile End in 1772. But the goat's companion on the voyage was still going strong, if slow, in 1900, in the zoological gardens, and might proudly have carried on its back the words, "I knew Captain Cook."

CHAPTER IX

The Dreaded Heath

HOUNSLOW, which follows on the old road to Bath, after Spring Grove, has nothing to offer that can detain the traveller. It is now one of London's many dormitories. It looks back on a past in which its prosperity came from the coaching traffic, and its unpleasant association with highwaymen, who found the wild Heath beyond it a profitable ground for their calling. Hounslow is also associated with military matters. It was the scene of several famous camps and still retains its barracks. Being the gateway to the West, since the days of the Romans, on the way to Staines (Pontes), Hounslow has seen all the successive stages of transport, but it was in the grand coaching days that it reached its heyday. Prior to this, most of the travellers had passed through it on foot or on horseback, and in the Middle Ages this was so perilous, since the undergrowth all around made such a good lair for robbers, that a law was passed in 1485 enforcing the clearing of the thicket on either side of the road to a depth of two hundred feet.

The seventeenth century saw the beginning of the vogue of the coach. *The Flying Coach* came through here in 1669, making the journey from London to Oxford in two days. The swift mail coach carried the wealthier travellers, the poor journeyed in the cumbersome wagons that made still worse the frightful condition of the roads. These wagons, covered, with twelve horses, considered eight miles an hour good going. In the heyday of Hounslow, which was the first stage for changing horses on the outward journey, as many as three hundred coaches passed through in a day, and there was stabling to accommodate a thousand horses. Since Hounslow was only one stage from London, few tarried there, and the whole place was always in a bustle with innkeepers, ostlers, waiters, postboys, coachmen and travellers anxious to be on their way. It must have been a pleasant sight; it delighted Washington Irving, on his visit to England.

"Wherever an English stage-coachman may be seen, he cannot be mistaken for one of any other craft. He has commonly a broad, full face, curiously mottled with red; he is swelled into jolly dimensions by frequent potations of malt liquors, and his bulk is increased by a multiplicity of coats. He wears a broad-brimmed, low-crowned hat; a huge coloured handkerchief about his neck, and has in summertime a large bouquet of flowers in his buttonhole, the present, most probably, of some enamoured country lass. His waist-coat is commonly of some light colour, striped, and his small clothes extend far below his knees, to meet a pair of jockey boots."

There were also the private postboys and postilions in gay livery. The public ones wore beaver hats, generally white, yellow jackets, and carried a flower in their mouths or behind their ears. They were all hell-for-leather lads. A good postboy once rattled my Lord Fitzroy Somerset from Piccadilly to *The George* at Hounslow in forty minutes. The same journey takes the same time to-day in a car, capable of 70 m.p.h., such is modern traffic congestion.

The state of the roads in the era of the stage-coach often made travel dangerous. The road was generally a bog two or three feet deep in mud in winter. The dust in summer blinded the horses and choked the passengers. Fog, snow and ice added to the calamities that threatened road users, who were often pitched headlong into the mud either from the furious driving of competing coachmen, or from falling into holes, or losing the track. The highwaymen had little difficulty in overtaking the coaches, and since they knew the country well and could cut across it, they generally got safely away. Often they were in league with ostlers and innkeepers who kept them posted with information and supplied them with hiding-holes. The rich traffic of fashion to Bath made Hounslow Heath, with its wild expanse and adequate cover, an ideal place for the highwayman's calling. Most of them were men made desperate by circumstances, soldiers who, after long years of service, were turned callously adrift and took to robbery since they had no other means of livelihood. But not all the highwaymen belonged to the most desperate and depraved order of society. Youths who had got into loose habits, gentlemen fallen on evil days, were to be found in the ranks of these desperadoes whose end was inevitably the gallows at Tyburn.

Macaulay wrote of them:

"The mounted highwayman, marauder known to our generation only from books, was to be found on every main road. The waste tracks which lay on the main routes near London were especially haunted by them, such as Hounslow Heath. It was necessary to the success and even the safety of the highwayman that he should be a bold and skilful rider, and that his manner and appearance should be such as suited the master of a fierce horse. Sometimes, indeed, the highwayman was of good family, and education. A romantic interest therefore attached, and perhaps still attaches, to the names of the free-booters of this class."

John Gay, on a remark from Swift, while staying at Twickenham, made a highwayman, MacHeath, the central figure of *The Beggar's Opera,* and it is singular to note, that, just as we fear to-day that the heroic criminals of the film may swell the numbers of those in real life by their influence on the young, so in Gay's time we learn that Sir John Fielding informed the Bench of Justices that he had protested to Mr. David Garrick upon the wisdom of performing this play "which was never presented upon the stage without creating an additional number of real thieves and highwaymen, as witness the increased robberies on Hounslow and Hampstead Heaths."

Two names are outstanding among the robbers who had a
halo of romanticism placed over their heads by popular fancy.
These were Dick Turpin and Claude Duval. Turpin's great
fame was founded on a desperate ride he was supposed to have
made to York on his horse Black Bess, which Macaulay was
prepared to prove a complete myth. Claude Duval has become
a fine figure of gallantry because it was related that somewhere
on the Heath he stopped a lady's coach and took from her £400,
of which he offered to return £300 if she would dance a *coranto*
with him at the roadside, which offer she accepted. Most versions make no reference to the cash basis of this gallantry.

The story as generally related has much highfalutin. Duval
and his band overtook a coach in which sat a knight and his
lady. The lady is supposed to have been playing the flageolet.
Not to be outdone Duval played also on his flageolet. "Sir," he
said to the knight, "your lady plays excellently and I doubt not
she dances quite as well. Will you please to get out and let me
have the honour of a dance with her upon the Heath." "Sir,"
replied the knight, "I dare not deny anything to one of your
quality and good mind." So they danced, the lady delicately in
her gown, the Frenchman elegantly in his high riding-boots.
The dancing finished, he conducted the lady back to her coach.
As the knight was getting in, "Sir, you have forgotten to pay
for the music," said Duval. "No, I have not," responded the
knight and, pulling out a bag of a hundred sovereigns, gave it
to Duval, who took it with a very good grace, answering, "Sir,
you shall have no cause to repent this liberality of yours." And
gallantly raising his hat, he rode off with his companions.

Thus the beau-ideal of the fraternity. Alas, for all his gallantry, the end was the same. Apprehended in a drunken brawl,
he was hanged at Tyburn in 1670, aged twenty-seven. His trial
became the meeting-place of fashion, his cell was so thronged
with the fair of high rank that eventually the authorities had
to prohibit further visits. He became the hero of innumerable
ballads, and after execution his body was buried in the centre

aisle of St. Paul's, that charming Inigo Jones church in Covent Garden, with a rhymed epitaph on his tombstone:

Here lies Du Vall: Reader if male thou art
Look to thy purse: if female, to thy heart.

This church has the distinction of holding the remains of more celebrated persons than any other church in London except St. Paul's Cathedral and Westminster Abbey. Duval has there for company Robert Carr, Earl of Somerset; Samuel Butler; Sir Peter Lely; Wycherley, the dramatist; Grinling Gibbons, the carver; and Dr. Arne, the composer of "Rule Britannia."

It is quite probable that Duval, the young chief of a formidable robber band, had exquisite manners. His origin procured him the graces. Born in Normandy in 1643, he served in Paris as a page to the exiled Duke of Richmond. This was the Duke who eloped with La Belle Stuart, brought up in the exiled Court, whom Charles II was so anxious to marry that he contemplated divorcing his wife, which the Duke forestalled by running off with La Belle. At the Restoration the Duke came to England, bringing Duval with him. Subsequently he left his service and passed, via the Heath and the gallows, into legend as a prince of highwaymen.

The vogue of the highwaymen lasted into the nineteenth century when the Bow Street Runners made their calling more perilous. In 1750 an Old Etonian named Parsons, an army officer, who reverted to the Heath to pay gambling debts, was hanged at Tyburn. This way out of difficulties suggested Sheridan's answer to his son. They were living then near to the Heath, and when young Sheridan, being short of money, asked his father for some, the dramatist replied, "My dear Tom, you will find a case of loaded pistols upstairs, and a horse saddled. The night is dark and you are only half a mile from Hounslow Heath." Whereupon the witty son of a witty father replied, "I

understand what you mean, but I tried it last night. I stopped
your manager from Drury Lane, who told me you had been
beforehand with him and robbed him of every penny he had in
the world!"

Hounslow Heath was, unfortunately, on the royal route to
Windsor. After the Peace of Ryswick, in 1697, crowds of old
soldiers in their desperation resorted to the Heath. They were
ruthless, since there was only one penalty, hanging at Tyburn,
and their skeletons gibbeted in chains on the Heath. On this
occasion, a company of masked horsemen waited for the passing of the nobility returning from a Court at Windsor. "Lord
Ossuslton got away with a loss of two horses," records Macaulay, "the Duke of St. Albans with the help of his servants beat
off the assailants. His brother, the Duke of Northumberland,
less strongly guarded, fell into their hands. They succeeded in
stopping thirty or forty coaches and rode off with a great booty
in guineas, watches and jewellery."

There was a royal occasion when the highwayman had a
shock. One day in June, 1741, a masked man held up a coach,
when three small heads bobbed out of the window. "Who are
these pretty dears?" demanded the highwayman. "The grand-
children of your King," came the terrified response from the
nursemaid. And so they were, the three heads belonged to the
family of Frederick, Prince of Wales, and one of the children
was destined to rule as George III. "God bless his Majesty!"
replied the highwayman, and let the coach pass.

By the middle of the eighteenth century the highwaymen
and footpads had become such a pest that there was a public
outcry. The passage of the Heath became a thing of terror to all
travellers. In 1749 a special body, called the Bow Street Runners, popularly known as "Robin Redbreasts" from their scarlet waistcoats, was instituted to patrol the roads and apprehend
robbers. A famous chief among these runners was John Town-
send who became a terror to the highwaymen. He was ruthless
and incorruptible. When once asked about a new "drop" for

the scaffold, he replied that "though this would take twelve criminals at a time, it would really only hang ten comfortably."

The roads across the dreaded Heath were spaced with gibbets from which dangled the dead highwaymen. They were first hanged at Tyburn and then taken to Hounslow and hung in chains along the roads as a gruesome warning to the brotherhood. As late as 1800 there were thirteen gibbets between Hounslow and Heston. A favourite spot was where the present highway out of Hounslow is bifurcated, one road going to Staines, the other being the old Bath Road as it goes to intersect the new Great West Road.

Hounslow has other and less gruesome memories. It has been associated with several notable military events, and its close link with the Army accounts for it having been the place where the first polo match was played in England, in 1868, when the 10th Hussars introduced the game from India and played a match with the 9th Lancers. And it is from Hounslow Heath that our present splendid Ordnance Survey had its start, for it was here in 1784 that General Roy measured his first base for trigonometrical survey. It is roughly five miles long, running from near Cranford Bridge to Hampton. The work was so accurately accomplished that when, in 1792, the main ordnance survey of the British Isles was begun, a new line was measured and it was found to be only two and three-quarter inches different from Roy's measurement. The work created the greatest interest: Sir Joseph Banks was there, as President of the Royal Society, interested in all scientific experiments, King George III honoured the operations with his presence and doubtless accepted Sir Joseph's hospitality, for the President "ordered his tents to be continually pitched near at hand, where his immediate guests, and the numerous visitors whom curiosity drew to the spot, met with the most hospitable supply of every necessary and even elegant refreshment."

This base line was measured with long glass tubes, and was marked by a small gun at either end. One of the guns may still

be found, just off the Bath Road, near *The Magpies*, beyond
Crawford, and the motorist, studying his one-inch Ordnance
Survey, will find "General Roy's Base" still marked on it, the
beginning of a vast enterprise.

The most notable military event at Hounslow was provided
by James II. From the day he ascended the throne, anticipating
trouble with the Commons, he began to build up a large camp
at Hounslow, designed to overawe the capital. James, plotting
to re-establish the Catholic religion, was soon in collision with
the people. The Test Act brought the matter to a crisis. The
arrest of the Seven Bishops and their trial sealed James's fate.
He had collected at Hounslow fourteen battalions of foot, and
thirty-two squadrons of horse, amounting to thirteen thousand
fighting men. The Londoner, overawed at first, soon turned the
great camp into a fair.

"Mingled with the musketeers and dragoons, a multitude
of fine gentlemen and ladies from Soho Square, sharpers and
painted women from Whitefriars, invalids in Sedans, monks in
hoods and gowns, lacqueys in rich liveries, pedlars, orange girls,
mischievous apprentices and gaping clowns was constantly
passing through the long lanes of the tents. From some pa-
vilions were heard the noises of drunken revelry, from others
the curses of the gamblers." The acquittal of the Seven Bishops
marked the end of Hounslow Camp, and of James as King.
"Nowhere had the news of the acquittal been received with
more clamorous delight than at Hounslow Heath," wrote Macaulay. "James was in Lord Faversham's tent when the express
arrived. He was greatly distressed and exclaimed in French, 'So
much the worse for them.' While he was present respect prevented the soldiers from giving a loose rein to their feelings, but
he had scarcely quitted the camp when he heard a great shouting
behind him. He was surprised and asked what the uproar
meant. 'Nothing,' was the answer, 'the soldiers are glad that the
Bishops are acquitted.' 'Do you call that nothing?' retorted
James."

Two years later Marlborough was reviewing the soldiers of another camp gathered there to repel the threat of the King of France to put James back on his lost throne.

In a sense Hounslow was destined to figure again in military history as the place where, in 1826, something that might be termed the first tank was displayed. An inventor named Gurney ran his famous steam carriage along the Bath Road in the "thirties." Its incredible performance of fifteen miles per hour soon drew the attention of the military authorities to its possibilities. Accordingly a demonstration was arranged near the Bath Road beyond Hounslow, with the Duke of Wellington present as head of the Army. A number of soldiers clambered on to the steam carriage which then, to the wonder of all, proceeded to do a series of manœuvres over the rough Heath, making little of the obstacles it encountered. The Duke was highly pleased at the success of this demonstration and warmly congratulated Mr. Gurney. "It is scarcely possible," he said, "to calculate the convenience as would be deemed from such an invention as this in war time, and that, if fitted with sheets of armour, no enemy could withstand its charge."

Here is the genesis of the tank which made its first appearance in battle on September 15th, 1916, on the Somme, though the Duke could not foresee petrol driven engines and tractor belts.

Gurney's steam coaches met with a rough passage in civilian circles. The coach proprietors, overawed at this new vehicle, banded themselves together to destroy it, which they succeeded in doing. Since they were large payers of tolls they had the road trusts behind them, and in addition an alarmed and ignorant public lent its opposition to this "dangerous" mode of transport. Great ditches were cut to break the axles, and in the end the steam coach was driven off the road. Horse traffic had triumphed, but not for long. The coach traffic on the Bath Road was doomed. In 1838 the Great Western Railway opened a line as far as Slough, in 1840 it extended to Reading, in 1841 to Bath and Bristol. The fine flower of the coaching days on the Bath Road had been ten years earlier, with fifteen day and night coaches and two mails running between London and Bath.

Ruin now fell upon the whole coaching fraternity; the road was deserted, the stables were empty, the inns without travellers. Brentford, Hounslow and Colnbrook fell from considerable prosperity to mere shadows of their former selves. They have never really recovered, except perhaps Hounslow, which has grown as a suburb of the metropolis, not very elegantly, though it is scarcely as horrible as C. S. Harper wrote of it at the end of the nineteenth century.

"Rurality is in its last ditch, while civilization has established a precarious outpost beside it. Flashy villas jostle the market-gardener's cottages; and respectability, even yet, sits self-satisfied in some surviving prim Early Victorian drawing-rooms, amid its chairs upholstered in green rep, its horse-hair sofas and cut-glass lustres, while on either side the vulgar herd sits at open windows in its shirt sleeves, and smokes black and exceedingly foul pipes and gazes complacently upon the clothes hanging out to dry in the garden."

All rurality has completely vanished in Hounslow. Its gardens have now been changed to factory sites within earshot of the incessant rumble of traffic on the Great West Road. But in fairness let it be recorded that one looks in vain for the vulgar herd sitting in its shirt sleeves at open windows. The herd, less vulgar, I hope, in artificial silk and grey flannels, is sitting at the cinema smoking Virginia cigarettes.

For a kinder version, we have to go to the diary of an earlier traveller, the gentle Pastor Moritz, who was in England in 1782, and walked from Richmond to Oxford via Isleworth—"a spot that seemed to be distinguished by some elegant gentlemen's country-seats and gardens." He walked along the road through Hounslow to where it joins the Great West Road, now villa lined as far as *The Traveller's Friend*, a favourite haunt of Dick Turpin. Moritz's report of the scene also tells us of the

astonishment with which a coaching age regarded a man who
was mad enough to walk.

"It is a charming, fine, broad road; and I met on it carriages without number; which, however, on account of the heat, occasioned a
dust which was extremely troublesome and disagreeable. The fine
green hedges, which border the roads in England, contribute greatly
to render them pleasant. This was the case in the road I now travelled, for when I was tired, I sat down in the shade under one of
these hedges, and read Milton. But this relief was soon rendered disagreeable to me, for those who rode, or drove past me, stared at me
with astonishment; and made many significant gestures, as if they
thought my head deranged. As far as Hounslow the way was very
pleasant, but afterwards I thought it not quite so good."

One wonders what Pastor Moritz would have thought of
Hounslow one hundred years later when the town was left
stranded by the vanished coach traffic, and before the garish
villas, with horse-hair sofas and cut-glass lustres, bore proof of
a new prosperity. Tragic was its plight in the interim. It had
kept 2,500 horses, which Lord William Lennox estimated
brought in a revenue of £5,000 a week, apart from money spent
at the inns by travellers. The stables stood empty, and on one
inn was displayed the sign "New Milk and Cream Sold Here!"
The furnishings of the inns came under the hammer, and one
once prosperous innkeeper was glad to set up as cobbler. The
railways also took off the roads the vast herds of cattle that
were driven every year towards London. Ten thousand head of
cattle and one hundred thousand sheep had passed yearly
through Hounslow, which later went by railway truck. Desola-
tion swept over a once festive scene, and the rhymer lamented
the tragedy of once prosperous Hounslow.

> E'en Bessy's self, so long the bar's fair boast,
> The cookmaid's envy and the bagman's toast,
> Whose winning smile was so well known to fame
> That, for a ray, each traveller duly came—
> E'en she—so hopeless, Hounslow, is thy case—
> Hath packed her traps and bolted from the place.

Poor Hounslow, those who have been unkind enough to say they would not bury a dog in it reveal their ignorance of its ancient etymology, for in Domesday it is called Honeslanu, signifying "dog's mound." The railway has since made handsome amends, and now brings thousands of workers daily to their suburban homes. And it is kind to remember that the beauties of this small town and its surrounding countryside once stirred the poet to song:

> *Pure is the air, the prospect unconfined,*
> *And various are the sports unbend the mind,*
> *Shall ancient Hounslow then be lost to fame,*
> *And dull oblivion desecrate the Name?*
> *No—from the Nine we this advice receive*
> *That in their records Hounslow's name shall live.*

How rash the nine Muses were few motorists on the Bath Road know, for Hounslow, like Brentford, is now by-passed by the new Great West Road out of London.

CHAPTER X

The Berkeleys of Cranford

EMERGING FROM HOUNSLOW on to the great highway, we soon approach Cranford, leaving Heston aerodrome on our right. I owe it to Miss Whissitt that I stopped at Cranford on our return from the Osterley Park and Spring Grove excursion. The village lies back a mile off the main road and so is missed by the hurrying motorist for whom Cranford is marked only by the new *Berkeley Arms,* part of an outcrop of Frenchified architecture, machicolated, with donjon towers, as if Viollet le Duc had strayed into the English office of a building contractor and said, "Let's see what we can do for the Bath Road, and make the air traveller from Paris feel at home when he alights."

This entrance to Cranford is a little startling. It suggests fearful possibilities in the competitive line. Plain Slough, slightly jealous, might go medieval in the German manner and wall itself in, à la Rothenburg, thus retorting to Cranford-Carcassonne. As we come to Cranford we cross the scene of the wildest part of the former Heath, which was all open land until the Enclosure Act of 1820. The River Crane, which gives its name to the village, crosses the Bath Road, and few motorists are aware of the small river flowing under the bridge, where, until the first bridge was built in 1750 for the Bath Road traffic, there was a ford. Before we came to it, Miss Whissitt asked me to turn right, at the corner where *The Berkeley Arms* stands in all its Gallic splendour, and down what remains of a once splendid avenue of oak trees. It is still an impressive drive, and leads one to the village itself which has numerous pleasant English houses set back in gardens. No one would imagine, looking through these iron-wrought gates and over old brick walls into well-kept gardens, that Hyde Park Corner is only some twelve miles away. One of these houses, the Firs, now burnt down, George III acquired for his dentist, so that he might have him on call midway between London and Windsor, and in this same house lived a retired brewer named Cox, who grew there the first Orange Pippins, to which he gave his now famous name. By the working of fate there lived at *The Cedars*, the man who destroyed the Bath Road coach traffic, and the prosperity of Cranford-Brunel, the designer of "The Great Eastern," who, as chief engineer to the Great Western Railway, planned the first railway to Slough.

Presently, following Church Road, a gateway and lodge house appear on the left, at the beginning of a long drive.

"Here we are," said Miss Whissitt.

"What are we going to see—can I go in?"

"Yes—this is Cranford Park. It's now public property. I shall show you a church with some beautiful monuments, and near it a country seat of the Berkeleys."

"What Berkeleys—the Berkeleys of Berkeley Square?" I asked, derisively, as we drove down the long gravel drive, until we came to a narrow, humped bridge.

"That's just who they are! Now look!"

I looked. The prospect was certainly a pleasant and surprising one. The River Crane, flowing placidly through the level park, had been made to feed the ornamental water on either side of the bridge.

"It was on this water Fanny Kemble used to sing to Grantley Berkeley when he was a small boy."

I was about to ask who Grantley Berkeley was, but I kept silent. Miss Whissitt would tell me all there was to know in her own time. Ahead lay the charming little church, near it towered up a massive red brick Georgian house.

"We're just in time," said Miss Whissitt, as we drew nearer. "In a few months it won't be here. *Vraiment!*"

I looked startled. It seemed as if that immense brick house would always be there. It sat overpoweringly on the flat parkland, and dominated the low church. Miss Whissitt explained that the Berkeleys had deserted the house some twenty years ago, it was falling into ruin, and the local Council had bought the park for public use and was pulling down the old house.

"Very sad," sighed my companion. "What a story that house can tell!"

With little encouragement Miss Whissitt told it, with such detail that I inquired if she had lived with the family. No, but when she was working at Osterley Park she used to walk over here and became very friendly with the agent and the caretaker.

"We'll do the house first," said Miss Whissitt, as we got out of the car, and led the way into a large cobbled yard with a magnificent range of stables surmounted by a splendid clock, said to have come from Hampton Court two hundred years ago. These stables once housed the hounds of the Berkeley Hunt, whose most famous exploit, under the mastership of that roaring Georgian buck, the Honourable Grantley Berkeley, must have been, in 1827, the hunting of a stag right from Cranford up to the threshold of the British Museum.

We walked round the outside of the house first, across a lawn that had become a wilderness. The enormous brick mansion towered up, sadly derelict, with broken frames and windows, fallen gutters, and ominous cracks in the walls, and everywhere a growth of parasitical ivy. The columned entrance porch still retained something of its former dignity. There were old people in Cranford who remembered the Berkeleys at the great house. Then, in 1918, a score of vans drew up at the door, and, loaded with furniture, wended their way through the village. The Berkeleys had departed, leaving the old mansion to decay, in a lost battle against the encroachment of the rising tide of cheap "distinctive homes" lapping the fringes of the park.

That procession was a sad symbol of the march of time. Almost the last sensation of many given to the villagers of Cranford by the wild Berkeleys had been a prize-fight, staged for a royal guest, the Prince of Wales, later Edward VII, when professional pugilists fought, bare fisted and stripped to the buff, cheered on by the guests of Cranford House attired as Georgian bucks in white top hats, coloured waistcoats and silk knee-breeches.

On the south side, above the derelict lawn and its ha-ha, there rose an astonishing double bay, each with its verandah, and long French windows with shutters. The green roofs of these twin verandahs had broken away from the wall fastenings and slipped down. It was a sad scene of decay. Who had opened those windows in past days, and from those semi-circular verandahs looked out across the level park towards the distant Bath Road?

"Curious, isn't it?" asked Miss Whissitt, as if in answer to my speculation. "The first old house had another built round it. One of the Berkeleys, the Admiral Sir George, retired here when he left the Navy. He had been in command of the old wooden men-o'-war. H.M.S. *Leopard* was under his command, in 1807, when it had its encounter with the U.S. frigate *Chesapeake*, leading later to the war of 1812. When the Admiral retired and came here he built those two bays and put on the verandahs. They resembled the galleried sterns of 'the old wooden walls of England.' He used to step out on to them and sweep the Bath Road with his telescope, over the green sea of the park, and imagine he was afloat again! *Drôle, n'est-ce pas?*"

Miss Whissitt gazed over the park in which some cows were grazing.

"Oh, that reminds me—Edward Jenner and vaccination," she exclaimed, suddenly.

I stared at her, wondering whatever she meant.

"Those cows," went on my companion, "you know Jenner got the idea of vaccination for smallpox from studying cowpox? He used to come here. The Berkeleys' chief seat was—it still is —Berkeley Castle, in Berkeley, Gloucestershire. Jenner's father was the clergyman there, and this connection resulted in Edward Jenner visiting Cranford. It's odd how things link up, isn't it? I've no doubt that's how he came to meet your Sir Joseph Banks, who must have come over here a lot from Spring Grove, for the Berkeleys entertained everybody. Banks got young Jenner the job of preparing and arranging the zoological specimens which he had collected on Captain Cook's first expedition—and Jenner was offered the post of naturalist in the second expedition. Those cows brought it all back."

From cows, Jenner and vaccination, I led Miss Whissitt on to the Berkeleys.

The family, one of the oldest in England, I learned, is still living at Berkeley Castle, which is one of the best preserved feudal strongholds, with its circular keep, battlements, dungeon, towers, moat and portcullis gate, in the Kingdom. Here Edward II was foully murdered in 1327.

> Mark the year, and mark the night,
> When Seven shall re-echo with affright,
> The shrieks of death, thro' Berkeley's roofs that ring,
> Shrieks of an agonizing King!

—sang Gray. The Berkeleys, immensely wealthy and powerful, have lived in their castle in feudal splendour since 1223. The dungeon chamber still exists in which Edward II was confined, immediately over the stench of a dead horse, purposely put there in the hope of inducing a putrid fever, which the king's constitution resisted, resulting in a fiendish death by violence. The family was the last to have a private jester, Dickey Pierce, who, when he died, in 1728, had his epitaph written by Dean Swift.

Such was the famous family which acquired Cranford in 1618.

In addition to the estates in Gloucestershire and the Cranford estate, there was a large revenue from Berkeley Square and other London properties which had grown tremendously in value since the days of the Elizabethan lord whose mother had a country residence in Kentish Town, and a town residence in Shoe Lane, Fleet Street. The Earl himself hunted the country of Gray's Inn Fields and "about Islington" with one hundred and fifty servants in livery.

The most remarkable inhabitant of Cranford was the fifth Countess of Berkeley. She lived to be over eighty and began life as the daughter of a butcher, whose liaison with the Earl resulted in a sensational appeal to the House of Lords. Fanny Kemble, writing of this redoubtable old lady, related that on one occasion, sitting at the high table at Cranford, she filled her claret glass till the wine appeared to form a rim about it, and then, raising it steadily to her lips, looked round the table, drank the contents without spilling a drop, and said: "Not one of my sons could do that!"

She had six sons, four illegitimate and two legitimate, by the Earl of Berkeley, and her story is one of the most remarkable in the annals of the Peerage.

Young Viscount Dursley, later the fifth Earl of Berkeley, was in command of a regiment of militia when his attention was attracted by the three Miss Coles, the pretty daughters of a butcher in Gloucester. They had a habit of sitting in the window over their father's shop, and drew the attention of all the young blades of the regiment. Presently one sister, Susan, went into the service of Lady Talbot in London, another, Mary, went as lady's maid to a vicarage in Kent. Later on Mary was sent for by Susan, who represented that she had made such an excellent marriage that she could not allow her sister to remain in a humble position. So to London went Mary, to reside in her sister's house. It soon became clear that Susan

was not married, but under the "protection" of someone. She
had received from Lord Berkeley a sum of money for inducing
her sister to come to town, and to become Berkeley's mistress.

If it was not the fashion in the eighteenth century it certainly was not considered unusual for a man in Society to support a mistress. Miss Cole, or Miss Tudor as she chose to be
known, was installed at Berkeley Castle and at Cranford,
where she played hostess to all the Earl's friends, from the
Prince of Wales, later George III, and the Royal Dukes down-
wards, all of whom made frequent calls at Cranford, whose
pheasant shooting was renowned. In general, she assumed the
position of a wife, and seemed quite content, as was Lord
Berkeley.

She bore him four sons, William Fitzhardinge in 1787,
Maurice in 1788, Augustus in 1789 and Francis in 1795. When
she was expecting her fifth child, Mary Cole urged upon the
Earl her desire for a proper marriage, and acceding to her
importunings, a marriage ceremony was performed in May,
1796, and she became the Countess of Berkeley. In November
of this year she gave birth to Thomas Moreton, who thus became the heir, as Viscount Dursley, and four years later to a
sixth son, Grantley; these two sons, being born in wedlock,
were legitimate.

The scandal of Berkeley's menage would soon have been
forgotten had it not been that a remarkable claim was put
forth in 1797 by the Earl and his wife, who declared that the
first son, William Fitzhardinge, was the rightful heir by reason
of a prior marriage in 1785. The astonishing reason given for
the suppression of the first "marriage" was that the entry of
the ceremony in the parish books had been purposely destroyed
by a clergyman, and Lord Berkeley's silence regarding the
marriage was due to his desire to save the clergyman from
punishment! He explained his leaving his wife two days after
the "marriage" by saying it was in order to keep the cere-

mony secret on account of the improper conduct of Lady Berkeley's sister, Susan.

Lord Berkeley stopped at nothing to bolster up his preposterous claim. He obtained access to the parish register in which the birth of Moreton, the legitimate heir, was registered, and made an entry in his own handwriting, stating that the title "Lord Dursley" had been given in error, as this was his fifth son born in wedlock. When the claim came before the House of Lords, the evidence was so "cooked" that the claim was speedily disposed of, and by this time Admiral Sir George Berkeley, the Earl's brother, was so suspicious of every and all marriages that he started another appeal to the House of Lords to prove that all the children were illegitimate and he was the heir-presumptive!

Lord Berkeley now dropped his claim, but he proceeded, in the disposition of his wealth, to do everything that gave emphasis to his recognition of Fitzhardinge, the first-born, as the legitimate heir.

Here the matter might have ended, but for the death of Lord Berkeley. Fitzhardinge, or Colonel Berkeley as he was now known, laid claim to the title and estates, and so drilled were the other members of the family, even including Moreton the rightful heir, that they supported his claim to legitimacy and all that went with it.

This time the House of Lords referred the matter to Committee, and a remarkable trial followed. Fitzhardinge suborned witnesses and found an ally in his mother's uncle, William Cole, who subsequently threatened to betray his employer, and levied blackmail upon him. The trial left Colonel Berkeley without a shadow of a claim, and such severe strictures were made upon the evidence he had manufactured, for even the coffin-plates in the family vault at Cranford had been tampered with, that he would have been in grave peril but for the

Prince Regent, who, out of regard for his dead friend, the Earl, took no action, as suggested by the House of Lords.

The future conduct of the heir proper, Moreton, Viscount Dursley, revealed a strain of almost excessive chivalry. Maintaining that the results of the trial, confirming the myth of the first marriage, cast an aspersion on his mother's honour, he declined all his life to accept either the viscounty or the earldom. He retired to Red House, a dwelling in Cranford village, and there lived to a ripe old age as plain Mr. Moreton Berkeley. His other legitimate brother, the heir-presumptive, Grantley Berkeley, died shortly before him.

Meanwhile Colonel Berkeley, deprived of the earldom he coveted, retired to Berkeley Castle, in possession of the huge revenues from the estates, and made new plans to get ennobled. At the Castle and at Cranford two mistresses reigned in succession, one possessing the incredible name of Mrs. Bunn. The result was that while Colonel Berkeley cut a figure in Society, the wives of his royal and noble friends never came to his houses. A crony of the Prince of Wales, and much in evidence in fashionable Brighton society, his common tastes drew him into the company of actors and actresses, and at one time the master of Berkeley Castle actually played with them as an amateur.

His plan for achieving a peerage could only have been conceivable in an age of the greatest political corruption. Although of a stout Conservative family, it was intimated to him that if he returned three of his brothers to Parliament as Liberals the Whig Government would advance him to a barony. With the important Berkeley interests this was not difficult. Three brothers were duly elected to Parliament, and Colonel Berkeley became Lord Segrave. But this was not enough. Smarting under his illegitimacy, he craved an earldom. The price, he learned, was four brothers in Parliament. He cast around for another brother, and was aided by Grantley Berkeley, the heir-presumptive to Moreton, a truculent, roistering buck who combined in his character all the worst features of the bully-cum-gentleman in that hard-drinking, hard-hunting and knuckle-fighting age. Later, Grantley Berkeley, cheated of the cash perquisites promised him by Lord Segrave, could say and write nothing hard enough about his eldest brother.

With the fourth brother safely lodged in the House, Lord Segrave now found himself promoted to the Earldom of Fitz-hardinge, but notwithstanding this, which seemed a complete abandonment of his claim to the earldom of Berkeley, More-ton, the rightful earl, persisted in his own renunciation. His mother, who as Mary Cole had shown much aptitude in man-aging Lord Berkeley's estates that all affairs devolved upon her, continued, long after she was Countess, to keep her grip on things, particularly at Cranford Park, which became the dower house and where her younger children passed much of their time.

There was a wild strain in most of this brood, legitimate and otherwise. The youngest fought a duel in Osterley Park and it was he who, with a professional pugilist, guarded the door of the Regent Street bookshop when his brother Grantley walked in and thrashed puny Mr. Fraser because, as proprietor of a magazine in which had appeared a caustic criticism of More-ton's first novel, he refused to divulge the name of the critic. This brutal assault landed Grantley Berkeley in court where he had to pay £100 damages. Two days later, Dr. Maginn hav-ing confessed himself the critic, he called him out and fought a pistol duel, wounding him. A great rider to hounds, Berkeley was a foremost patron of prize-fights and cock-fights, and the unfortunate servants and grooms at Cranford were called upon to stand excessive punishment as boxing partners of the pu-gilistic brothers.

Berkeley, placed in Parliament by his designing brother, soon quarrelled with him, and spent £30,000 to retain his seat against his brother's interest at the next election. A roaring blade of the twenties, there were some artistic streaks in this aristocratic bully. He lived for his hounds, and his appreciation of nature was deep and real. Much of his life was passed at Cranford Park, or at Springfield, a house in the village. He wrote romances in the three-volume fashion of the age. He was the Member who secured ladies the privilege of admittance to the Strangers' Gallery in the House. He wrote books on hunting, a long, romantic poem called "Love and the Lion," and a pamphlet on the potato disease. With his brother Moreton, he explored every inch of the country around Cranford, consorting with gamekeepers and such company as gathered in local inns.

He lived long enough to span two distinct ages. His father had driven down from London to Cranford in the family coach, with four long-tailed horses that took one hour to cover the twelve miles. It was his father who, driving out to dine with Mr. Justice Bulstrode at Hounslow, one November night in 1774, had been held up by a highwayman. Lord Berkeley seized the weapon pointed at him, thrust it against the highwayman's body, and discharged it. The man's clothes were set on fire, but he managed to ride some distance away before falling dead. His accomplices were afterwards discovered to be a gang of amateur highwaymen, all youths in good positions in London.

There was a romantic halo over highwaymen's heads, and Lord Berkeley's shooting was not considered sportsmanlike. The public, which cheerfully flocked to their hangings, did not like to hear of them shot. Lord Chesterfield, whose reputation was then under a cloud for having prosecuted for forgery the celebrated Dr. Dodd, his son's tutor, with the result that he was hanged, was unwise enough to ask Lord Berkeley, sneeringly, how many highwaymen he had shot lately. At once came the stinging retort, "As many as you have hanged tutors, but with much better reason for doing so."

Grantley, the son of this gentleman who, in 1784, had seen

the first mail driven to Bath and Bristol, saw sixteen day and night coaches pass through Cranford in 1830, the heyday of its prosperity, when five hundred horses were stabled there for the Bath Road traffic. He lived to see that prosperity fade away when railways traversed the kingdom. He entertained at Cranford the Duke of St. Albans when the pheasant-shooting was so famous that the Duke tied up his left eye with a scarf "to avoid the trouble of having to shut it so often when I fire," and the Duke of York declared he had had the biggest bag of his life. A sportsman, a naturalist, a hard liver all his life, he lived on to be an old man in the village he loved and where his boisterous life had been spent. And looking back on those youthful scenes, his pen became lyrical:

"To those dear woods and fields at Cranford then, a long farewell, woods where in summer song-birds flocked from the more open and well-trodden fields to pour out their lovely melody in security. Where the last quiet notes of the murmuring turtle-dove were taken up by the nightingale . . . to the river through the willows and the park where Miss Kemble once entranced my soul by singing to us as the boat floated down the stream, memories of heroism and love, adieu to all!"

When Grantley Berkeley died in 1881, a picturesque if turbulent figure who was born in the opening year of the century passed away. To the end of his days he dressed the part of a Regency buck, with two or three coloured satin under-waistcoats, around his neck three or four gaudy silk neckerchiefs, and on his head a flat cocked hat, a "character" who had dined and wined with Beau Brummell and Count d'Orsay. His yellow chariot with the crimson lining was as well known to every turnpike man on the road from Cranford to London as was his tawny orange plush coat in the hunting-field. Whatever he was, he stands forth from the shadows thrown by the old mansion, a full-blooded, boisterous giant, one of the seven astonishing sons of their astonishing parents.

II

Miss Whissitt, having led me into the courtyard formed by the stables and the back of the house, boldly approached a door and pushed it open. We found ourselves in an immense Georgian kitchen, with great ovens, heavy iron roasting spits, and a kitchen-table that was like a split oak tree. I saw, in imagination, the army of servants coming and going; my lord's French chef, the robust English cooks in their white aprons, the apple-cheeked scullery and stillroom maids, and, perhaps, a loitering young footman delaying the busy preparations with his flirtatious bantering. Over all rose the odour of pheasants roasting, numerous pies full of fruit from the kitchen-garden, and all the ingredients for the elaborate dinner-party that evening. For His Royal Highness, the Duke of Kent, His Grace the Duke of St. Albans, Lord William Lennox and the famous Sir Joseph Banks were dining with his Lordship after the shoot.

Miss Whissitt marched on as if she owned the manorhouse of the Berkeleys, across the stone-flagged floor, down a corridor and into a large room, probably the servants' hall, where she greeted the caretaker like an old friend. In her charge we toured the house, a sad spectacle with its great shuttered windows, its library with mildewed, empty book-cases, and long drawing-room, whose floor was rotting away. We ascended the winding stone staircase, past an apse holding an immense Apollo in black plaster, to the first landing, part of which had fallen away into the corridor below. Here came successive bedrooms, some with balconies overlooking once trim lawns and rose gardens, now a jungle of weed and wild briar. In this room, with its delicate, flowered wallpaper, the French maid dresses the Countess's hair, and helps her into a new Empire gown, which Lady Blessington has made so fashionable this season. Meanwhile my lady reads a gossipy letter from Lady Holland. Lord Holland is laid up with gout. Madame d'Arblay, whose new novel is just out, which my Lord Byron has so highly praised, has just called, with an account of her visit to Dr. Herschel's wonderful telescope at Slough—has her lady-ship yet seen it?

The toilet is finished. Before the dinner-bell rings she has just time to go into the nursery. It has been rather stupidly placed over the library. To deaden the sound, the spaces between the joists have been packed with sea-shells, a most novel idea, which has quite cured the nuisance. In the nursery, where young Moreton and Grantley and some visiting cousins are being taught proficiency with the globes, Miss Woburn dutifully rises with her charges. She is newly engaged, having been compelled to earn her living owing to the recent death of her father, a poor clergyman. Her ladyship felt very doubtful about engaging someone with no experience, but Dean Brush most strongly recommended her as endowed with every moral and religious virtue. According to the Dean, she is well quali-fied to teach Latin and Greek, history and mathematics. She has the rudiments of Hebrew, some Spanish, French and Italian, and can instruct in dancing and the elements of the natural sciences. Her father, an improvident man, doubtless, was a Fellow of his College. Miss Woburn was at a good school and had as school-fellows Miss Mary Mitford and Lady Caroline Lamb, but twenty pounds a year seems a lot for one so young. Too young and pretty—but she will be kept safely interned in that "no man's land" between the servants' hall and the drawing-room.

"This was the nursery," said Miss Whissitt, as we stepped into a large room. "Look!"

She stooped, where a floor-board had been prised up, and I found the space between the joists packed with small sea-shells.

"To deaden the sound over the library," she explained.

I picked up a small shell as a souvenir. They say that shells still hold the voice of the sea. Perhaps this one held the voices of the nursery:

"No, Master Moreton, pass the globe to Lucy—(poor bairn, what a shame! He is really His Lordship, and they're cheating him out of his rights)—Now recite your tables."

At the foot of the staircase we passed on into the octagonal entrance hall, and as we stood in the half-light on those cold stone flags, and looked at the peeling walls, I thought of other days when the hoofs of horses on the gravel and the jingle of harness had been heard as the family coach, with cockaded grooms on the box, drew up at this front door. The butler and his underlings had scurried into this hall, and James, with powdered hair, had stood to attention.

A grandson of these Berkeleys, Percy Armytage, a Court official who had spent much of his boyhood here, and lived on in the vicinity until after the Great War, has given us a glimpse of that coach. He describes the migration from Cranford to Berkeley.

"Clothed most unsuitably in a little Lord Fauntleroy velvet suit, I climbed into a high-bodied chariot, painted bright yellow; it was drawn by four horses and the postilions wore crimson liveries. There was only one seat inside, and this being reserved for my grandparents, I was accommodated with a brocaded footstool. The dicky behind was occupied by my grandparents' maid. The front of the chariot was enclosed by a sheet of plate glass, curtained at each end. From my lowly perch I first became acquainted with the eight miles of road between Cranford and Slough. From Slough to Stroud the coach, including the occupants, was taken by rail on a truck, horses again drawing it on the last stage of the journey."

The day came when the railway took them all the way, when at last the carriage and horses no longer clattered bravely up the drive to this hall door. And standing in this barren entrance hall one other picture from the same source comes into mind. It is a Sunday morning, in the quiet of the summer landscape, where only the lowing of cows and the birdsong break the country quiet.

"As the old church bell was tinkling, we assembled in the hall, each with a large Book of Common Prayer. We would await the coming of the Reverend Hickes, a genuine sporting parson, who farmed, hunted, engaged in all the prevailing amusements, revelled in a good dinner with vintage wine, yet never forgot he was a parish priest. At about five minutes to eleven Mr. Hickes would arrive, always with the remark 'We are ready now, Sir.' Thereupon, with Mr. Hickes leading the way as if it had been a funeral procession, and we following grandfather and grandmother who were immediately behind him, the household marched solemnly into church. The Rector himself handed us to the family pew and then disappeared behind an old three-decker pulpit, from which he presently emerged in a white surplice, which he afterwards changed into a black gown for the sermon."

Let us follow these ghosts in their walk from the vestibule of the manor-house into the church only a few yards distant. A former church was here in Saxon times, and in the Domesday Book the priest held thirty acres of land in a manor that consisted of eight villeins, two cottagers and three slaves. The Berkeleys came here in 1618 when Elizabeth, Lady Berkeley, purchased the manor, a tenure that lasted for three hundred years. During her lifetime a fire destroyed much of the church, which was then rebuilt by her, the parishioners contributing a shilling in the pound. It still has much fifteenth-century work, and some frescoes, monogram symbols of the Virgin Mary, surmounted by a royal crown, belong to that period. On stepping into the little church its general loveliness reveals at once the hand of an enthusiast at work. Here is no sad, decaying house of God, but a radiant little church, with everything most carefully tended. Its rector, one of a line dating from 1310, the Rev. Maurice Childs, has tackled the restoration of St. Dunstan's to its original beauty, with reverence and humour. For this church of the Knights Templars set in Cranford Park, with its lich-gate and castellated tower overlooking the stables and the manor-house, is rich in monuments of the successive lords of the manor.

In the north wall of the chancel Mr. Childs opened up a little Tudor doorway which had been blocked up by the elaborate tomb of the Astons. It now opens so that when he celebrates for the quick and the dead he looks out upon the green graves of those who have gone before.

The Aston tomb was in a sad state of decay. With rare enterprise it was not only completely dismantled but was rebuilt with a new canopy, and the knight's family, his two ladies, four daughters and infant son were sent to the cleaners, and returned with all their ruffles, breeches, doublets, and stomachers restored to their original colours, so that the kneeling family strikes a note almost of gaiety in this cheerful church.

At the time we visited St. Dunstan's, Sir Roger Aston had not joined his family. Insufficient funds had not yet allowed him to go to the dry-cleaners, and there he was, kneeling on the belfry floor, rather dowdy, with a pathetic card hung round his neck. "Won't you please give something so that I can be restored to my family in the chancel." As Miss Whissitt remarked, as I gave five shillings towards his renovation, it was not every day one could subscribe to the wardrobe of a knight.

Sir Roger Aston, Lord of the Manor of Cranford in 1604, was Barber and Gentleman of the Bedchamber to James I of England, and Keeper of the King's Great Wardrobe. This means he was something more than a supervalet, for a barber in the Jacobean days had onerous duties. There is more in the barber's striped pole and basin than meets the eye. The white ribbon round the pole indicated the fillet for bandaging the arm in bleeding, and the basin was to receive the blood—not from an unlucky slip on the throat of the patron. The barber was, in short, something of a surgeon, and by an Act in the reign of Henry VIII they were united with the Company of Surgeons, it being specified they should confine themselves to the minor operations of blood-letting and drawing teeth, while the surgeons, debarred from "barbery or shaving," tackled the bigger jobs.

Sir Roger, then, added the rôle of dentist to his occupation of wardrobe keeping, and, if he practised dentistry in that era, he must have had some skill as a sculptor since contemporary teeth were carved out of solid blocks of ivory! Was he plumber to His Majesty also? For if he "filled" the royal teeth, he filled them with lead, as was the French practice in the seventeenth century, an operation delightfully termed *plombage!* Is it for this reason that the inscription on Sir Roger's tomb dryly praises the knight as "a deligent and trustie servant to his King . . . and for ye painfull and faithfull service he hath donne"?

Sir Roger, therefore, must have been a good handyman for His Majesty to have about him. He married twice and had four daughters and an infant son, who died soon after baptism. Here they all are, an entrancing family, almost life-size, in coloured alabaster, with their personal histories inscribed underneath them. The artist-sculptor must have enjoyed making this monument. It shines with blue, yellow and vermilion, with ruffles and stomachers, lace and jewellery and stars, with proud escutcheons and "coloured shoon." Let us linger over lovely young Ann, in a green dress. Poor child! She wanted to marry for love the dashing young blade who courted her, but the affair did not prosper because the young man could not produce a competent dowry. It was not the real excuse, for James could not endure anyone to come between his passion for the handsome Leicestershire youth whom he made an earl at twenty-four, a marquess at twenty-five, a duke at thirty, and the richest noble in his kingdom. So poor Ann never married the William George Villiers, destined to fall at the age of thirty-six to an assassin's dagger. The future Duke of Buckingham married Kitty Manners, daughter of the Earl of Rutland, who adored him despite his faithlessness, and gave him the family we have seen in Van Dyck's picture at Osterley Park.

Poor Ann Aston passed into oblivion, save for this lovely monument. Its creator was William Earl, who was Clerk of the

Works to King James. The contract for the work, completed shortly after Sir Roger's death, is still in existence. For three hundred years his work was left to fall into ruin, and was in danger of collapse, when Mr. Childs started his task of a general restoration of the church and its contents.

Opposite this monument there is a more restrained work, but exquisite, the tomb of the Lady Elizabeth Berkeley, who bought the Manor in 1618. She was the widow of a son of the eleventh baron, a cousin of Queen Anne Boleyn, and her son succeeded as Lord Berkeley. Lady Elizabeth lies in a shroud of white marble on a black slab, and the workmanship is so human and exquisite that for a long time it was believed it came from the chisel of the great Bernini, creator of the colonnade of St. Peter's. It has since been discovered that it is his influence which shows in the work. Nicholas Stone, master-mason to James I and Charles I, sent his son to work in the studios of Bernini at Rome, and the coats of arms that decorate the tomb were all wrought there.

Near the Aston tomb there is a memorial plaque to Sir Charles Scarborough. He was a famous physician and mathematician who, if he saved Charles II, James II and William III much pain, to all of whom he was chief medical attendant, must also have caused mental agony to generations of English schoolboys, for he was the translator of Euclid into English. Considered an incomparable anatomist, he must have been a genial soul, even allowing for the fulsomeness of ancient epitaphs, which in his case tells us he was "among doctors of the English a Hippocrates, among their mathematicians a Euclid; blessed with a gracious character, kindly affectioned to all, and equable in every duty of life. Of citizens, husbands, fathers, friends, the best."

He had a country house at Cranford, to which he came from his house in St. Martin's-in-the-Fields. It is quite probable that he was physician to Lord Berkeley. He was the friend of all the well-known men of his day. Scarborough was intimate with

Waller and Cowley, the poets, with Harvey, discoverer of the circulation of the blood, who left "my velvet gown to my loving friend Mr. Dr. Scarbrugh, as well as all my little silver instruments of surgerie," and with Pepys, the diarist. What is more likely than that Berkeley brought him to the notice of Charles II, for we find him, in May, 1660, going with Berkeley, in a distinguished company, to the Hague to escort Charles II back to England and his throne. There was also present on that occasion Samuel Pepys, who has left a lively account of the King's return from the Hague.

On the eve of the sailing Dr. Scarborough dined with Pepys. "At supper the three Doctors of Physique again at my cabin; where I put Dr. Scarborough in mind of what I heard him say, that children do, in every day's experience, look several ways with both their eyes, till custom teaches them otherwise; and that we do now see with but one eye, our eyes looking in parallel lines." And so the decanter went round, and the company in the cabin discussed all manner of things.

There was another occasion nearly three years later, when Pepys went to a lecture at Chyrurgeons' Hall to hear a lecture and have a fine dinner in learned company. After dinner, by way of entertainment, Dr. Scarborough took Pepys and some of his friends to see the body of a lusty seaman hanged for robbery. "I did touch the dead body with my bare hand: it felt cold, but methought it was a very unpleasant sight," records Pepys. Thereafter, back at table, they discussed hanging, how one Dillon made a silken halter for himself, not for honour only but because "it do slip close and kills, that is, strangles pleasantly; whereas a stiff one do not come so close together, and so the party may live the longer before killed. But all the Doctors at table conclude that there is no pain at all in hanging, for that it do stop the circulation of the blood; and so stops all sense and motion in an instant."

Sir Charles Scarborough's career almost had a sudden and tragic end in May, 1682. He accompanied the Duke of York on

board H.M.S. *Gloucester* in a naval excursion to Scotland. The
pilot ran the ship aground, and some two hundred men were
drowned, including several of the royal suite. The Duke of
York got safely into a boat, but Sir Charles was desperately
struggling in the water when one of the accompanying vessels,
with Pepys on board, came up and rescued the doctor in the
nick of time, for he was almost dead with cold.

In the chancel nearest to the altar there is another monument
to a remarkable man of even wider fame, Dr. Thomas Fuller,
chaplain to Charles I and Charles II, who was rector of Cranford from 1658 to 1661. He, too, joined his friend, Dr. Scarborough, and his patron, Lord Berkeley, and went to meet
Charles II in 1660, who made him a D.D. His fame rests chiefly
on his book *The Worthies of England,* published after his death,
and one of the great successes of the seventeenth century. But
he had always had a pen in his hand, and when he died, in a
Covent Garden lodging during a visit to London, "he cried out
for pen and ink to the last." He was, indeed, in an age when
men of letters starved, almost the first author to make an income with his pen.

The son of a Bishop, who watched his nephew's interest,
Fuller, sometimes accused of being a turncoat during the troubled age in which he lived, had really no political passions, and
only wished to exhibit goodwill to all. He survived the Cromwellian age, and basked in the Restoration without making
himself a martyr, and Charles II had a great respect for his
frank honesty. A charming personality, a considerable scholar,
witty, and urbane, he was welcomed in all company. When he
preached, so popular was he, it was said he had two congrega-
tions, one in the church and the other listening through the
windows. He suggested his own epitaph—"Here lies Fuller's
earth," which was not used, being considered too flippant, but
such was the veneration in which he was universally held that
when he died, after preaching in the Royal Chapel of Savoy,
more than two hundred members of the clergy on horseback

accompanied his body to Cranford, where the Dean of Rochester preached a panegyric.

Pepys knew him, of course, and esteemed him—"He tells me of his last and great book that is coming out, that is the History of all the Families in England, and could tell me more of my own, than I knew myself." Later, reading the *Worthies,* he even forgave him the omission of his own family—"much troubled that he says nothing at all." When he heard him preach in the Savoy on May 12th, 1661, he recorded that it was "a poor, dry sermon. And I am afraid my former high esteem of his preaching was more out of opinion than judgment." But Pepys was too harsh. Dr. Fuller was failing. Three months later he wrote, commenting on a form of fever about, "among others, the famous Tom Fuller is dead of it." It remained for Coleridge to pronounce judgment on the worthiness of the author of the *Worthies,* and like Lamb he praised him highly. "Fuller was incomparably the most sensible, the least prejudiced, great man of an age that boasted a galaxy of great men."

III

Fuller was succeeded at Cranford by an equally remarkable man. This was John Wilkins, who, six years after leaving Cranford, became Bishop of Chester. Like Fuller he had been private chaplain to Lord Berkeley, and thus came to have the living of St. Dunstan's. He made only a short stay, leaving in 1663, but his fame as a writer who mixed the romantic with the scientific had been long established. He was of an inventive turn of mind, and astonished the inhabitants around the Heath by sailing over the land in a wind yacht he had devised, which he describes as a "land-sailing carriage" in his book *Mathematical Magic*. While at Cranford he took a great part in the founding of the Royal Society, of which he was appointed chairman. He, too, steered clear of trouble during the Civil War, the Commonwealth and the Restoration, and succeeded in being

Cromwell's brother-in-law and on good terms with Charles II. He evidently inherited his curious turn of mind from his father, an Oxford goldsmith who was termed "a verie ingeniose man with a verie mechanicall head."

Wilkins early attracted notice in 1638 with the publication of *The Discovery of a World in the Moon,* which was "a Discourse tending to prove that 'tis probable there may be another habitable world in that Planet." In other words he was putting in a word for the theory of the man in the moon. In a second edition he put forth the possibility of reaching the moon by "volitation," little knowing that, three hundred years later, only a mile away at Heston aerodrome, man would be flying through the skies at three hundred miles an hour, and would have achieved non-stop flights of four thousand miles, if not from planet to planet, at least from continent to continent.

In 1640, greatly daring, Dr. Wilkins put forth "A Discourse concerning a new Planet, tending to prove that 'tis probable our Earth is one of the Planets." Wilkins was right, and his probability became a scientific fact. Just over one hundred and forty years later, not more than seven miles away. Herschel added another planet, Uranus, to the list.

Dr. Wilkins never ceased to speculate on the curious. A year after his discourse on earth as a probable planet, he turned to telepathy, or was it an intelligent anticipation of broadcasting? For he called his new publication "Mercury, or the Secret and Swift Messenger, showing how a Man may with Privacy and Speed communicate his thoughts to a Friend at any Distance." His visitors were always certain to be entertained by some new speculation or scientific experiment, such as his "rare burning glass." No wonder he became something of a "best seller" in his day. We find Pepys, who knew him, of course, on May 15th, 1668, recording, "And so to my bookseller's, and carried home some books—among others Dr. Wilkins's *Real Character*" and, again, on the 17th—"And so home, and made my boy read to me part of Dr. Wilkins's new book of the *Real Character,* and so to bed."

There are memorials of less celebrated people in Cranford Church, but some of the inscriptions suggest they were quite as delightful. William Smythe, Esquire, for instance, who married the daughter of the first Earl of Berkeley, and died in 1720 aged eighty. A medallion shows a life-like head of Mr. Smythe, who was a poet, painter and critic; and somehow, for once, one believes the panegyric on his monument in the nave. We learn he was "no less blessed in the high birth of his bride than in his own intellect. For he was a man of such pleasant speech and such bodily beauty that one could not tell which added greater grace and nobility to the other; and he possessed as his favourite pastime, the pastime of every eminent and distinguished man—the arts of painting and poetry. How subtle a judge he was in the former and how elegant a spectator, is shown by the exquisite ornaments in his house!" How pleasant to have known Mr. Smythe. No wonder he captured the peer's daughter.

There is one more memorial deserving of notice, that of Moreton Berkeley, the sixth earl who, out of chivalry to his mother, would never assume the title, and who was borne to his resting-place in this churchyard on the shoulders of those among whom he had lived all his long life, greatly beloved. There is a Berkeley hatchment, the escutcheon of arms placed over the entrance to a great house where the head of a family died. This one, bearing the arms of a widower Earl, was erected over the portico of Cranford House, where it hung for a year before being transferred to the church.

There is another curious memorial of a noble earl; this is a sanctuary lamp hanging over the south end of the altar, which incorporates the coronet of the fifth earl, Mary Cole's lover. It was thrown into the eastern vault and lay neglected there for a century.

One of the windows, in coloured glass, is remarkable in that it contains staves and music notes of an anthem. This singular design is ascribed to Mendelssohn, who often stayed in the vicinity with the friend it commemorates, a lover of music.

The real music in the church has changed for the better in

the last sixty years. The singing was once dependent upon a barrel organ which only had three tunes. The village school-mistress turned the handle, and began her operation when Parson Hickes gave a lusty blast upon a whistle. The three wheezy tunes had to serve alike for psalms and hymns without the slightest regard for metre or length of line. It was hardly more terrible than the harrowing hell-fire sermon that came from the three-decker.

"Well," said Miss Whissitt, as we came out into the late afternoon, "it was worth coming to see, *n'est-ce pas?* I regret that old house going—I'd rather like some of the bricks for a garden house, as a memorial—but at least the church and the park are safe."

We paused as we came to the ornamental bridge over the Crane. There was a boat on the water, with a woman and a boy in it. I thought of Fanny Kemble singing to Grantley Berkeley. The evening sunlight lay red on the mansion house and the church tower. In the Manor of the Knights Templars few things remained the same, except the orbit of the sun and moon over this parkland and the course of the Crane, all known to worthy Dr. Fuller and "ingeniose" Dr. Wilkins.

"Oh, no, there are a few things left," said Miss Whissitt as I lamented. "There's a meadow still called the Quintain Field, where the knights and the villagers practised the art of tilting. I wonder if Richard Clinker-a-Dagger, who is in the parish register, ever changed his weapon for the lance?"

I made no answer. The bridge was narrow and the road was rough; and as I turned the car towards the Bath Road I looked for the ghostly coach of the Berkeleys, with postilions in crimson livery and horses jingling as the proud earl and his redoubtable countess came home to Cranford.

CHAPTER XI

Colnbrook's Grim Legend

SOON AFTER LEAVING CRANFORD we cross the bridge over the Crane. Who was Jack England, one wonders, who, according to a record in a neighbouring church, killed William Rowls in a duel at Cranford Bridge on July 1st, 1784? A mile down the Bath Road brings us to Harlington Corner where *The Coach and Horses* is still preserved. The old inn sign, with its painting of a coach and horses is delightful, as also are the bow windows and weathered tiles. Half a mile behind this inn lies Harlington. It is strange that Arlington Street, off Piccadilly, owes its name, as also a certain Lord, to a slip on the part of a clerk in Heralds' College. Sir Henry Bennett, a member of the notorious Cabal ministry, who lived at Harlington, was raised to the Peerage, in the manner of politicians who have cost their country dear. He chose as his title Earl of Harlington, but a careless clerk, perhaps *sans* aspirate himself, dropped his Lordship's aitch and thus Sir Henry became Lord Arlington, with the result that the street he owned off Piccadilly has been Arlington Street ever since.

At the edge of Harlington village stands Dawley Farm, a fragment of a former house which Lord Bolingbroke converted into a wonderful mansion, and where he lavishly entertained the men of genius of his age. It is said he spent on this country retreat more than £23,000, vowing he would end his days there. Pope, who was a frequent visitor there, tells us that he paid an artist £200 to paint his hall in stone-colour with trophies of rakes, spades, prongs and other agricultural implements, a striking effect in chiaroscuro.

The men of letters who visited Bolingbroke at Dawley included Voltaire, Dean Swift, Gay, Dryden and Pope. It was here that Swift read to a company, which included his host, Pope and Gay, the manuscript of *Gulliver's Travels*. He had begun to read it at Pope's villa at Twickenham, but did not finish it, and the reading was completed to the reassembled company the next evening at Dawley Farm. Bolingbroke's vow that he would end his days there was not fulfilled. In 1735 he had to exile himself in France, and Dawley was sold to the Earl of Uxbridge, who pulled down all except the one wing still standing.

The Bath Road now runs over a flat plain which for generations has been famous for its fruit and vegetables. Some of these fields still remain well cultivated, but the cheap house and the sprawling factory are devouring them. On the left-hand side we soon come to a little thatched inn, *The Magpies*. Almost behind it, a plot called "King's Arbour" takes its name from the fact that George III, who used this road when travelling between London and Windsor, had an establishment for changing his coach horses, as it was beneath the royal dignity to have them changed at the posting inns. It was from this place that Major-General Roy's survey line started its run to Hampton.

It is curious that there are two old inns, one called *The Magpies* and another *The Old Magpies*, within a few hundred yards of each other, and looking at them it is not easy to say which is the older, though perhaps the thatched roof gives the vote to the second. These inns mark the site of a tragedy. One evening, in April, 1798, a Mr. Mellish was returning with some friends from a day's hunting with the King's hounds when their coach was attacked by three highwaymen. One seized the horses' heads, while the two accomplices robbed the occupants of their purses and watches. When they were allowed to proceed, one of the robbers fired a parting shot into the back of the coach, which wounded Mr. Mellish in the head. He was assisted into *The Three Magpies* and a surgeon was sent for from Hounslow. The surgeon, too, was held up by the same gang, and on arrival was too late to assist the wounded man, who died forty-eight hours later. The highwaymen were never caught.

Approaching the hamlet of Longford the temptation is to take the straight road, which now leaves the old Bath Road, by-passing Colnbrook. But to do this will rob us of much interest, and since we are in no hurry to arrive and want to see everything of interest, we keep to the left of *The Peggy Bedford,* which marks the fork. A glance to the right, across the level heath, reveals the beautiful battlemented tower of Harmondsworth, with its graceful belfry canopy standing out in silhouette above the level landscape. And the specialist in barns will find in this village a remarkable specimen of fourteenth-century carpentry. It is a veritable forest of oak, a cathedral one hundred and ninety feet long, the largest tithe barn in England, with threshing floors in the third, seventh and tenth bays where the ancient yeoman threshed out the wheat with the primitive flail. Monastic in its origin, it was built by the Benedictines, who had a Priory here. It is divided into a nave and aisles, and has resolutely withstood the gales of this windswept heath through nearly six hundred years.

The Peggy Bedford, which marks the parting of the ways at Longford, has forgotten its original name and taken that of its famous landlady. It was originally *The King's Head,* and was a famous house of call for the coaches. The old inn has completely disappeared and the present one is pseudo-Tudor, which, nevertheless, was gutted by fire in 1937, and rose again from its ashes. The original inn claimed to be nearly seven hundred years old, and it gathered fame to itself from a remarkable old lady, Peggy Bedford, whose portrait, complete with bonnet and brooch of mid-Victorian days, may still be seen on the inn's crockery. Her hour of fame was when Queen Victoria's barouche drew up at the inn. Peggy nursed a baby in long clothes

who reigned later as Edward VII. It is perhaps unkind to be
sceptical and ask why a landlady of all persons was allowed to
nurse the heir to the Throne, but it may have been done surrep-
titiously while the royal infant's nursemaid was making a call!
An access of loyalty has often resulted in strange happenings.
I remember seeing for sale in a Lincolnshire inn, at a shilling a
bottle, the water in which the same royalty, later become Prince
of Wales, had taken a bath after a hunting excursion.

Whatever Peggy's real title to fame, she survived the coaching age, and has achieved the popular fame of an inn signboard.
Longford, which now lies on our track, took its name from a
ford, where the River Colne, in one of its many branches,
crossed the road. We are now approaching the border of Mid-
dlesex, and about to pass into Buckinghamshire. This stretch
of the road, for the two miles between Longford and Colnbrook,
was well worked by the highwaymen, who caught the coaches
coming out of the latter place, and in Longford two highwaymen who repeatedly robbed the Bath Mail were gibbetted in
1722. But there is no ghastly spectacle today to mar the exquisite glimpse of Windsor Castle seen southwards across the
level meadows.

In this glimpse southwards from Colnbrook, we are looking
at the very cradle of English history. A mile away, its church
tower visible, lies Horton, which nurtured the young Milton,
and not two miles distant lies Runnymede, the Thames, and
Magna Carta Island, where on that day of June, 1215, the
Barons wrested from King John the charter that laid the foundation of English liberty and became a pattern to all mankind.

The cottage-fringed road as it draws across successive bridges
into Colnbrook, has two curious objects, seldom noticed by the
swift motorist. They are a pair of large iron pumps, each
mounted on a small hillock, standing by the roadside. What
are they for? They are somewhat rusted, their great handles
are padlocked to the pump. It is many years, obviously, since
water flowed through their cast-iron spouts. Are they to give

water to the village? For one is placed on the very edge of ancient Colnbrook. But the other is nearly two miles away, and no one would be likely to transport water that distance. Moreover, there are plenty of wells in this flat landscape, as well as the various branches of the Colne.

For the solution we must go back to the heyday of fashionable Bath. The winter season had proved so successful that Beau Nash planned a summer season. His plan was carried into effect, but a serious drawback to the advent of the fashionable world soon began to manifest itself. The travellers, the beaux and the belles, complained of the choking dust that rose from the highway as they journeyed to Bath. Roads that were quagmires in winter and commended in 1754 as being only two feet deep in mud, became deserts of dust in summer. The coaches moved through dense clouds. One was choked on the top of the coach or compelled to keep the windows closed and stifled within it.

Beau Nash's ingenuity did not fail him. He constructed along the highway from London to Bath a series of pumps. He built them over pits which collected the winter and spring rains. The pumps were placed in the charge of pumpers, men with numbered brassards, whose duty it was to water the road along which the coaches travelled. They can be found, as here at Longford and Colnbrook, only where the original road had not been widened or the growth of building has not entailed their removal. The Colnbrook specimens are in excellent preservation.

One must tell the sad truth about Colnbrook. It has had a glorious and prosperous past, its present seems to lack a redeeming feature, unless it be the richness of the pasture and farm-land, so lush and well-watered, that surrounds it. There are moments when some vestige of ancient beauty can be surmised. Its long winding street, lit by soft moonlight, attains a romantic beauty like the more squalid canals of Venice under the kindly veil of night. But by day its air of desertion and decay, its straggling untidiness, have a depressing effect. Even its renowned *Ostrich Inn,* enticing the visitor with gruesome legend, presents nothing but dull rooms, and a courtyard whose background is a gasometer. And yet we must not omit Coln-brook. It commanded the Bath Road once, and if ever a village street was full of ghosts, of spectral coaches and horses, this High Street is full of them, its cobbles and its mud trodden by the feet of the long dead generations ever since the Kings of England kept state at Windsor Castle. The street is still nar-row, for it is said that it was made by the stones laid by the Romans across this marshy land. One wonders how the tearing coaches made their way into the village without head-on colli-sions. Fate has been unkind to the place. It had no historic church, no beautiful period building, no market square, no vil-lage green. And yet twice it has been alive with currents of traffic, once when all the coaches of the Bath Road made it one of the chief stages, and again, after a century and a half of neglect, when the first motor traffic to Bath flowed through its narrow street. Then came the straight Colnbrook by-pass, leav-ing it stranded, and again it fell asleep, forgotten of the world.

And yet with a little imagination we can make the old place live again. There are a few bones of the skeleton that will carry the trappings of history; and at its poorest it is splendidly rich compared with that arid macadam speed-track, the by-pass, spaced with truck-drivers' cafes, glass-houses and garages. It is a road so straight, so inviting to the driver who must "let her all out" that few, as they rise over the arch bridging the Colne ever notice that enchanting vista of Windsor Castle, dove-grey or silver, floating over the left horizon.

The importance of Colnbrook in the eighteenth century may be surmised by the number of inns that still survive—*The Ostrich, The George, The Catherine Wheel, The White Hart,* all of which have their roots in history. Pride of place goes to *The Ostrich,* a long, double-gabled Elizabethan inn claiming descent from a hospice founded in 1106 "for the good of travellers in this world and the salvation of their souls in the next."

Why *The Ostrich?* one asks. The suggestion has been made that the word is a sort of orthographic compromise between Hospice and Ostrich. And the question then arises how old is the bird, to English knowledge, since it is a native of a land not discovered until 1497, when Vasco da Gama rounded the Cape. And confusion is added to confusion by a further ornithological transition, for somehow, in the reign of Henry I, it was known as *The Crane*. Whatever the name, two things the birds had in common were the length of their legs and their bills.

It seems likely that it was at *The Ostrich* that Edward the Black Prince, returning from the war, with King John of France as his prisoner, was met by his father Edward III. The inn became the house of call for all guests going to Windsor Castle, and here the visiting ambassadors tidied up and robed themselves before being conducted into the royal presence. Froissart in his *Chronicles* mentions four ambassadors from Philip, King of France, sent to Edward III, in 1337, to do homage for the Duchy of Guienne, who "dined in the Kynge's chamber, and after they departed, laye the same night atte Colnbrook." Henry VIII and his Queen Catherine stayed at *The Catherine Wheel*. Queen Elizabeth, inevitably, slept in Colnbrook, though three inns contest the honour, and the obvious solution would be that so itinerant a sleeper slept at them all in turn. But *The George*, an eighteenth-century hostel whose red brick façade greets one on entering the village, has a good claim to the great Eliza, though she was not then a Queen, but a prisoner on her way from Woodstock to Hampton Court in 1558. The halt was a forced one, for the wheel of her coach came off. The tide of the Civil War flowed in and out of Colnbrook, and *The Ostrich* was honoured for a space with Prince Rupert and his staff, before proceeding to the battle with the Londoners at Brentford.

The fame of *The Ostrich*, however, is most popularly based on a gruesome story of the Sweeney Todd variety, which is not

even dimmed by the fame of having housed Dick Turpin, who
did a jumping act from his bedroom window on to his horse in
the courtyard when the Bow Street Runners were after him.
During the reign of Henry I, *The Ostrich* and Colnbrook
achieved wide fame as the scene of the foulest murders imag-
inable. The first English novelist, Thomas Delaney, made it the
subject of his romance, *Thomas of Reading*. The inn was then
kept by one Thomas Jarman and his wife, and was a favourite
house of call for the rich clothiers who, with their packhorses
loaded with bales, journeyed from the West of England to the
London market. They carried, on the return journey, large
sums of money from their sales, and the cupidity of the innkeeper and his wife was thus aroused. With one of these travellers, Thomas Cole, they became very friendly. He stayed
frequently at their inn, and entrusted to them large sums of
money for safe keeping, not always a wise proceeding, for the
innkeepers were often in league with thieves, as John Clavel, a
reformed highwayman, confessed in 1628.

> *Oft in your clothier's and your glazier's inn,*
> *You shall have chamberlains that there have been*
> *Placed purposely by thieves, or else consenting*
> *By their large bribes, and by their often tempting,*
> *That mark your purses drawn and give a guess*
> *What's there, within a little, more or less.*

The unfortunate traveller in those days had, therefore, to
take his cash to bed and risk being murdered in his sleep, or to
trust to the honesty of his host. The evil pair at Colnbrook were
not such crude thieves. They got rid of the evidence by em-
ploying a murderous device. The bed was fastened over a trap-
door. "In the dead of night, when the victim was sound asleep,
they plucked out the bolts, and down would the man fall out of
his bed into the boiling cauldron below, in which they fer-
mented their brew, where being suddenly scalded and drowned,
he was never able to cry or speak one word."

Thomas Cole, it seemed, had a presentiment of doom. He

arrived at the inn in a most melancholy mood. "With that, his
hostess, dissembling, answered: 'Doubt not, Master Cole, you
are like enough by the course of nature to live many years.'
'God knows,' quoth he, 'I never found my heart so heavy
before.' "

It seemed that he would never go to bed. "Certain musicians
of the town came to the chamber and Master Cole being there,
drew out their instruments, and very solemnly began to play."
But soon he begged them to be gone, and retired to bed, full of
foreboding.

"When they had listened at his chamber door, they heard
the man sound asleep. All is safe, quoth they, and down into the
kitchen they go, their servants being all in bed, and pulling out
the iron pins, down fell the bed, and the man dropped out into
the boiling cauldron."

But they had forgotten the clothier's horse in the stables,
which had strayed out. Inquiries were started and eventually a
warrant was taken out for the arrest of Jarman and his wife.
The innkeeper was caught hiding in Windsor Forest, and both
were hanged after confessing to sixty murders.

The figure sixty suggests a gleeful boastfulness on the part
of *The Crane*, or *The Ostrich*, which has ever since made profit
out of its notoriety as a place of murder. To-day it is sleeping,
like the rest of Colnbrook, on its past. Its only link with the
world of fashion that once thronged its long streets is the London bound motor-bus from Slough, which kindly ignores the
by-pass and connects Colnbrook with the outer world; for its
so-called railway-station is a distant and grass-grown affair.
Strange to think that less than two hundred years ago gallant
bucks, dainty ladies, and great figures in the social life of England, clamoured for beds and scrambled for meals in the over-
flowing inns of the village; and that as long ago as 1544 it
possessed a bailiff, twelve burgesses, a Market and a Fair. It
had also a court of summary jurisdiction, curiously called a
Court of Pie Powder, a corruption of the French *pied-poudreux*,

dusty-footed—a court for travellers involved in disputes with traders or other itinerant persons. What a gay scene this place offered in the Middle Ages, when its great fair lasted three weeks, and was attended, so runs the record of the Court, "by many foreign merchants, buying Gascon wine, Milan armour, Venetian glass, Genoese silk and velvet Flemish clothes, Spanish iron, besides all sorts of English produce." It knew the clamours of war also, long before dashing Rupert and the Royalist Army made it their headquarters. In 1400 forty thousand men lay camped in its meadows, gathered together to march on the usurping Henry IV at Windsor Castle, and restore the deposed Richard II to his throne. But he was too quick for them, slipped away to London, and raised an army so threatening in size that Richard's camp melted away.

The meadows saw more peaceful scenes, as when in 1521, according to the accounts of the Duke of Buckingham, 6s. 8d. was paid to Henry VIII's falconers for "showing my Lord game with their hawkes, between Colbroke and Houndslowe."

II

Before we leave Colnbrook and join the by-pass again, we pass into Buckinghamshire and come to a road running from the left of the street. It leads to Horton, a mile distant, and if we care to go on foot, a path runs through the fields. I discarded my car at this point and took the path because, for me, it was hallowed ground. How often, along this path, the feet of young Milton had trodden in his journeyings between his father's house at Horton and Colnbrook. He spent five of the most impressionable years of his youth at Horton. His father, the retired scrivener, had settled in this village in a house near the old church. Milton was here between 1632 and 1638, having settled down at home immediately after coming from Cambridge, where he had taken his master's degree. He was then nearly twenty-four years of age. The elderly Milton must have been quite unlike the traditional father, for he did not urge upon him a professional career but seemed quite content that his son should pass his time browsing among books. Milton himself has told of this period:

"At my father's residence, whither he had returned to pass his old age, I, with every advantage of leisure, spent a complete holiday in reading over the Greek and Latin writers; not but that sometimes I exchanged the country for the town, either for the purpose of buying books, or for that of learning anything new in mathematics or music, in which sciences I then delighted. I had passed five years in this manner, when, after my mother's death, being desirous of seeing foreign lands, and especially Italy, I went abroad with one servant, having entreated and obtained my father's consent."

He was not idle in these years, and from the quiet loveliness of Horton and its meadows he distilled some deathless lyrics. He wrote here, in 1634, *Comus*, and in 1637 *Lycidas*, with *L'Allegro* and *Il Penseroso* and his *Sonnet to the Nightingale* somewhere in between. They reflect in many passages the landscape around him at Horton, which had changed very little in three hundred years, thanks to the isolation of this village, although but a mile from the old Bath Road. When I climbed the tower of the old church, upon whose turret he had often stood, I saw, as he had recorded:

> *Meadows trim, with daisies pied;*
> *Shallow brooks and rivers wide;*
> *Towers and battlements it sees*
> *Bosomed high in tufted trees,*

for there, across the Thames, lay Windsor's noble pile, and the spires and roofs of Eton College.

He knew that College, having walked to it to call upon the Provost, Sir Henry Wotton, who, on receipt of a copy of *Comus* from the poet, had written a graceful letter of thanks. "I should much commend the tragical part, if the lyrical did not ravish me with a certain Doric delicacy in your songs and odes;

whereunto I must plainly confess to have seen yet nothing parallel in our language."

Milton's mother having died in 1637, he had decided to travel, and it was natural he should apply for advice and letters of introduction to Sir Henry, who had been James I's ambassador in Venice on three occasions. For Italy was Milton's goal.
He wrote, therefore, to solicit the Provost's aid, and received a charming reply, for the young Milton had obviously delighted his elderly friend on their first meeting, when Milton had walked the five miles through Datchet and along the bank of the Thames to Eton. He regretted that he had not been aware that Milton was still residing at Horton. "I would have been bold, in our vulgar phrase, to mend my drought (for you left me with an extreme thirst) and to have begged your conversation again . . . over a poor meal or two," wrote Wotton, and then, as requested, proceeded to give him some advice, and letters of recommendation. Passing on some advice he had once received himself from a wary Italian diplomat, he cautioned Milton to observe, *"I pensieri stretti ed il viso sciotto"*— "thoughts close, looks open." This kindly, gifted man died a year later, aged seventy-two, and did not live to hear Milton's report on the return from his travels.

The quiet family life at Horton must have been broken up by the death of Milton's mother. A day came at last when the aged father stood with his two sons, Christopher and John, and his daughter Anne, beside the grave opened in the chancel of the old church. Doubtless the neighbours were present in that band of mourners, among them Squire Bulstrode Whitelock, who was Cromwell's friend, and, later, ambassador to Queen Christina of Norway. The coffin was lowered, the mourners returned to their homes in the village, and a plain, blue stone on the floor of the chancel recorded that "Here lyeth the body of Sara Milton, the wife of John Milton, who died the 3rd of April, 1637."

The next year Milton went on his travels to Paris, Florence,

Rome and Naples, impressing all whom he met by his scholar-
ship and grace. He had planned to go on to Sicily, but news
came of the rising storm engendered by King Charles's strife
with his Parliament, and he hurried home in July, 1639. There
must have been some visits to his old home at Horton, but the
following year his father and his brother Christopher moved to
Reading, and Milton's connection with Horton came to an end.

The home of the Miltons was pulled down in 1798 and nothing now remains to mark the association of the poet with this
quiet village, save the memorial stone in the chancel, and the
verses he wrote that took their imagery from the hedges and
fields around.

> *The tufted crow-toe and pale jessamine,*
> *The white pink and the pansy freaked with jet,*
> *The glowing violet,*
> *The musk-rose and the well-attired woodbine,*
> *With cowslips wan that hang the pensive head.*

They are all still to be seen in the meadows and cottage-
gardens of Horton, and the musk roses were in bloom on the
hot June afternoon when I interrupted the sexton at his scyth-
ing in the beautifully kept churchyard separating the church
from the road. In Milton's day there was a large house, called
Place House, which actually adjoined the church tower. The
owners ornamented the grounds with small canals.

The first curious object that caught my eye in this restful
place was the strong churchyard wall, with bays at intervals.
The bottom courses of this old wall have large square bricks
which suggest formidable strength for building. The great
house was built in Queen Elizabeth's day, and was not pulled
down until 1785. It could not have been very beautiful, jammed
up against the church, but it must have been a familiar sight
to young Milton. What was beautiful in his day and still is, was
the wooden porch to the church and the fine Norman arch with
double rows of zigzag ornamentation.

The church inside is solidly built, with strong Norman piers to the arches and a splendid oak roof. But it is to the chancel that one turns, and there, in the centre, is the dark, plainly lettered stone slab marking the grave of Sara Milton. It does not require a great effort of the imagination to see that small group of mourners, the family headed by the retired scrivener, his two sons, including the young Milton, and his sister. In this year death took two he loved, his mother in April, and a short while afterwards his college friend Edward King, drowned in the Irish Sea. He wrote subsequently a noble elegy, *Lycidas*, in which he also severely attacked the degraded condition of the church. Is it with this first sad ceremony by his mother's grave in mind that he opens the poem with:

> *Yet once more, O ye Laurels, and once more,*
> *Ye Myrtles brown, with Ivy never sere,*
> *I come to pluck your Berries harsh and crude,*
> *And with forc'd fingers rude,*
> *Scatter your leaves before the mellowing year.*

It is pleasant to think that before she died Sara Milton had some knowledge of her son's springing fame. She must have smiled if he read her his sonnet beginning:

> *How soon hath Time, the subtle thief of youth,*
> *Stolen on his wing my three-and-twentieth year!*
> *My hasting days fly on with full career,*
> *But my late spring no bud or blossom sheweth.*

She had doubtless rejoiced in the success of that Mask, *Comus*, which had been dedicated to Viscount Brackley (ancestor of that young Viscount we have seen at the Syon marriage reception) and performed by him, his brother Thomas, and his sister Lady Alice Egerton before Lord Bridgewater and a distinguished company at Ludlow Castle one Michaelmas night, 1634. Did her proud heart ever see it in print? For in the year of her death it had been published by "Humphrey Robinson, at the signe of Three Pidgeons in Pauls Church-yard."

Her modest son had not openly declared his authorship, but it was well known, and in offering it to Brackley, the "much-promising Youth" as Milton termed him, he spoke of the frequent copying that "hath tired my Pen to give several friends satisfaction." We can hear the enthusiastic guests at the Ludlow Castle performance exclaiming, "Oh, we would like a copy, Mr. Milton," and so into print Milton went. If Sara Milton never saw the book, perhaps she saw her son busy on the proofs. But she was not to know that greater visitation of the Muse when a blind old poet, defeated in all his political hopes, lucky to escape the scaffold, and "fallen on evil days" wrote *Paradise Lost*, retired from the triumphant forces of the Restoration. She had no fore-knowledge of the eminence in state and literature awaiting him, nor of his perils, afflictions and disappointments. In the year of her death if she worried over him it was because he had declined to enter the Church, and now, at twenty-eight, sat at home reading and studying, with no clear aim in view.

So Sara, aged sixty-five, a victim of the plague then visiting Horton, was laid to rest. It marked the break-up of the Milton home in that village, for young brother Christopher was soon married and took off his father to live with him at Reading, and Milton went off on his travels, marred by the death of another dear friend Charles Diodati, and the growing political turmoil at home.

We can climb the steps to the crenellated tower, and see before us, very little changed, the view that young Milton knew so well, the level lush meadows, the distant aspect of Windsor Castle and Eton College, the silver Thames, and that path through the fields to Colnbrook.

Straight mine eye hath caught new pleasures,
Whilst the landscape round it measures;
Russet lawns and fallows grey
Where the nibbling flocks do stray.

CHAPTER XII

Herschel of Slough

HAVING LEFT THE SCENE of Milton's young manhood, we regain Colnbrook, and journeying westwards again join the end of the new by-pass, with Slough ahead. We soon come to a cross-roads with a road leading to Datchet and Windsor on our left. This was the route favoured by the royal equipages which joined the Bath Road here on their journeys from Windsor to London. What a stirring sight it must have been on a sharp, frosty morning to see the officers of the guard riding ahead, followed by the postilions in their scarlet liveries, drawing the leather-sprung four-wheeled coach, with the royal arms emblazoned on its half-glass doors, in which sat the bewigged George III. It was no easy journey in 1800, and the coach might be overturned, or stuck in the mire, though the turnpikes were effecting a great change.

Slough suffers both from its name and its appearance, but nothing seems to check its growing prosperity. Its main street, incorporating the Bath Road, now stretches some two miles along the quagmire from which it probably derived its name, until it reaches the elevation of Salt Hill. Up till the nineteenth century Slough scarcely existed as a place, being a few houses in the parish of Upton-cum-Chalvey. Smarting under its name it attempted in 1890 to change it to Upton Royal, without success. It has had its revenge in completely swallowing up Upton, and a population which was 1,000 in 1800, and 7,000 in 1900, has grown to 55,000 in another forty years. Slough owes its prosperity in the first instance to an Army transport base during the Great War, and then the acquisition for factory sites by a private-trading concern of the derelict area, rendered ghastly by a quarter of a million Army lorries rotting in the rain. Since we must have factories, the Slough enterprise shows how inoffensively, and sometimes artistically, these can be built. A comparison of the Victorian brick labour-prisons with these citadels of light and cleanliness, strikingly demonstrates the social progress of fifty years in the industrial world.

But if little can be said for Slough, an American main street without a single distinguished building, it is an excellent place to get away from and much history and beauty sit on its threshold. Two miles or so southwards lie royal Windsor, and Eton College, with shining reaches of the Thames. A mile to the north is the world's most famous churchyard, Stoke Poges, where "the rude forefathers of the hamlet sleep" with the poet Gray, who gave their obscurity noble immortality in that flawless Elegy.

On its right hand and its left Slough, at these cross-roads, can send us into realms of literary and historic interest. It happens that by this very cross-road, but a few yards distant, hidden by the new façade of *The Rose and Crown*, which commands the turning to Windsor, there is a house where history was made, although written in the stars, and where, a little over a hundred years ago, distinguished visitors from all over the world felt themselves privileged to call. For only a few yards distant, in a house that shuts itself off from the world by its plain exterior, dwelt Sir William Herschel who added a seventh planet to the known total of six.

It was not likely that any traveller in 1790 was unaware of Herschel's presence in Slough. His fame was over the earth, but even if that failed to mark him in the traveller's mind, there was a tangible reminder of this singular man of genius. Archibald Robertson, travelling through Slough in 1792, observes that "near this village, on the left of the road to Eton and

Windsor, stands the house of the celebrated Dr. Herschel; by whose extraordinary improvements in the construction of telescopes many discoveries have been lately made in the noble and useful science of astronomy. The apparatus, which gives motion to his grand telescope, is seen from the high road. The establishment of Dr. Herschel is at the expense of His Majesty, and is one of the numerous instances in which the king displays a love of genius and science, and a disposition to patronize them."

Let us anticipate the end of our journey and jump to Bath on the first day of the year 1767. The fashion has gathered at a benefit concert in the Assembly Rooms, a small but select company. Mr. Linley, the conductor, is the father of the beautiful Miss Linley who, with her exquisite voice and beauty, is the rage of Bath. Gainsborough has not yet painted her, nor has R. B. Sheridan courted her; the larger world lies before her, but her present domain lies very much at her feet.

The soloist on this occasion is a young man who has newly come to Bath from Leeds, where he has achieved something of a reputation as a musician and a composer. He has been engaged at Bath as an organist, but to-day he shows his versatility. He performs a solo concert on the violin, one on the hautboy and a sonata on the harpsichord, all of which are well applauded, which results the next day in a letter from Mr. Derrick, Beau Nash's successor as the Master of Ceremonies, inviting him to join the established Band of Musicians who perform at the Pump-room and the subscription concerts.

The young musician, William Herschel, late of Hanover, is delighted to accept. It is an addition to his salary as organist and his casual income as a teacher of music. Agreeable, gifted, and twenty-eight years old, Bath likes him. He is just emerging from a struggle for existence in a foreign land. The son of an oboist in the Hanoverian Foot Guards, he has been a hautboy in this same regiment at the age of fourteen. But the life was a poor one, and six children at home, in a country impoverished by war, made the Herschel household aware of privations.

William Herschel had visited England with the Guards in 1756. It was a rich land, its people were friendly. A year later he returned, to write his name in English history.

It seemed at first he would be a musician. His career began to be fixed at Bath, to which he had called his devoted sister Caroline to keep house for him. He had a faithful patron in Lady Lothian, and the gracious young German music master began to practise his profession in the houses of the county society. By 1771 he was earning nearly four hundred a year. His brother, Alexander, had joined the household at Bath. The trio was complete, and it was only shattered by death. Immediately on her arrival at Bath, Caroline appeared as a concert singer. She was determined to be useful, with English lessons before breakfast, and housekeeping in the morning. "The remainder of the forenoon was chiefly spent at the harpsichord, showing me the way how to practise singing with the gag in my mouth. And by way of relaxation we talked of Astronomy."

At the age of twenty-seven she was launched on her career as a singer, and as general assistant to her adored brother. She kept the accounts, cleaned the house, cooked, and copied music. Her eager mind absorbed everything, even algebra, geometry and trigonometry, which her brother taught her in her spare time.

At thirty-five, well-launched on his career as a musician, William began to feel the interest of mathematics and astronomy. He turned to them at first as relaxation. In April, 1773, the musician bought himself a quadrant. He suddenly felt an ambition to study the whole of the heavens. He wanted a telescope, bigger than the biggest ever made. He would have it, he vowed. One day Caroline was dismayed to see William and Alexander turning every room in the house into a workshop. They began with a four-foot telescope, then progressed to a twelve, fifteen and a twenty-four-foot telescope.

The next nine years were devoted to music for a living and astronomy as a passion, to music scholars by day and tele-

scopes and stars by night. It soon became evident that their
first house was not large enough for the instruments. So in 1774
William Herschel moved into a house whose grass plot had
room for the giant twenty-inch telescope he was preparing.

The burden increased on the stalwart shoulders of sister
Caroline. While the brothers frantically polished mirrors for
sixteen hours at a stretch, she read to William, copied music,
cooked, "and by way of keeping him alive I was even obliged to
feed him by putting the vitals by bits into his mouth." They
moved again and this time the telescope had to be erected in
front of the house where it soon attracted attention. "His lodging," wrote a visitor, "resembled an astronomer's much more
than a musician's, being heaped up with globes, maps, telescopes, reflectors, etc., under which his piano was hid, and the
violincello, like a discarded favourite, skulked away in a corner."

In 1780 at Bath, the divine afflatus was directing one young
musician to the planet Uranus, and, at Bonn, a still younger
musician to the Fifth Symphony, so curiously works the passionate spirit of genius. Up till now William had not met a
fellow astronomer, but a Dr. Watson made his acquaintance
while he was trying to find the height of the lunar mountains by
measuring the shadows they cast. He wrote a paper on the subject, which the doctor forwarded to the Royal Society. It drew
the attention of the Astronomer Royal. There was a young man
at Bath worth watching.

But Herschel had rather shocked the cautious Astronomer
Royal, by doing exactly what Dr. Wilkins of Cranford had
done, stating his belief that the moon was inhabited. The Astronomer Royal begged Herschel to withdraw this unorthodox
passage before the paper was read to the Society. He withdrew
it, but in a private letter stuck to his guns. "I beg leave to
observe, Sir, that my saying there is an absolute certainty of
the Moon's being inhabited may perhaps be ascribed to a certain Enthusiasm which an observer, but young in the Science of

Astronomy, can hardly divest himself of when he sees such wonders before him."

Years later he knew he had erred, that the moon had no atmosphere and therefore no possibility of life.

He was now within a few months of a stupendous discovery that was to establish him among the great astronomers of all ages. Early in March, 1781, he had moved again to 19 New King Street, Bath, and had set up his seven-foot telescope in the garden, before the furniture had moved in. On the night of the 13th he noticed "a curious either nebulous star or perhaps a comet," crossing his steady sweep of the heavens. It was not an accident, he affirmed.

"It was that night *its turn* to be discovered. I had gradually perused the great Volume of the Author of Nature and was now come to the page which contained the seventh Planet."

On April 23rd, 1781, a letter addressed to "Mr. William Herschel, Musician, near the Crescent, Bath" from the Astronomer Royal, who had now examined the planet, confirmed the momentous discovery of this amateur astronomer. Sir Joseph Banks, the President of the Royal Society, now came on the scene. In December William Herschel was elected a Fellow.

The Bath Season having come to an end, the new Fellow began to erect in the garden a stand for a twenty-foot telescope. Raising scaffolds, experimenting with metals for casting reflectors, and incessant polishing, he worked in a frenzy. "In short," moaned hard-driven sister Caroline, "I saw nothing else and heard nothing else but about those things when my Brothers were together." And she observed, a little caustically, that Alexander was always alert enough for starting anything new, but soon lacked perseverance and faded away. It was Caroline who came to the rescue, making catalogues, calculations "when I found that a hand sometimes was wanted: measures to be made with the lamp micrometer, etc., and a fire kept in, and a dish of coffee necessary during a long night's watching; I undertook with pleasure what others might have thought a hardship."

When we look at Uranus let us remember devoted, enduring, sister Caroline. It was her planet as well as William's.

To-day it is not easy for us to comprehend the immense mechanical difficulties with which astronomers had to contend, even as late as the eighteenth century. To pursue his investigations, Herschel ground his own mirror or reflecting spectrum, and this involved a furnace, and mixing and casting the amalgam from which he made it. There was in addition the enormous labour of polishing, and the making of eyepieces. Telescopes were either refracting or reflecting instruments. In the refracting instrument, the observer looks along to the tube, but in the reflecting instrument he looks back down the tube on the mirror used in the place of a transparent lens—in those days a too costly object, and much smaller than Herschel desired. To look down the telescope, from its rim on the mirror, and not obstruct the view with his own head, Herschel slightly tilted the mirror so that the focus of the object fell on the rim, where he placed the magnifying eyepiece through which he looked. Since the observer had his back to the object he was reflecting, he had to have some means to reach the upraised rim of the telescope. In small telescopes a scaffolding sufficed; in his forty-foot telescope he devised a cradle in which the observer was wound up to the vantage-point.

It all seems very primitive now when giant telescopes with multiple magnifying lenses are raised and revolved with automatic mechanism, and a telescope weighing tons swings with the ease of a compass. But Herschel had to be a mechanic, a scaffold builder, a carpenter, a polisher, and a furnace-man as well as an astronomer. For his mirrors he had to experiment with mixtures of tin, copper and antimony. Sometimes months of work were marred in the casting or polishing. In all these labours he was assisted by Alexander and Caroline. They had to make their own tools, to grind and polish, spending many hours at the lathe. Caroline went from the oven to the bench, from the harpsichord to the mirror. William Herschel, fresh from teaching a fine lady the violin, or conducting a concert in the Assembly Rooms, for which he composed glees and catches, went, through the hours of the night, to labour on his beloved telescope. They were a trio sustained by a passionate obsession.

William Herschel had now only one desire, to escape from the drudgery of conducting and teaching music, to give his whole life to the study of the heavens. After the momentous discovery of Uranus, and recognition by his peers, deliverance was at hand. His telescopes were now acknowledged to be greatly superior to those in the Royal Observatory at Greenwich. Sir Joseph Banks, who interested himself in this man of genius, began to cast around for a means of freeing him for science. George III had founded a private observatory at Kew. It was expected that the astronomer there, an old man, would soon retire. Banks began to make plans on Herschel's behalf, only to discover that the position had been earmarked for the astronomer's son. But the King was interested and asked to see Herschel and his telescope.

So the seven-foot wonder was packed and went with its designer from Bath to London. After some waiting, he was summoned to Windsor. "Last night the King, Queen, the Prince of Wales, the Princess Royal, Princess Sophia, Princess Augusta, etc., saw my telescope and it was a very fine evening. My Instrument gave a general satisfaction; the King has very good eyes and enjoys Observations with Telescopes exceedingly." Thus he wrote to Caroline and Alexander. Hopes that help would be forthcoming from the royal fount were not in vain. Herschel was given a pension of £200 a year and the King ordered five ten-foot telescopes, and later contributed £4,000 towards the monster forty-foot telescope.

The life at Bath had come to a triumphant end. The planet was called *Georgium Sidus* in tribute to the King, though never popularly known by that name, and soon was universally known as Uranus. In buoyant spirits the Herschel household migrated to Datchet, to be near the royal patron. How they would all manage on two hundred a year, the faithful Caroline, almost in tears, had no idea. Sir William Watson, hearing of the amount of the pension, caustically exclaimed, "Never bought Monarch honour so cheap!" But the die was cast, the music-master of Bath was no more. The royal astronomer set up in a ruinous house at Datchet to explore the heavens.

He was now in his forty-third year, about half-way through life, could he have known, in this summer of 1782. The one sad fact was the separation from brother Alexander whose musical engagements, and his livelihood therefore, were all at Bath. But the stars were too strong for him and he frequently returned to the starry fold.

Much of William Herschel's time was now spent showing the King and the Royal Family the stars through his seven-foot telescope. But he was hard at work on the construction of the twenty-foot instrument. A band of workmen were engaged and trained to the work of construction. Alexander took long vacations from Bath. The place was a hive of industry. Raised up perilously some fifteen feet on a flimsy scaffold, William swept the heavens by night, and hammered, turned at the lathe, and polished by day. Orders began to flow in for the new famous Herschel telescopes.

But Datchet soon proved an impossible place. The low marshes, the fog and the winter cold were too trying to one who worked in the open all night. He succumbed after three winters of exposure. A move had to be made. They found a new home at Old Windsor, but a cantankerous landlady drove them out. Finally, on April 3rd, 1786, they moved to Slough.

It was to be William's home for life, and Caroline's until, on the death of her beloved brother, she returned to Germany. She noted the aspect of the house in her Diary: "A very pretty garden of one acre, at the end of which was a gravel walk, with a row of high elms on each side. On the side near to Windsor, from whence there was an impressive view of the north side of the Castle, was a raised terrace with a few trees, just enough to break the scorching rays of the sun without impeding the view."

The house they had found was just off the Bath Road, behind *The Crown Inn,* on the road that leads to Windsor. A handful of houses clustered at the cross-ways where the hamlet of Slough was growing out of Upton-cum-Chalvey. Established in the new house, the work on the giant forty-foot telescope went forward. Meanwhile the twenty-foot instrument revolved on its basis, though there were labour difficulties, for at Slough no steady out-of-door workman for the sweeping-handle could be met with. "Lost a Neb(ulous) by the blunder of the person at the handle," recorded Caroline. She was busy on her own work some nights: "I found I was to be trained for an assistant Astronomer. . . . I was to sweep for planets." So she swept the floors by day and the heavens by night.

On August 2nd, 1786, while her brother was away delivering, at the King's request, a telescope to the University of Gottingen, she discovered a comet and communicated the news to Sir Joseph Banks. Caroline's reputation was marching with her brother's. On August 6th she records: "In the evening Sir J. Banks, Lord Palmerston, and Dr. Blagden came and saw the Comet." The renowned Aubert wrote and congratulated her: "I think I see your wonderfully clever and wonderfully amiable Brother, upon the news of it, shed a tear of joy. You have immortalized your name. . . ."

Caroline had now her own small observatory. The rooms joining the house to the stables had been made into a small cottage. On the roof the "Newtonian sweeper" was installed, and here Caroline laboured, with a metronomic clock to tick the seconds in timing her observations.

By now the Herschels were such figures of renown that all the world began to call. The distinguished royal and other visitors at Windsor Castle found it a pleasant drive to call on the celebrated Dr. Herschel and his sister at Slough. The Visitors' Book in which they inscribed their names may still be seen in the house. It presents a pageant of the great figures of the age.

There was a very distinguished party on August 17th, 1787. The work on the forty-foot telescope was going rapidly forward. The great cylindrical tube, over fifteen feet in circumference, was lying on the grass plot in front of the house. King George arrived with Queen Charlotte, the Duke of York, the Princess Royal, Princess Augusta, the Duke of Queensbury, the Archbishop of Canterbury, and other company. One can imagine the stir at Slough corner as the carriages stopped and the postilions and coachmen in livery stood by the horses. But Dr. Herschel was always having notable visitors. He had put Slough on the map, just as he had mapped Uranus (*Georgium Sidus*, may it please your Majesty) in the heavens.

The King must have been in a gay mood. Sir Joseph Banks had suggested the visit. Herschel wanted financial help in building his new telescope. What was the singular fellow up to now? King George had come to see. The giant contrivance on the grass was examined. The King looked at the enormous tube which had not yet received its reflector or been raised skywards. Some of the company thought it amusing to walk through the telescope. The Archbishop of Canterbury found it not easy. "Come, my Lord Bishop, I will show you the way to Heaven!" cried the King, giving him a hand.

But the royal party were not the first through. Fanny Burney, now Madame d'Arblay and a lady of the Court, with her father, Dr. Burney, had been to visit the Herschels nine months earlier. "By the invitation of Mr. Herschel, I now took a walk, which will sound to you rather strange; it was through his telescope, and it held me quite upright, and without the least inconvenience, and so it would have done had I been dressed in feathers and a bell-hoop, such is its circumference." Dr. Burney and the Bishop of Worcester followed her through it.

At last, after immense labour, the great telescope was finished and rose on an enormous scaffolding into the air. Two giant mirrors had been cast, weighing nearly half a ton and four feet in diameter. The tube had had to be built in a barn near the house. The first mirror had proved too thin, but the disappointment vanished in the excitement of the first trial. Herschel was wound up in the cradle to the rim with its eyepiece, where he looked down the great tube. Caroline in a small hut at the foot of the telescope, registered its position as it revolved on its circular track, moved by a man at a handle. Seated in front of her recording dial and clock, she took down her brother's observations as he spoke to her down a speaking-tube.

Herschel soon discovered a sixth satellite of Saturn. Two months later he wrote to Sir Joseph Banks, almost jubilantly, "If satellites will come into the way of my forty-foot reflector, it is a little hard to resist discovering them. Now as a seventh satellite of Saturn has drawn me into that scrape, I must trust to your good nature to forgive me when I acquaint you with it."

By this time the forty-foot telescope was famous. Scientists all over the world knew of it and came hurrying to Slough to see it, as well as the fashionable hordes of idlers. They wasted Herschel's precious time, and asked ridiculous questions, but he treated all alike, patient, courteous and hospitable to all who approached him. Then when the crowd had gone and the daylight had faded, up in the cradle he went, calling down his observations to patient sister Caroline. It was the top of this great telescope and the immense scaffolding that supported it which Archibald Robertson saw from his coach on the Bath Road in 1792. It was a landmark for travellers.

There was another gentleman who saw it. Quick-eyed, nimble-minded Oliver Wendell Holmes saw it, and gave us his impression in *The Poet at the Breakfast Table*. He reveals

how from childhood the fame of this telescope had been known
to him.

"I was riding on the outside of a stage-coach from London to
Windsor in the year—never mind the year, but it must have been
in June, I suppose, for I bought some strawberries. But, as I was saying, I was riding down from London to Windsor, when all at once a
picture, familiar to me from my New England village childhood,
came upon me like a reminiscence rather than a revelation. It was a
mighty bewilderment of slanted masts, spars and ladders and ropes,
from the midst of which a vast tube, looking as if it might be a piece
of ordnance such as the revolted angels battered the walls of heaven
with, according to Milton, lifted its mighty muzzle defiantly towards
the sky. 'Why! you blessed old rattletrap,' I said to myself, 'I know
you as well as I know my father's spectacles and snuffbox.' And that
crazy witch, Memory, so divinely wise and foolish, travels thirty-five
hundred miles or so in a single pulse beat, and makes straight for
an old house and an old library, and an old corner of it, and whisks
out a volume of an old encyclopædia, and there is the picture of which
this is the original—Sir William Herschel's great telescope!"

That was in 1834. He was just in time to see it, for in 1839,
after standing for fifty years, Herschel's son demolished the
rotting scaffolding, leaving prone on the lawn some ten feet
of the base of the tube, and removing the great reflector to a
place of honour on a wall in the hall of the house.

The giant telescope had been something of a disappointment to its creator. It was too unwieldy, it took too long to
prepare for observation when time was short, it required too
many assistants. Herschel found the twenty-foot telescope
more accurate and easier to manipulate, and after a time went
back to its use. But it had its publicity value, though he cared
little for that. Sir William Herschel's great telescope was a
popular wonder of the age.

George III proved a good patron. He gave a second two
thousand pounds towards finishing the telescope, and recognized the services of the devoted sister, with a salary of fifty
pounds a year. She was greatly relieved "for nothing but Bank-

ruptcy had been all the while running through my silly head."
But in 1788 there was an event that overshadowed her. William was marrying a well-to-do widow, and she gave up her
place of housekeeper. She kept her bitterness to herself, and
on his marriage removed to adjacent lodgings. Mrs. Herschel
proved a lovable woman, and when a son was born, Caroline
found one more object on which to expend her devotion.

Caroline continued her work at Observatory Cottage, as the
converted stables in the grounds were called, and where she
did her "sweeping" on the flat roof with the four-foot telescope. In December 1788 she discovered a second comet, and
by 1793 she had seven comets to her credit. Her last and
eighth was noted on August 14th, 1795, with the aid of her
brother Alexander.

The years slipped by. Herschel wrote his last paper in 1817,
when he was eighty-two, and after years of observation declared "that the utmost stretch of the space-penetrating power
of the twenty-foot telescope could not fathom the profundity
of the Milky Way."

Among the many friends who gathered about the famous
astronomer at Slough was Dr. Burney. "Slough, Monday
morning, July 22nd, 1799, in bed at Dr. Herschel's half-past
five; where I can neither sleep nor lie idle," he wrote to his
daughter Fanny, the first of the lady novelists. Alexander, as
soon as the season at Bath was over, always came home to
Slough for a month or two, and, with his sister's aid, a great
polishing of the forty-foot telescope's mirror took place.

William's health was failing, but the communal sweeping of
the heavens went on. Occasionally he travelled, when Caroline
was left in charge of his boy, young John. A visit to Paris in
1802 resulted in a meeting with Napoleon, at which the First
Consul, as he then was, tried to pose as a man of scientific
learning. Herschel seems to have been more impressed with
Madame Bonaparte (Josephine) than with her husband. "She
is a very elegant lady and seems hardly old enough to be the

mother of her daughter." Of Napoleon, he said, "His vain air was something like affecting to know more than he did know." For James Watt, of steam-power fame, a visitor to Slough, he had warm admiration.

All through his life Herschel maintained the most affectionate relations with the family over in Hanover. There was a time when his young brother, Dietrich, "bolted." Herschel immediately laid aside his work and went off to the Continent in search of the runaway, who was eventually found in London, ill and penniless. The opening years of the new century saw Europe convulsed by Napoleon's adventures. Their native Hanover was overrun and ruined. Dietrich took refuge in Slough, ruined in health and fortune. He remained for four years. It was Caroline who always came to the rescue. "I hope I have acquitted myself to everybody's satisfaction," she wrote, having nursed William, Dietrich and her nephew, "for I never neglected my eldest brother's business, and the time I bestowed on Dietrich was taken entirely from my sleep, or from what is generally allowed for meals, which were mostly taken running or sometimes forgotten entirely." Surely she goes down in history as one of those devoted sisters, in the wonderful company of Dorothy Wordsworth and Mary Lamb. She so overworked herself that at one time she was threatened with blindness, and was kept in a darkened room for a fortnight to practise being blind, possibly a doctor's ruse to stop the nightly "sweeping."

Meanwhile news came to Slough of Napoleon's defeat at Waterloo. The forty-foot telescope now lay tarnished in the garden, an object of curiosity to the general public. When it was finally dismantled in 1839, Sir John Herschel, the famous son of a famous father, with his wife and family and household, assembled within the tube and sang a requiem which he had composed in honour of the great telescope. Sir John did something else which made photographic history. He took the first photograph of the scaffolding on a sensitive negative and fixed it for the first time in history. This negative is now in the

South Kensington Museum. In 1839 Sir John, wishing to ascertain more fully how far organic matter is indispensable to the decomposition of the salts of silver by light, used glass plates to receive, under water, a deposit—"murite" (chloride) of silver from a mixed solution of the nitrate with common salt. He wrote:

"After four and a half hours the chloride had formed a film firm enough to bear drawing the water off very slowly by a syphon. Having dried it, I found that it was very little affected by light, but by washing with nitrate of silver, weak, and drying it, it became highly sensitive. In this state I took a camera picture of the telescope on it." He exposed it with "the glass towards the incident light," and fixed the image with hyposulphite of soda, the solvent action of which on chloride of silver he had announced twenty years earlier. The negatives (as he called them, coining the word for the first time) were the first obtained on glass, and from them he printed a few positives, now lost.

Sir William Herschel's life was drawing to a close. The Prince Regent knighted him in 1816, and he lived on, in failing health, but loaded with honours, a gracious figure among the great men of his age until 1822, when he died at the age of eighty-three. Poor Caroline, his wife, and his son, followed his body across the road from the Slough home to Upton Church where he had been married and had worshipped.

And Caroline? It is by no means the end of her story. She was now seventy-two, and might well have sung *Nunc Dimittis*, but there were twenty-six years of sad but treasured recollections before her. As soon as her brother was buried she decided on her course, to join her brother Dietrich in Hanover. The scene of her childhood called her back. Her brother came to fetch her. On October 7th, 1822, she drove over to Windsor and took leave of the Princess Augusta and her friends there. On the 10th, at nine in the morning, she left Slough by coach, accompanied by her brother, her nephew and Lady Herschel. In that journey she closed a momentous chapter in her life and scientific history.

She lived on in Hanover, editing her brother's works, writing her memoirs, alert till the close of her life at nearly ninety-eight. She was the Great Aunt Caroline from England to ten of her grandnephews, honoured by the visits of royalties. Her nephew, visiting her when eighty-two, found that she skipped up two flights of stairs, was "fresh and funny" at eleven P.M., sang old rhymes and even danced. At eighty-five she was elected an Honorary Member of the Royal Astronomical Society. She rejoiced in her nephew's triumphant tour to the Cape, where he swept the whole southern hemisphere with their famous telescope. He received a baronetcy at the Queen's Coronation, on his return, and the Duke of Cambridge brought her the news. A little later Sir John himself brought her his five-year-old son to receive the great-aunt's blessing.

In 1846 the King of Prussia conferred on her a large gold medal, in honour of herself and her immortal brother. And so full of years and honours, aged ninety-seven years and ten months, "she fell asleep in happy peace," to quote her own words; for assiduous to the very end, she prepared her own epitaph, grandly declaring, "the gaze of her who has passed to glory was, while below, turned to the starry Heaven; her own discoveries of the Comets, and her share in the immortal labours of her Brother, William Herschel, bear witness of this to later ages."

Sir William was fortunate in his son John. From early youth he gave brilliant promise. After obtaining a Fellowship at St. John's College in 1813, he had thoughts first of the Church and then of the Bar, but finally he decided to assist his father, since Aunt Caroline was no longer able to work so hard in assisting her brother. Young John at Cambridge had been Senior Wrangler and first Smith's Prizeman. A few months later he was elected to a Fellowship of the Royal Society. After his return from the Cape of Good Hope he settled down in his father's old home at Slough from which many of his scientific papers are dated.

When he demolished the great telescope in 1839 he had completed the great work his father had begun, the telescopic survey of the entire heavens, in his laboratory in a corner of the garden. He was also the originator of the system of fingerprint identity and became Master of the Mint in 1850. At his death in 1871 he was buried in Westminster Abbey, close to Isaac Newton.

Observatory House, as it was now known, still continued its great tradition, for two brothers of the third generation carried on the work, Alexander Herschel and John Herschel. Alexander became a great authority on meteors. He lived at the old house for the last twenty years of his life. John finished their grandfather's great work, *Revision of the Comparative Brightness of the Stars*, in the same room as it had been begun a century earlier.

II

"Do you think there is anything to see inside?" I said to Miss Whissitt, as we turned round by *The Old Crown* at Slough and came to Observatory House.

"Let's have a look," she said, eagerly. "The front porch's Gothic Victorian, stuck on later, I'm sure."

We got out of the car. Across the road a large cinema, in new red brick, proclaimed "You Can't Take it With You" on a great placard.

"And who would want to!" snorted Miss Whissitt. "Shades of Sir William—look at this new palace of the celluloid stars. There were green fields here in his day."

Miss Whissitt's quick eye had seen a drive running down a brick wall. It was marked *Private*. While I hung back she marched bravely on. She came back after a few moments with shining eyes.

"Would you believe that at the bottom of that drive there's the dearest Regency villa, complete with verandah and French windows, in the heart of a lovely garden? It's only a few yards behind the shops in the high street; yet it's embowered in trees. I found an old couple living in it, and over their wall what do you think I saw—William Herschel's garden intact— and a shed that holds the telescope! They tell me a Miss Hardcastle lives there."

"I can't believe it," I retorted, following her back up the drive. I looked across the wall. There, undoubtedly, was a large-windowed house with a great wide lawn, flower-beds and trees—a kind of remote country rectory snugly set not a hundred yards from the roar of the traffic on the Bath Road through Slough.

Miss Whissitt marched back, up to the door of Observatory House.

"What are you going to do?" I asked, nervously.

"Call."

"But you can't."

"*Mais pourquoi non?*—they say Miss Hardcastle's charming."

It was too late to stop her: she had rung the bell.

"You suffer enough from this sort of thing—you should be allowed to do it yourself, once," declared Miss Whissitt, alluding to my cottage visitors.

The door opened. Yes, Miss Hardcastle was at home.

"Mr. Cecil Roberts and Miss Whissitt," she said to the maid, who asked us into the hall and disappeared upstairs.

"As if that meant anything to her," I said.

"We'll see," answered Miss Whissitt. "*Mon Dieu*—just look!"

Something like an enormous gong, polished, hung in the hall. It must have been four feet in diameter.

"The mirror of the great telescope—I'm sure," cried Miss

Whissitt, and with a thrill I knew she was right. At that moment the maid came in. Miss Hardcastle would be down presently. We were shown into a large sitting-room with windows looking on to the wide, tree-bordered lawn. It seemed impossible to believe one was a hand's throw from Slough High Street. There were Victorian portraits on the walls, mirrors and high bookcases. "I wonder who Miss Hardcastle is?" I asked, as we sat waiting. The next moment our hostess entered, a little, keen-faced, elderly lady. I apologized profoundly. But in two minutes we felt at home. She radiated goodwill and delight in all she had to show. Yes, it was all here, or almost all here, she said.

"The great telescope," I began.

"There's the circle of its old base—now a flower-bed," replied Miss Hardcastle. "But come outside."

She led us across the lawn to a low shed; in it was something that made my heart jump. There was no doubt about it. It was the end of the old tube through which George III had led the Archbishop of Canterbury. Our hostess raised a small door. We looked into the dark funnel whose mirror had caught the light of the stars. There were other things to see. Across the lawn there was an old cottage in a bower of green.

"Not Caroline's cottage—where she swept the stars?" I exclaimed.

"Yes, and come in here," replied our hostess, as we approached.

She led the way into a small shed, and there lay the famous twenty-foot telescope at which William, Caroline and Alexander had laboured so long, which had explored the heavens, making astronomical history, and which, when its survey of the Northern hemisphere had been completed, was carried to the Cape by the son, to survey the Southern hemisphere.

Our hostess led us indoors to the long library, after we had looked again at the great telescope's foundations on the lawn.

"Stand there," said my hostess, placing me in position, "and let me have the latest Star in my reflector," she added, playfully.

I looked down the long room across the hall, to a reflector hanging on the wall, which caught my image and magnified it. It was the twenty-foot reflector, in which, on that unforgettable night of March, 1781, Herschel had seen the unknown planet Uranus.

Miss Hardcastle opened a cabinet full of mementoes of Sir William and Sir John, among them the treasured Visitors' Book kept by sister Caroline. Many of the entries were in Caroline's own fine handwriting, but many were autograph signatures. Here was a cluster of royalties, over from Windsor, and Sir Joseph Banks from Spring Grove, and the royal dukes, and the ambassadors and their ladies. Diplomats and duchesses jostled foreign scientists and celebrities. Evidently it was the thing to call on Herschel and the telescope.

"Poor man, he can't have had a moment's peace, *c'est formidable*," cried Miss Whissitt.

"Oh, I expect he enjoyed it, really," said Miss Hardcastle.

In the study we found further mementoes of father and son; part of the foot-lathe; the clock with hammer and bell for timing and recording rotations of the telescope; the instruments with which Sir William discovered Radiant Heat, and much of the impedimenta used in that tremendous output of sixty-nine telescopes and four hundred mirrors. Yes, the large reflector hanging in the hall had belonged to the giant telescope.

Miss Hardcastle was standing just in front of a crayon copy of the Herschel portrait in the National Gallery, a fine head, drawn when the Sir William was forty-six. Suddenly I was aware of the astonishing likeness my hostess bore to the astronomer. I had to remark on it.

"Are you a relation?" I asked, overcome by curiosity.

"His great-granddaughter," laughed Miss Hardcastle. "I've impersonated him, too. Look!"

She picked up a portrait of Sir William in knee-breeches, stock and broad-brimmed hat.

"That's me—I drove round in a carriage as Sir William at the Runnymede Pageant last year!" laughed our hostess.

We went out into the garden again, stepping from the eighteenth century into the twentieth. I remarked on the growth of Slough in the intervening years.

"Horrible! Horrible! Once you looked across green fields to Windsor. Then the houses began to spring up. Why, even poor Queen Victoria got nervous watching them grow from her terrace. She made them put battlements on one row of villas to disguise them. The telescope used to stick up in the sky here— and now look what's appeared in the sky to-day!"

We looked. There was a kind of grid-iron on a long pole projecting high up over the garden wall.

"Whatever is it?" asked Miss Whissitt.

"The march of science—the new Television aerial at *The Old Crown*," exclaimed our delightful hostess, scornfully. "That's what the modern traveller sees now from the Bath Road!"

As we regained our car, I glanced at my watch and gave a cry of dismay. We had imposed ourselves on Miss Mira Hardcastle for almost two hours. It was nearly eight o'clock.

"Heavens!" I exclaimed, "I've guests for dinner at eight, and twenty miles to go!"

"Heavens is the right word," retorted Miss Whissitt. "You know, you'll never get to Bath at this rate. But what a delightful afternoon! *C'est la bonté en personne!* But why Mira, I wonder?"

The next morning the telephone rang.

"Mira—William Herschel's first two papers were written on the variable star, Mira—*et voilà!*" cried Miss Whissitt.

CHAPTER XIII

Montem and Maidenhead

THREE YEARS BEFORE the famous astronomer of Slough was born at Hanover there had been a remarkable scene in this Bath Road village, to which I called the attention of my young Austrian friend, Rudolf. His whole opinion of Slough, which had been unflattering, thereupon changed, and like the house in North End Road, it became hallowed ground. In 1741 Samuel Richardson was exciting the reading world by the issue of his novel, *Pamela*. When his anxious readers learned that the heroine had triumphed, the enraptured villagers of Slough rang the church bells for joy. Those who could not read the sensation of the hour gathered at a local forge near Salt Hill, and the literary shoeing-smith, in between shoeing horses on the Bath Road, read *Pamela* to an attentive audience.

Rudolf immediately wished to see the forge, and was bitterly disappointed when he learned it had long disappeared, but he reverently went to Upton Church, since those were the only bells of Slough in that era. The memorial of Herschel, which we found there, scarcely aroused his interest.

William Herschel did not hear the bells of Slough rung for the triumph of *Pamela*, but two other singular events he must have been aware of. Salt Hill, a rise in the Bath Road which follows immediately out of Slough, had an unhealthy reputation for highwaymen and footpads, whose lairs were Hounslow Heath on the east and Maidenhead Thicket on the west. The danger from these desperate characters was so constant that in 1783 there was a gathering of Slough notables at a well-known hostelry, Botham's Hotel, at Salt Hill, a coach halt and a favourite resort of honeymoon couples, for the purpose of protecting property and persons "from Rogues, Felons, Highwaymen and Footpads."

It had been in existence under the name of The Salt Hill Society for three years when William Herschel came to Slough and excited everyone by the erection of his great telescope. He must certainly have joined it, for it numbered among its members nearly all the local landed gentry—Lord Grenville, Lord Orkney, Lord Godolphin Osborne of Baylis House near by, the Duke of Buccleuch, the Duchess of Cumberland, at Cliveden, as well as the farmers and tradesmen of the district.

At this time there were no police, no Bow Street Runners, no civil guard. Slough was a tiny hamlet, with nothing between *The Old Crown* and Eton College except the Herschel house, the church, a few cottages and farms. The Bath Road was really a rough track, surfaced with rubble and stones over the thick mud in winter. Its dust was indescribable in summer, hence the roadside pumps.

Public morality was then in a singular state. The roads were infested by unfortunate men discarded from the Army and the Navy during the lull between wars, and, in the absence of any public assistance, they were driven to robbery and general crime. The scale of punishments was harsh and arbitrary. The landed gentry protected their game preserves fiercely, with hangings, floggings and transportation for life. As late as 1790 men were hanged for sheep stealing and transported for poaching. The Bath Road was gruesome with gibbets, and as late as 1804 George III had to order them to be taken down near Hounslow, as they made too ghastly a spectacle on his way to and from Windsor.

The Salt Hill Society had a purpose, therefore, in protecting those who lived around Slough. Its original object has now disappeared, but the love of tradition keeps it sturdily alive, and every year, since it was first founded and held its original meeting at Botham's hotel, it holds an annual dinner at which, though highwaymen have vanished and footpads are unknown, the health of the Society is loyally toasted. The last toast of the evening is always "Our Next Merry Meeting."

Was it at this hotel that the "week-end" came into existence? William Hickey in his *Memoirs,* relates how he and other roisterers used to go there from London, from Friday to Tuesday, "twelve or fifteen of us, attended by some of the most fashionable women of the time, where we spent three or four days together in all sorts of frolic and fancy."

On our way to Salt Hill, which is now a part of Slough opposite the recreation ground, a gap in the houses gives one a view of a grassy mound of earth, with a tree growing on top of it. It stands just off the road that runs to Eton, on the edge of the municipal playing fields. Of the hundreds of thousands who pass along the Bath Road at this spot scarcely one notices this historic mound. What it was originally no one knows; it has been thought to be the tomb of an ancient Briton, or a Roman surveying mount. Certainly it has been associated with a hallowed Eton College ceremony since 1561, and continued until 1847. This ceremony was known to all Etonians as Montem, from the cry *ad Montem,* to the Mount.

It was at first an annual festival, and in 1775 was changed to a triennial one. Salt Hill took its name from this event when the Eton boys, dressed in fancy costume, travelled the country around, and specially along the Bath Road, extracting tribute money, or "salt" as it was called, from everyone they encountered. It was very much like our own charity flag days, though much fiercer in its demands and manifestations. Later on a ticket was given to the accosted person to make him free of further demands. The sum of money thus collected, which often amounted to a thousand pounds, went to the Captain of Montem, the highest Colleger in the School, supposedly to meet the expenses of his university career, but much of it was absorbed by the costs he incurred in providing fancy costumes, a band, and a banquet at Botham's to close the day, when the exuberant boys thoroughly scared the good people of Slough with the scenes that followed.

The origin of this custom seems lost in obscurity, though it may have been a version of the Boy Bishop Festival so widespread in the time of Henry VIII. Certainly, in later years, Montem included a mock service with a boy dressed as a bishop, which so shocked Queen Charlotte in 1758, by its parody of religion, that this part of the festival was discontinued at her request. Later Montem was always held on a Whit Tuesday, instead of in January, owing to the better weather. William Malin, writing in 1561, describes the ceremony:

"At nine o'clock on a day chosen by the Master, the boys go to the Hill, just as they go to gather nuts in September. The devotion of Etonians gives a kind of sanctity to the spot. On account of the beauty of the country, the pleasantries of the greensward, the coolness of the shade, the sweet harmony of the birds, they dedicate the retreat to Apollo and the Muses, they celebrate it in song, call it Tempe, and extol it above Helicon."

After this we learn they indulged in all "the wit (salts) and humour that can be mustered," and finally, after orations and triumphs, returned from the hill to college. But Montem gradually became a form of polite blackmail on travellers. Pairs of scholars called Salt-bearers, dressed in white, with a handkerchief of salt in their hands, went on to the high roads and demanded tribute. No one escaped. The Bath coaches were held up; the proudest equipages were brought to a standstill. They even stopped the carriage of William III on one occasion, greatly to the surprise of his Dutch Guards who would have struck them down as highwaymen had not the King intervened.

In time the festival became more and more elaborate, the fancy dress more georgeous, the procession to Montem longer. Twelve servitors, or Runners, as well as Salt-bearers, went forth wearing fancy costumes, with satin money-bags and painted staves. They demanded tribute, each accompanied by a hired assistant with pistol, to protect him from real highwaymen. One of the Runners in 1835 described how he worked at Colnbrook from 7 A.M. to noon and gathered seventy-seven pounds—"We got saluted by beggars on Montem day as brothers of the profession." George IV and Queen Charlotte always gave fifty guineas apiece.

Doubtless William and Caroline Herschel, venturing abroad, were put under tribute. "June 7. Was the 'Montem,' of course much company," wrote Caroline in her diary in 1808. Probably she stayed at home all day entertaining the stream of callers. George III never missed a Montem in his unclouded years. Sometimes he drove the Queen there in a chaise, sometimes he went on horseback. The Duke of Cumberland was one of the royal party in 1799, and rode about with such lack of formality than an Eton boy, unaware of royalty, exclaimed, "I should recommend you, my friend, not to let your horse tread on *me!*" Following the example of George III—George IV, William IV, and Queen Victoria all graced the festival.

An elaborate procession set out on the great day from Eton College. It consisted of a Marshal followed by six Servants, a Band, a Captain with eight Servants, a Sergeant-Major, twelve Sergeants, a Colonel, four Polemen, four Corporals, a second Band, Salt-bearers, Servitors, Stewards, and a host of Servants, all attired in the most gorgeous and fancy costumes. When this procession reached the Mount a great flag was unfurled. At the end of the day the boys and visitors adjourned to dine at Botham's and *The Castle*. In later times these banquets became so costly and riotous that the Captain, when he had paid for costumes, servants, bands, wine and food, had very little left. After the banquet there was a general rough-house, particularly if the Captain was unpopular, when as much crockery was broken as possible, in order to swell the landlord's bill that he must pay.

The boys along the garden strayed,
With short, curved dirk high brandished—
Smote off the cowering onion's head,
And made e'en doughty cabbage feel
The vengeance of their polished steel.

The revellers then left Slough and Montem in peace, and in the evening the Terrace of Windsor Castle was like a carnival with all the boys in fancy costume mingling with the great crowd of sightseers.

But a day came when the abuses became too grave. The railway coming to Slough brought an undesirable element. The festival had outlived its singularity, the boys got out of hand, it began to be resented by the sober public, and seemed a waste of time and money. Tradition, however, dies slowly at Eton. When Provost Hodgson proposed bringing Montem to an end even Queen Victoria and Prince Albert, who had been present in 1841 and 1844, were reluctant to see it pass. But after a second approach, backed by the Headmaster, Hawtrey, and a number of notable Etonians jealous for the reputation and dignity of the school, the royal pair assented to the change.

So in 1847 there was no Montem. There were loud protests, and an open threat of rebellion by Etonians at the universities, who planned to march on to Montem, but on the festival day all passed quietly. Thus, after nearly three hundred years, the grass on Montem was allowed to grow undisturbed. Singular to relate, Etonians took no care as to the fate of the famous mount. It passed into various private hands, and sported in turn a gazebo, a summerhouse, and a hawthorn tree. When I approached the venerable hillock, having passed it scores of times coming out of Slough, I found it was part of a private garden. But it could be approached from a park laid out by an enterprising Corporation. The view from it must have changed greatly since last the Captain's flag fluttered on its summit, but Windsor Castle still nobly dominates the skyline across a dreary valley of shacks, houses, sheds and gasometers.

"Oh, yes, sir!" said the official keeper of the greens and the swimming-pool. "We've lots of people come to look at it—I'd a gentleman from America yesterday, who said it was a shame the way we neglected our historic spots. He said they think the world of it over there."

Whatever we may think of it to-day, and it is merely a neglected hillock with a romantic history, there were many who shed a tear for the passing of Montem. An Etonian's *Farewell*, written in 1832, shall be ours, before we take the dreary stretch that brings us to Maidenhead.

"I love that no-meaning of Montem. I love to be asked for 'Salt' by a pretty boy in silk stockings and satin doublet, though the custom has been called 'something between begging and robbing.' I love the apologetical *mos pro lege* which defies the police and the Mendicity Society. I love the absurdity of a Captain taking precedence of a Marshal, and a Marshal bearing a gilt baton, at an angle of forty-five degrees from his right hip, and an Ensign flourishing a flag with the grace of a tight-rope dancer; and Sergeants paged by fair-skinned Indians and beardless Turks; and Corporals in sashes and guarded by innocent Polemen in blue jackets and white trousers. I love the mixture of real and mock dignity; the Provost in his cassock, clearing the way for the Duchess of Leinster to see the Ensign make his bow; or the Headmaster gravely dispensing his leave till nine to Counts of the Holy Roman Empire and Grand Seigniors. I love the crush in the cloisters and the mob on the Mount. I love the clatter of carriages and the plunging of horsemen. I love the universal gaiety, from the peer who smiles and sighs that he is no longer an Eton boy, to the country girl who marvels that such little gentlemen have cocked hats and real swords. Give me a Montem with all its tomfoolery—I had almost said before a coronation—and even without the aids of a Perigord-pie and a bottle of claret at the Windmill."

The prosperous coaching inns on Salt Hill, patronized at Montem, vanished when the coming of the railway from London to Slough sounded the death-knell of the hostelries on the Bath Road. The Great Western Railway planned their first line to Slough, but the opposition of Eton College and the Court was so strong that not only was the railway kept out of Windsor, it was also forbidden to erect a station at Slough. The station, therefore, was Taplow, officially, but there was nothing in the Company's Act that forbade them to stop at Slough. They therefore hired two rooms at a public house near the site of the present station, and tickets were issued over the bar. In vain exclusive Eton College applied for an injunction.

Slough has one more claim as a pioneer village. The public telegraph was first used to Slough signal-box. No one except the railway would patronize this new invention. Then one day in 1845, a man named Tarvell poisoned his sweetheart and escaped to London, but a description of the man was telegraphed to the police and he was arrested. It seemed almost a miracle, and after that the telegraph leapt into popularity.

II

There is nothing to detain us on our road from Salt Hill to Maidenhead, but before we come to the Thames, we can make a swift side visit to Cliveden, in its woods above the river. We turn off by *The Dumb Bell*, appropriately named since it is a favourite headquarters for boxers in training. Cliveden rewards the visitor, if he is lucky enough to gain admission, with a magnificent vista of the Thames, but it is the history of the house on this site which we call to mind. It is the scene of the first rendering of *Rule Britannia* in Arne's masque, *Alfred*, performed at Cliveden for the occupant, Frederick, Prince of Wales, the dissolute father of George III. Two Clivedens have been burnt down since that occasion, the first fire having been caused in 1795 by a servant girl reading in bed. The house in which Dr. Arne's bellicose air was first heard, in an age when Britannia really did all she threatened to do, was then occupied by one who was probably the most dissolute man in the kingdom, in a reign notorious for its rakes. This was the second Duke of Buckingham, whose pictures, smuggled to the Continent, we have seen at Osterley Park, including the Van Dyck portrait of the boy-Duke with his mother and family.

The Duke of Buckingham, in his rake's progress, counted among his affairs one with the Countess of Shrewsbury, a wanton at the court of Charles II. As is so customary in these cases, the Earl was jealous of his wife's virtue, and, feeling outraged, challenged Buckingham to a duel. Shrewsbury was killed and it is said that while it was being fought, the Countess, disguised as a page, held Buckingham's horse. The fatal duel over, the pair fled to Cliveden, the Duke's house, where he "slept with her that night in his bloody shirt," according to Pope, who heard it from one Spence. I feel the story is too sordidly romantic to be true. The guilty wife disguised as her lover's page, yes, perhaps; the homicidal lover sleeping forthwith with his mistress, a widow of a few hours, probably; but without changing his blood-stained shirt—never!

In half a mile we are at Maidenhead Bridge with the town's centre a mile beyond. In the Naughty Nineties, when peers waited at stage doors to woo chorus ladies, Maidenhead was the favourite retreat of seduction, which gave an ironic touch to a place so singularly named. There is little ground for the agreeable legend that Maidenhead owes its name, if not its reputation, to a head, sent as a relic here, of one of St. Ursula's eleven thousand peripatetic virgins, whose wanderings are so delightfully depicted by Carpaccio in the Accademia at Venice.

Here is the headquarters of pleasure boating on the Thames, with far-famed Boulter's Lock a short distance along by Cliveden Woods, but only the bridge shall detain us here, for its views, its history and its own graceful architecture.

There is more history connected with the bridge than with the pleasant old town, which, curiously, was for a long time south of the Bath Road, in the parish of the celebrated Vicar of Bray. The town owes its prosperity to the river and the road, which here crosses the Thames for the first and last time, dividing Buckinghamshire and Berkshire. In 1297 Edward I gave a grant of "pontage" for the maintenance of the bridge, which was almost derelict. In the rebellion of the Earls against Henry IV in 1400, the bridge was successfully held by the Earl of Kent, to protect the retreat of his friends. It was again the scene of a skirmish against a king when, in 1688, an Irish regiment held it for James II, but in the night the good folks of Maidenhead beat a Dutch march, and the Irish fled.

The bridge had always had the patronage of Kings. As early as 1451 Henry VI incorporated the Guild of the Brethren and Sisters of Maydenhithe, which from 1352 had charge of the bridge. There was a curious service in 1423 in which a Richard Ludlow was admitted to the "hermitage of the bridge" after vowing "that I will lead my life to my life's end, in sobriety and chastity; will avoid all open spectacles, taverns and other such places." He promised also that all goods given him "receiving only necessaries to my sustenance, as in meat, drink, clothing and fuel, I shall truly, without deceit, lay out upon reparation and mending of the bridge." In short he would be an exemplary bridgeman.

The Guild, dissolved at the Reformation, was revived by Queen Elizabeth. Whenever in these days I cross this charming bridge, I am inclined to wonder if the ancient Guild has ever died out. One always sees some of the Brethren, accompanied by a few sisters and supported by the balustrade, divided in their attention by the flow of traffic over and under the bridge.

The scene from this bridge to-day has lost much of the additional charm once added to nature by the lines of elaborate house-boats, with their fronts gay with flowers. The motor-car and the quiet week-end has killed the river as a gay and fashionable resort, and the house-boat will soon qualify for the South Kensington Museum.

There was one exciting scene on the bridge on October 31st, 1913. A toll continued to be collected at this bridge long after the cost of its erection had been wiped out. The indignant public, backed by the Town Council, after various lawsuits, seized the

gate and threw it into the river, and the road to Bath was freed
from the toll-keeper.

One looks in vain for the old *Greyhound Inn,* which used to
be in High Street, and was the scene of a meeting between the
captive King Charles I and his children. Taken to Caversham
as Cromwell's prisoner, he was permitted to write to his children, the Duke of York aged fifteen, the Princess Elizabeth,
thirteen, and the Duke of Gloucester, a tiny boy of seven who
could not remember his father. The Prince of Wales had escaped to France. These three children were held in custody by
the Earl of Northumberland at Syon House and St. James's
Palace. On July 4th, 1647, Charles wrote from Caversham to
the Duke of York, the eldest of the three.

"I am in hope that you may be permitted, with your brother and
sister, to come to some place betwixt this and London where I may
see you . . . but rather than not see you I will be content that you
come to some convenient place to dine, and go back again at night."

Maidenhead was selected as the meeting-place, and the royal
father met his children and had them dine with him at *The
Greyhound,* a scene of reunion that affected all who witnessed
it. The King was then permitted to take his children back to
Caversham for two days, where Cromwell himself witnessed the
parting with considerable emotion. The Parliament party
showed clemency in this matter, for this was only the first of
many meetings permitted between father and children. They
were to meet again at Syon House when King Charles went over
to see them from Hampton Court; and vice versa, until that
last sad day in January, 1649, when he bade them farewell at
St. James's Palace, and walked thence to the scaffold.

The Greyhound was burnt down in 1735, while the landlord
and his wife had gone to London to prove a Will. We learn that
"out of the thirty-six Standing Beds, only three Feather Beds
and one Pewter Dish was saved; even all the Plate, Money and
Books were lost; it was accounted one of the best-furnished

inns in England." One wonders why the pewter dish was saved at the cost of so much.

In connection with the fire three maids were tried at the Assizes. One of them turned King's Evidence, but despite this the other two were acquitted. "Her behaviour in Court, and her character in Abingdon (where she was born) so much incensed the inhabitants against her that she was obliged to have a Guard from the Court to her lodgings, to prevent her being torn to pieces by the populace."

There is another inn with a history. Children delight in *The Bear* with the luminous eyes. This splendid animal, erect but chained, with red electric lamps for eyes, stands over the porch. It would have been dear to Edward Lear who created the *Dong with a luminous nose*. This inn recalls an old coaching inn, its predecessor, and has long since outlived an accusation in Court, in 1489, of "charging an unlawful price for provisions."

Coach travellers, on arriving from London, had the dreaded Maidenhead Thicket before them, so they preferred to sleep the night at *The Bear* and journey on by daylight in the morning. But *The Bear* is famous for the story of James I's encounter with the Vicar of Bray. The King, hunting with his hounds, lost his way and came alone into the yard of *The Bear*, where, unrecognized, he asked what he might have for dinner. "Nothing, Sir, It is Lent, and all the fish is bespoke, and dressing for dinner for the Vicar of Bray and his curate," said mine host. The King then commanded the landlord to ask the Vicar if a strayed gentleman might dine with them. Permission was given, and the King entered into conversation with the company, but at the end of the meal there was some outcry when he said that, having left home in haste, he had no money with which to pay for his share. The Vicar was indignant, but the curate exclaimed, "Oh, sir, do not speak thus to the gentleman. I'll pay his reckoning, and think myself well repaid for his entertaining conversation."

The King had scarcely thanked the curate when the gentlemen attending the King came to the inn and asked if His Majesty had been seen, whereupon James showed himself on the balcony, to the utter confusion of the Vicar. On his bended knees he asked pardon. He did not know, and if— "Man, I forgive you. You shall be Vicar of Bray still, I promise you," replied the King, and turning to the curate, "As for you, good fellow, there's a Canonry of Windsor vacant and you shall have it."

This cannot have been the celebrated Vicar of the Restoration song:

> *For this is law I will maintain*
> *Until my dying day, sir.*
> *That whatsoever King doth reign*
> *I'll be the Vicar of Bray, sir.*

Dr. Fuller, who writes of him in his *Worthies*, tells us this was a vicar who, living in the reigns of King Henry VIII, King Edward VI, Queen Mary and Queen Elizabeth, to keep his office was in turn a Papist and then a Protestant, and then again a Papist and a Protestant. "He had seen some martyrs burnt (two miles off) at Windsor, and found this fire too hot for his tender temper."

Whatever Vicar it was, it is worth while to go to Bray, a mile south of Maidenhead, to see the splendid lich-gate, dated 1448, in rooms above which the weathercock Vicar is said to have resided. In 1736 Thomas Darvill, the landlord of *The Bear*, was authorized to pay the sum of £20 to anyone who gave information that led to the arrest of any highwayman or robber when within five miles of Maidenhead Thicket. This sum, as at Salt Hill, had been raised by exasperated local inhabitants, and was additional to the £40 paid by Act of Parliament.

There is another inn at Maidenhead which has been immortalized by a picture. This is the popular riverside hotel, by the bridge, Skindle's, which has a place in J. M. W. Turner's fa-

mous painting, "Rain, Steam and Speed," which shows a train
crossing a railway bridge over the Thames, with the hotel building included.

But let us be on our way, for though there is some history
there is little to see. Perhaps, knowing this, the local council
send the motorist on a curious detour round the town on the
way to Bath. One day it will be by-passed, and go back into
the sleep of centuries. The air is relaxing, and life flows lei-
surely along the narrow High Street, the road known to Kings
and Queens and to Commoners. Pepys, coming home from Bath
on June 17th, 1668, passed through it, having "set out with one
coach in company, and through Maydenhead which I never saw
before to Colebrooke by noon; the way mighty good." Was it
known to an earlier and more famous traveller? Perhaps so, for
Shakespeare writes in *The Merry Wives of Windsor,* wherein
we met the Fat Woman of Brentford:

"There is a friend of mine come to town, tells me there is
three cozen-germans, that has cozen'd all the hosts of Reading,
of Maidenhead, of Colebrook, of horses and money." He was
alluding to the Duke of Wurtemberg, who, with his suite, had
once travelled that way, grossly abusing the hospitality shown
to them: but he may have slept at *The Bear* himself and have
paid an unlawful price for provisions!

The lover of architecture will find little in Maidenhead to
delight him save the bridge, but he should not neglect, as he
goes over the hill to open country, the line of Victorian villas,
some with attendant monkey-puzzle trees, that have a charm of
their own. They have delightful verandahs, with diapered green
metal awnings. You feel their owners went to the City each day,
carrying little black handbags, and the single servant with a
tiny white cap rested her tired feet, in button boots, on the
kitchen snippet rug.

Over the hill and down again brings us to Maidenhead
Thicket. It is scarcely a thicket now on the road to Bath, but
when I turned right to go homewards to my Chiltern cottage, I

pass through the heart of this ominous lair of robbers. Mrs. Montagu, the famous Queen of the Blue Stockings, wrote to her husband on November 7th, 1764, "A chaise was robbed in Maidenhead Thicket yesterday but I passed unmolested; but I imagine there is much robbery for the machines have four men to guard them and gentlemen's equipages have often a great number armed to the teeth."

The Vicars of Henley would only be induced to take services in Maidenhead by being offered an annual £50 for the risk. There was one poor parson who had a frightening experience as late as 1782. This was our friend Pastor Moritz who on his walking tour went through Slough and Maidenhead. He was too early by three years to see his fellow countryman, and the great telescope that became a landmark, and he was also too late in the year for Montem at Salt Hill, though he has something to say about it.

"I took my way through Slough by Salt Hill to Maidenhead. At Salt Hill, which can hardly be called even a village, I saw a barber's shop; and so I resolved to get myself both shaved and dressed. For putting my hair a little in order, and shaving me, I was forced to pay him a shilling. Opposite to this shop, there stands an elegant house and a neat garden."

What was the house which faced this shop where he paid too much for a hair-cut? It was probably Baylis House, a seat of the famous Lord Chesterfield, which still reminds us of the age of leisure and letters. But to continue with the Pastor:

"Between Salt Hill and Maidenhead, I met with the first very remarkable and alarming adventure that has occurred during my pilgrimage. Hitherto I had scarcely met a single foot passenger, whilst coaches without number every moment rolled past me; for there are few roads, even in England, more crowded. . . . The road now led me along a low sunken piece of ground between high trees, so that I could not see before me, when a fellow in a brown frock and round hat, with a stick in his hand a great deal stronger than mine, came up to me."

The result of the encounter was that Moritz was only spared
from parting with one of his few shillings by the coming up of
a coach which frightened off the footpad. Such was hiking in
1782. No wonder he arrived at Maidenhead, "a place of better
note," with a thirst. He ordered some mulled ale "for which I
was obliged to pay ninepence" and heard them say, as he
passed on, "A stout fellow!" which, with his knowledge of
English, did not seem a compliment. "This, though perhaps not
untrue, did not seem to sound, in my ears, as very respectful. At
the end of the village there was a shoe-maker's shop; just as at
the end of Salt Hill there was a barber's shop."

Poor Pastor Moritz! A shilling for a shave at Salt Hill, a
footpad on the way, ninepence for mulled ale in Maidenhead,
and called "a stout fellow" on leaving! At the Thicket he left
the Bath Road, and got safely through that traveller's nightmare.

The footpad pest of which we know so little to-day was one
result of the utterly callous treatment of poor people in the
eighteenth and early nineteenth centuries. Men who had been
press-ganged into the Services were thrown on to the streets
after years of strenuous service, and then were treated with the
utmost severity of the law for being destitute. A few voices
were raised in protest, and it is a singular thing that one verse,
written in Maidenhead, voiced the rising indignation which
compelled a more humanitarian treatment of paupers. This
verse, set to music and known throughout the land, was the
Pauper's Drive:

> *Rattle his bones over the stones*
> *He's only a pauper whom nobody owns.*

It was written by Thomas Noel, who lived in Maidenhead at
the beginning of the nineteenth century.

Beyond the Thicket to Knowl Hill follows the pleasant passage of Littlewick Green. We have come at last to the open
Bath Road. It is a fair country—with no trail of villadom over

the fields. Three times approaching Knowl Hill, I resisted the temptation to go two miles south to Shottesbrooke, but on a fourth occasion I succumbed, lured there by observant Archibald Robertson, to look at the tomb of "the very learned Mr. Henry Dodwell. . . . This extraordinary man, it is recorded, travelled over most parts of Europe on foot, reading as he walked; and carried with him books fitted to his pocket." I hoped that learned Mr. Dodwell might prove as singular in death as he was in life, but was disappointed. Mr. Dodwell has for company Henry VIII's Serjeant of the Bakehouse.

The noble church rewards one, however, as also a glimpse of the great house in its park, the home of that Francis Cherry whom Queen Anne called "one of the honestest gentlemen in her dominions." He was highly hospitable as well as honest, for he kept seventy beds for his friends. The church, it is said, owed its origin to a hard-drinking knight. Having nearly drunk himself into the grave he vowed to reform by "taking water-drenches, water gruel, water soups." He carried out his vow, and built a church to St. John.

And the patron Saint that I find the aptest
Is that holiest water-saint—John the Baptist.

Knowl Hill serves to remind one of the great age of the noble rich eccentric, when a man might travel across Europe with twenty servants, a chef, bedding and cooking utensils, or build a grotto underground, and a folly above it. On a road coming from Marlow and intersecting the Bath Road the traveller is greatly puzzled by milestones marking the distance to Hatfield. Why Hatfield, of all places, which, right across country, would seem to have no possible connection with the Bath Road. But there we err. The whims of the rich and illustrious were never thwarted in the eighteenth century, particularly the whims of the Cecils. The Marquis of Salisbury, seated at Hatfield, and his neighbour the Earl of Essex, made yearly visits to Bath. All cross-road journeys being atrocious in their day they were compelled to make the journey to Bath, via London, a long detour which, subjecting them to fearful jolting over the cobblestones of London aggravated their gout and their tempers. So my lords promoted a road of their own, making a straight line from Hatfield to Knowl Hill, which cost a lot of money but saved them twenty miles of agony on their way to make the cure and meet the fashion.

We can keep to the by-pass from Hare Hatch, thus missing insignificant Twyford, forgotten on the old road, but it would be a pity to omit a side visit of half a mile to Sonning, which, with houses, a charming old Thames bridge, lock and weir, walled gardens, and the perfect vicarage lawn fit for "the sly shade of a rural dean" deservedly won a prize as the prettiest village in England.

And now "step on the gas," as our American friends say, for a speed of a hundred miles an hour is not enough to blur the vision of a dreary marriage of bedraggled rusticity and villadom that prepares us for the industrial drabness of Reading, which a cruel fate has ordained to possess a wonderful history and scanty proof of it. But before we enter Reading, let us recall a strange scene on this highway in the year 1827. George Sanger, who ennobled himself and called himself Lord George Sanger, of circus fame, was born in Reading, the son of a father who had been press-ganged into the Navy, and who fought at Trafalgar. Later, the elder Sanger settled in Newbury as a showman with a peepshow on his back. The young Sanger prospered greatly in the circus business. One day his circus encountered a rival menagerie, and each tried to secure a pitch first. The contest soon degenerated into a free fight. The wild beasts, like their owners, roared, the horses took fright, and the elephants added to the mêlée by smashing the wagons. In this pandemonium of horses, elephants, lions and human beings, Lord George's caravan was turned over and burnt. In the end those who were not carried to hospital wounded were careering

over the countryside in quest of escaped members of the menagerie, and one gentleman, driving home in a "whisky," was
astounded at seeing a kangaroo give one great leap across the
Bath Road.

CHAPTER XIV

The Worthies of Reading

I FELT LIKE APOLOGIZING to Rudolf for Reading. He shared that singular taste which most Teutons, visiting England for the first time, so often display. His heart leapt up at the mention of Manchester and the industrial north. "Chimneys, smoke, money! that is why you are rich!" he cried. Elsewhere I had encountered very solemn young Germans, wearing very short shorts, sturdily pushing bicycles up hills on their way to Manchester of all places. Afterwards they went to Stratford, but only afterwards. When I suggested that Reading was a dull industrial place and quoted the rhyme:

> 'Mongst other things so widely known
> For biscuits, seeds and sauce,

he was at once eager to visit the town, when, after a few days at Pilgrim Cottage, we rejoined the Bath Road. But in showing him industrial Reading I discovered a town that is sorely maligned. It had as much history as any town in England that I knew, but that it possessed anything really worth seeing, historically considered, I was yet to learn.

The Saxons seem to have been the first to seize on this undulating place at the juncture of the Kennet with the Thames, and the Danes seized it and fortified it. Then the Normans followed, and it began to acquire importance when William the Conqueror's son, King Henry, founded the "Noble and Royal Monastery of Reading." He also intended the place as a memorial to his father, his mother and all his ancestors. He planned it on a generous scale and sent over from the great Benedictine monastery at Cluny a prior and seven brothers as a nucleus of the new shrine.

On June 18th, 1121, in the presence of his nobles, the king laid the foundations. An army of workmen brought the building to a habitable condition in two years, and King Henry's friend, Hugh de Boves, was appointed the first Abbot. When, some years later, he became Bishop of Rouen, the fame of Reading Abbey had already been established. King Henry, who lived fourteen years after founding the Abbey, was buried there in January, 1136, before the high altar in the presence of King Stephen, the barons, and a great gathering of the common people.

The Abbey he had founded between the Thames and the Kennet ranked among the three greatest in England. So very little of it remains that it is difficult to conceive to-day what a vast edifice fell before the rage of Henry VIII and his vindictive servant, Thomas Cromwell. It consisted of a great church and offices, surrounded by a massive wall, with the Kennet and the Holy Brook on the fourth side. There were four embattled gateways, and a large public court, called the Forbury, in front of the Abbey. The church itself had a nave with a double row of eight piers. There were cloisters, a great Chapter House, a Monks' Dormitory, a Refectory 167 feet long, an Infirmary, a Leper House, isolated, and a Hospitium, where the hospitality was on a generous scale to a very large assembly of pilgrims and travellers.

For four hundred years this great Abbey grew in power and splendour until that day of doom when its last and thirty-first Abbot was hanged in front of its gateway. King Henry richly endowed the Abbey, which was consecrated by Thomas à Becket in 1164. Henry's daughter, Matilda, the widow of the Emperor Henry IV of Germany, returned to England bringing with her the reputed hand of St. James. "Know ye," wrote the King, "that this glorious Hand of the Blessed St. James the Apostle, I, at her request, send to you and grant for ever to the Church of Reading." It was enshrined in a golden reliquary, and drew thousands of pilgrims. Richard Coeur de Lion coveted the reliquary so much, since it was covered with precious stones, that he took it from the monks, but left them the Hand.

What became of this Hand? It was there, apparently, when Henry VIII's assessor visited the Abbey in 1538. *"Imprimis, two peeces off the holye crosse. Item Saynt James Hande,"* he wrote in his inventory, and added, "I have lokkyd them upp behynde the high awlter and have the key in my keeping." After that, darkness obscures the history of the Hand for several centuries. Then, in 1786, some excavations were being made among the ruins, when some workmen uncovered a box containing a hand. It was at once asserted to be the lost hand of the Apostle, and was kept in Reading Museum, labelled "the hand of St. James" until 1855, when it was privately purchased for £30, and passed eventually, through a donor's hands, to the Catholic Church of Marlow on Thames, where it may be seen to this day.

The Roman Catholic Archbishop of Westminster rejected the Hand when it was offered to him. It sounded too cheap for the genuine article. It is a delicate left hand, somewhat Oriental in character. It is known that St. James had his left hand struck off when he was beheaded, and the cathedral of Santiago de Compostella claims to possess the body, with the left hand missing. "We must believe it, it is more interesting, *nicht wahr?*" said Rudolf, on hearing the story, when I appeared sceptical. "And you cannot prove it is not the Hand," to which there seemed no answer.

The Abbey witnessed many great events in history. Henry II held a Council there in 1184 to elect a new Archbishop of Canterbury. The next year it saw the visit of Heraclius, the Patriarch of Jerusalem. He came to implore help for saving Jerusalem from capture by Saladin.

The interview with Henry II took place in the chapter house, in a setting of great splendour. The Patriarch was accompanied by the Master of the Hospitallers of Jerusalem, in the great cloak of that historic order, but the appeal was made in vain. The King was sympathetic, but in true English fashion evaded the point by consulting a committee, and the idea died of prolonged discussion. It was in vain the Patriarch shed tears and handed to the King the keys of the Tower of David, and of the Holy Sepulchre. Henry was no crusader. Bitterly disappointed, Heraclius returned to Jerusalem, and in due time the Sultan Saladin captured it.

History at Reading Abbey is marked in the thirteenth century by the composition of the earliest known English song, written for six voices. The original manuscript, written by a monk of the Abbey, is now in the British Museum. It is a far cry from 1240, when the monk wrote his song in the Calendar of the Abbey, but it rings as true to-day as then, a perfect song of the English spring.

> *Summer is icumen in,*
> *Lhude sing Cuccu!*
> *Groweth sed, and bloweth med,*
>   *And springeth the wude nu—*
>   *Sing Cuccu!*
>
> *Awe bleteth after lomb,*
> *Lhouth after calve cu;*
> *Bulluc sterteth, bucke verteth,*
>   *Murie sing cuccu!*
>
> *Cuccu, cuccu, well singes thu, cuccu!*
> *Ne swike thu naver nu;*
> *Sing cuccu, nu, sing cuccu,*
> *Sing cuccu, sing cuccu, nu!*

One can almost see the musical monk looking out of his cell on the April meadows across the Kennet, hearing the cuckoo, and taking a brush, as he turns to his scroll of parchment. The colours from that far-off day, as the music with its tones and semi-tones, are still plainly legible on the old parchment.

Perhaps the most splendid assembly ever gathered together in Reading Abbey was when John of Gaunt married Blanche of Lancaster, on May 19th, 1359, and thereby gave England three Kings, Henry IV, V and VI.

John was nineteen, a tall, soldierly bridegroom, whom Chaucer described as "a wonder, wel-faringe knight!" The bride, his cousin, was a beautiful golden-haired girl of eighteen, who figures in Chaucer's the *Book of the Duchesse*.

> *As the someres sonne bright*
> *Is fairer, clerer, and hath more light*
> *Than any planete, in heven,*
> *The mone, or the sterres seven,*
> *For al the worlde, so had she*
> *Surmounted hem alle of beaute,*
> *Of maner and of comlinesse. . . .*

This royal marriage filled the Abbey with the splendour of robes, flags, jewels, and the shining armour of the barons, knights and esquires. Edward III, John's father, his three brothers, Edward the Black Prince, Lionel and Edmund, were present at the ceremony performed by the Lord Bishop of Sarum. And it is very probable that one great scribe, who had sung the virtues of the royal pair, Master Geoffrey Chaucer, the King's "well-beloved yeoman," was present in that dim church.

The solemn office, the chanting, the sprinkling with holy water are ended. The brilliant procession moves out into the sunlight of the Forbury, to the ringing cheers of the populace. And now all go to the King's Meadow for the grand tournament. There is a three days' jousting, with all the great barons of the land in the lists. Later to London the whole cavalcade moves, the tournament proceeds, this time with royalty in the lists. For here are two royal prisoners, King David of Scotland,

and that King John of France whom we have seen, brought as
the Black Prince's prisoner, to the meeting at Colnbrook with
his father on his return from the French wars. But to-day these
prisoners are honoured guests, and in the lists with the King
himself, the Black Prince and the barons.

Ten years later that beloved young bride was carried to her
tomb in St. Paul's Cathedral, where in due time her husband
joined her, after long lamenting:

> *Now that I see my lady bright,*
> *Which I have loved with all my might,*
> *Is fro me deed, and is a-goon.*

Their tomb was by the north altar, and Henry IV, their son,
erected a noble monument in alabaster portraiture.

In the course of time the power of the Abbots became very
great. The town outside their walls was wholly in their grip
and also the farms of the surrounding country. Then gradually
the struggle for independence by the burghers brought conflict
between Abbots and townsmen. A bitter quarrel developed and
lasted two hundred years, but the gradual rise to power of the
wealthy guilds, with the increasing population, and prosperity
from the cloth manufacture, found the Abbots unequal to the
struggle.

But they never lost control. To the end, during which there
was fierce fighting between the Abbot's bailiffs and the burghers, the Mayor was appointed by the Abbot, from three names
submitted to him. The struggle went on desperately, until one
Thomas Mirth was the last mayor to be elected by the Abbot.
For it was now the era of the great storm, and under the rage of
that monster, Henry VIII, the Abbey and all those in it were
smitten with ruin.

Hugh Faringdon was the Abbot, and he stood so well in his
King's favour that he received from him a silver loving cup.
Then came Henry's denunciation of Rome, his seizure of the
Headship of the Church of England, his fury against Wolsey

d all those faithful to the Church. That evil genius, Thomas
omwell, saw in the dissolution of the monasteries and the
zure of their properties an enormous revenue for the royal
asury. Cupidity united with licence. In one year nearly a
ndred monasteries were suppressed. The King wanted bigger
ne. Accusations of treason were made against the Abbots of
e three great Abbeys, Colchester, Glastonbury and Reading.
a September 1st, 1538, Abbot Hugh had permitted an inven-
y of the relics. Six months later his loyalty was challenged.
d he deny the King's spiritual supremacy? Yes. An honest
urchman, he would not recant. The Pope was the Church's
oreme head.

Together with the Abbots of Colchester and Glastonbury,
ringdon was imprisoned in the Tower. He was doomed, and
s trial was an utter mockery. Wrote the fell Cromwell: "Re-
embrances—the Abbot Redying to be sent down and to be
ed and executed at Redying with his accomplices." So in his
n hall at Reading he was tried for treason and condemned.
a November 15th, 1539, the last act of this ghastly drama was
rformed. Together with two of his monks he was tied to a
rdle and dragged through the streets. Then with a rope round
s neck he was brought to the gibbet before the gateway of his
n Abbey, where he was permitted to address the crowd, kept
soldiers at an inaudible distance. He boldly proclaimed his
th; then followed the hanging, the disembowelling, the quar-
ing, in all its grisly order.

It was the end of Reading Abbey. Two hundred monks were
nt adrift to starve. The treasury was plundered, the vest-
ents and plate were seized for the King. The fabric of the
eat Abbey fell before the ruthless dismantlers who melted its
ad roofs, tore out its pillars, doors and windows. For a time,
e remaining fabric housed the royal visitor, and then the once
lendid edifice fell into utter ruin, a quarry for builders, a lair
r bats. What remained of it by 1643 was demolished in the
rce bombardments of the Civil War. A mine destroyed three-

quarters of the nave and the north transept. The Abbey had
come a vast rubbish heap.

And yet Time has not wholly effaced this great Abbey. '
gateway, before which Hugh Faringdon with the halter aro
his neck took his last look of the world, is still intact bef
that great courtyard, now a public garden. The massive w
of the chapter house recall the vanished majesty they hous
A portion of the ancient dormitory still survives, and serve:
public offices. There is irony in the fact that where once
infirmary stood there now rises the discarded Reading G:
grandiose and castellated, a specimen of red brick mid-\
torian architecture masquerading as a *cinquecento* Ital
stronghold.

From the river by the gaunt chapter house, and the w
where the monks went down to the gate on the Kennet, you
see the row of cells beyond a forbidding high wall that lo
down on the prison yard. In one of those cells Oscar Wi
wrote his confession, *De Profundis*. Within a few months
his release in 1897 he wrote *The Ballad of Reading Gaol*,
as one looks up from the ruined Abbey to that cell of a rui
man, the words of his dreadful ordeal come to mind:

> *I know not whether laws be right*
> *Or whether laws be wrong;*
> *All that we know who lie in gaol*
> *Is that the wall is strong;*
> *And that each day is like a year,*
> *A year whose days are long.*

II

The motorist to Bath can so easily get a poor impression
Reading. Little is done to entice him to linger. He rushes up
London Road, and climbs Castle Street and is gone. The
toric Reading lies on his right. Let us follow the King's R
into the town the old way of the traffic and turn up to

rket-place. Linger here, for a dozen styles of architecture
et the eye, Elizabethan, Queen Anne, Georgian, Victorian.
e entrance to the Corn Exchange strikes the romantic note,
obelisk by Soane, over the public lavatory, rounds off the
ongruities.

his market-place was ever a lively centre; to-day it delights
eye with a miscellany of goods for sale in windows as vari-
in character as their contents. William Darter, looking back
he year 1812, remembered the pillory here, with a delin-
at in it. "I saw Mr. Moody, the coach proprietor, bring two
ets of eggs from Mr. Millards, and he threw them so well
the poor fellow, whose head and arms were fixed, was lit-
y covered with yolks of eggs and other matter, and to com-
the affair he was bespattered with refuse from Hiscock's
hter house."

fore us, at the top of the market-place, stands St. Law-
's Church, and to the right we come to the old Abbey gate-
and the Forbury gardens. The church once had a "piazza,"
caded walk on the market side. It was built in 1620, and
me incomprehensible act of vandalism it was pulled down
undred years later.

s Whissitt, bless her, sent me inside St. Lawrence's
h, which formed part of the great gateway leading to the
ntrance of the Abbey. Had I seen Mrs. Martha Hamley
ng before her *prie-dieu* on the north wall, asked Miss
itt. It was *tellement remarquable*, and must have a special
st for me. For Mrs. Hamley was born a Miss Seakes of
y-on-Thames. She lived at Henley until she was mar-
s she died in 1638, and Pilgrim Cottage was built in
Miss Whissitt had no hesitation in connecting Mrs. Ham-
h Pilgrim Cottage. "She must often have walked up the
Road and seen the charming new cottage, and as the
tion was so small, it's quite likely she knew the first ten-
ere, and visited them. So when you look at her, remem-
knew your cottage," said Miss Whissitt.

I was quite prepared for her to prove that young Miss Sea▌
met Mr. Hamley at a party in my cottage. It is by no me▌
improbable that she knew the place, so I did look at her w▌
added interest. Strictly on its own merits the monument ▌
serves attention. The dear old lady wears a hat over her w▌
ple, and also a beautifully laundered ruffle. She is most c▌
fortably settled on her knees, and obviously enjoys praying

There are other monuments in this splendid twelfth-cent▌
church, whose north chapel has a fifteenth-century timbe▌
roof of seven cants divided into panels. To the right of the a▌
steps there is the jolly family of Master Thomas Lydall. ▌
divided into two arched compartments; on the left kn▌
Thomas and his three sons, on the right, facing them, kn▌
Mistress Margaret Lydall, with her six daughters in three
pairs behind them. Beruffled and gowned, they look as if ▌
had just walked into service on a morning in 1600.

Mrs. Hamley has for a companion on the north wall or▌
Reading's great characters. This is John Blagrave, in cloak▌
ruff, who died in 1611. It was he who gave the vanished p▌
to the church. An ingenious gentleman, he was called "the
ere of the mathematick." His life interest is represented ir▌
half-portrait by the globe and the quadrant he holds i▌
hands, and the symbols carved on the frame. He published
eral "ingeniose" works, among them *The Mathematical J*▌
written, as he announced on the title-page, by "the same
willer to the Mathematicks." It was a treatise on "Th▌
miliar Staffe, as well for that it may be made visually ar▌
miliarlie to walk with, as for that it performeth the Geome▌
measurements of all Altitudes." It was in fact a giant p▌
compasses. He wrote a treatise also on "The Art of Dyal▌
wherein he talked learnedly on sundials of all kinds.

His will expressed the nature of this ingenious gent▌
who must have had a playful turn, for all his scientific se▌
ness. He had no less than forty nephews and he left th▌
legacies, but one particular legacy still provides Readin▌

an annual entertainment. He left the sum of twenty nobles to be competed for annually by three maidservants of good character and five years' service under one master. The maids appear on Good Friday before the Mayor and Aldermen in the Town Hall, and cast lots. Harassed housewives will learn with astonishment that maids with a five-year service qualification still present themselves.

One of John Blagrave's forty nephews, Daniel, had to flee the country. He signed King Charles' death-warrant, and was threatened with the gallows. The Blagrave family were well established in the Elizabethan era, and by Southcote house are the remains of their property, a fifteenth-century tower, a guard-house, and a moat thirty feet wide. It is certain that the eminent deviser of walking-sticks and dials was well to the fore when Queen Elizabeth visited this church in 1602 and found it decked with flowers and rushes in her honour. One wonders if he presented her with an "ingeniose" walking-stick. As a small boy he may have seen the young Edward VI when he came to Reading in 1552, and Queen Mary with her Spanish husband, Philip of Spain, two years later.

One feels certain that Mr. Blagrave was an elegant young man, which means that he went to Mr. Laud's the master tailor, whose sign hung out in Broad Street. Mr. Laud had a very sound business, and he held his head high, for his brother-in-law had been a Lord Mayor of London who was knighted by Queen Elizabeth. He had also, at the time Mr. Blagrave patronized him, a very bright son, little Willie Laud, destined to become Archbishop of Canterbury, to prove a tyrant in the dreaded Star Chamber, and to lead King Charles on a course that brought them both to the scaffold. And yet he was withal a man of great learning and piety, who endowed the Reading Grammar School, founded the Oxford University Printing Press, and enriched the Bodleian Library. But John Blagrave, being measured for a new doublet, and seeing a boy's round face peering at him from the sitting-room behind the shop, could foresee nothing of this, though he lived long enough to see young Laud become President of St. John's College, Oxford.

The clothiers of Reading, of whom the elder Laud was an important member, prospered greatly. In 1628 they built themselves the Oracle, on the corner of Minster Street and Gun Street, where all their woollen cloths had to be examined and measured, to prevent fraudulent dealing. The clothiers formed a powerful guild that was the backbone of the opposition to the autocratic abbots.

By the tower in St. Lawrence's, near to the splendid font, there is a monument to William Douglas. For virtue John Blagrave paled before the peerless William. His astonishing virtues entitled him to become the patron saint of solicitors. We are told that he was a "batchelor, and honest man and an eminent conveyancer, remarkable for his zeal for his king, love for his country, duty to parents, generosity to relations, sincerity to friends, integrity to clients, benevolence to the distressed, love to all men." After this panegyric his nephew, William Boudey who must surely have benefited from that "generosity to relations," improves upon his uncle's astonishing virtues:

So great his patience
Yt he bore the acute pain
of ye gout for forty yrs
with thankfulness.
So good his judgment
that he never made
in all his practice
any one material error,
nor lost one sum
entrusted to his care.
So generous his soul
that to educate and maintain
all his relations
was his chief pleasure.
So cheerful his temper
that his conversation
was coveted by all.

Now, blest of God,
Enjoy thou the reward
of true Christian charity.

This paragon of virtues, at whose shrine all maligned bachelors should lay flowers, passed from perfection in 1732, aged seventy. A little overcome by merit, let us go out into the fresh air, walk along under the vanished piazza, and so come to the only remaining Abbey gateway, the scene of Abbot Hugh's execution, and thence into the recreation gardens that adjoin the Abbey ruins.

On entering these be not dismayed by the astonishing bronze lion that snarls at you. It is colossal, it shames the lions of Trafalgar Square, and yet it is both comic and pathetic. Comic because I cannot help feeling something has gone wrong somewhere in its proportions, for in certain aspects it is grotesque; pathetic, because this immense lion commemorates some three hundred soldiers who died in a forgotten Afghan campaign. They died very gallantly, these few hundreds, but their memorial entirely dwarfs a later memorial to tens of thousands of Berkshire lads who fell in the Great War. Looking at these memorials one wonders just how small in progressive diminution will be the next memorial to the next greatest war.

It seems as if Reading does not wish one to see the ruins of her Abbey. Access to them is under a small bridge in one corner of the grounds. I thought I had seen them, and was bitterly disappointed until Miss Whissitt discovered I had only seen an odd wall. Once through the tunnel under the bridge, the massive ruins exist in sufficient majesty to conjure up the great scenes of which they were the background. Here is the chapter house, wherein Parliaments met and great decisions were taken. Memorial tablets recall Henry I handing a staff to the first Abbot, and the last Abbot going to the gallows with the halter round his neck.

There is a pillar by the central tower that has witnessed the beginning and the end of the Abbey's life. Was it here that

Chaucer leaned while watching the marriage of John of Gaunt, or that the funeral cortège of King Henry halted on its way to the vault before the High Altar? Was it here Thomas à Becket paused to look over the great assembly at the consecration, and that the Patriarch Heraclius knew he had failed? The long wall of the dormitory still exists, which housed those two hundred monks who were "a noble pattern of holiness and an example of delightful and unwearied hospitality," according to a grateful contemporary.

Down across the gardens, on an island near what was once the King's Meadow bordering the Thames, and where now the railway-lines close in around the station, King Henry II, with Abbot Roger, watched the Trial by Combat of Henry of Essex and Robert de Montfort. Henry, Earl of Essex, Standard Bearer of England, accused of treachery by Robert de Montfort, fought here before the King and all the nobles of the realm. He was struck down in the field, and, repenting his crime, he became a pious monk. He artfully explained his defeat by declaring that he was menaced by the vision of a knight he had wronged, accompanied in the sky by Edmund, the Martyr King.

III

There are two Readings. There is the thriving manufacturing town of biscuits, seeds and sauce, which so excited Rudolf, and there is the Reading of the old Bath Road. Let Miss Mary Russell Mitford describe it for us. She was educated at the Abbey School, the famous young ladies' academy in Reading, where, in 1780, Jane Austen was a pupil, and also the wholly forgotten Mary Martha Butt, who, as Mrs. Sherwood, found fame as the authoress of that masterpiece of sadistic virtue, *The History of the Fairchild Family*. This famous school had moved to Chelsea in 1798, when Mary Mitford went to it, and had for schoolfellow the amazing Lady Caroline Lamb.

Little Miss Mitford was caught up to fame by her book *Our Village*. From the start she was destined to an odd mixture of fortune and misfortune. Her dissipated father, a feckless doctor, bought a lottery ticket in Mary's name, and won £20,000. He came to live in Reading in a new red brick house on the London Road, and sent Mary to school. Like so many men of sudden fortune he got building mania, pulled down the house, built a new one, and by 1820 was penniless and dependent upon the pen of his gallant, gifted daughter. She carried the spirit of a knight errant in a lumpy body, and only her eyes, gleaming in a spotty face, betrayed her genius. No one ever heard her complain, or saw her spirit falter through a long life of incessant industry and a desperate fight with poverty. She radiated kindness and optimism from her little cottage at Swallowfield. It is through her quick, kindly eyes we can see Reading, or "Belford Regis" as she called it in 1846.

"Clean, airy, orderly and affluent; well-paved, well-lighted, well-watched; abounding in wide and spacious streets, filled with excellent shops and handsome houses—such is the outward appearance, the bodily form of our market town."

The Reading of Mary Mitford survives in places. There is Albion Terrace in London Road, and a block of stucco houses in Castle Street. There are delightful Georgian brick houses, with Victorian metal verandahs, down London Road. In Castle Street we find a charming brick house, with a bay at each end, a Georgian survival, once the celebrated *King's Arms*, more modern than *The Crown* in Crown Street, where, in 1798 Pitt stayed on his way to visit his mother at Burton Pynsent, and where Pepys came on June 17th, 1688.

"Rose and paying the reckoning 12s. 6d.; servants and poor, 2s. 6d.; musick, the worst we have had, coming to our chamber door, but calling us by wrong names."

In Castle Street, which mounts the hill out of the town, along the Bath Road, there are "opulent" Victorian villas, Georgian

brick mansions, and other houses making a delightful medley
ranging from Elizabethan to Edwardian. On the left we can
admire the fine seventeenth-century Lynford House, with its
twin gables and barge-boards. Almost opposite is the quaint
tiled *Sun Inn,* a humble neighbour of St. Mary's Episcopal
Church, built in 1799 on the site of a gaol, which is grandly
classical, with its Corinthian hexastyle portico and a tower belfry, the Greek Revival cheek by jowl with late Elizabethan.

The Bear, The Crown, The George and *The King's Arms*
were the great inns of the coaching days. Oliver Cromwell was
presented with wine and sugar at *The Bear,* in token of sub-
mission; at *The George* one may still see how the coach turned
in to the courtyard and went out at the farther end into Minster Street. Many a "Flying Machine" must have clattered in
for its weary passengers to lay their limbs in lavender sheets at
the end of the day's run from London.

In 1718 Thomas Baldwin, of *The Crown Inn* at Slough, was
making history. He ran Flying Machines from London to Bath.
He announced in April that he was ready to "begin Flying from
the aforesaid places during the Flying Season, which is a
Performance never done before." The dizzy journey was accomplished in two days, if the coach was not overturned. The
Princess Amelia preferred to make the journey to Bath in a
sedan-chair, carried on men's shoulders. She rested at *The Bear.*

By 1761 they were "flying" to Bath in one day, starting
eleven o'clock at night, and arriving late the next evening.
Reading and other towns were filled with dismay at this loss of
custom. The first coaches were stoned, and horrible stories
were told of overturned coaches, wrecked by this dangerous
speed.

The motorist doing the London to Bath journey in his Flying Machine to-day would do well to linger in Reading, like his
predecessors, otherwise he will miss much entertainment. And
let not the visitor, dining, be abrupt with the young waiter who
may not be as smart as he should be, but may render as great a

service to literature as that young waiter at *The Bear* in December, 1793, but for whom *The Ancient Mariner* might never have been written.

Young Samuel Taylor Coleridge ran away from his college at Cambridge to London, and finding that authorship would not support him, took the King's shilling and enlisted in the 15th Light Dragoons, stationed at Reading. He was a shocking soldier, and not knowing what to do with this odd recruit, they made him nurse a sick comrade. One day he astonished the officer by pinning some Greek verses over a stable door, and, on examination, confessed to being a Cambridge scholar. Captain Ogle, in command of the troop, consulted genial Dr. Mitford, always in the bar of *The Bear* in Bridge Street, where the officers were quartered. He urged that the learned recruit should be discharged. This was not easy, but a servant in the dining-room, overhearing the conversation, volunteered to enlist in the place of Silas Tomkyn Comberbache, as Coleridge had called himself. The discharge took place at the Doctor's house, and with a joyful heart Coleridge went back to Cambridge. One wonders whether, on departing, he kissed the little girl who, by winning a lottery, brought the Doctor to live in Reading, and who, at a time when Coleridge had lapsed into drugs after years of brilliant promise, won fame for herself with *Our Village*.

The visitor, if it be wet, may spend a rewarding hour in Reading Museum where he may see a Greek two-handled cup dredged out of the Thames, and a Roman marble funeral urn which had been used for centuries as a flower-pot. But these relics pale beside the largest legacy from Roman Britain, gathered here in the Silchester Collection.

At Silchester, or Calleva Atrebatum, as the Romans called it, a whole Roman town was unearthed at the beginning of this century, with baths, forum, temples, colonnades and villas. Then it was all covered up again, but not before many of the astonishing objects found in the settlement had been sent to Reading Museum. There we can see a tessellated pavement, with the name of the town inlaid, knives, lamps, bottles, styluses, jewellery, pottery, and the tools of the blacksmith, carpenter and potter. How near that Roman day is when we look on a pipe with "Clementinus made this pipe" inscribed on it!

And then, musing on the grandeur that was Rome, we can wander a few hundred yards to the ruin that was once an Abbey, afterwards a palace where lodged Henry VIII, Edward VI, Queen Mary and Philip and Queen Elizabeth, and last of all the royal visitors, Charles I, while the plague raged in London. Returning by moonlight through the quiet streets to our own inn, our mind prepared by the relics of Roman and Tudor England, we may stumble upon a Georgian scene—the steaming horses, the bustle of ostlers, the clamour of cramped passengers just off the London-Reading Stage Chaise, a new wonder made with steel springs, whose lamps glimmer in the yard of *The George*.

Inside the parlour all ears are given to an excited gentleman who relates how, beyond Slough, two highwaymen stopped the coach and robbed them all of their purses and watches, but had the effrontery to return a shilling to the driver, to drink their health!

CHAPTER XV

The Newbury Town

THE ROAD CLIMBS STEEPLY up Castle Hill out of Reading, past a number of villas almost ostentatious in their prosperity, and, reaching a plateau, gives us a panorama of the Kennet valley. Soon Victorian prosperity degenerates into modern Georgian "instalment" houses. Prospect Park, a noble recreation ground, brings dignity back again. Just beyond it let us turn in at the winding drive that takes us to Calcot Park. We are not calling on the ancient family of the Blagraves, who succeeded the romantic Childs. The house is now the clubhouse of a Golf Club, and we are frankly trespassing, but without the heinous offence of walking across the greens.

Anyone curious to see in what taste and quiet splendour the eighteenth-century gentleman lived can see it here. You enter under a great arch into a rear courtyard, formed by beautiful stable buildings, and are confronted by the dignified back entrance of the great house. The date 1755 is on the front of the house, which has a columned portico commanding the park to the south. There are a lake, some noble trees, and a splendid drive, but it is the mellowed old Georgian House, sound and sensible, with white sash windows in its weather-reddened face, that commands admiration.

This was the site of the home of Frances Kendrick, who became known in ballad and legend as The Berkshire Lady. She was the daughter of Sir William Kendrick whose effigy is in St. Mary's, Reading. She was a young maid of considerable wealth and determination. An heiress to over five thousand pounds per annum, and the Calcot estate, she did not lack suitors. But she had her own ideas about a husband. Then one day:

> *Being at a noble wedding*
> *In the famous town of Reading,*
> *A young gentleman she saw*
> *Who belonged to the law.*

Either the young man was timid, or blind. The lady went straight to the point. She sent him, anonymously, a challenge either to marry her or to fight a duel. The young barrister, Mr. Benjamin Child by name, was greatly astonished and intrigued. Accordingly, he made a rendezvous with the fair unknown in Calcot Park, and was astonished to find, at the hour fixed, a masked lady with a rapier, who was quite prepared to fight. She would not tell him who she was—he must take a chance.

> *"I will not my face uncover*
> *Till the marriage rites are over;*
> *Therefore take you which you will,*
> *Wed me, sir, or try your skill."*

The young man took the chance. The lady unmasked. She was as beautiful as she was rich, and proved to be the young lady with whom he had flirted at the ball. It would seem, if legend be true, that Mr. Child himself was a singular person. We turn from romance to oysters in considering his career. Years afterwards, in a room in Calcot House, he had an enormous collection of empty tubs which he kept as proof of the innumerable oysters he had consumed in the course of his life. Long after the death of his wife in 1722, aged thirty-five, the chosen, oyster-eating husband was buried beside her in the Kendrick vault in St. Mary's. He had sold the old home, and then refused to quit it, so that the new owner was forced to pull off the roof to eject him, whereupon the poor oyster-eater took refuge in a cottage in the wood, where he ended his days.

After Calcot we come to Theale village, which has nothing much to detain us. The coaches often stopped at *The Crown* to regale the passengers with cakes and ale, the long London-Bath journey being divided, gastronomically, into breakfast at Colnbrook, dinner at Reading, cakes and ale at Theale, Newbury supper and sleep, Marlborough for breakfast, Chippenham for lunch, and Bath for high tea.

Let us turn off the main road at Theale and, a mile to the right, enter the magnificent gates leading up the drive to Englefield House. We are not trespassing, for access is given to the church, charmingly situated in the heart of one of the best kept parks in England. Beautifully trimmed grass verges border this avenue sweeping up the hill to the house and the church.

Englefield House answers fully to the description of a noble pile. It has been greatly enlarged in the course of centuries, but its singular abutment on the wooded hills at one end found its origin in a device of Sir Francis Walsingham, who sumptuously entertained Queen Elizabeth here. He built a long gallery to the house from the hillside above it, so that she might mount to the first floor without going up steps.

Early in its history the house belonged to the Englefields, one, Sir Thomas, having been Speaker in the Parliament of Henry VIII. A member of this family, Sir Francis, born about 1520, got into grave trouble and had to flee the country. His religious scruples did not prevent him from benefiting by the plundering of Reading Abbey by Henry VIII, from whom he received its manor of Tilehurst, nor did he refuse a knighthood from Edward VI. But he was soon in trouble with the young monarch, and found himself in the Tower for permitting Mass in the house of Princess Mary, to whom he was Groom of the Chamber.

Under the Catholic Queen Mary, his star rose, and in his fanatical zeal he hurried many heretics to the stake and the block. The ascension to the throne of Queen Elizabeth saw a speedy reversal of his fortune. He fled the country and became a leading Popish plotter. He took up his abode in Spain, and drew a pension from Philip of Spain. His estates confiscated, he remained in exile until his death, some forty years later, of which the last twenty were passed in blindness and comparative poverty.

But it is not of the unhappy fanatic, but of Sir Edward I like to think, who, on his retirement from the Low Counties where he had been Minister, spent his time in enlarging the house and making a garden. There is an intimate, modern note in his letter to a friend in which he said he had confirmed himself in his opinion of a happy country life, adding, "If you help towards Englefield Garden, either in flowers or invention, you shall be welcome thither." He, too, entertained Queen Elizabeth to dinner in his house.

In the little church we can see the memorial scroll to Sir Thomas, and we can, by squeezing ourselves in at the back of the organ, vandalistically imposed on the side chapel, continue to see the charming memorial to Sir John, his wife and children, all kneeling at prayer in most life-like devotion. There is another memorial scroll notable, not for its intrinsic merit, but because the inscription came from the pen of Dryden, and because its elaborate eulogy gives no clue whatsoever to the person thus memorialized. Actually the scroll celebrates the virtues and memory of John Paulet, Marquis of Winchester, who fell at the battle of Newbury, fighting on the Royalist side. The Marquis lived at one time at Englefield House, and a connection of the family is there to-day.

Emerging from the Park gates, Bradfield is at a short distance on our left, but we must not be tempted, either by that delightful College where the Bradfield boys give a triennial performance of a Greek play in the open-air theatre, which both for quality and setting are worthy of the Attic Drama, or by a desire to look at the place, where, according to a seven-

teenth-century chronicler, there was an "ill spirit whose mani-
festation was never so busy and never made such a harvest or
had such a latitude of power given to him to ramp up and
down in any part of the earth, as he hath had lately in this
island."

Bradfield had also another rare spirit in John Pordage, as-
trologer, and rector there in 1647. "While preaching he fell
into a trance and rushed out of the church and went to his
house where he found his wife, Mistress Pordage, cloathed all
in white lawn with a rod in her hand. Ten other women came
in and all fell to dancing the Hays about the flower pots." The
Rev. Pordage's mysticism, alas, brought him into trouble during the Commonwealth, when he was twice accused of heresy.
He was deprived of his living in 1655, but was reinstated after
the Restoration.

On the Bath Road again we soon come to Woolhampton,
and a memory of the excursion made by Hazlitt and his friend
Pigott comes to mind. They had been to see a prize-fight at
Hungerford. They were walking to Newbury when a post-
chaise passed them and they hailed it. In it they found two
dismal fellows who, having lost their way, had been driving
about the countryside all night, and had arrived at Hungerford
half an hour after the fight was over. "We parted with these
two gentlemen, who had been to see the fight, but had returned
as they went, at Woolhampton, where we were promised beds,
and we turned into an old bow-windowed parlour with a carpet and a snug fire; and after devouring a quantity of tea,
toast and eggs, sat down to consider, during an hour of phil-
osophic leisure, what we should have for supper."

The road here is swift and straight. The lush meadowland
lies backed by woods above the valley of the Kennet. One
wonders why this stretch of the road has been so heavily bar-
ricaded on either side by telegraph wires. The telegraph poles
of England, unlike those of any other country, are demure
and straight, but even so they are not things of beauty. One

day they may be as rare and curious as are now the pumps on this road.

At Thatcham the name of the place is self-explanatory. They were thatching four of the old cottages that line the road as I passed. It is a village of entrancing roofs, before it degenerates into a drab housing estate. It seems notable for breeding the kind of boy who wins the V.C., for Thatcham boasts of two of them. In the church we may wonder whether Francis Baily, an astronomer who lies buried here, did anything to excite interest. Actually he provided astronomers with a phenomenon to which he gave his name, and he was the first man to weigh the Earth.

Sir William Herschel knew him well, he was a frequent caller at Slough, and Sir John Herschel wrote his life. He was born in Newbury in 1774, where his father, who came from Thatcham, was in business as a banker. Young Baily was so learned and "ingeniose," as they would say, that he soon got the nickname of the Philosopher of Newbury. But his father was firm, and into the City went young Francis. He broke the shackles at twenty-two and in 1775 off he went to the United States, whence, of the future capital of Washington he wrote home: "Game is plentiful in these parts, and what may seem remarkable, I saw some boys who were out a-shooting actually kill several brace of partridges in what will be one of the most public streets of the city." He also added that building lots, uncleared, were selling from threepence to one shilling per square foot.

Sailing home, he was taken prisoner by a French privateer. Had he acquired an accent? For we learn that he was released as an American citizen and safely reached England. He now went into business as a stock-broker where he made a modest fortune, but his heart was in astronomy, so he retired at fifty, and in a few years had made a great name in astronomical circles. He reformed the Nautical Almanac, revised the catalogue of the stars, corrected the calculations of the pendulum,

so that our clocks have become more accurate, revised and corrected the British standard of length, so that ladies now buy a
correct yard of material, and gentlemen can walk an exact
mile, and then, as a make-weight as it were—he weighed the
Earth!

But this was not all. He immortalized his name by giving
the astronomical world Baily's Beads. This phenomenon,
named after its discoverer, is seen during a total eclipse of the
sun. Just before the disc of the moon completely covers the
sun, the smooth crescent of overlapping sunlight is broken in
several places, giving an appearance somewhat like a string
of beads. This is due to the irregular outline formed by the
mountains on the rim of the moon's disc. Baily first saw this
phenomenon on May 15th, 1836, during an annular eclipse of
the sun. His discovery started a series of eclipse expeditions,
including the totality of July 8th, 1842, which he observed at
Pavia. He died in 1844, and was buried in the family vault at
Thatcham. And here we leave one more celebrated astronomer
on the Bath Road.

At Thatcham an unknown traveller comes out of the night,
via an 1837 newspaper cutting. He has left Reading in darkness in *The Beaufort Hunt*, the crack coach. "Twenty minutes
before twelve you arrive at Cooper's Cottage at Thatcham,
where you find a good substantial supper laid out, consisting
of ham, beef, fowls, meat pies, etc., with waiters to carve and
attend on you, and as twenty minutes is allowed you have
plenty of time to discuss the various articles before you. As
you pass one of the up-coaches, the down-coachman wishes the
up-coachman a good night, and the down-guard does the same
to the up-guard. In the dead of night when all is still, you
reach Hungerford."

Before leaving Thatcham a glance at the local police-station
transported me to Venice. It was not the architecture of the
station but an erection over the roof such as one sees over most
Venetian houses. Lacking gardens, the Venetian builds a small

platform high up over the roof of his dwelling. It serves many purposes. He can hang out the family wash to dry—a colourful process in Italy—and here he can sit in the evenings and take the air, the glorious panorama of Venice, and its lagoons spread out below him. This platform is called the *altana*. What was the Thatcham policeman doing with an *altana*—was it to keep an eye on motorists along the Bath Road?

At that moment the local police force drew up on a bicycle, twelve stones of ruddy British beef.

"I'm interested to see you've an *altana*," I observed.

"No, she's a red setter!" replied the policeman.

I laughed. I had not noticed the dog following the cycle.

"I mean that platform up there—is it for the washing—or a look-out?" I asked.

"Oh, that! No, sir, it holds the air raid warning siren—can't you see it—that round thing, sir!"

I saw it, then. What a commentary on our civilization. Two hundred years ago this road was at the mercy of highwaymen, and now again it was at the mercy of more deadly invaders. Here, high over the sleepy village, was the noisy symbol of impending doom.

A few pleasant miles of road, still running parallel to road, river and telegraph wires, brought me to Newbury. One entered it by Speenhamland, once a suburb on the track to the important Roman settlement of Spinae, but now absorbed by Newbury whose T it crosses. Speen, (Spinae), was the junction of the important Roman highways running from Gloucester (Glevum), Bath (Aquae Solis) and Silchester (Calleva Atrebatum). Spinae itself was a Roman hill station, but the Romans spread themselves all over this countryside and Speenhamland was an outskirt. Driving into Newbury one goes, therefore, over the very stones of ancient history.

Coming to the eighteenth century, it is of the famous Speenhamland inn *The Pelican*, now vanished, that one thinks. Quin, the witty retired actor of Bath, perpetrated a famous quatrain, which may or may not have been libellous:

The famous inn at Speenhamland
That stands below the hill,
May well be called The Pelican
From its enormous bill.

It saw many great personages, and witnessed some stirring scenes, including one on October 17th, 1822, when William Cobbett, returning from a visit to Jethro Tull, near Hungerford, attended the market-ordinary at the inn, and afterwards addressed an audience. So great was the throng that all doors and windows were crammed to hear the famous reformer, and hundreds were turned away.

The glories of the old inns, *The Pelican* and *The Castle,* have passed away. Mr. Colton, the "gentleman coachman connected with some of the best families in Newbury," a clergyman's son, whose passion got the better of all other ambitions, no longer handles the ribbons, covering the distance between St. Martin's le Grand, where the Royal Mail started, and Newbury, fifty-eight miles, in the magnificent time of five hours, fifty-three minutes, if you please. He lies now in the local churchyard, and cares nothing for the smelly auto-bus that does the journey in less than a third of the time. His were the "flying" days, when the Newbury coach was started in 1752 and soon produced rival services.

"The Flying Stage Chaise, made with Steel Springs, as easy as any Post Chaise, to carry Four Passengers at Ten Shillings each Passenger to or from London, by the Proprietors of the Newbury Stage Coach who take this method merely for their own Defence and not for the sake of Opposition."

At the beginning of this century there died in Newbury an old man of eighty, a celebrated whip, who remembered the day of doom when his employer said, "John, we must think of some other line of business, and go with the times, as we cannot keep the coaches on the road much longer." He little thought on that sad day he would live to see the enemy, the new railway, brought low by the motor-car, and the ruined inns, such as had survived, gain a new prosperity.

Before we pass Speenhamland, and turn at the old round Clockhouse that separates the main thoroughfare of Newbury from the Bath Road, let us recall the famous Speenhamland experiment in social reform. It was here that a departure in Poor Law Relief was made, an attempt to fix a minimum wage and to establish a scale of poor relief according to the price of wheat and the number of children in a family. The Speenhamland scheme was tried in many parts of the country. The intention was good, the results disastrous. Riots broke out. The high-handed squires and farmers imprisoned, whipped and branded the farmhands. In 1795 the scheme was changed, with even more disastrous results. A body of magistrates meeting at Speenhamland devised a system of rate-subsidy to pay wages. It killed all thrift, ruined the workman and trebled the poor-rate expenditure.

But Speenhamland has happier memories than this. Up a side-street there is a little building which was once Newbury's Theatre, and afterwards degenerated into cow-sheds. It had a quaintly classical façade; it entertained the Fashion who halted overnight *en route* to Bath. The stars of the theatrical firmament glittered behind its snuffed candle footlights, it knew the voices of Edmund Kean, Fanny Kemble, the Infant Roscius, and the celebrated Mrs. Jordan, mistress of the Prince Regent, later George IV.

Since we have an evening to spare, on our way to take the cure at Bath, let us spend it at Newbury and go to the theatre. Egad, sir, there's not a vacant room in *The Bear*, and two of my lady's postilions are sleeping in a loft, together with my black boy. By the pay-desk entrance, mine host, Mr. Carey, has just pinned up a notice—so that's what lusty young Harry and cherry-lipped Susan are doing in this year of grace!

"John Carey has again taken *The George* and *Pelican Inn* at Speenhamland for his Son and Daughter, and hopes for the continuance of those Favours on their Son and Daughter which will be ever gratefully acknowledged *by* the Young People."

Well, good luck to 'em! Stap me vitals, it seems only yesterday one dangled young John on the knee and put a toy duck in his tin bath!

And what do we see to-night? Zounds, there's plenty going on. When my lady's done having her hair pomaded over that fantastic contraption of her French hairdresser's, we'll hurry off—if we can get any service in the coffee-room.

To-night

The Conquest of Algiers
or British Bravery Triumphant
written by an officer of the Navy.

The Bey's Palace at Algiers.

A Sea View with the *Queen Charlotte*
lying at anchor.

A complete and correct reproduction of the entire
Quarter Deck of the *Queen Charlotte*.

The British and Dutch Fleets,
Passing in a line of battle before the
Town of Algiers.

Representation of the desperate and glorious
Engagement.

The Blowing up of the Town, Fort and Shipping
And the Total Defeat of the Algerines,
To the Immortal Honour of the British and
Dutch Navies.

By the Desire of Captain Montague, the Officers, Non-Commissioned Officers and Privates of the Woodley Troop of the Berkshire Yeomanry Cavalry.

Mr. Wilson will, at the end of this play, go through his wonderful Evolution on the Tight Rope, his unrivalled Exertion commencing with his celebrated Gavotte, with several Equilibriums, during the Performance of which he will throw an Extraordinary Somersault over the Orchestra and will dance his much admired Fandango, accompanying himself on the Castinets, as expressly composed for him by Signior Baptisto, first violin of the Theatre Royal, Madrid, concluding with his justly admired Tambourine Rondo.

Egad, that's a brave entertainment! But Mr. Wilson has plenty of competition to-night. There Mr. Theweneti (from Germany) at *The Globe Inn,* with his Microcosms, and "a Pyramid with two Serpents pursuing each other with peculiar activity." And what's this, pray?

Olympic Circus on the Marsh, Newbury

The celebrated young Saunders and his Sister. Tight-Rope Dancing by Young Saunders; and the celebrated Miss Saunders, whose elegant performance on the slack wire has created so much surprise in the Metropolis, will exert herself in that Department, after which the well-known Prodigy of the Brute Creation

Toby the Sapient Pig.

Toby performed before the Royal Party at Windsor, before the Officers of the Oxford Blues, before Dr. Keete, of Eton College, and when in London was sent for to perform before the following persons of distinction, at their own private houses; viz, His Grace the Duke of Wellington, Duke of Argyle, the Earl of Liverpool. The Sapient Pig has perfect knowledge of the Alphabet; understands Arithmetic, and Reading, will Spell and cast Accounts, Tell the points of the Sun's rising and Setting.

Some pig, 'pon my faith. I wonder if it was safe from Dr. Keate. The old brute flogged my boy at Eton till the blood came. There's a Sapient Pig for you! Well, shall it be Mr. Wilson with his wonderful Evolutions, Mr. Theweneti with his Microcosms, or the young Saunders and the Sapient Pig? I'll let my lady decide.

II

The motorist to Bath often misses Newbury. He rushes through Speenhamland, past the clock-house, up the hill to Speen and on. Rudolf was with me on the sunny July morning that I went down Northbrook Street, its main thoroughfare, crossed the quaint bridge, and turned into the market-place which appropriately commands the top of Cheap Street. Just round the corner was the old Cloth Hall, now a museum.

How old was Newbury, asked Rudolf, with his passion for facts. Had it a *Schloss?* No, it had no *Schloss* now, I replied, but there had been a castle once, as may be seen from the town's arms—a castle with three domed towers. Rudolf was distressed to find the *Schloss* had vanished. "We always keep them in Austria," he said. "Our poor aristocracy have to live in them—where does your poor aristocracy live?"

That was a question I was not prepared to answer, though when I gratified him an hour later by showing him Donnington Castle, in a ruinous state, he observed sympathetically, "The last poor aristocrat must have been very cold."

Newbury's castle has vanished, but we have the legend of a boy there. In 1152 John Marshall was defending Newbury Castle, for the Empress Matilda, against the usurping King Stephen, who laid siege to the castle. The King commanded the Constable to deliver up the castle. After a long siege a truce was asked for by the besieged, that they might communicate with the Empress. It was given by King Stephen on condition that John Marshall's young son, William, a boy of fourteen, was delivered to him as a hostage. The truce ended, John Marshall refused to deliver up the castle, whereupon Stephen threatened to hang the boy.

A contemporary poet gives us a full account of this siege, and valiant young William's part, in a long poem called *L'Histoire de Guillaume Le Maréchal.* This extraordinary poem, consisting of 19,214 octosyllabic lines in thirteenth-century French, was discovered in 1880 by a Mr. Paul Meyer at Middle Hill. He remembered having seen it at the sale of the Savile collection in 1861, when it was bought for £380. Mr. Meyer traced the manuscript, bought it, and published it. It deals with the siege of Newbury Castle, with its defence by John Marshall, Earl of Pembroke, Marshal of England, who in his old age was the Regent of England in the first three years of the reign of the boy-king Henry III, but most of all with young William, the hero of the piece. When the King found himself defied he was in great rage and anger, says the poet—he ordered the boy to be carried to the gallows and hanged.

> *And the child whom they carried,*
> *Who suspected nothing of his death*
> *Saw the Earl of Arundel*
> *bearing a very handsome lance;*
> *he said to him with simplicity,*
> *"Sire, give me that lance."*
> *When the king heard this childish speech,*
> *for all the gold which is in France*
> *He would not let him be hung that day,*
> *but with simplicity and gentleness,*
> *of which his heart was full,*
> *he took the boy in his arms*
> *and said, "Of this pain I release you*
> *'certes; you shall not die of it to-day."*

So the boy was reprieved until some of the soldiers counselled that the boy should be placed in the catapult (*perrière*) sling and hurled at the wall of the castle. So to the catapult the evil counsellors hurried the boy, who upon seeing it, naïvely exclaimed:

> *"God help us! What a swing!*
> *It is very right that I should swing myself in it!"*

which hearing, the King cried remorsefully:

" 'Certes, he would have a felon's heart
who could suffer in any way—
that he should die this martyrdom,
he knows too well how to say pretty
childish things."

So young William was again reprieved until other evil counsellors suggested tying the boy on to a battering-ram and attacking the wall of the castle under his father's eyes.

Such a squeeze shall he have, know this,
of which he shall be soon beaten in
like a drum.

So they hung out the ram's head, a great millstone, over the
battlements, as a threat, which the boy, seeing, asked:

What plaything this could now be
that they were hanging at his window.
When the king heard him say this
he began to laugh heartily
and said, "William, such play things
for you would not be good nor fine.
He is a great sinner who harms you
for you have never done him wrong,
from such toys I quit and release you,
you shall never die by me."

So William remained safe in the King's custody. The child
played a soldier's game with him, and defeated him, and his
boy's prattle and lovely ways delighted the King through the
long siege. At length a peace was arranged, King Stephen departed, the hostages were freed.

And William came to his father;
great joy had his mother of it,
and the three brothers and the sisters
who had for him great grief
because of the great tortures which they heard of.

It now only remains for the poet to close his long poem with a lyrical comment on the future grace of this handsome boy whose innocence and courage served him so well.

In short time and in a few years
was William grown up and tall,
and was of body so shapely
that if he had been carved by art
there might not be, truly, such handsome limbs,
for well I saw them and well I remember them,
he had very beautiful feet and beautiful hands.
Who looked at him well from without,
to him he seemed so well made and straight
that, if he were to judge aright,
he could decide that on the whole
there was none more shapely in the world.
He had the hair brown
and the eyes, but of his person
he seemed a great enough man
to be emperor of Rome.

Happily we know the subsequent history of young William Marshall of Newbury. He lived to be a great and famous man. William succeeded as Earl of Pembroke and became the Great Protector. He accompanied the young Prince Henry on a crusade who, dying at Turenne, gave him, as his best friend, his cross to carry to Jerusalem. On his return from the Holy Land he was present at the wedding of Richard Coeur de Lion, and bore the royal sceptre. He was with King John at Runnymede, and in company with the Master of the Temple induced the King to sign the Magna Charta. He defeated the French Army and obliged the French King, who had actually fortified himself in the Tower, to sue for peace and evacuate England.

He died in 1219 at Caversham, near Reading, and was given a great funeral procession by the monks of Reading Abbey. After resting before the high altar, while high mass was celebrated in great pomp, the body was taken to Westminster Abbey for another mass, and then borne in state to the Temple

Church. There he now rests, beneath a martial effigy, clad in chain mail. Thus ended the saga of the boy hero of Newbury Castle.

III

Rudolf, on hearing the story of Newbury Castle, seemed well satisfied. William wholly fulfilled his conception of an aristocrat living in a *Schloss*.

However, it is not William but Jack who is the most celebrated inhabitant of Newbury. His is the true "poor boy to rich man" story which always delights the village, and there was something very taking about Jack of Newbury, as he is known in local history. His real name was Smallwoode, before he was so identified with the town that its name became his, though early in his career he took the name Winchcombe, from the Gloucestershire village in which he was born. It is related that he entered a monastery there as a novitiate, but escaped and entered the service of a clothier, whose widow, in true apprentice style, he married, thus gaining a flourishing business which he greatly increased. He was a likeable lad, according to Mr. Delaney, who published a pamphlet about Newbury's hero, in 1596, which he called a "delectable Historie." Jack was a good mixer:

"He would spend his money with the best, and was not at any time found a churl of his purse. Wherefore being so good a companion he was called of old and young, Jack of Newbrie. . . . Jack would no sooner get a Crowne but straight he found means to spend it; yet had he ever this care, that hee would always keepe himselfe in comely and decent apparel, neither at any time would hee be overcome in drinke, but so discreetly behave himselfe with honest mirth, and pleasant conceits, that he was every Gentleman's companion."

The widow had a strong affection for him, but Jack had to be brought up to the scratch. Rich and buxom, she was sought by a wealthy Tanner, a bachelor Tailor and the Parson of Speenhamland. She kept them all dangling, but by a stratagem married Jack in the chapel attached to the Hospital of St. Bartholomew. Alas, it seems she was given to gadding about and staying out late. One night she was so late that Jack locked her out. At last, after long moaning on the doorstep, Jack took pity on her, slipped on his shoes and came down in his shirt, whereupon, the door being opened, she went in quaking. Just as he was about to lock it again, she confessed that as she had waited by the door her wedding-ring had slipped forth. "Good, sweet John, come forth with the candle and help me to seek it." No sooner had he done so than in she slipped and locked the door on him.

His troubles ended with her death, and she left him a wealthy man in possession of a flourishing business. All the ladies of Newbury, and all the mothers with daughters set their caps at him, but he scandalized them all by marrying one of his own servants, a bonny maid from Aylesbury. The scene of their wedding, as narrated by Delaney, sounds like a page from Spenser:

"The Bride being attyred in a Gowne of sheepes russet, and a Kirtle of fine worsted, her head attyred with a filliment of gold, and her hair as yellow as gold hanging downe behind her, which was curiously combed and pleated, according to the manner in those dayes.

"Shee was led to Church between two sweete boys with Bride laces and Rosemary tied afront their silken sleeves, the one of them was sonne to Sir Thomas Passy, the other to Sir Francis Hungerford; then there was a faire Bride cup of silver and gilt carried before her, wherein was a goodly branch of Rosemary gilded very faire, hung about with silken Ribonds of all colours.

"Next there was a noyse of musicians that played all the way before her; after her came all the chiefest maydens of the Countrie, some bearing great Bride Cakes, and some garlands of wheat finely gilded, and so she passed into the Church."

We are told that the Rhenish wine supplied at the feast was as plentiful as beer, that the feast lasted ten days "to the great relief of the poor," that Jack's father-in-law had £20, and broadcloth enough to make him a coat, and his mother-in-law enough for a gown, with the injunction, "when this is worne out, come to me and fetch more."

It was a happy marriage and all Newbury went to the wealthy clothier's wedding.

When James IV of Scotland invaded England, Henry VIII called up levies. Jack was commanded to supply four pikemen and two cavaliers. Instead he supplied "fiftie tall men, well-mounted in white coates (from Jack's factory), and red caps with yellow feathers, demilances in their hands; and fiftie armed men on foot with Pikes, also in white coats."

Jack himself headed them in complete armour on a goodly Barbary horse, with a lance in his hand "and a faire plume of yellow feather in his creste." Naturally he excited attention when he attended the assembly of the levies, where Queen Catherine reviewed them for her fickle husband, Henry. As soon as she saw the Newbury cohort she asked who led them, whereupon Sir Henry Englefield replied that it was Jack of Newbury. "Good Sir Henry, bring the man to me that I may see him," she commanded. Whereupon Jack and his men approached and fell upon their knees, Jack making a pretty speech as a poor clothier, whose hands were his looms and all at His Majesty's disposal.

The day came when the whole army marched towards Flodden Field, but it was not wanted, as news came that the Scots had been defeated and their King slain.

The ballad-writers were not going to be thus cheated of their saga. They marched the boys of Newbury to Flodden Field, where they covered themselves with honour:

> *Come, archers, learne the News I telle*
> * To the Honoure of your arte,*
> *The Scottyshe King at Flodden felle*
> * Bye the poynte of an Englyshe Darte.*
> *Thoughe Fyre and Pyke dyd Wond'rous thynges*
> * More wonders stylle dyd wee*

And ev'ry Tongue with rapture syngs
Of the laddes of Newberrie.

The Bonnie laddes of Westmorelande
And the Chesshyre laddes were there,
Wythe Glee they took their Bows in Hande
And wythe shouts disturb'd the Ayre.
Awaye they sent the Grey Goose Wynge,
Eche kylle'd his two or three,
Yet none soe loude wythe fame dyd rynge
As the laddes of Newberrie.

Jack had a house in Northbrook Street, the main thorough-fare then as now, leading to the bridge over the Kennet and the church. It was here he lavishly entertained Henry VIII and Queen Catherine. They were accompanied by Cardinal Wolsey, with whom Jack once had a passage of words, concerning a petition on the wool trade, in which Jack came off victorious, remarking bitingly, "If my Lord Chancellor's father had been no hastier in killing calves than he is in the dispatching of poor men's suits, I think he would never have worn a mitre"—a neat thrust at the butcher's son.

Jack entertained the royal guests lavishly. He covered the floor with Newbury broadcloth instead of rushes, valued at a hundred pounds a cloth, which he presented to the King. Following a sumptuous banquet, Jack escorted the royal pair over his house. They saw two hundred looms worked by two hundred men, each with a boy making quills. There were a hundred women carding, who sang as they worked, while two hundred maidens were employed in spinning "in petticoats of stammel-red, and milk-white kerchiefs on their head," and white smock sleeves tied in silk at the wrists. There were also eighty poor men's children picking wool at a penny a head, plus food, and fifty shearmen and ninety men in the dyehouse.

The work-people gave the King a warm welcome and after-wards presented a masque. When Henry came to leave he wished to knight his host, but Jack humbly declined, requesting the King to let him "live a poore Clothier among my people in whose maintenance I take more felicitie than in all the vain titles of Gentilitie."

He died at an advanced age, a wealthy and loved Newbury man. A son succeeded Jack of Newbury, and it was a descendant, an heiress with £30,000, who married Lord Bolingbroke, the "English Alcibiades" whom we have already met at Dawley Farm.

Jack gave to his town the noble church, finished in 1532 by his son. He and his wife are recorded by the brass on their tomb. The old room, doomed by the beetles and stripped of its lead roof for bullets in the Civil War, has been carefully replaced. The interior of this fine Tudor church is notable for a series of windows in modern stained glass, one of which, with a medallion portrait of Jack the woollen clothier, shows the Good Shepherd among his sheep.

The fine Jacobean pulpit would probably not be in existence to-day but for the ingenuity of someone who encased it in plaster during the Civil War to preserve it from the iconoclastic Puritans. This was the pulpit used by William Twisse, a sympathizer with the Cromwellians, who, nevertheless, gave the last sacrament at his house to Lord Falkland, the young Royalist who fell in the battle of Newbury. Convinced that a battle was inevitable, and having a presentiment that it would prove fatal to himself—"I am weary of the times and foresee much misery to my country, but I believe I shall be out of it ere night"—he took the sacrament early in the morning. That same evening his body passed the rector's door, slung lifeless and unrecognizable across a horse on its way to *The Bear Inn,* where, with the bodies of Lord Sunderland and Lord Carnarvon, it awaited burial.

One other rector of this church must be mentioned who, living in happier times, escaped the fate of Dr. Twisse, whose bones at the Restoration, together with those of Cromwell's and Blake's, were dug up in Westminster Abbey and thrown into a pit. This other rector, who missed becoming a Canon of Windsor through "bogling long with himself whether he should take it or not," was Benjamin Woodbridge. He had the singular distinction of being the first graduate of Harvard College. He went to America in 1629, when a boy, and was Harvard's first student in 1642. He returned to England while a young man and became rector of Newbury, which living he held for the first two years of Charles II's reign. He then refused to conform and became the Minister of the United Presbyterians and Independents. In 1672 he was again licensed to teach in the Town Hall. Until his death in 1684 he was revered as "a godly able and painefull minister."

We cannot see this church without recalling a singular trial which took place in the choir, where five commissioners held a heresy trial in 1556. They were the High Sheriff; the Bishop of Salisbury's representative, Sir William Rainsford; Sir Richard Brydges; the parson of Englefield; and Henry Winchcombe, grandson of Jack. The accused were Julius Palmer, Master of Reading Grammar School; John Gwin, and Thomas Askew, who were tried for denying the Papal supremacy. The horrors perpetrated by religious fanaticism provide one of the blackest chapters of man's cruelty. Oddly enough, Palmer, while Reader of Logic at Magdalen College, was expelled for being in favour of the Roman Doctrine, under the rule of Edward, but he was burned at the stake for being in opposition to it under Queen Mary, his conversion being due to witnessing the suffering of Protestant martyrs.

On the evening of the second day of the trial, being condemned, Palmer and his companions were led from the choir by the town bailiffs to the fire. While Palmer was speaking at the stake one of the bailiff's servants threw a faggot at his face, wounding and blinding him. The indignant sheriff broke his staff over the wretch's head. It was this sheriff who, in an attempt to seduce Palmer from the way of martyrdom, said, "If thou wilt be conformable and shew theyself corrigible and repentant, in good faith I promise thee meat, drink, books and £10 yearly so long as thou shalt dwell with me; and if thou shalt set thy mind to marriage, I will procure thee a wife, and a farm, and help to staff and fret thy farm for thee." It was an offer few would resist, but resist Palmer did. One cannot help wondering whether the loving eye of the sheriff's daughter prompted this offer to the young Romanist of twenty-four.

Even Winchcombe's appeal was ignored—"Take pity on thy golden years, and pleasant flowers of lusty youth before it is too late," he said, to which Palmer in his fanatical zeal retorted, "Sir, I long for those springing flowers that shall never fade away!"

A tradition still lives in Newbury to the effect that the man who threw the faggot, blinding Palmer, was himself struck with blindness, and that his descendants in Newbury to this day have an affection of the eyes. I feel it is rather hard on all Newburians with defective eyesight that they should be branded as descendants of the faggot-thrower! The wish to impose poetic justice is often the foundation of such legends.

In an age of indiscriminate bombing and gas attacks it ill behoves us to point a remonstrative finger at our forebears, but as late as 1754 a Newbury girl was committed to prison for two months and ordered to be publicly whipped each Friday between two and three o'clock, and three years later Ann Fisher was whipped at the post on a Market day for stealing a leg of pork. In 1791 a wretched woman who stole a few trumpery articles was led round the town at the cart's tail and then given three months' solitary confinement. Newbury possessed a ducking stool which frequently had victims. The high standard of art and social elegance in the eighteenth century was offset by incredible brutality and coarseness.

IV

The church visited, Rudolf and I turned our steps to the ancient Cloth Hall, once the headquarters of the Clothiers Guild. It has been carefully restored and has splendid Jacobean woodwork. Behind it, facing the modern car park, where grain barges once tied up at a wharf adjoining the Kennet, is a long tiled barn with an outside wooden gallery, once the corn stores. What gossiping and bargaining must have gone on there between the Berkshire gaffers, while the sails flapped on the barges and men sweated carrying in sacks of corn. The corn tradition is strong in Newbury.

My irrepressible curiosity led me to push open the door of a building in the market-place. It was the Corn Exchange, a superb example of mid-Victorian elegance. It still functions as a corn mart, which accounted for all the little desks arrayed in a semi-circle that made me think, at first, that I had stumbled on a school. "Corn and Seed market to-morrow," said a man painting a sign. But my mind wandered from seed to grease-paint. There at one end of the galvanized arch, whose retaining walls carried an immense hot-water pipe for warming Newburians, was the local stage, complete, with drop scene, curtain, and orchestra. It had a dowdy, romantic air, looking exactly like those twopenny coloured theatres that the boys of my era cut out from sheets and glued together with such meticulous and sticky fingers. Had the ghosts of that orchestra struck up *Ta-ra-ra Boom de-ay!* I should not have been surprised. But I do the dear Corn Exchange an injustice. It has its triumphs to-day. A yellowing playbill with a photograph of Paul Robeson bears his autograph, with the comment, "I enjoyed singing in the Hall very much and felt extremely happy."

The market-place presents a delicious medley of styles. There is a bank gone somewhat Venetian, the inevitable Georgian house turned into a solicitor's office, several inns, ranging from *The White Hart* to *The Hatchet,* and various oddments charm-

ingly out of line, added to and taken from. A passion for classical pilasters seems a common bond in all this decoration.

The peak of Rudolf's delight was achieved by the sight of
the town's stocks, preserved in the museum. He could not believe that as recently as 1872, one, Mark Tuck, had, within the
memory of those living, been placed in the stocks.

"What had he done, please?" inquired Rudolf, of the attendant.

"That isn't a thing one can say, sir. It isn't nice," was the
wary answer.

Nothing could have excited curiosity more. Rudolf was like
a terrier with a rat.

"What did he do, please? Can't you say?"

"Well, sir I could but I wouldn't. It was something in
church."

"He sang?"

"Oh, no, sir—he could do that."

Rudolf appealed to me. I took up the questioning.

"I won't be saying, sir, it isn't decent for Christian ears."

"If my ears aren't Christian?" I suggested.

"It's not a thing I can say, sir—it isn't nice. He was a dirty
old man."

"A dirty old man—oh, for not having a bath he was put in
the stocks!" cried Rudolf.

"Dirty in this sense means indecent," I explained.

"You've said it, sir," said the attendant, greatly relieved.

"Said what?" inquired Rudolf, eyes agog.

But there the trail came to an obstinate end. Baffled, we left
the museum. For the next month, at odd intervals, Rudolf
would return to the problem of the man in the stocks.

"Why did they put him in the stocks—he kicked someone in
church."

"Probably that," I agreed, anxious to end the problem.

One other exhibit aroused Rudolf's curiosity. It was an engraving of a great number of people in front of a house, one

shearing a sheep, some sewing, one measuring a gentleman's back. The picture was called *The Newbury Coat*. I was urged to find out what this picture represented. It proved to be one of Newbury's famous episodes.

In 1811 there was a prosperous cloth manufacturer, John Coxeter by name, who owned the Greenham Mills at Newbury. One day, talking to a number of gentlemen about the great improvements in his mill, he said to Sir John Throckmorton of Buckland House, who was of the company, "I believe that in twenty-four hours I could take the coat off your back, reduce it to wool, and turn it back into a coat again."

Sir John, at a dinner-party later, remembering Mr. Coxeter's boast, offered to lay a wager of a thousand guineas that between sunrise and sunset a coat could be made, the wool for which should have been that morning growing on the sheep's back. The wager accepted he went to Mr. Coxeter to ask for his help.

On June 25th, 1811, at five o'clock in the morning, Sir John arrived at the Greenham mill bringing with him two fat Southdown sheep. These were shorn at once, the wool was washed, spun and woven. Next the cloth thus made was scoured, pulled, tented, raised, sheared, dyed and dressed. The weaving was entrusted to Coxeter's son, renowned for his speed. The work was so far advanced by four o'clock in the afternoon that the cloth was finished. The Tailors now came upon the scene. A Mr. White, the Tailor of Newbury, with nine of his men, completed the coat in two hours and twenty minutes. By this time, the news having got abroad, a great crowd had gathered to watch the end of the task, which was completed at twenty minutes past six.

A platform had been erected on the lawn in front of Mr. Coxeter's house, and when Sir John Throckmorton appeared wearing the coat, nearly five thousand people cheered him. A feast followed; the two sheep who had lost their wool were roasted whole and distributed among the crowd, together with

120 gallons of beer, given by Mr. Coxeter amid general rejoic-
ing. Mr. Coxeter also gave a private dinner-party to forty gentlemen, and Sir John, who was wearing the now famous coat, a
hunting kersey of a dark Wellington colour. Sir John slept that
night at the *Pelican Inn* after an exciting day.

This historic occasion in the annals of Newbury was por-
trayed in oils by Luke Clint, who faithfully reproduced each
person taking part in the proceedings. It was an engraving of
this painting which excited Rudolf's curiosity in the Cloth Hall.

This was not by any means the last appearance of the Newbury coat. It was shown at the Great Exhibition at the Crystal
Palace in 1851, and Sir Robert Throckmorton provided for the
precious coat a special mahogany case with a plate-glass front,
after which the coat, now a Throckmorton heirloom, returned
to Buckland Hall, and is still in the possession of the Throckmorton family.

Having seen the church we began to look for Jack of Newbury's house which we had been told was in Northbrook Street.
But nowhere could we find anything that looked like a Tudor
house. There was a Tudor café, so I went in and asked a waitress if she knew where Jack of Newbury's house was.

"No, I don't know anyone of that name," she replied.

"But surely—he's the most famous character here—his house
is——"

"I've never heard of him," she replied. "What does he do?"

At this Rudolf rudely burst into a peal of Austrian laughter. I thought it wise to retreat. My next attempt was with a
solemn-looking schoolboy.

"Can you tell me where Jack of Newbury's house is?" I
asked him.

"Yes—it's Marks and Spencers."

"What!" I exclaimed.

"What is Marks and Spencers?" demanded Rudolf.

"You know Marks and Spencers!" exclaimed the astonished

schoolboy, scornfully regarding Rudolf. "It's the biggest shop here."

I thanked the boy. It did not seem possible that Newbury would sacrifice its historic past to its industrial present.

We came to Marks and Spencers. It had a special line in cheap flannel trousers that would have sent Jack of Newbury into bankruptcy. The boy's story was true. As a slight recompense for the shock we had suffered we learned that of the old house only one fifteenth-century gable end existed in a side-street. The street was almost a passage. The gable had a lovely oriel window and a carved verge board. With that, and a façade of flannel trousers, we had to slake our thirst for the authentic house, which had disappeared a few years ago, together with an inn, *Jack of Newbury,* on part of the site, the whole of which had been doomed by the deathwatch beetle, discovered too late.

And yet Northbrook Street, stretching from the pillared clock-house, an unnecessary obstruction on the Bath Road, to the quaint old bridge over the Kennet, is full of charm and interest. It is England of the market town, the coloured jumble of sixteenth, seventeenth, eighteenth, nineteenth and twentieth centuries, with roofs of all shapes and hues, a medley of chimney-pots, broken lines of windows, overhanging stories, irregular lintels and wavering façades of plaster, stone, wood and brick. The sunlight gave it all a cheerful look, the pavements were thronged with happy shoppers, cars raced through to Winchester, errand boys wobbled on cycles.

I thought of the scenes this street had witnessed. Here had passed that young William Marshall, taken as a hostage to the castle by the wharf. Here rode in a bright cavalcade, in the year 1507, the young Duke of Buckingham, Lord High Constable of England, "Bounteous Buckingham, the mirror of all courtesy," attended by twenty gentry, fourteen valets, twenty-nine grooms, with fifty-nine horses for his household and twenty-eight for himself. He was doomed to the block on Tower Hill, the fourth of his family in succession to die by violence.

I thought of Chaucer, *en route* from Winchester to Reading, sleeping perhaps at the hostel maintained by Winchester College for its scholars proceeding to New College, Oxford. Here passed the royal procession of Edward II, going to Sandleford Priory in 1320, and the retainers of Simon de Montfort, riding with his wife the Princess Eleanor, who held the manor of Newbury. A Newbury woman, Matilda Farou, had been cured of dropsy by touching the fillet round his corpse, after the battle of Evesham in the year 1265. And over an earlier bridge at the end of this street had ridden another lord of the manor, Roger Mortimer, Earl of March, paramour of Queen Isabella, "Hangyd uppon a comyn galowys of thevys" as a chronicle records in 1330, that same Earl who had taken Edward II prisoner, destined to a fearful doom in Berkeley Castle. But the greatest of all cavalcades had surely been that of Henry VIII and his queen, Catherine of Aragon, escorted by stalwart Jack of Newbury, to the door of his house in this street.

Lastly, I wondered whether it was at *The Bear* or *The Pelican* that Samuel Pepys heard such good music, on the evening of June 16th, 1668, unlike his experience the next day at Reading.

"Come to Newbery, and there dined—and musick; a song of the old courtier of Queene Elizabeth's and how he was changed upon the coming in of the King, did please me mightily, and I did cause W. Hewer to write it out."

The next day between Newbury and Reading he lost his way, but found it again, and reached Reading by the evening.

All these ghosts I saw in busy Northbrook Street, and on my way to view St. Bartholomew's Hospital I halted on the bridge over the Kennet, with its arched balustrade and quaint shops. There was a day when the old bridge had "shoppes" on it, a miniature Ponte Vecchio, for then, as now, the market-place, Northbrook Street, and the bridge constituted the business centre.

Pause on this bridge and note the four delightful arches of plaster Regency period at each corner. It is easy to miss three of them, for they have been incorporated, two on the left into butchers' shops, and one into W. H. Smith's, the booksellers. But the National Provincial Bank has proudly made a feature of its arch. It is now an entrance, and with admirable restraint it has only added a quaint model of Bishopsgate, a centre arch with two postern gates, once set in London Wall and destroyed in the Great Fire. Since the Bank now has its headquarters in Bishopsgate, it has taken this gate for its crest. So here the crest, an arched gate, appears in miniature on the real arch rescued from its former incorporation in a hatter's shop. It may be said, therefore, that these four arches, each with a fluted tympanum, now house banking, butchery and literature.

Across this bridge, on his way to the apothecary, came John Bandewyn, the town's "leche" or physician, in 1440, who paid half a pound of pepper as rent for his house in West Street.

There was nothing democratic about Newbury in those days. When the lords of the manor had ceased to rule, an oligarchy, consisting of thirty-one rich burgesses, with a mayor and six aldermen, held the town in their grip. The Signory of Venice was not more powerful. They ruled the Guilds, who in turn ruled the tradesmen and craftsmen. The government of each guild was in the hands of a master and two wardens appointed by the mayor. No one could keep a shop without permission, masters had to submit their apprentices to the mayor and aldermen who inquired of their birth, whether freemen or aliens, and "the cleanness of their bodies," after which they were registered. Nor were they allowed to lounge on the bridge or stand at street corners. Shooting with the long bow at the butts was compulsory to "keep them honestly exercised during the holidays," and on Sunday, work or play being strictly forbidden, they had to attend service at the parish church, after which they might take "lawful exercise." The pendulum has swung viciously in the opposite direction since those days.

Newbury, however, still has good and intelligent apprentices. I found one at a garage in Newtown Road. A first attempt to find Bartholomew's Hospital drove me to inquire of a street-sweeper. "There's a 'ospital alright, but not St. Bartholomew's —it belongs to the town," he replied. After two more vain inquiries I found the youth at this garage.

"They think a hospital means a hospital—it's the almshouses you want. I can tell you all about them, they're over there," he said, as he poured petrol into my car.

He seemed to know a lot about Newbury. I congratulated him. Jack of Newbury had not been born in vain.

"I take an interest in anything like that, sir," said the bright youth, and added, proudly, "I've got a beetle in the town museum."

But it was Bartholomew's and not beetles I sought. First of all I came upon a delightful group of almshouses round a court. In the centre there was a wheel window, and the name Raymonds, with the date 1716. The name and date are misleading, for the almshouses were bequeathed by a London alderman in 1676 to his grandson, Jemmett Raymond, as a home for poor persons. They bear comparison with the almshouses across the road, St. Bartholomew's, a much older foundation, for it was receiving favours from King John as early as 1215.

The present delightful building dates back to 1698, and has projecting wings and gabled roofs. It was originally designed for six poor men and women who were to have gowns, coats and pocket-money every year. The wealthy clothiers were always charitable, and another almshouse provided six poor old maids with peats and faggots.

The good work has not ended in Newbury. Across the road I espied a lovely old Tudor building which excited my curiosity. Under an arch one passed into an old English garden. This is now a haven of rest for nurses and old ladies, and the enterprise of a local doctor has resulted in a second haven, a Tudoresque companion house, cleverly matched. North of St.

Bartholomew's is the Litten House, once the chapel, wherein
Jack of Newbury was married. Street widening has docked it,
and the vicissitudes of Time have made it in turn a chapel, a
grammar school, where Francis Baily was educated, an hotel,
and a private house.

V

And now while on the Newtown Road we will go a little afield
and visit a famous Bluestocking at Sandleford Priory two miles
south, up the hill, above the enchanting valley of the Enborne
stream, with a view of the Downs to the south. This is the road
to Winchester, and as lovely an English scene as one sees in
many a day.

There is little of the ancient Priory to be seen. The house,
set back in a splendid park, is chiefly eighteenth century. But
we have not come to see the Priory, but to visit the home of
the famous Mrs. Montagu, a brilliant woman who entertained
in her London house Dr. Johnson, Burke, Reynolds, and a host
of celebrities. She was the foremost of the Bluestockings, so
called, it is believed, after a Dr. Stillingfleet, a member of the
coterie, who wore blue worsted stockings. The ladies declared,
"we can do nothing without our blue stockings," so stimulating
to good talk was the amusing doctor.

One of William the Conqueror's knights founded the Priory
of Sandleford. By 1439, the Priory, and particularly the Prior,
Simon Dam, had got a bad name. He was deprived of his office
after an inquiry by the Bishop of Salisbury at St. Lawrence's,
Reading, and was publicly deposed in Newbury Church, April,
1440. He must have been a gay monk, for a certain Thomasia
de Rise, who figured in the evidence as "Thomasia with the
Black Brows, of London," was found living in the monastery.
The Prior had also pawned the chalice. Thirty-eight years later
the Priory was deserted and became a private dwelling.

We are not concerned with the Priory until it came into the

possession of Edward Montagu, a grandson of the first Earl of Sandwich, and described by a contemporary as "a mathematician of great eminence, and a coalowner of great wealth." It was clear that coal did more for him than figures. Amiable and elderly, he liked to puzzle friends with mathematical problems, and was never so happy as when the price of coal was high, "but he urged other owners to incur the odium of making the advance." In 1742 he married a young heiress, Elizabeth Robinson, endowed also with brains. She was twenty-nine years his junior, and sacrificed love and romance in favour of comfort and reliability. Her great friend was the Duchess of Portland, so she had the entrée of the worlds of fashion, wealth and wit. She loved London, and had travel conditions permitted would have been a great week-ender, but she was faithful to Sandleford in summer. Nevertheless, she braved incessant journeys, risking highwaymen, drunken Jehus, and accidents.

"Fortune, who favours the bravery of men, looked enviously at our female courage; and perhaps alarmed to see wheels that turned faster than her own, did very uncivilly lay some stumbling block in the way of our chaise-horses; down they fell prostrate in the dust," she wrote of one journey.

She was always on the move, going to Bath or Tonbridge, accompanying Mr. Montagu on business tours of his collieries in the north, or visiting at great houses. For Newbury she had no great affection. It was "a melancholy example of the decay of trade." The Newbury bargeman stole her white peacocks and poultry. Happily the Duchess replaced the peacocks, sending them by carrier from Slough. She was fragile, had a dread of smallpox, was frequently inoculated, and suffered from hysteria and the spasms. Yet she survived a dose of eau-de-Luce, a mixture of sal ammoniac and quicklime, poured down her throat by a servant, while in a fainting fit.

Whatever the state of her body, her mind was strong and bright. She battled with obstreperous Dr. Johnson and defeated him. Her interests were wide. Every year she entertained her colliers in Northumberland, and young chimney-sweeps in London, for whom she gave an annual Saturnalia at Montagu House, her splendid dwelling in London. It has been suggested that she built many of the innumerable chimneys at Sandleford out of her devotion to sweeps.

She was a great letter writer and left sixty-eight cases of them, each containing over one hundred and fifty. No wonder she ordered her pens by the hundred.

She was extremely hospitable, and the position of the Priory, half-way between London and Bath, made it a convenient rendezvous. Her letters reflect the events of her time, and the agitations they provoked. 1766 was a stormy year in Anglo-American relations. The downright Tory lady had no uncertain opinions.

"There is a cruel tax going to be lain on the cottagers, who are to pay the tax if they have seven windows, so these unfortunate wretches must live without light and air—all this to please America. To please North America the duty is to be taken off molasses and a heavier duty to be lain on wheels. I wish our ministers were shipped off to their friends in America."

It is odd to think that the blocked-in windows which are such a feature of our old country houses owe their blindness to the American Revolution. Dear Mrs. Montagu became hot with resentment. She finds the young Sams, kicking up their heels in the transatlantic colony, useful scapegoats.

"The Country gentleman is to pay £10 a year for his coach and 1s. 6d. a window. There is not a more oppressed creature in this nation than a Country gentleman, obliged to keep up an old mansion and an old name, ashamed to appear below every upstart in his parish."

How familiar it all is, and income-tax had not yet been invented! What would Mrs. Montagu have said to a loss of thirty to fifty per cent in tax on Mr. Montagu's coal royalties? She would probably have thrown down her pen in mute indignation.

She weeps tears for the poor squires and finishes by vigorously chastising the American whipping-boy.

"I grieve for the gouty squires and their fat wives who will not be able to let the coach and old Dobbin and Whiteface tug them to church, or to visit a neighbour, while your American drives his gilded car, and six bays, tho' perhaps his Father was transported for felony."

Poor Mrs. Montagu! She did not live to see the noble revenge taken by the gouty squires whose sons took to themselves American wives and thus kept the roofs on the old halls. Her views were not shared by her husband, who opposed Lord North's American policy, nor by her brother Mathew who wrote vigorous pamphlets in favour of the rebellious colonists. We see Mr. Montagu hurrying off to a political meeting in 1774.

"Mr. M. set out at eight this morning (for Reading) in a new suit of clothes, new laced hat, and laced postilions to his chaise, and two smart footmen attending him; you would have thought he was going to a wedding."

In these days the political enthusiast lends his car to bring democracy to the polling booth, in those days it was his carriage.

"It was intimated his carriage carrying voters would be honourable and useful, which was accordingly sent, and our Servants to their honour came home sober, tho' many a Coachman, Postilion and Footman was scattered in the road."

They were great days when every man knew his betters, and the village curtsied to my lady. Harassed housewives will wonder at the easy assurance of Mrs. Montagu who, coming to the help of a poor curate, "placed" his daughter, remarking, "She is too light, too giddy for a servant, but time and experience may mend her."

The overtures between Mrs. Montagu and Dr. Johnson were a little strained. They were carefully polite, but it is plain she thought him a boor, and Johnson thought her vain. It is obvious he would feel ill at ease in her palatial house in Portman Square, where she held receptions for six or seven hundred people. It was here she made the famous room decorated with feathers, immortalized by Cowper.

> *The birds put off their feathery hue*
> *To dress a room for Montagu.*
> *The Peacock sends his heavenly dyes,*
> *His rainbows and his starry eyes.*

At Sandleford she made many alterations, turning with some qualms the ancient chapel into a dining-room. She got an Archbishop to give it his benediction to salve her conscience, and ease her palate. Her devotion to Sandleford was very real, if seasonal. Returning from Paris in 1776, she wrote to a friend:

"From a gay Parisian Dame visiting the Beau Monde, and conversing with the Beaux Esprits of the Academies, I am at once metamorphosed into a plain Country Farmeress. I have the same love for my pigs, pride in my potatoes, solicitude for my Poultry, care of my wheat, attention to my barley, and application to the regulation of the dairy as formerly."

She gave rustic parties as well as elegant ones, entertaining to beer and supper fifty haymakers with their families. She had a natural pride in her estate, sitting snugly on a slope, with a prospect of the downs, a singing stream, a bridge and a Tudor inn beyond her gates. But her eye was always on the great world. "The Duchess of Montagu is come to Town much mended by the Bath waters. The Duchess of Buccleugh has the proper sloping kind of shape, which promises great joy to the noble family, and in a short time."

Mr. Montagu died aged eighty-four in 1775. It had not been a love match, but they were very happy together. Then for

twenty-five more years lively Mrs. Montagu settled down to
enjoyable widowhood, which lasted until 1800, when she died,
aged eighty.

She had made the best of both worlds, town and the country,
enjoyed intelligent society, employed the best architects and
garden designers, and had taken the full flavour out of life on
ten thousand pounds a year in a century when the pound had
real value. Sir Joshua Reynolds painted her, and we might
agree with her epitaph in saying she "might be justly deemed
an ornament to her sex and country."

VI

As one enters Speenhamland a turning off the Bath Road,
before one comes to the clock-house, leads to Shaw House. The
parish, which comprises two villages, Shaw and Donnington,
lies on the slope of the Lambourn valley not far from its junction with the Kennet. Let us go to Shaw House and Donnington
Castle. They tell us a story of wars in their past, but to-day
they epitomize the beauty of the peaceful English scene. Shaw
House was built in 1581 by Thomas Dolman, a successful Newbury clothier. He made a great fortune with a factory in Northbrook Street. Evidently his retirement threw a number of people out of work, which gave rise to the lament:

> *Lord have mercy on us miserable sinners!*
> *Thomas Dolman has built a new house, and has*
> *turned away all his spinners.*

To this Dolman retorted by carving Greek and Latin inscriptions on the frieze of the house, the point of which must have
been lost upon his illiterate employees.

The house itself is a noble example of its period, built in
red brick in the form of an H, with porches on either side,
gabled in the third storey and lit by magnificent stone-mullion
windows. On the calm sunny day of July when I first saw it,

serene beyond its great gates, set back behind wide lawns, looking towards the stream with its bridge, mill house, and the valley where Newbury lies, it was impossible to believe that once the noise of fierce battle roared about its walls, and men fell in a death grapple on its garden ramparts. A later Thomas Dolman, who had inherited this Elizabethan mansion, was a zealous Royalist, and during the second Battle of Newbury, on a Sunday morning, October 27th, 1644, the house, fortified by Dolman, bore the brunt of the Cromwellian attack. The garden on the east side was the scene of a desperate fight, with the dead piled up on the ramparts, and afterwards the owner proudly took for a motto:

> *King and law*
> *Shouts Dolman of Shaw.*

In an upper bay window is an inscription marking a bullet hole and stating that while Charles I was dressing on the morning of the battle, someone fired a shot through the window, narrowly missing the royal target. Four old cannon captured in this fray line the south front of the house. After the battle, the King retired on Donnington Castle, in the belief that he had lost the battle, whereas the Royalists were in a strong position. It was a fatal decision which may have lost Charles the Civil War and all its consequences. His retreat to Donnington Castle heartened the dismayed Parliamentarians.

From Donnington Castle he went to join Prince Rupert in Bath. Both sides afterwards claimed the victory, and unfortunate Newbury, as after the first battle a year earlier, had the expense of burying the numerous dead. It is said the Dolman's motto arose through "King and Law" having been agreed upon as the password on the eve of the battle, and that young Thomas Dolman announced it to the Army by the command and in the presence of the King. With Dolman at his side the King fought hand to hand in the gardens of Shaw House, the last English King to fight in person.

It is a far cry from the noise of that battle to the peace of to-day. The churchyard adjoins the grounds of Shaw House, and beyond stretches a park towards Donnington Castle. From the old churchyard, through the lich-gate, one has a glimpse of a silver stream, lush meadows, and the wooded uplands of the Lambourn valley.

There is nothing exceptional in the church, except that it has been a repository of local history. The spurs, sword, gauntlets and visored helmet of a Sir Thomas Dolman decorate his memorial on the left wall. His father, Thomas, had entertained Charles I and his Queen, and he in turn entertained Queen Anne in 1703, on her way from Bath, for which he was knighted.

The manor passed later to James, Duke of Chandos, whose widow lies buried in the church. This was the Duke who was the target of Swift and Pope. Their satires on him were merciless. Dr. Johnson accused him of too great a fondness for pomp and show. He had received his dukedom from George I. Swift quarrelled with him and wrote:

> *James Brydges and the Dean had long been friends;*
> *James is beduked; of course the friendship ends;*
> *Be sure, the Dean deserves a sharp rebuke,*
> *For knowing James, to boast he knows the duke.*
> *Yet since just Heaven the duke's ambition mocks,*
> *Since all he got by fraud is lost by stocks,*
> *His wings are clipped, he tries no more in vain*
> *With bands of fiddlers to extend his team.*
> *Since he can no more build, and plant and revel,*
> *The duke and dean seem near upon a level.*

The lampooned duke copied his predecessor at Shaw House in the matter of a bequest. Sir Thomas Dolman, in his will dated 1710, left ten shillings a year for a sermon to be preached on his birthday. Either the sermon rate went up, or the Duke thought he would have a better or longer one, for he left by his will of

1735, "at the request of Cassandra his duchess," twenty shillings for a birthday sermon.

When I asked the sexton if the birthday sermons were still preached, he said he did not know, but that the sermons the parson preached were good ones (whether ten-shilling or twenty-shilling ones), which proved him a tactful sexton. He obliged me by showing me the grave of a rector who had lived to be ninety-two, John Horatio Nelson, a relative of the great admiral.

Donnington Castle is just a pleasant walk along the valley. It is a picturesque ruin, but the gateway and its twin towers, with a few rooms in the tower, are still standing. From this gatehouse the layout of the whole castle, with its bastioned walls, can still be traced. The view from the embattled turrets is superb, and one realizes, at once, how it dominated the countryside. Rudolf, who accompanied me on this occasion, declared it was "a satisfactory *Schloss*," and when I pressed him for the reason for his qualified praise, he said a good *Schloss* should be well up a mountain. "But you have no mountains, so no English *Schloss* is a real *Schloss*," he added, patronizingly. But his estimate rose when he discovered it possessed a dungeon, the inalienable asset of every true *Schloss*.

It was built, under licence from the King in 1386, by Sir Richard Abberbury, who refounded the delightful almshouses down by the bridge. He sold it in 1415 to Thomas Chaucer, the son of Geoffrey the poet, and butler to Richard II. It is sad to record the fact that all legends declaring that this was Geoffrey Chaucer's castle, or that he ever lived in it, or planted the oak tree called Chaucer's Oak, are completely false. Chaucer died in 1400. In vain, therefore, does a later poet, Miss Mitford, apostrophize the castle:

> *and wipe from Chaucer's bowers*
> *The last rude touch of war!*

The ownership of the castle was settled upon Thomas
Chaucer's daughter and her husband. This Alice Chaucer married at the age of eleven Sir John Philip and was a widow
within a year. Constant widowhood seemed to be poor Alice's
lot. Later on she married Thomas Montagu, Earl of Salisbury.
He was killed in the blockade of Orleans in 1428, and his body,
boiled in oil, was shipped home for burial. His brother-in-arms,
the young William de la Pole, Earl of Suffolk, then took command, and later married Montagu's widow. Thus it came about
that Alice Chaucer lies to this day in Ewelme Church, a Duchess of Suffolk, in a splendid tomb, with the Order of the Garter
on her arm. Her husband, the Earl of Suffolk, created Duke of
Suffolk in 1448, seemed born to misfortune. He was captured
by Joan of Arc, and as a soldier lost for his country Maine,
Orleans, Anjou, Rouen and Bordeaux. This aroused the wrath
of the nation. He fled to France, but on May 2nd, 1450, his
ship was intercepted by the man o'-war *Nicholas* midway between Dover and Calais. "Bring up the duke on board," said
her commander, and as the unfortunate man stepped on to the
deck of the *Nicholas*, he was greeted with, "Welcome, traitor!"

For two days he was held in close confinement while the commander awaited orders. On the third day a cockboat came
alongside, with a block, an axe, and an executioner, to whom
Suffolk was immediately handed over and beheaded. Alice
Chaucer, mistress of Donnington Castle, was a widow for a
third time. She lived until 1475 and saw her son married to
the sister of Edward IV.

Her husband Suffolk had greatly strengthened and enlarged
their castle, which must have been a pleasant haven after being
a prisoner of the Maid of Orleans. It was soon forfeited to the
Crown, and thus came into the possession of Henry VIII, Edward VI, and subsequently Queen Elizabeth, who gave it to
Charles Howard, Earl of Nottingham, whose son, Lord Howard of Effingham, was the Lord High Admiral who defeated the
Spanish Armada. It is pleasant to think that after his great sea-

battles he enjoyed the tranquillity of the Berkshire landscape viewed from the turrets of this castle.

The castle makes no figure in history for almost another twenty years after the Admiral died, until 1644, when it was stoutly held for King Charles I by Sir John Boys. He had held the castle gallantly all through the first battle of Newbury, despite an attack by four thousand Parliamentary soldiers for twelve days. Having beaten down three of the towers, they demanded its surrender and received a defiant reply from Boys, "I have not learned yet to obey any other than my sovereign." Defied and defeated, the enemy withdrew. In the second battle of Newbury, 1644, the remains of the castle under Boys still dominated the road to the west, and it was here Charles retreated after his engagement at Shaw House. When the King had gone, Boys still defiantly held on. One day the whole Parliamentary army stood massed before the walls and Boys was peremptorily commanded to "deliver it up to them, or else they would not leave one stone upon another," to which the defender stoutly retorted, "I am not bound to repair the castle; but by God's help, I will keep the ground." For two months it was besieged in vain, then Charles came to its rescue. It capitulated finally only when news came of the King's surrender to the Scots, and the end seemed certain. Then stalwart Sir John marched out with his men, flags flying, drums beating, accorded full military honours by an admiring enemy. It was then demolished, except for the noble gateway we now see standing, flanked by its twin towers.

In recent years someone has tried living in it, and a gallant attempt has been made to create a *salle d'armes* and an upper reception-room. But the perilously winding stairs to the turrets, the lack of water, electric light, and other domestic refinements must have defeated the gallant attempt. Unlike Sir John Boys, it seems probable the last tenant suffered defeat at the hands of domestic servants, who, if oblivious of the stairs, must have been very conscious of the ghosts who haunted the ruined castle on nights when a cold wind whined around the battlements.

The old castle has had a companion near it for some centuries, Donnington Priory. Those who remember *Tom Brown's Schooldays* will recall the pride that Tom and his father, the Squire, took in the Berkshire landscape. It was from this old priory that young Tom set forth, in fiction, for his adventures at Rugby School, for it belonged to John Hughes, father of Thomas Hughes, author of the greatest classic among school tales.

When I asked the small boy who had conducted us to the Castle what his name was and he said Tom, I asked him his surname, hoping it might be Brown. Alas, it was White! But he had read the story, greatly to my surprise, and on my saying, "Then you're not Tom Brown," he retorted, brightly, "Oh, no, I'm not that Tom. I go to a better school here." I felt my guide well merited a shilling.

CHAPTER XVI

The Lively Lady of Benham

OUT OF NEWBURY, again on the road to Bath, we climb up the hill to Speen, which lies on a ridge between the Kennet and the Lambourn, running through beautiful valleys. This village is the Spinae of the Romans, but nothing now remains to mark their sojourn here. Speen Church is down in the valley, charmingly situated, but without any distinctive merit. It has a plaque by Canova, a memorial to the Margrave of Anspach.

And thereby hangs a story, fully known to Miss Whissitt; but we must mount the hill and travel a couple of miles farther along the road to Bath. There will then appear before the traveller, on the left, a pair of magnificent gates, with twin arches and rubricated pillars, and a drive leading down into a thickly wooded park. The well-kept sward before them, as well as the sturdy elegance of the gates themselves are a fitting introduction to Benham Place which lies, embraced in woods, facing the Berkshire Downs rising across the deep valley.

The fifth Earl of Berkeley, whose romance with Miss Cole, the butcher's daughter, we have followed at Cranford, had four sisters of whom one, Elizabeth, born in 1750, married, at seventeen, the sixth Lord Craven. This gentleman undoubtedly married a handful, though he had his own weakness for the fair sex. His wife complained that he disliked remaining longer than three weeks at a time in any one place. If this were so, it is certain Lady Craven thought three weeks too long, judging by her tireless wanderings.

Lord Craven was a descendant of that Lord Craven who employed a remarkable gentleman called Sir Balthazar Gerbier to build him a mansion at Hampstead Marshall, which lies across the valley, opposite Benham Place, and takes its name from the young hero of Newbury Castle. This Lord Craven had for his mistress the Queen of Bohemia (the Queen of Hearts), mother of Prince Rupert, who died in his town house in Drury Lane. He had a passion for building, and having pulled down Coombe Abbey, commissioned Sir Balthazar, a renowned miniature painter, to build him a mansion in the manner of Heidelberg Castle.

Sir Balthazar Gerbier's career was almost as fantastic as his name. He had come to England as an odd job man for the splendid Duke of Buckingham, for whom he collected pictures, arranged masques and revels. As a sideline he acted as ambassador, and rumour charged him with selling an English State secret to the Infanta for twenty thousand crowns. His fate trembled in the balance when Buckingham was assassinated, and but for this ill-chance he might have ousted Inigo Jones as the architect of the day. But he did not do badly, and at Hampstead Marshall he did grandiosely. He lived to see his Heidelbergian labours finished. He died in the house while visiting it in 1557, and lies buried in the church.

During his astonishing career he had raised troops, tried to form an academy, built houses, recommended Rubens to Queen Henrietta, gone on embassies for King Charles, and had himself and his family of ten painted by Van Dyck, a picture now one of the glories of Windsor Castle.

Within fifty years of its erection the house at Hampstead Marshall was burned to the ground, and nothing now exists of it except eight pairs of gate pillars, three in the park and four in the wall of the great garden. It is another pair that we see at the entrance to Benham Place. The sixth Lord Craven built this latter place, or rather Lady Craven, with her husband's permission. It was a stately mansion with an Ionic

façade, overlooking a lake fed by the Kennet. It once had a
wooden bridge "in the Chinese taste," as Archibald Robertson
records, and a right of way which became such a bone of con-
tention that years later the lady went into exile in a high
dudgeon.

Lord Craven's wife, married at seventeen, bore him seven
children. In her copious diaries she recorded that he was proud
and stupid, while she was beautiful and clever, and that eventually, after thirteen years of married life, he declined to live
with her, settled £1,500 a year on her, and advised her to take
herself off. But this she had done already, according to the
scandalmongers of Bath.

That she was indiscreet there is no doubt. She had a passion
for amateur theatricals and scribbling. Beautiful, well-born,
she was typical of those eighteenth-century butterflies who
sipped the honey of the earth and gave nothing in exchange
save a history of extravagant instability. Unhappily she did
not confine her passion for romance to her mediocre verses.
There was a much discussed affair with the Duc de Guines,
French Ambassador at the Court of St. James. This brought
the matrimonial quarrel to a head. The world, however, did
not really care, and even censorious Dr. Johnson paid visits
to "the beautiful, gay, and fascinating Lady Craven," and
Horace Walpole wrote her verses. After all, in comparison
with her brother, the Earl of Berkeley, her irregularities
seemed feeble.

Lord Craven at one period was undoubtedly fond of her.
He built her a theatre at Benham, in which she acted in one
of her own plays, afterwards produced at Drury Lane with a
prologue spoken by Sheridan. Romney was delighted to paint
her; she was always good copy for the newspapers.

When the break came she left Benham Place, took with her
the youngest son, Keppel, to whom she was devoted, and settled in a house at Versailles. One of her visitors here was the

Margrave of Anspach, a German princeling, who was the
nephew of Queen Caroline and of Frederick the Great. She
visited his Court, where his wife, the Margravine, was living,
and amused it with her theatricals. But Lady Craven found installed there the Margrave's *chère amie* the famous actress,
Mademoiselle Clairon, who at once took umbrage at the presence of this rival. The mistress of many years standing, fifty-
five years old, naturally lost to a lively, young and beautiful
woman of rank. Lady Craven drove her rival from the field
and reigned for four years at the royal villa. She had the
royal theatre at her disposal, wrote plays for it, and acted in
them. While there she angled to get the Order of the Garter
for her bovine Margrave, without success.

Prior to her advent at the Margrave's Court, she set the
world by the ears with a grand tour taken in company with a
Mr. Vernon. She visited St. Petersburg and was received by
the Empress Catherine at her Court, having been preceded by
the amazing and bigamous Duchess of Kingston. She found
St. Petersburg "a very congenial asylum." From this capital
they went to Moscow, and thence to Constantinople, no mean
achievement for a lady of fashion in 1786. Here she remarked
that "the dresses seem calculated to set off to the best advantage everything that is hideous, and destroy everything that is
beautiful." She went to the divan and sat down with a Pasha
who had a tame lion instead of a spaniel. She visited the
Tauride and was fêted there "for since Iphigenia I am the first
Lady heard of in that Country."

She came home via Varna, Bulgaria, and Bucharest, where
the Prince of Valachia gave her an Arab horse, then Vienna,
with a call at Anspach, and on to England, taking with her
"the proud satisfaction" of having pleased the Margravine.
"Your courtiers," she wrote to the Margrave, "have assured
me that I am the only person they ever saw her like, and she
told them the sound of my voice did her good." One wonders!

II

The Margrave having decided to sell his Principality to Frederick the Great, he visited the Court at Berlin and took Lady Craven with him. They felt compelled, though reluctant, to recognize her, and all tongues wagged. The Margrave disposed of his inheritance for £100,000 a year, a bargain not honoured after his death, and, highly satisfied with the deal, the pair returned to Anspach, where they were greeted with the news that the Margravine was dead. A little later they descended on London, to find it would not receive them. So off they went on their travels again. While in Lisbon news came of the obliging death of Lord Craven, within nine months of that of the Margravine.

The erring couple were now free to marry, and they lost no time. Craven had died on September 26th, 1791, and they were married in the British Embassy chapel on October 30th. There was a galaxy of foreign nobles present, French dukes, Spanish dukes, Portuguese dukes, but the English were conspicuously absent. They now set out for England to live in a style of magnificence. The Margrave had lost his wife and sold his principality. He was extremely rich and complaisant. The new Margravine was beautiful, energetic, and determined to shine.

They took a house in Fulham which had been lavishly decorated by the egregious Lord Melcombe, or "Sillybub" as the rich sycophant was derisively called. It had a gallery eighty-two feet long, converted into a marble ballroom by the Margravine. A small theatre was built, and Brandenburg House, as it was called, was ready for the conquest of society by the wife of His Serene Highness Christian Frederick Charles Alexander, Margrave of Brandenburg, Anspach and Bayreuth. Two years later the Emperor of Germany created her Princess Berkeley, a title which George III firmly declined to acknowl-

edge. The Margravine was mortified but she was not subdued.
She reigned at Brandenburg House, where we find her nephew,
Grantley Berkeley, the buck we have met at Cranford, at
what he called "the resort of the gay world of both sexes." In
1799 her son, the new Lord Craven, sold to her Benham Place,
inherited from his father. So back she went to it, with a new
husband. An era of splendid hospitality and lavish entertainments began. The Margrave soon developed a preference for
country life, and his wife set up a playhouse in the grounds.
She wrote ten plays, all produced in one of her two theatres.

The Margravine of Anspach soon established herself as the
Bountiful Lady of Newbury, with her distinguished, royal, and
silent husband in the background. Newbury was a little non-
plussed by a Prussian Princess and Margravine, born in England, "disguised with an immense quantity of rouge and burnt
cork on her eyebrows," as a friend remarked, but her charm,
infectious gaiety, talent and titles soon overcame the town. If
any hesitated, the generous donations to all social and charitable causes won them over. She was, whatever she was,
irresistible.

They had only just settled in Benham, one of the finest man-
sions in Berkshire, whose park wall borders a mile of the Bath
Road, when the Napoleonic invasion threatened England. The
Margravine in person presented a handsome standard to the
Newbury troop of Yeomanry, assembled in the Market Place.
The curate of Newbury, Mrs. Montagu's kinsman, solemnly
blessed the standard. A public dinner took place in the Town
Hall, with the Margravine in the seat of honour. A specially
written song, sung by the composer, evoked loud cheers from
the replete assembly.

> And if a Winchcombe could excite
> Our gen'rous sires to arm,
> Much more shall Anspach now invite,
> Possess'd of every charm.

which showed the Margravine of Anspach was one up on Jack of Newbury. In a quarrel a year earlier over a right-of-way with a local Colonel who had now come to heel, she did not hesitate to assert herself, declaring she would oblige any residents near her provided "they don't forget *what she is,* and the obligations the whole nation as well as Berkshire are under to the best of princes, and most excellent of men, her present husband."

What the most excellent of men ever did for England, except letting his wife spend his money here, was never clear. Her devotion suffered a great blow in 1806 when the Margrave, fourteen years her senior, died at Benham. The funeral was elaborate even for the times. His Serene Highness Christian Charles Frederick Alexander, Margrave of Brandenburg, Anspach and Bayreuth, Duke of Prussia, Count of Sayn, etc., was buried in Speen Church. The procession was headed by two mutes, twenty-five gentlemen, two by two, with silk scarves and hatbands, a Groom of the Chamber, mounted on a horse dressed with black velvet and escutcheons, carrying the Crown and Cushion. The coffin, covered in crimson velvet, was ornamented with gilt nails, crowns, and lined with white satin. The Margrave's horse, put in mourning, followed with a groom. There were eight coaches and six, containing, among other mourners, two clergymen, two medical men, six pall-bearers, the Margravine, Lord Craven, and the local gentry. Four footmen in state liveries brought up the tail.

Did the Margravine, one wonders, have any misgivings as her spouse was interred in Speen churchyard? For the Resurrectionists were abroad in the land. This was the name given to the body-snatchers, who maintained the supply of corpses for dissection. As much as twenty pounds was paid for a "healthy" specimen. The district of Newbury was a favourite nocturnal hunting-ground of these ghouls. To thwart them, deep interments became the vogue, with a stone of great weight clamped to the bottom of the coffin.

Even so the Resurrectionists were successful. They simply opened the ground at the head of the coffin, forced it, and drew out the body. Having considerably removed the death trappings and replaced them, the body went into a sack and on to a spring cart *en route* for the dissecting theatre. Speen churchyard itself suffered this desecration, a late Mr. Pearce, the local workhouse-master, having vanished from his coffin. There might be Resurrectionists with a special taste for royal bodies, but at Speen this best of princes and most excellent of men was interred, whatever the risk.

The bereaved Margravine, who as a solace received personal property of the value of £150,000, devised an elaborate monument to her husband. It was a splendid cenotaph at a cost of £5,000, and was for many years a familiar landmark to travellers on the Bath Road. A Mr. Villebois, who bought Benham later, and had no reverence for Anspach memorials, tore it down and sold the materials by auction. The monument had a memorial plaque by Canova comprising a medallion of the Margrave and a representation of his widow weeping over his urn. This was sent to Speen Church and erected near the place of burial. But it has fared almost as badly as the cenotaph. The Vicars of Speen do not seem to have liked the Margrave or the Margravine, judging by the scant courtesy shown to the monument. It was shorn of its dedication: "Sacred to the Memory of the best of Sovereigns and men," and became, on arrival at Speen Church, coldly: "In Memory of," since the Vicar had grave doubts as to the Margrave's orthodoxy. It was subsequently torn from its place near the body and exiled to the obscurity of the lower wall of the church tower. Here I found it, a pleasing work by Canova, in gloom and neglect, and then only because I chanced upon the Vicar in the church and asked for directions. It was graciously given, but with the chilling observation, "I can't think why people want to put up things like that." Poor Margravine, poor best of princes and most excellent of men!

A widow, now fifty-five, it might be expected the Margravine of Anspach, Princess Berkeley, would settle down to mourn her spouse and tend his grave. She had idolized him, for king or husband, she could not exalt him sufficiently. But no, within eighteen months she suddenly appeared at Anspach to take possession, as sole heiress, of her husband's properties. Under an agreement with the former King of Prussia, she received an annuity of £2,000, payable after the decease of her husband. This was ratified by the King's successor, but not a shilling of it was paid. A Rothschild offered to make an advance, upon arrears. She declined, hoping, and keeping her faith in His Majesty, in vain. But she was a wealthy woman. The Anspach plate was said to be worth £80,000.

Two years after her return to Benham, this tireless lady projected a newspaper entitled *Courier de Brandenburgh*. A first number appeared, resplendent, with the Anspach crown and eagle. It had no successor. She was still busy concerning her husband's monument and place of burial, and tried for his remains to be removed "to the more stately tomb-house of the Berkeleys in the cathedral which owed its existence to their piety" at Bristol. But nothing came of this.

The wretched squabble over a public pathway on her estate arose again. She would brook no compromise, and declared her abdication from Benham and the neighbourhood. The declaration had a royal air, "I take this method of assuring the people of Newbury and all the worthy Yeomanry of the County of Berks, that I only wish I had now ten times as much landed property as I have; to have ten times the means and opportunities of proving my attachment to it."

She left, nevertheless, taking with her her beloved son Keppel. Benham was to know her no more. Ferdinand IV, restored King of the Two Sicilies, an old friend, gave her two acres of land at Naples, and here, on a beautiful spur of Posilipo, commanding a magnificent view of the Bay, she built the Villa Craven. Here Lady Blessington visited her in 1823, and was enraptured with it. Its mistress, now seventy-two, had lost all the beauty immortalized in the portraits by Romney, Reynolds and Gainsborough. She occupied her time writing her *Autobiographical Memoirs*, published in her seventy-sixth year, and in gardening. A visitor who had long known her, wrote home:

"I have seen her, a few years before her death, working in her garden, spade in hand, in very coarse and singular attire, a desiccated, antiquated piece of mortality, remarkable for vivacity, realizing the idea of a galvanized Egyptian mummy."

This is too unkind, and has no reverence for age. The first flush of the romance, the beauty of the flesh had gone, but as her autobiography shows, her loyalties remained, above all her devotion to the long-dead Margrave. She died in her seventy-eighth year, at her villa, in the presence of her son. Gardening passion hurried her end, for she persisted in digging on a wet day, and caught a chill. She was buried in the British cemetery at Naples. The wit, the fluent pen, the beauty, rank and passion had all come to a little dust. There remained the affection of her children which, through all the vicissitudes of her life, she had never lost.

III

There is nothing to detain us between Benham Place and Hungerford. The road curves, grows prettier and more rural. Near Halfway, so called because it is half-way on the journey between Bath and London, a sham castle, once a toll house, looms up on the horizon, commanding this road. It is quaint, and as beautiful as plaster Gothic, castellated, ever can be. Hungerford now begins to appear beyond a growth of villas, tea-gardens, and garages. In the town, which stands on the border of Berkshire and Wiltshire, we cross a bridge over our companion, the Kennet, and pull up at *The Bear*, which juts out into the road to remind us of its ancient importance.

The moment I entered a ladylike voice said, "Hello!" I turned and saw a parrot and a page-boy. The bird and not the boy had greeted me. Polly, completely untethered, must have derived literary ambitions from the notable scribes who have stayed there, for she straightway walked on to my arm and picked out of my pocket the fountain-pen with which I have written this and a score of books. An alarmed Boots immediately dashed forward, informing me that the bird had a passion not to write but to chew. The pen recovered, my next surprise was the sight of that rare object, a Parliament clock.

My companion Rudolf could not understand my intense interest in the clock. It seemed to him that its face was out of proportion to its body. I explained that this was deliberately so. In 1766 the Government, exercising its ingenuity, brought in a window-tax and a timepiece tax. Both of these, according to Mrs. Montagu, must have been due to the revolutionary colonists in America. Since people objected to paying taxes on their windows and watches, they blocked up their windows, and put away their watches. Enterprising tradespeople and inn-keepers, seeking to attract customers, bought clocks made with specially large dials and numbering, and put them in their public windows, a useful display much appreciated.

The clock tax was so futile and unpopular that it was repealed within a year, hence the rarity of these clocks. Invariably the dials are embellished with period decorations, and the good honest faces, with their bold lettering, are as attractive as they are quaint. The explanation quite satisfied Rupert, derisive after the sight of that Halfway toll-house *Schloss*.

But there was true excitement in store for him after lunch. Did we know, asked the Boots, that Hungerford was famous for its trout and cray-fishing?

Hungerford cray-fish, match me if you can,
There's no such crawlers in the o-ce-an!

runs a local rhyme. Old Fuller wrote, "Good and great trouts
are found in the river of Kennet near Hungerford; they are
found in their perfection in the month of May, and yearly decline with the buck. Being come to his full growth, he decays
in goodness, not greatness, and thrives in his head till his
death." John o' Gaunt granted the right of free fishing to the
inhabitants as far back as 1366, but the charter was stolen or
lost some two hundred years later. The rights were then
bought back.

Producing a large slice of bread, the Boots led us to a bridge
behind *The Bear* and we leaned over the swift streamlet above
the trout farm, and watched the fish scurrying and gobbling
our bread. As we lingered over the parapet, above the clear,
weedy stream, feeding the trout, I thought of another trout
stream, the Traun above Gmunden, with Rudolf slipping off
his shirt and leather shorts and braving the icy stream, sleek
and adept as an otter in those treacherous currents, to disentangle the Englishman's line. Rudolf must have known my
thoughts, for with a sad smile he looked at me and said, "I
wonder who fishes the Traun now the English don't come,"
and a shrug of his slim shoulders expressed all of Austria's
tragedy. I could see again his green Tyrolean hat with the
"flies" stuck in the band. In another week he would vanish
from this exile's refuge, to seek a new life in far Tanganyika.

The motorist to Bath is apt to miss Hungerford's High
Street for it lies beyond the fork to Salisbury, over the canal
bridge. Just over the bridge I found a perfect bow-windowed
hairdresser's shop and waited for an old gentleman to come
out, who perchance had had his peruque curled or been bled,
but in vain. Two houses here have amusing upstair and down-
stair entrances off the street and bridge—which do they use,
one for dining and one for sleeping?

Hungerford is at its gayest during its Hocktide festival. A
jury is chosen out of a hat on Easter Tuesday and is summoned to a Hocktide Court on the following Tuesday, which

is known as Tutti Day. While this Court assembles at the Town Hall, an ancient and battered brass horn, said to have been presented by John o' Gaunt, is blown from the balcony. Numerous ancient rules are then read out, three bailiffs are appointed to look after the Fisheries, and two as Ale Tasters. In former days there were also two Searchers and Sealers of Leather, with two Tasters of Flesh and Fish.

After this the Tutti-men set out bearing long staves bedecked with streamers of royal blue ribbon, and bouquets of hot-house flowers. Their name is said to be derived from a West of England word, "tutty," meaning nosegay. The duty of the Tutti-men is to collect a penny from each person in every house. They are accompanied by a man with a basket of oranges. Any lady refusing to contribute has to submit to being kissed. On each of the staves is a spike with an orange on it, this being presented to the lady kissed, and another orange put in its place. It would seem obvious that the appearance of the stave bearer decides whether the lady decides to have an orange or give the penny. The Tutti-man is at the mercy of this decision.

At the conclusion of this ancient and, we hope, pleasant foolery, the Court assembles for lunch, and oranges and hot coppers are thrown to the children in the street. A brave mixture called "ye ancient Plantagenet Punch," doubtfully said to be made from a recipe of John o' Gaunt's day, is drunk. Newcomers to the ceremony, called colts, are shod by having nails driven into their feet, when they are expected to contribute to the cost of the aforesaid Punch. In the evening there is a Banquet, at which the Constable presides, seated in an old chair with the horn suspended over his head between the two Tutti-poles. At the stroke of midnight the immortal memory of John o' Gaunt is drunk, and after *Auld Lang Syne* and *God Save the King*, the horn is blown again and the Constable leaves the hall to be carried in a chair to his home, when Hungerford settles down again into its usual quiet. Who started this elaborate rigmarole no one knows, but it is now honoured in tradition and provides Hungerford with a happy festival.

Like all old towns its records are deeply interesting. It had a stocks, pillory, whipping-post and ducking-stool for offenders. It regularly whipped men and women in public, the cost of flagellation varying from twopence, in 1658, for whipping "one, Dorothy Miller," to one shilling, in 1676. But let it be recorded that fourpence was given in 1678 to a poor man that was whipped. The public executioner named Savage received five shillings "for his extraordinary paines this yeare and whippinge of several persons."

Hungerford's position on the road from the West resulted in a great number of vagabonds and destitute travellers being thrown on the mercy of the town. In 1660, for instance, it relieved the daughter of a merchant who had lost everything in a shipwreck, three ladies whose husbands had lost £900 by the "Turkes," some "pore seamen who had been captives to them," a gentleman who had fought for the King "twenty years beyond the sea," and a "pore minister from Ireland and two Frenchmen." In 1667 there are traces of the Dutch war, in relief given "to six prisoners out of Holland" and to a "pore surgion" with them. But who was the proud hidalgo for whom the Constable paid 1s. 7d. for a "Spanish lord's lodging and diet"? Poor creatures, for a brief moment they stand illumined in the light of charity, and pass thence into the darkness of Eternity.

The trout fed, we returned to *The Bear,* and talked with the wife of mine host, a successor in office to that Robert Brabon who kept house here in 1537 and gave evidence against two highwaymen who stayed at *The Bear* after committing highway robbery. Three years later Henry VIII settled this hostelry upon Queen Anne of Cleves, as part of her dowry, and, later, on her ill-fated successor, Catherine Howard. It was inevitable that Queen Elizabeth should have slept here, and

while not doubting the authenticity of the claim I firmly refused to view the bedroom of that ceaselessly itinerant sleeper.
No wonder her coachman died here in 1601, worn out, poor
fellow.

The real event in this history of Hungerford took place on
December 6th, 1688. The whole of England was in a state of
turmoil. King James II, by his attack on the liberties of his
people, and his determination to reintroduce the Roman Catholic religion, contrary to his solemn vows, had provoked a
revolution. The King's son-in-law, William, Prince of Orange,
had landed in England, and, welcomed by a powerful army of
revolutionaries, had, on December 6th, advanced as far as
Hungerford on his road to London. Here he rested at *The Bear
Inn*. Fighting had broken out at Reading between King James's
imported Irish troops and the revolutionaries, resulting in a
complete defeat of the King's mercenaries. On the morning of
the 8th, the King's three commissioners, headed by Lord Halifax, arrived to treat with Prince William, bearing a private
letter from the King, now in a state of panic. Macaulay has
recorded the scene at *The Bear*.

"They expressed a hope that the Prince would favour them with a
private audience, but they were informed that he had resolved to hear
them and answer them in public. They were ushered into his bedchamber, where they found him surrounded by a crowd of noblemen
and gentlemen. Halifax put into William's hands a letter from the
King and retired. William opened this letter and seemed unusually
moved. It was the first letter which he had received from his father-
in-law since they had become avowed enemies."

For once in his life the taciturn Dutchman was moved.

"He requested the Lords and gentlemen whom he had convoked
on this occasion to consult together, unrestrained by his presence, as
to the answer which ought to be returned. To himself, however, he
reserved the power of deciding in the last resort, after hearing their
opinion. He then left them and retired to Littlecote Hall, a manor-
house situated about two miles off, and renowned down to our own
times, not more on account of its venerable architecture and furniture

than on account of a horrible and mysterious crime that was perpetrated there in the days of the Tudors."

The events which rapidly followed that meeting of William
of Orange and the Commissioners, resulted shortly in the flight
of James II to France, and the end of the reigning house of
Stuart in England. It gave rise eventually to a series of Jacobite
risings, including the ill-fated and romantic episode of Bonnie
Prince Charlie.

The Bear Inn had seen other historic occasions; Charles I
had made it his headquarters from November 16th to the 19th
in 1643. When the eighteenth-century traffic was increased,
with all the Fashion flocking to Bath, it touched the height of
its prosperity.

Until 1744 the road to Bath had been through Chilton Foliat,
past Littlecote Park, to Ramsbury and Marlborough. In 1744
an Act was passed for repairing the turnpike road from Newbury to Marlborough, and, by arrangement with the Duke of
Somerset, the road was now carried past Froxfield, and through
the Savernake Forest, the only forest in the kingdom held by a
private person. By this road went the royal Georges, the great
Earl of Chatham, Lord Nelson, visiting his father at Bath, and
the elegant Beau Brummell, all known to my host at *The Bear*.
Pepys, naturally, had been a forerunner of all these. He was
here in 1688, complimentary to the trout and rude to the town.
"So came to Hungerford where very good troutes, eels and
cray fish. Dinner, a mean town."

And ere we quit *The Bear Inn* let us recall that great wit
and practical joker, the cleric, Sydney Smith. He had a friend,
a pluralist, at a time when it was not scandalous for a parson
to farm out several livings among semi-starved curates. On
hearing that his friend was arriving at *The Bear Inn* he ordered
for him, in advance, seven dinners, telling the landlord to prepare for a dean, an archdeacon, a canon, a prebendary, a
rector, a vicar, and a perpetual curate!

CHAPTER XVII

The Littlecote Drama

SINCE WE ARE SENSIBLE MOTORISTS, in no hurry to arrive, and prepared to accept any delay that can offer adequate justification, we will take, for a part of the way, the valley road, following the gentle Kennet, which was the earlier Bath Road. To the traveller of the early eighteenth century this was known as the "Ramsbury Narrow Way" to Bath. When the new road from Hungerford to Marlborough was opened in 1744, the conservative spirits stuck to the old one, although it was three miles longer. There is a complaint of a coachowner that his man would drive the coach the old way, despite the awful surface, as a rhyme celebrated:

> From Hungerford we swiftly cross'd the plain,
> Too soon we came to the destructive Lane.
> O fatal way! Here rocks and craggy stones
> Our limbs distorted, and unlock'd our bones;
> The long-worn axle to the coach, alack,
> Here gave a dismal, unexpected crack.

Nothing would deter the conservative coachman. His passengers dwindled away, going by the new road through Savernake Forest, until finally, in despair, the owner dismissed the ancient, and replaced him with a driver who took the new way.

The old road leads us to Chilton Foliat, Ramsbury, and eventually to Mildenhall, almost a suburb of Marlborough, which was the Roman settlement of Cunetio, where five

Roman roads met. But as far as Mildenhall we will not go, although this quiet valley road, now forgotten by the world, is as lovely as any that England can show, with its old mills, cottages, lush meadows, wooded slopes and little bridges over the weedy stream.

The first right turn along the Bath Road out of Hungerford brings us in a couple of miles to Chilton Foliat, beautiful as its name. We are now in Wiltshire, famous for its great rolling downs, its sheep, bacon, cheese and cloth. But as yet no downs are in view. Here by the little bridge is a perfect Gray's *Elegy* village. The river becomes almost a lake, bordered by cottages with their flowery patches of gardens. Through the old lich-gate, along an avenue of limes, we come to the medieval church. It is a place of angels carved by long dead craftsmen; two winged ones greet us at the door, inside there are twelve more with shields painted in red and gold. This is not the end of the angelic cohort, they perch on the pews and the choir stalls, and are usefully employed to bear up the chancel roof, decorated with the familiar Tudor rose, also in colour.

This is one of those happy places where everything is just right. There is the great Elizabethan Manor house, Littlecote, with an ancient family, and a dark legend. There is an amiable river full of scurrying fish. The old church, the lich-gate, the carved font, the lime avenue, the trimmed lawns, the crusader knight, Sir Sampson Foliat, lying on his stone tomb, who founded the thirteenth-century church, all these things are to be found in this village.

On the sunny July afternoon I entered there, it supplied, as correct furnishing, two oldest inhabitants, bearded, leaning on sticks as they warmed their bones in the sun, a tiny urchin wheeling his tinier sister in a potato box, a patient gentleman by the bridge, a sexton cutting the churchyard grass, an old lady in a bonnet tying up her hollyhocks, and a cat riding on the back of a great bay mare. Let time stand still, I thought, here is perfection. No mid-European Jew making an English historical film in America's Hollywood could create a better "set" than this at hand. And across those meadows where the Kennet flows, backed by the grave woods clothing the dark hillside, stands Littlecote Park, gabled, mullion windowed, sinister in its ancient beauty, with its dark legend of the sixteenth century.

The Great Hall of Littlecote, again, would delight the Hollywood impresario. It is a perfect setting for *The Ghost Goes West*. If legend is not false, the ghost has not gone west but has remained faithful to the home site, and the haunted chamber. The Hall is hung with pikes, helmets, cuirasses, and leather jerkins, relics of the Civil War, and of the Royalists who made the house their rendezvous. Its owner, Colonel Alexander Popham, whose suit of armour hangs over a door, led Popham's Horse in many a gallant encounter.

And here in this hall, on Sunday December 9th, 1688, the Commissioners dined and met William of Orange again, come on from *The Bear*. The spurred boots of Peers, Generals and Bishops clanged on its stone floor. The trimmer, Lord Halifax, King James's representative, encountered his old friend Bishop Burnet, a William of Orange man. "Do you wish to get the King into your power?" asked Halifax. "Not at all, we would not do the least harm to his person," replied Burnet. "And if he were to go away?" asked Halifax, diplomatically. "There is nothing so much to be wished," said Burnet. The tip was given. King James slunk away by night. The throne changed hands, bloodshed was averted.

In the closing years of the fifteenth century Littlecote was built by the Darells. History has little to say concerning them until, in the reign of Queen Elizabeth, one of the Darells, "Wild Will," as he was called, found himself arraigned by the Attorney-General, Sir John Popham, according to the story. Seven miles distant there is the village of Great Shefford, which has the distinction of having had a vicar, about this time, John Prince, the founder of Princeton. Here one dark

night a messenger on horseback who arrived to summon a
midwife, declaring that a Lady Knyvett, of Charlton, near by,
was in child labour. But he insisted on blindfolding the midwife before taking her on the pillion behind him on the journey. He then took a devious route so that the alarmed woman
began to be very suspicious. Finally they came to a great house
where the midwife performed her office for a young masked
lady. No sooner was the child born than in strode a wild-looking
man "having upon him a gowne of black velvett," who, without a word, took the child from the midwife and threw it on a
blazing fire in the ante-room, crushing it with his boot into
the flaming logs. A horrible story this, which Scott, the novelist,
took much pains to collect from local gossip when the legend
had been current for over two hundred years.

The story then continues that the midwife contrived to cut
away a piece of the bed-curtains, and on being blindfolded
again counted the stairs as she was led away. Immediately
upon her return home she went to a magistrate, was taken
back to Littlecote, which she suspected of being the house,
where the hole in the curtain corresponded with her fragment,
and the stairs were the same number as she had counted.

Darell was tried for murder before Popham—whom Scott
erroneously makes Lord Chief Justice, which he was not until
thirteen years later—and to the public fury he was acquitted.
It was said Popham had received Littlecote Park as a bribe
to procure a *noli prosequi*. Legend again lets the imagination
run, and it was said Wild Will Darell came to a violent end.
He was seen on horseback flying down the road, pursued by
the apparition of a burning infant, and that he met his death
by being thrown from his horse while in flight.

Now, however lurid and fantastic the legend may seem, embellished by the rustic imagination, it is not wholly fiction. It
is difficult at this distant day to disentangle rumour from fact,
but certain things have been established. Darell had an unpleasant reputation as a seducer. He had, according to the story,

one mistress at Littlecote, and it is known there was another, a somewhat terrifying lady, an elderly charmer, Lady Anne Hungerford, whom Wild Will had seduced from her husband. Her letters, addressed to "deare Darrell" are still extant, and in them she complained of having been accused of adultery and trying to poison her husband, charges that seem well founded, despite her hope of being acquitted of such "vill and abomynabell practisces."

Darell, it is known, as well as his amatory excesses, got heavily into debt, and had a passion for litigation that ruined his estate. He offered in 1583 a sum of £5,000 to Lord Chancellor Bromley, to be his "goode friend"; so that he knew how to bribe the Law. Again, at the beginning of the nineteenth century a deposition came to light, wherein Mrs. Barnes, a midwife of Great Shefford, made a statement to a magistrate, a cousin of Darell's, in which she narrated the story of her visit and its events on that night of horror. True, she does not mention Littlecote or Darell, but the cousin might wisely have suppressed all names.

Then again, nearly three hundred years after the alleged affair, an original letter was discovered, written by Sir H. Knyvett, husband of the Lady Knyvett whom the midwife was supposed to attend, that gave foundation to the horrible story. A Mr. Bonham, whose sister was known to be living with Darell as his mistress, received this letter, which requested that "Mr. Bonham will inquire of his sister touching her usage at Will Darell's, the birth of her children, how many there were, and what had become of them; for that the report of the murder of one of them was increasing foully, and would touch Will Darell to the quick."

Whatever the truth, here is the basis of the tragic story which hangs over the old house and its haunted chamber. Darell died at Littlecote, eleven years after the midwife's death, and he was buried in the Darell Chapel at Ramsbury, which we shall see presently. It is a fact also that Littlecote passed to Sir John Popham on Darell's death in 1586, and has been in that family for over three hundred years.

Legend had not finished with the house after Wild Will's death. About 1861 a child, Francis Popham, was lying ill in a room above the entrance to the house, which has a forecourt with tall iron gates. The nurse, alarmed at the child's condition, sent an urgent message to the parents, away visiting. The next night, as she was watching by the child's bed, she heard, greatly to her relief, the gates flung open, the noise of a coach on the drive and then a peal of the bell. When the parents failed to come up to the room the nurse went to a casement and looked down. There was no coach, no horses, not a sound in the still moonlit night. The parents arrived the next day, but their child was dead. Years later the child's father found an old manuscript in the muniment room in which it made mention of the legend that, on the death of the heir, Wild Will drives up to the door. In Chilton Foliat church there is a monument to this child, Francis Popham, the heir to Littlecote, who died in 1861. It is a pathetic little figure, six months old, resting on a cushion in a window of the chancel.

On our way to Ramsbury the road gives us a distant front view of the great Elizabethan mansion, a gloomy edifice of long roofs and gables set at the foot of a darkly wooded hill. It is the very place for a lurid drama. Alas, many of its treasures were dispersed at a sale. Mr. Justice Popham's chair, the thumbstocks he used for extracting confessions, and the tragic bed of the legend, as well as much of the armour, were sold and taken away. The original curtains of the bed, with the patch thoughtfully returned and sewed on, were intact until 1840, when General Leybourne-Popham, pestered to death by ghoulish visitors, found he could endure it no longer and burnt the curtains.

There is a gossipy portrait of Sir John Popham in *The Scandals and Credulities of John Aubrey*, written round about 1680, sufficiently near in time to the events at Littlecote to mix current gossip with recent facts. Aubrey's account of Popham is full-blooded and frank. "He for several yeares addicted himselfe but little to his studie of the lawes, but to profligate company, and was wont to take a Purse with them. His wife considered her and his condition, and at last prevailed with him to lead another life, and to stick to the studie of the lawe, which upon her importunity, he did, being then about thirtie yeares old. He was a strong, stout man, and could endure to sit at it day and night, became eminent in his calling, had good practice; called to be a serjeant, and a Judge."

Aubrey then relates the Littlecote tragedy, asserting Popham received the place as a bribe, and continues:

"I have seen his picture, he was a huge, heavie, ugly man. He left a vast estate to his son, Sir Francis (I think ten thousand pounds per annum); he lived like a hog, but his sonne John was a great waster, and died in his father's time. . . . Old Sir Francis he lived like a hog, at Hunstret in Somerset, and all this while with a moderate pittance. Mr. John would say that his wife's estate was ill gott, and that was the reason they prospered no better. She would say that the old judge gott the estate unjustly, and they would thus twitt one another, and that with matter of trueth."

The Pophams are no longer at Littlecote, having sold it a few years ago, but they are still at Hunstret.

There is one object at historic Littlecote for which we shall look in vain. In 1730 a Roman tessellated pavement was discovered there consisting of a *templum* and a *sacrarium* which measured forty-one feet by thirty-three, and seemed to have been the floor of a temple. The *templum* had a border with a picture of a two-handled cup, a sea monster, dolphins and tigers. The *sacrarium* had semi-circles of rich patterns with, in the centre, Apollo playing his harp, four symbolic nude female figures; Spring, holding a flower in her hand, and seated on a deer; Summer, on a panther and holding a swan; Autumn, riding on a bull and holding a vine, and Winter, on a goat, empty-handed. Where is it now? In the British Museum or Reading Museum? No, not at all. Listen to Mr. Archibald Robertson, writing in 1792, on his journey to Bath. He said not a word about wild Will Darell, the legend was perhaps too lurid for his refined classical taste.

"Littlecote Park was noted for a pavement found there, in the year 1730, but destroyed in 1733. This extraordinary pavement, the largest ever found in England, was discovered by Mr. William George, steward to Edward Popham, Esq., two feet underground. By him an exact drawing was made from it, in its proper colours, and afterwards engraved by Vertue, at the expence of the Society of Antiquaries."

And that is all—"but destroyed in 1733." But, by George, what did William do with it?

Two memorials of that discovery do remain, however. One is a reproduction in needlework of the pavement, kept at Littlecote Park. The other is the Rudge cup which takes its name from the site of the Roman villa with the pavement. This cup tells a strange story. A letter of Lord Hertford's, dated 1725, gives the details.

"Not far from this pavement a well was discovered, but filled with rubbish in the cleaning of which were found several bones of beasts, four or five human skeletons, and some medals of the lower Empire. But what is more curious is a brass cup about four inches in diameter and three deep. The outside of it is wrought and has been enamelled in red, blue and green."

It has been conjectured that this cup, which bears the names of military stations on the Roman Wall in Northumberland, was owned by a Roman officer of high rank, to whom it was given as a memento of his service on the Great Wall. He may have thrown it into the wall as a votive offering, as was the Roman custom. The cup passed from Lord Hertford, afterwards fifth Duke of Somerset, to his daughter, who became the

Duchess of Northumberland, and is now preserved as a priceless relic at Alnwick Castle. So needlework at Littlecote, and a
cup at Alnwick bear witness to the vanished pavement.

The history of Chilton Foliat is overshadowed by the grim
story of Littlecote Park. The church itself, lovely to linger in,
has a pleasanter story of those who have worshipped there and
passed on. It has had distinguished patrons, who have been
lords of the manor. Henry VII, Henry VIII, Queen Catherine
of Aragon, Queen Catherine Parr and Queen Elizabeth have
in turn possessed the manor. In 1523 Queen Catherine of Aragon wrote to Sir Edward Darell, vice-chamberlain and keeper
of the park of Chilton Foliat:

"We will command you to deliver or cause to be delivered three
oaks convenable for timber . . . for the reparation of the church,
which is in great ruin and decay."

From these oaks came the structural timbers, now encased
in the present roof and bell frame. In its earliest form the aisle
had a low flat roof and battlements, but when the south aisle
was enlarged in 1840 the mistake was made of putting battlements around the new sloping roof. Now, as the rector, Rev.
W. H. Pelham, has pointed out, the idea of battlements was to
protect a man when he was shooting with his bow and arrow.
He could not do this standing on a sloping roof. In 1925, therefore, the roof was altered to its former shape, in keeping with
the battlements.

The first known rector of this old church was William de
Eton, who had the living in 1297. We know very little of him,
but we do know something about Lewis Morgan. When he died
in 1598 he bequeathed a cow to his church-wardens which was
to be loaned out to the farmers, its earnings going to the poor
of the parish. He had the ingenious idea that when the cow
began to give out, one of her calves should earn revenue, so
that, in theory, the charity cow should never die. The rector

under Charles II rejoiced in the name of Timothy Topping, and it is certain he preached sound, jolly Restoration sermons. The original high-backed pews of his day were cut down in 1840 to the present low pews; mercifully the mellowed wood was retained.

In the Churchwardens' Account Book, there is the item, "To a pair of Oaken Stocks, and putting up and painting, £1 1s.," under the date 1773, and the habits of the age had not greatly changed in its treatment of wrongdoers even as late as 1813, for there is another entry, "At a vestry meeting held in the Parish Church of Chilton Foliat, the following Resolution was carried by a majority of the parish then present: 'That a strong substantial parish cage or lock-up house be forthwith built for the Confinement of Refractory Disorderly persons in some convenient retired place within the parish.' "

One cannot help wondering where was the site of that convenient retired place, with its caged occupant, and was Mr. Harris present at the vestry meeting? He lived at the manorhouse, Chilton Lodge, and was then thirty-two. Romance and literature were nearly joined in matrimony through him, for he fell in love with, proposed to, and was accepted by Miss Jane Austen. But by the next morning the great Jane had changed her mind and rejected him. He found consolation in a Miss Frith, two years later. How different would *Emma* have been had it been written at Chilton Foliat in Wiltshire instead of at Chawton in Hampshire, one wonders.

Among the holders of the manor we find Thomas, Lord Berkeley, in 1397, an Earl of Warwick in 1432, a Duke of Somerset in 1448, the various royal holders already mentioned, Sir Edward Darell in the year that Henry VIII died, father of Wild Will, and then the long line of the Pophams from 1589 until 1929. There is one notable figure living at Chilton Foliat in 1670 whom I greeted like an old friend. In the village of Fawley, up above Pilgrim Cottage, lies the effigy of Sir William Whitelock, and down at Fawley Court, by the River

Thames, lived his son, Sir Bulstrode Whitelock, who was Cromwell's ambassador to the amazing Queen Christina of Sweden. As he departed on that mission his wherry lay at the mouth of the Thames, held up by contrary winds, which enabled him to receive the news that his dear third wife had been safely delivered of his "thirteenth" child, a son. I have told his story at greater length in *Gone Rustic,* but after recounting the accouchement on that November day in 1653, of his third wife, I never expected to encounter her again. She seemed gone into oblivion. And now to my surprise and delight, here she turns up again, with her prolific husband, living at Chilton Foliat, in the manor-house, since the lord of the manor, a Popham, lives at Littlecote. And at Chilton Foliat the chapter closes concerning the lady who gave Sir Bulstrode his thirteenth child, for she died there, as also her husband.

She was buried there in 1684, while Sir Bulstrode, dying nine years earlier, was carried to Fawley to sleep by the father he had honoured with a beautiful memorial. For company Lady Whitelock had that thirteenth child, Samuel, who died and was buried at Chilton Foliat in 1690. Samuel broke the thirteen tradition and had only two sons, one of whom, Bulstrode, dying a bachelor, perhaps frightened by his grandfather's record, left all his money to his nieces, who put up a tablet to his memory which we may read to-day. It is pleasant to relate of Samuel thirteen, that he was "the best neighbour unto the poor in the parish, and a man in much esteem with ye rich."

One is tempted to linger long in this delightful church. It has a fine barrel ceiling, a sixteenth-century rendering of a medieval hammerbeam roof; two hatchments, the armorial shields once placed over the portal of a deceased nobleman or knight, and after twelve months transferred to the church; and a stained glass window to Elizabeth Mills Reid, the wife of Whitelaw Reid, the American Ambassador to Great Britain from 1906 to 1912. It is the gift of her daughter, Lady Ward, who lived in the village. The Ambassador's wife loved this old church. Her nephew, a young American who joined the British Air Force during the War, and was killed when flying near the village, lies buried here; and to the church she gave a cross, some candlesticks, and the carved angels on the reredos. Again I had a thrill when seeing this memorial window to Mrs. Reid. The splendours of the hospitality dispensed by her at vanished Dorchester House, Park Lane, were long before my day, but when a very young man, visiting the United States for the first time, I was taken to tea, at a house near Rye, New York State, where I met a distinguished old lady who had many stories of the Edwardian era in London, when she had reigned there as American Ambassadress.

But regretfully we must away from Chilton Foliat, its old church, thatched cottages, silver weir and bridge above the slow stream.

II

Let us hurry on past Littlecote Park to the ancient village of Ramsbury, two miles distant. We shall have gone from *The Boot* to *The Bleeding Horse*, the respective inns of Chilton Foliat and Ramsbury. As we enter the latter place, we see the immemorial elm in the little square, a giant fellow, over twenty feet in circumference, shelter for men and birds, and a grand chattering place for both. Ramsbury has one long quaint street. No one stops in it and there everyone makes a mistake. It has been forgotten by Time, and yet it wears the mantle of former greatness. Its church was once a cathedral, and in A.D. 909 became the seat of a Bishop, from which Christianity was diffused among the rude Saxons. In the next one hundred and fifty years there were ten Bishops of Ramsbury, and three of these became Archbishops of Canterbury. Soon after the Norman conquest the Bishop removed his see from Ramsbury and established it at Old Sarum, and then Salisbury. The day of little Ramsbury's

ecclesiastical glory was over. The Bishops resided there, however, as late as 1524, when there is a record that Bishop Ande-
ley of Salisbury "died in his palace at Ramsbury."

But the old village does not depend on its past for its charm.
I am sorry for the Queen Anne house by the church gate. It has
fallen on evil days. Its kitchen end is now a lawyer's office. Its
main rooms stand empty. There are beautiful old bow windows,
and ironwork balconies, and the first floor window-lintels have
delightful beaded plaster ornamentation. A stately portico
speaks of a patrician state within. Alas, the old house overlooks
a gravel yard and garage, where once, it is certain, Miss Phœbe
tended the hollyhocks, the lavender and the love-in-the-mist.

Shameful it is to look at so shabby genteel an old lady, but
stopping in the main street I shaded my eyes and peered in.
Two Ionic columns supported the ceiling of the drawing-room
recess. A bow-fronted grate, rusty and forlorn, dreamed of the
days when Aunt Serafina, once very gay in London, now poked,
with blue-veined hands, its fire to make a blaze for young Master Charles, descended at the door from the Bath and Bristol
coach. As he entered, the coach has gone on, with a great clatter
of hooves and a tootling on the guard's brass horn, to Marlborough.

I tremble for the fate of this charming old house, a period
piece. A noisy school stands cheek by jowl, droning the daily
lessons in its ear. It has seen better days, and, like Aunt Serafina,
how full of life and laughter it once was! Let us lament a while
and then go past it into the church. The present building dates
back to the twelfth century, but some portions of a Saxon cross,
and the stone lids of coffins, one a Bishop's, point to an earlier
origin. The monuments are a joy. Here is the grandiose tomb
of Sir William Jones. He lived at the splendid old manor with
the lion gates and the ornamental water where the Earl of Pembroke once entertained Cromwell. Jones was Charles II's
Attorney-General, and considered the greatest lawyer of his day
in England. He is certainly a grand old fellow, half reclining

here, with long curled wig, and the ribboned gown of a legal luminary. For company he has a descendant, another William Jones, whose widow was living at Ramsbury Manor when our Mr. Archibald drove by in 1792 and noted the "handsome park, adorned by clumps of stately trees, with other wood judiciously distributed."

On the left of the chancel of this church lies the Darell Chapel. It contains the tombs of the Littlecote family, dating from 1450. Here Wild Will lies buried, but, alas, what once were splendid tombs, doubtless, are now barren stones in a barren chapel. The Puritans stripped off the brasses, fulfilling their hatred of all beauty. There is a little comic relief in two other monuments. One is to Elizabeth Batson, who was distinguished in "the half blood," but even more distinguished in "the whole blood," being a Yorkshire Lascelles. Her life, we learn, was prolonged "by cheerfulness and temperance," to ninety-two years, when she departed this world "without a struggle." And why not, she surely had had enough of it. The other monument is in memory of a remarkable gentleman called Jonathan Knackstone, "whose eminent virtues endeared him to all good men while living and whose death cannot be sufficiently lamented in this degenerate age."

We had always thought we had a monopoly in degenerate ages, but Mr. Knackstone's biographer was probably right. That dreadful George II had been running all over Europe with his Hanoverian troops, for which the British paid, and now the Young Pretender was invading the kingdom, while Prime Minister Pelham was struggling to consolidate the huge national debt piling up. Terrible times, egad. Lucky Jonathan Knackstone to be out of them. In life as in death he had been fortunate. "He was never known to murmur though deprived by nature of the organs of hearing and speaking. Piety, justice, paternal affection, humanity, benevolence, were practised by him with an undeviating constancy. He died March 18th, 1745, aged 63."

Just in time, indeed, for Pitt was to follow, and the Seven Years' War and the battle with the Bourbons were ahead. Even patient Jonathan might have murmured, though how, without the organs of hearing or speaking, is difficult to comprehend. Did Mr. Knackstone live in the Queen Anne house by the church gate, I wonder, and practise there his formidable list of virtues? With the question unanswered we will leave the thatched cottages of Ramsbury, their choice gardens and water meadows, *The Bleeding Horse,* the tenth-century Holy Cross, and return to the Bath Road via Chilton Foliat.

But arrived here we take the smaller road branching to the right, passing the back of Littlecote Park, and by delightfully named Cake Wood, come down through undulating fields to Froxfield on the Bath Road. As we are about to join the road our curiosity is raised by high walls, long, red roofs, Gothic pinnacles, and some near gardens. We are coming down by the back of the Somerset Hospital, whose long, dignified front faces the main road.

It is certain that had I been on that main road into Marlborough, so conducive to speed, I should have passed the building. An almshouse, it seems, and that is all. But it is very much more. Let us climb up the steps, pass under its clock-tower and cupola, through the castellated gate-house, and so gain the great quadrangle with a Gothic church in the centre of the long, green lawn. Here are the little homes of the "Twenty Clergy and Thirty Lay Widows, Founded and Endowed by the late Most Noble Sarah, Duchess Dowager of Somerset, A.D. 1694."

Who was this Most Noble Sarah who provided this charming oasis of peace for tired, impoverished old ladies? The plan of the whole "College," as it is called, is so delightful that one is curious about its donor. The Duchess was a widow, and the Duke had died leaving no direct heir. Apart from certain manors passing by entail to the next holder of the title, her patrimony was unfettered. She left by her will of May, 1686, a large sum of money to be laid out in "furnishing a Hospital and Chapel at Froxfield," together with a sum for buying "tables, bedsteads, and such desirable furniture; and seats, Bibles, cushions and other necessaries for the Chapel."

So well has the trust thus created been managed that the income has greatly increased in the two and a half centuries that have passed. Leases of farms and land having fallen in, the revenue, as it increased, has been applied as she wished to the support of more widows. These are drawn chiefly from the widows of clergymen, though others are eligible.

As I entered the quadrangle, and read an inscription on a chapel given by a Marquis of Ailesbury, I wondered if I was trespassing, but, enchanted by the rows of neat cottages, the latticed mullioned windows, borders of flower-beds, and framed porches, an old lady, straight as a poplar tree, came out of one of the doors, smiled at me, and invited me to look inside her little house. She seemed a woman of about seventy, with an old world courtesy that gave her small domain a manorial dignity. She took me up to the little bedroom, so nun-like in its severe simplicity, showed me the kitchenette, and invited me to sit in her living-room.

"It's like an oasis of peace," I remarked, looking out through the door on the long green lawns, and the evening sunlight falling across the flower-beds and windows of the houses opposite.

"That is just what I said," replied my hostess, "when I reached here after being battered from pillar to post."

I looked at her refined face and guessed the tragedy of the poor gentlewoman, widowed and in reduced circumstances.

"We have gardens," she said. "Would you like to see them?"

We passed out under an arch and up some steps which she took in a sprightly stride.

"The gardens, you see, are allotments, in the same order as the houses, so we know just where we are."

I looked across several acres of flower-beds.

"Do you all do this yourselves?" I asked, astonished.

"Nearly all of us—a few hire the porter to help them," she

answered. "But I must show you one garden, a gem, kept by an old friend of mine."

She led the way up the path until we came to a perfect lawn, surrounded with a deep bed of roses, delphiniums, lavender bushes and phlox. It was a gay, most orderly garden, bearing every sign of loving and assiduous care.

"Isn't it lovely?" asked my hostess. "She does it all herself, and she's eighty-six!"

Our way back lay along a high terrace that looked down on the long mellow roofs of the quadrangle. We talked of flowers and books, of peace and war, of politics and politicians, for her late husband had been an official of the House of Commons, and for forty years she had lived within the shadow of Parliament. As we parted at the gate I thanked my gracious hostess, and asked if I might come again, perhaps in the Spring.

"Certainly if I am here," she said.

"But you are not going away?" I asked.

"Well, I might, any time," she said, with a quiet smile. "You see, I'm eighty-two."

And then I understood. And before I passed out under the gate-house into the roar of the traffic running down the Bath Road, I looked across the quiet lawns at the long rows of little green doors where, in the calmness of old age, some fifty gentle old ladies waited to embark on that last voyage, and meanwhile tended their gardens. Surely the shade of the kindly Duchess visits this tranquil spot.

III

Within a few miles the scene suddenly changes on the Bath Road. A dense forest looms up, its entrance marked by a lodge. But the lodge no longer guards the entrance to the Savernake Forest. A public road now cuts through two miles of the northern verge of this private forest, the property of the Marquis of Ailesbury. It is a woodland scene of great beauty, and the highway, bordered by giant trees, with wide vistas of forest and open greensward, becomes more like a private drive than a public road. The road was once a private way, but it is now, by concession, a public thoroughfare cutting through the great forest, which, by its owner's generosity, is accessible to the public.

These massive oaks and beeches of Savernake are magnificent in their grandeur. The forest has, nevertheless, for all its wild appearance, been cultivated, and certain avenues reveal careful planning in the past two centuries. There is a point where eight separate walks converge, each offering a cloistral avenue of foliage to the sight. At this point a great column has been erected, originally brought from Brandenburg House, when the Margravine of Anspach bought the house from Bubb Doddington for her lavish London entertainments. He had erected the column as a memorial to his wife, whose heart rested in the urn which crowns it.

The inscription at the base of this column could only have been conceived in the eighteenth century. It carries the blend of pomposity, cant and sophisticated romance which gives such an air to these formal inscriptions.

"This column was erected by Thomas Bruce, Earl of Ailesbury, as a testimony of gratitude to his ever-honoured uncle, Charles, Earl of Ailesbury and Elgin, who left to him these estates, and procured for him the Barony of Tottenham."

Good old Uncle Charles! Well might a grateful nephew raise a column to him. And—with an eye to further royal favours?— the inscription proceeds:

"And of loyalty to his most gracious Sovereign, George III, who, unsolicited, conferred on him the honour of Earldom."

One wonders. Why drag in that word unsolicited? And now, Uncle Charles and King George having been hospitable, Thomas turns to the Almighty:

"But above all to Piety, to God, first, highest, best; whose blessings consecrate every gift, and fixeth its true value. 1781."

And then, on the opposite side, Thomas throws another bouquet at the human fount of all honours:

"In commemoration of a signal instance, of Heaven's protecting providence over these kingdoms, in the year 1789, by restoring to perfect health, from a long and afflicting disorder, our excellent and beloved Sovereign, George III."

Thus the noble earl celebrated the mad King and madder statesmen who, seven years earlier, had lost the British their great American colony. The column is splendidly placed on a height from which one may command a view of Tottenham House, the marquis's seat, a mile and a half away down the straight avenue.

This forest of Savernake is perhaps the most beautiful small forest that England can show, the oak, the ash, and the thorn flourish, as they did in the days of the Norman Conquest. These vast aisles and green naves made by the great beeches, with their clean, smooth trunks, give a cathedral air to the forest, which will change suddenly into open spaces of downland, wild forest growths of bush and bracken, glades where the herds of deer start away at a sound. It is the forest of Titania and her court, it is ancient England of the royal huntsmen and the serfs. Its history is woven with that of the English people.

How old is this beautiful domain, once a vast expanse, and even now, in private ownership, sixteen miles in circumference? In 933 it was given to the Abbey of Wilton. In the Norman days its hereditary wardens were the Sturmy family. Their name is in the Domesday Book, and King John confirmed one, Thomas Sturmy, in his wardenship and knighted him. This family were here until 1426, when the daughter of the last male of the line died. She married a Seymour, whose fame was in the ascendant, for in a house on the edge of the forest, one descendant, Jane, was married to Henry VIII, and the wedding feast was held in the great barn still standing at Wulfhall. Jane, unlike so many of Henry's wives, did not lose her head, but died giving birth to the future Edward VI, in 1537, Henry's only son. Jane's brother was Edward, the Protector Somerset, and another brother Thomas, married Katherine Parr, Henry VIII's widow.

In due time Savernake passed by marriage from the Seymours to the Bruces, who, as Marquises of Ailesbury, are still there. But one of them, the fourth Marquis, almost brought a wealthy family to complete ruin. He was a "throw-back," if there was ever anyone in this family so degenerate to throwback to. Heir to this noble demesne, the only forest owned by a private subject, the fourth Marquis, then known as Lord Savernake, was born in 1863 and educated at Eton. He began his rake's progress early and set a hot pace to all the Victorian rakes and rattlers. Vine Street Police Station knew him well. A brawler, a bully, he would smash in the face of anyone who got in his way. His language was such that a contemporary Prime Minister said "his mind was a dunghill of which his tongue was the cock."

In 1886 he succeeded to his grandfather as the fourth Marquis, and thus at twenty-three inherited the forest of Savernake, Tottenham House, other estates and properties, and an income of eighty thousand pounds a year. Within a year of his inheritance he was expelled for life from the Jockey Club, for fraud in connection with the running of a horse. At twenty-one Lord Stomach-ache, as he was nicknamed, had married a barmaid, Julia Haseley, aged twenty-three, known as Dolly Tester. She was the daughter of a baker at Brighton. "The Marchioness Dorothy, née Tester," a London paper described her, "late of the refreshment department of the Theatre Royal, Brighton, and more recently of the chorus at the Empire and elsewhere." They were married at a registry office, and Lord Savernake described himself as "Bachelor, Cab Proprietor, Kendall's

Mews." He certainly dressed the part of a horsey tipster, with a high collar, a bird's-eye blue belcher for a necktie, a drab box-cloth coat with large mother-o'-pearl buttons, a low-crowned, broad-brimmed coachman's hat, and a tight pair of trousers.

The rake's progress, through wine, women and horses, did not last long. In 1892, six years after he had succeeded, he was in the Bankruptcy Court with liabilities of £345,402, of which £244,211 were unredeemable. This wretched, depraved young man died two years later, aged thirty, leaving a trail of ruin behind him. He had sold his Yorkshire properties in 1887 for £310,000, and in 1891 he had tried to sell the Wiltshire estate, comprising Savernake Forest, for £750,000, but the heir-presumptive spent £20,000 fighting the sale, which the House of Lords refused to sanctum. His heirs have had to struggle with a grievously encumbered estate ever since. His widow, despite her origin, was a woman of aristocratic bearing and superior manners. She subsequently exchanged her title of Marchioness of Ailesbury for that of Mrs. Waddle Webster.

Happily there is another Marquis, the fifth of his line, still living at Tottenham House, whose great façade of Bath stone looks down the long avenue towards the column. He served his country in the South African War, and standing now as he welcomes us, in the great hall, he is a typical English country gentleman. He wears an old coat, leather-patched at the elbows, trousers long neglected by a valet, and, at a casual glance, is the archetype of those stories in which the lordly owner of a vast estate is tipped by the tripper for showing him the way through his own grounds. But a closer look reveals behind the monocled eye and in the courtly manner, a good shot at a covert, and a perfect host at the table.

The great forest, he tells us, is now being taken care of, by arrangement, by the Forestry Commission, but the symbol of his ownership still hangs there in a corner of this great hall, the ivory horn mounted in silver and curiously carved, given some six hundred years ago by a king to a Sturmy as the symbol of office as hereditary warden of the forest.

From this hall, with its flanking wings carrying heraldic shields with the Garter motto, we look out, at either end, north-west, up the great ride to the column, south-east, over the deer park towards the old Roman road running to Wilton. Thus the Roman way of the Caesars and the forest of the Norman Conqueror, are in the view of this Grecian-style mansion occupying the site of the palace of the Plantagenet Seymours, a panorama comprising nearly two thousand years of British history.

We returned to the Bath Road, down the five-mile-long avenue of beeches, over a road falling into disuse, but well worth the risk of breaking the chassis springs. The last lodge gate on the Bath Road is only two miles from Marlborough, which soon lies below us on the slope of a great down, with the Kennet running through the valley. The steep hill which commands a lovely view of Marlborough spread out below us was long a nightmare to coach traffic, which often became stuck in the mud or was overturned on the execrable surface. But we have no such worries to-day. Marlborough lies enticingly below us. If Reading be famed for biscuits and seeds, Marlborough might claim equal distinction as the town of boys and tea-shops.

CHAPTER XVIII

Lovely Marlborough

FOR SOME REASON the guide-books are inclined to be disparaging when dealing with Marlborough. When they call it "disappointing" they lie sadly. It gave me, on first acquaintance, the same kind of thrill as when I saw Rothenburg. It is a time-weathered symphony of red roofs and gables, with a High Street that has not its superior in the British Isles. At least that is how I felt about it when, turning round up the steep corner by the Town Hall, I saw with astonishment that long, wide street, set on the slope of a hill, closed in at either end by a church.

It is a new town, in the sense that little survives of a date earlier than 1653, when it was swept by fire. Its houses on either side of the High Street date from the end of the seventeenth century. Evelyn visiting it in 1654 recorded that it was "now new built." Pepys, in 1668, alluded to "the pent houses supported with pillars that make a fair walk." The pillars and the overhanging floors of the shops are still there, making a charming arcade. But to see Marlborough properly you must walk up and down its High Street four times; once, from the east end to the west, to look at the shops, roofs, gables, yard openings and houses on the lower south side; once, from the west end to the east to see the buildings on the upper north side; once, down the middle of the street to enjoy the picture on either hand; and a fourth time for the sheer delight of enjoying a street, warped, gabled, overhung, bow-windowed,

many-chimneyed, that begins with a church and a Town Hall
at one end, and ends with a church and a school at the other,
both bottle-necks which should never be widened.

It is a High Street which is at the same time the main Bath
Road, a market-place, and a bazaar of tea-shops, if I may mix
the metaphor, out of which could walk, with a background as
correct as their period costumes, John Evelyn, Samuel Pepys,
Nell Gwynn, Lord Chatham, Lord Chesterfield, Nelson, Jane
Austen, Garrick, Horace Walpole, Benjamin Franklin, the
Duke of Wellington, George III, Beau Brummell, Byron, Prince
Albert and Queen Victoria. Actually we shall see the boys of
Marlborough College coming out of St. Patrick's or Polly's tea-
rooms with their "people." Some of them, it may be, not so free,
pass by, carrying their text-books in folded cushions called
"kyshes," which serve a dual purpose for sitting on and carry-
ing books.

When Marlborough began no one is quite sure. The Romans
were at Cunetio, a litle way off. Its very name is open to dis-
pute. It comes from Maerleah, meaning a cattle boundary, says
the prosaic historian; it comes from Merlinbergh, since Merlin
the wizard, of King Arthur's Court, lies buried under the Castle
Mound, says the romantic historian. The town's arms evidently
plump for the romantic version, for its motto runs *Ubi nunc
sapientes ossa Merlini?* though it cautiously asks if Merlin's
bones be there. Marlborough had a new grant of arms in 1635,
when it added a castle, and a shield with a bull, two capons and
three greyhounds. This pictorically perpetuates the tradition of
the aldermen and burgesses presenting to the mayor, on their
admission, a leash of white greyhounds, a white bull, and two
white capons.

The Mound is still here, high, bold, and venerably old, certainly as old as Stonehenge. It commands the western gateway
of the town. The Romans might certainly have used it for a
station. William the Conqueror had a castle on it and set up a
mint. It remained a royal castle for five centuries. Henry I

kept Easter there in 1110. The third Henry was very fond of it
and brought over a Florentine to rebuild and decorate it. King
John, of Magna Charta fame, married his Queen Isabelle there,
and during his reign it was held by the Dauphin of France, at
the invitation of the rebellious barons. It passed down the ages
and through various hands to the Protector Somerset. The Seymours used it as a residence until it fell into ruin and became
an heirloom of Lady Elizabeth, who married Sir Hugh Smithson, created Earl and later Duke of Northumberland, the re-
builder of Syon House and Alnwick Castle. Earlier it had figured prominently as a castle held by King Charles in the Civil
War. Charles II and his Queen stayed there on his progress to
the West, and were received by Lord Francis Seymour, who
built near by the new house which is now part of Marlborough
College.

It was in this house that the Countess of Hertford, afterwards Duchess of Somerset, kept a court of bad poets and ob-
scure painters. She reigned in an age of folly, when overdressed
ladies sat in grottoes and arbours and listened to bad verses
from tame poets. Lady Hertford had among her courtiers Dr.
Watts, who tried in vain to teach her son his "repetitions," but
succeeded in passing from the sublimity of "O God, our Help in
Ages Past" to the asininity of "How doth the little busy bee."
But human gadflies rather than bees must have been his chief
inspiration.

Mr. Thomson, who wrote *The Seasons*, dedicated the *Spring*
part of it to his hostess, "When nature is blooming and benevo-
lent like thee." But he was a drunken little sot, and when the
Countess found he was passing his time drinking hard in a
grotto with her husband, instead of courting the Muse, she sent
him packing.

Another member of that queer menagerie wandering amid
the sham ruins, reciting by artificial cascades, and posing amid
the Arcadian foolery immortalized by Watteau, whose shep-
herdesses and milkmaids would have had the vapours at the

sight of ticks and dung, was the Countess's protégé, Stephen Duck, the "thresher poet," whom her ladyship had rescued from useful work on the farm to create useless verses for the boudoir. She introduced him to Queen Caroline, who gave him a pension and made him a Yeoman of the Guard. Swift's biting comment lives longer than Duck's quacking:

> *The Thresher Duck could o'er the Queen prevail,*
> *The proverb says "no fence against a flail,"*
> *From threshing corn he turns to thresh his brains,*
> *For which her Majesty allows him gains;*
> *Tho' 'tis confessed that those who ever saw*
> *His poems think them not worth all the straw.*
> *Thrice happy Duck! employed in threshing stubble,*
> *Thy toil is lessened, and thy profits double.*

The poet eventually became a parson, and, poor man, despite his name, drowned himself in a fit of madness.

The Mound which Duck decorated with verses was better served by his patroness who put on it an octagonal summer-house. It now carries a water-tank, fed by a spring that supplies the College. There was a twelfth-century tradition that "whereof whosoever drinketh thenceforth he will speak barbarous French." This may account for the fact that the tongue of Marlborough College is rarely the tongue of Paris; and the French master cannot be blamed.

When the Northumberlands inherited the house they were much too busy building elsewhere, and disposed of it. Later, it was opened as *The Castle Inn,* and entered on an era of splendour and importance. Everybody went to Bath, and as a consequence everybody stayed at *The Castle Inn.* It was the thing to do. A list of its patrons would be a list of all the great figures of the late eighteenth and early nineteenth centuries. Stanley Weyman in his novel, *The Castle Inn,* has given us a vivid reconstruction of the inn and the Fashion that gathered there. It was here that the great Lord Chatham, one of the few men, as

Macaulay observed, who added inordinate vanity and show-
manship to true greatness, staged a halt in his journeying to
London that created a sensation throughout the country. Even
now it is not known whether it was calculating strategy or temporary madness induced by gout that produced this excursion
in ostentation. Chatham shut himself up in his room for three
weeks, and while Burke thundered in the House of Commons,
and his frantic ministers appealed to him to return, he remained
invisible, unapproachable, dumb. But the whole world knew he
was there. *The Castle Inn* and the town seemed to swarm with
his servants, for he had made it a condition of his stay that, in
addition to his own retinue of grooms and footmen, all the inn
servants, waiters, page-boys, grooms and stable-boys should
wear his livery.

That was in 1767, and the inn had a century of prosperity
until 1843, when the railways, having driven the coaches off the
roads, and the fame of Bath having declined, *The Castle Inn*
closed its doors. But in August of that same year it entered
upon a new life of prosperity and renown. The Rev. Charles
Plater opened it as a public school primarily designed for the
sons of clergymen. It had a stormy passage for some years, and
then began a record of uninterrupted success. To-day the
school, occupying the old wing which, with its classic portico, is
known as C House, gives new life to Marlborough, whose boys
enliven its streets, and make merry in Brew, the little tuck-shop
at the High Street corner by St. Peter's Church. The Bath
Road traffic passing down that street and corner passes also the
green lawns of the former inn. It curves again at another corner
where the town gaol has been transformed into the school gym-
nasium, and, on a road leading straight for the Downs, passes
under the arch that, like a Bridge of Sighs, unites the school
buildings on either side of the road.

It was a kindness as well as a practical thing for the War
Memorial Hall to have been built facing the road, across a
paved court and garden. Its eight stone columns strike the

classic note, and let those critical of its vivid colouring remember how the Greeks painted their temples with blues, greens and purples. The interior provides a splendid auditorium and stage. Behind the hall, as if to strike the ultra-modern note in architecture, the chemical laboratories rise to a latticed rotunda. Hidden behind this is the open air swimming-pool, where a frieze of naked boys maintains the Grecian note, though very English are the joyous voices that rise from the troubled waters. It will be observed that this pool is irregular in shape, due to the fact that the makers utilized the moat of the ancient castle. Behind the bathers, on a green slope, like a backcloth to this classic scene, is the white horse cut out of the turf of Granham Hill in 1804 by the industrious boys of a local academy kept by a Mr. Greazley in the High Street. The guests at *The Castle Inn* must have seen it for some forty years, and in the eyes of Marlburians it is affectionately regarded. It has passed into song on the lips of boys leaving the school at the end of the last term.

> *And when to Marlborough, old and worn,*
> *We shall creep back like ghosts,*
> *And see some youngsters yet unborn*
> *Run in between the posts,*
> *Ah, then we'll cry—thank God, my lads,*
> *The Kennet's running still,*
> *And see! the old White Horse still pads*
> *Up there on Granham Hill.*

Since it is not yet the hour which we have appointed for meeting young Peter, who will conduct us over the school, and then take us to the right tea-shop, we will turn in at St. Peter's Church, closing in the High Street, opposite the school. It is fortunate it is a church, otherwise some "improver" of the highway would sweep it out of existence, for it makes an acute angle for the motorist, and doubtless many a coach had a narrow escape from being overturned or collided with by some dashing young rake careering along in his post-chaise.

The Marlborough which Charles I knew, when he lay here
with his troops, disappeared in the great fire that swept it in
1653. It broke out in a tanner's yard near St. Peter's rectory
and in a few minutes, under a strong driving wind, soon caught
all the thatched roofs. No thatch was allowed in Marlborough
after that experience, hence the lovely old tiles seen everywhere
to-day. And one good thing Cromwell did for Marlborough. He
raised a national subscription for rebuilding the ruined town,
which Evelyn, the diarist, saw rising from its ashes when he
passed through in 1654, and ascended the Mount "by windings
for neere half a mile."

St. Peter's escaped the fire, but it did not escape a nineteenth-
century "improver" who removed many of the features of a
church dating back to the Norman conquest, and left it with
a leaning north-west pinnacle on its battlemented tower. Two
men, one very famous and one very notorious, are connected
with this church. It was here that Thomas Wolsey took his first
step towards the Cardinal's hat, and the great power he
wielded. The butcher's son was ordained here in March, 1498,
when he was twenty-seven years of age. He just failed to fulfil
the wish expressed by his father, in his will, that his son should
be a priest within a year of his death.

The other man connected with St. Peter's was Dr. Henry
Sacheverell, one of those fanatical notoriety-mongers which
every age breeds. His father was rector of St. Peter's, and he
was baptized here. He grew into a particularly pestilential parson. A rabid Tory, the Whigs played into his hands by impeach-
ing him. His violent sermons were ordered to be publicly
burned and thus achieved the notoriety he sought for them. He
made a triumphal progress from London after his trial, and returned later when Queen Anne gave him a living. He followed
the customary rôle of the canting opportunist. A rich admirer
gave him an estate, and he made doubly sure of his good fortune by marrying his admirer's widow.

A third man, known to fame in his day, has his memorial

here. This is Sir Nicholas Hyde, who was Lord Chief Justice, and met his death in 1666 by catching gaol fever from a prisoner he tried at Norwich. This mishap resulted in the custom, still maintained, of laying bunches of aromatic herbs before the judges in Old Bailey trials, to give them protection. Poor Sir Nicholas was ill-fated, for this charming memorial shows him and Lady Mary, "his wife that is" kneeling at a *prie-dieu*. It is a touching memorial to the deaths of his three little children in an epidemic in 1626; Robert, buried January 24th, Francis, January 28th, and Elizabeth, February 28th. "We shall goe to them but they shall not return to us," runs the pathetic quotation underneath. Wholly delightful are the figures of the bereaved knight and his wife, he in a ruffle and doublet, a gilt belt and red shoes with gilt buckles, she in an elaborate stomacher and full kirtled dress. The work suggests an Italian influence, with its delicate ornament and marble frame.

We journey to the east end of the High Street to visit St. Mary's, which lies between the new Town Hall, a not very fortunate substitute for the old Market Hall, and the sloping Green with its charming medley of eighteenth-century houses. St. Mary's suffered from the great fire, and its present ugliness owes much to the Puritans who restored it with their customary lack of taste. Fortunately, a fine Norman doorway escaped both the fire and the Puritans. Could they but have known it, paganism took a real revenge on the religious fanatics, for there came to be built into the new church, somehow, a stone figure of Fortuna, carved about A.D. 300, which it is assumed came from the nearby Roman town of Cunetio.

From the church a lime walk leads one to the village green. Call at the Council House, where a pleasant office boy will give you a town guide; use this pretext to see the offices he now works in, a lovely old house with a great staircase, a view into a garden, and from its white, sashed windows a prospect of the sloping green. Then walk along Silverless Street, in a hundred yards of which are a score of quaint, leaning houses whose windows have watched the fashion go by, with patches and powder and pomaded hair, the Beau Brocades and Lady Teazles *en route* for the waters of Bath.

We are now *en route* ourselves to meet Peter, our cicerone. He is waiting, in typical Malburian sports kit, a white sweater, loose white shorts and greyish stockings which it seems fashionable to allow to slip down the legs. The pink and white of fifteen accompanies an infectious smile. Being of a nice nature he contrives to hide his boredom at taking us over the school.

We go first to see an inter-house polo match in the pool. The horse on Granham Hill looks cool against the emerald turf, the sun-dappled water is threshed to a white foam by desperate brown limbs, the crowd cheers. As we leave the pool a frightful noise of bagpipes out of, or in tune, according to one's fancy, assails the ears. Through the window of a tin hut a small boy marches up and down, his cheeks puffed out, the bagpipe under his arm. He is in the isolation hut, practising a pibroch that surely must wake Merlin under the mound.

We cross a long open court, tree-lined. Facing it stand the columns of C House Porch, a seventeenth-century colonnade removed from another mansion. The open door in the wide hall gives a vista of the smooth, green lawns on the opposite side, and the terrace of the Master's Garden. As I pass through this porch there comes to mind another Malburian, Charles Hamilton Sorley, with the quick flame of youth burning in his ardent face. He was fated to die at twenty, a boy-captain, killed in action, with most of the poetry he might have given the world locked in him. I thought of him

> *Who could scarcely leave*
> *The Downs on a December eve:*
> *Was at his happiest in shorts,*
> *And got not many good reports,*

to use his own words. Aloud, I quoted the unfulfilled wish of his friend,

God grant, dear Voice, one day again
We see those Downs in April weather,
And sniff the breeze and smell the rain,
And stand in C House Porch together.

Peter looked at me wonderingly, and the swiftness of the generations lost in the maw of Time was borne in upon me when I discovered Sorley's name meant nothing to him. But he listened patiently, and for a moment the ghost of another schoolboy was evoked in C House Porch. We looked in the Adderley library, cool and quiet save for the whir of a mower down the long lawns of the terrace. In the inn days it was two rooms, later converted, as one room, into the school dining-hall. Thence we went to the present dining-hall. Curious to know what was in a row of lockers under the windows, Peter raised for me a lid, revealing an assortment of jam pots.

"So here the little Erics feed," I exclaimed.

"Little Erics?" said Peter, resentfully.

"*Eric, or Little by Little*—you know your Eric?"

"No—never heard of him!"

I sighed again. Never to have known that little prig Eric— I realized then the enormous, unbridgeable gap between Peter's boyhood and mine own.

"Eric belongs to the Victorian band of young prigs—the Goodchild Family, Little Lord Fauntleroy," I explained. "I fear you must read *Eric;* it was written by one of your head-masters, Dean Farrar."

Later, in W. H. Smith's bookshop, I tried to buy *Eric, or Little by Little,* but Eric had not been heard of. To console us the kindly bookseller took us up a wide well staircase and showed us the Jacobean room over the shop. It has splendid panelling, magnificent fireplaces, and some lovely old leaded windows looking down on the High Street. In the centre window was a curious sundial, the gnomon plate itself being a pane of coloured glass in an oval leaded frame. In the middle of the glass a fly is transfixed. It has been debated whether the unfortunate fly got into the molten glass, or whether it is a painted fly. Whatever it is, real or fake, it is extraordinarily life-like. Peter could not resist wagering it was a real fly put there to be symbolical.

"Why symbolical?" I demanded.

"Time flies," he retorted, at a safe distance.

It is believed that this shop was once a convent. There is a way of escape over the roofs. Later it was the Mayor's House. Since it survived the fire of 1653 it may well be that in this room the Mayor ransomed some of the "disaffected" townsmen when Charles I attacked Marlborough and took them prisoners.

Walking down one of the widest High Streets in the Kingdom we can still see the place which Pepys in 1668, when visiting with Mrs. Pepys, their "boy" and two maids, called "a pretty fair town, for a street or two, and what is most singular is their houses on one side having their pent-houses supported with pillars, which makes a good walk."

I thought what a good walk it made as Peter took me off to tea after viewing the Chapel, with its panels bearing the names of distinguished old boys, and its frescoes showing the influence of another O.M.—William Morris. The tea-shop was full of youth and noise. It stood in the High Street by an archway that had once led into a coachyard. Gardens fell away behind, towards the limpid Kennet flowing through the level meadows. Opposite rose the gables of a new shop, so cleverly faked that I thought it was Jacobean. I would rather a dozen fakes like this than the wicked brick monster of a Post Office that massacres this time-mellowed street. Over the fake shop I deciphered the motto carved on the barge-boards. "A Word fitly spoken is like Apples of Gold in Pictures of Silver," which young Marlborough derisively snorted at.

It being six o'clock, the college curfew imminent, Peter rose from the table, and after a polite speech of thanks, took leave of me. But I lingered in Polly's Tea Shop, by the bow-window commanding a view of the old street, since I had made a friend in the person of a French poodle. I once wrote some lines to a friend's French poodle, and these I proceeded to quote to my new, unclipped acquaintance, whose tail wagged encouragingly.

Timorously treading, the curled darling goes,
A Harlequin dog, on delicate toes;
Elegant gentleman!—do you suppose
He's a Prince of the Blood with his Bourbon nose?
Though ruffled, he dances with royal disdain
A pavan for a poodle, to music from Spain.

To speak to a dog successfully is often an introduction to its owner. It was so this time. The dainty poodle's charming mistress joined in the conversation, which went careering from French poodles, verses, bow-windows, the old High Street, to St. Peter's Church. My enthusiasm for the Nicholas Hyde memorial slipped out.

"But we live in old Sir Nicholas Hyde's house," said the poodle's mistress.

And that was how the door of The Hermitage, an old, gabled house, with a priest's window over the porch, set back on a green lawn behind excluding walls, a few yards from the High Street, came to be opened to me. So I sat and talked under the roof where in almost the space of a month poor Sir Nicholas and Lady Mary had seen their three children carried out for burial, and where a young nephew visited them, Edward Hyde, later Earl of Clarendon, author of the odious Clarendon code, and scapegoat for Charles II, when it was politic to discard him.

Another hospitable door opened to me that day. No doubt I was a noticeable figure, gaping there on the pavement by St. Peter's Church. But I had just been thrilled by what seemed to me a discovery and a coincidence. Inside the Church, looking up from a portrait of blatant Dr. Sacheverell, my eye had caught the prominent face of a clock. It was the great bold face more than the date, 1746, that gave me the clue to its probable history. I suspected it had once been the advertising device of an innkeeper across the way, for I was not deceived by its religious quotation substituted for the name of the maker.

Outside again, ruminating and gazing at the clock on the tower, a lady near me volunteered a comment. The clock-face was much larger than it appeared. She had been told that when the clock had been on the ground for repairs, ten workmen had taken their lunch on its face. This led to the other large face inside the church, whereupon the lady supplied a clue upon which I fastened eagerly. The clock I had seen, she had heard it said, had been the property of *The Castle Inn,* and when it closed its doors, had been given to the Church. *Incroyable!* as Miss Whissitt would certainly have said.

"Won't you come in, my husband will be most interested?" asked my informant, and so another door opened, and I was in the Rectory. Through that door I had another surprise. The windows of the drawing-room beyond looked southwards over lawns sloping to the banks of the Kennet. The town behind me was completely shut out; this was a rectory in the heart of green Wiltshire. With the slightest prompting the kindly rector began to delve through that pleasant disorder so becoming in parson's dens. He produced paper after paper. The local rector is generally the repository of local history. The father of his flock—if anyone knows, he is likely to know. Substitute the English for the Spanish setting, and Browning has drawn his portrait for all time.

> *You saw go up and down old Marlborough*
> *A man of mark, to know next time you saw,*
> *His very serviceable suit of black*
> *Was courtly once and conscientious still . . .*
> *He took such cognizance of men and things,*
> *If any beat a horse you felt he saw . . .*
> *So, next time that a neighbour's tongue was loosed,*
> *It marked the shameful and notorious fact,*
> *We had among us not so much a spy,*
> *As a recording chief-inquisitor,*
> *The town's true master if the town but knew!*

That is often how a local rector strikes me, a contemporary. And of course my rector knew things I had not heard before; how the flint walls on the outside of the rectory had come from the old walls of the Castle, part of a deal done by a Jacobean rector, Nicholas Proffet by name, and judging from his shrewd dealing, Proffet by nature, for like the Vicar of Bray he continued to remain at the Rectory from the time of Charles I until long after the Restoration. To his honour he had protested against the King's execution, despite the harsh treatment Marlborough had received at Royalist hands, for over forty of the townspeople had been transported as prisoners to Oxford, where one notable citizen died in the gaol there.

While talking to the Rector, I thought of another and much earlier Cecil who is reported to have breathed his last at the Rectory, though another house contests the claim. Was it here, on the night of May 1st, 1612, Robert Cecil, first Earl of Salisbury, founder of a long line of statesmen, famous in their country's service, stayed on his way from a sojourn at "The Bathe"? He was ill, and was hurrying home to Hatfield, which he was not destined to see again, for he died in the parson's house three weeks later. One wonders if, while in the neighbourhood, he visited Wilton, and the brilliant Countess of Pembroke, Sir Philip Sidney's sister, who, according to Aubrey, had for one of her gallants, "crooke-back't Cecill, earl of Salisbury."

A straying odour of the rectorial dinner warned me I must be gone, pleasant as it was to linger with such genial company, so bearing a sheaf of booklets I stepped into the quiet High Street. The charabancs and the motors had gone, the schoolboys had all been locked up, tranquillity brooded over the place. It had been a grand day. The level light of the sun over a hundred gabled roofs made of the glowing tiles an "incarnadined sea." Now might Mr. Pepys be walking abroad. Presently, he will return to *The Hart,* and there have Mrs. Pepys read to him. He recorded it all in his diary, paying a tribute to *The*

Hart—"a good house. . . . My wife pleased with all, this evening reading of 'Mustapha' to me till supper, and then to supper, and had musique whose innocence pleased me, and I did give them 3s. So to bed, and lay well all night, and long, so as all the five coaches that come this day from Bath, as well as we, were gone out of the town before six."

And as I thought of Pepys, making my way down the High Street, along came the musicians. They were itinerants playing their way to Bath. They played musique whose innocence pleased me, though it came, syncopated, via Hollywood. So preserving the Pepysian tradition I did give them 3s. So to bed, and lay well all night.

CHAPTER XIX

The Avebury Mystery

"I SUPPOSE," said Miss Whissitt, calling early one morning, about some old cottages the Rural District Council proposed pulling down, and which she was determined to keep up, "I suppose you're doing Avebury as soon as you've finished with Marlborough?"

I looked blankly at her, as I finished my breakfast.

"That marmalade reminds me," she said, pointing to a jar of Keiller's Dundee marmalade on my table.

"Why should marmalade remind you of Avebury?" I asked.

"Because at Avebury Mr. Keiller is doing a really marvellous work. He is digging out and re-erecting all the sarsen stones. I think Avebury's more marvellous than Stonehenge, about which such a fuss is made. It's just off the Bath Road, three or four miles out of Marlborough before you come to Silbury Hill," explained Miss Whissitt. *"C'est formidable.* I'll lend you some papers about it. Aubrey discovered it."

"Not *The Scandals and Credulities* fellow?" I exclaimed.

"That's the man," replied Miss Whissitt. "He found it when on a hunting expedition with the Seymours of Marlborough Castle, in 1648."

I was about to ask how and why Miss Whissitt came to know of Aubrey's rare book, but I checked myself. There is no end to Miss Whissitt's sources of information whether on chicken-pox, thatching or archæology. I looked up the "mago-tie-headed Mr. Aubrey," as an unkind contemporary called him. Let him introduce himself, writing in the third person. "Borne, longaevous, healthy, kindred in the countrie of Wilts, March the 12th, A.D. 1625, about Sun-rising, being very weake and so like to dye that he was christened before morning prayer."

Aubrey lived till 1697, out of estate and penniless, a child of misfortune but of such garrulous charm that he never lacked a table at which to sit, or a bed in which to sleep. His magpie mind collected every glittering fact, and his salacious, gossipy *Brief Lives* has been quarried by almost every writer on the great figures of Elizabethan or Stuart times. No story was too strange, no fragment of gossip too doubtful for his collection. Down at heel for most of his life, no party willingly omitted Aubrey, in drink or out of it. He knew something creditable or otherwise about everybody. His ceaseless enthusiasms carried him along, and his wandering pen has given us a lively portrait of a kindly ne'er-do-well "never quiet till all was gone, wholly cast myself on God's providence."

Some twelve years after his discovery of Avebury, buried under the accumulations of ages, King Charles II, talking one morning about Stonehenge, learned that Aubrey had said that Avebury "did as much exceed Stonehenge as a Cathedral does a Parish Church." The King thereupon commanded that Aubrey should be brought to him next morning. Says Aubrey:

"I brought with me a draught of it donne by memorie only; but well enough resembling it, with which his Majesty was pleased: gave me his hand to kiss, and commanded me to waite on him at Marlborough when he went to Bath with the Queen (which was about a fortnight later) which I did: and the next day when the Court were on their journie, his Majesty left the Queen and diverted to Aubrey (Avebury) where I showed him that stupendous Antiquity with the view thereof. He and His Royal Highness the Duke of York were well pleased."

What Aubrey had discovered in 1648, Dr. William Stukeley, the antiquary, studied a century later. He surveyed it, he wrote books about it, he concocted erroneous theories concerning the origin and meaning of this great megalithic monument.

As soon as one leaves Marlborough the nature of the country undergoes a complete change. The wooded landscape changes to the lonely spaces of the rolling downs. Here are no trees, lush meadows and streams. The great bald hills rise up under the wide sky, and the eye rests nowhere until the horizon fades away. Here is the home and burial ground of prehistoric man, of a race shadowy and forgotten, with no evidence of their existence in this dim past save the remote impressive barrows they raised on the bleak downs. A few miles out of Marlborough along the Bath Road we see these mounds, like breasts on the bosom of the earth. At the village of West Kennet, three miles along the road, we take a sharp turn to the right, following a narrow way, and become suddenly aware of a long avenue of parallel stones, great blocks, standing up on end, mute witnesses of the tremendous labour of a forgotten people.

It is an uncanny sight, this avenue of great stones. For what purpose, by what people were these sarsen stones put into their position? Yet this strange avenue is but the prelude to a stranger sight. It leads to a high circular rampart of earth enclosing an area of some 28½ acres, in which, like a beautiful parasite, there has grown up an old English village. Inside this vast rampart stand other stones, with three smaller circles within. The ravages of man, more than of Time, have greatly reduced the number of these stones, visible and standing. There was once some three hundred of them. Aubrey saw only a few, Stukeley was not much more fortunate. To-day, thanks to the labours of Mr. Keiller and his staff, the miracle of Avebury is returning. Fallen stones have been erected, buried stones have been dug out, and the site of lost stones has been traced and marked. What was once the outstanding archæological disgrace of Britain is being wiped out.

When Mr. Keiller began his excavations there were only

four stones standing, though Aubrey had seen seven. There are now over thirty in the great outer circle. To facilitate his work Mr. Keiller has had to purchase part of the village, remove derelict cottages, recover stones incorporated in walls and farm buildings. Little by little, with infinite patience and labour, the ancient monument is being restored.

The great bank enclosing this astonishing monument towers up some fifty feet from the bottom of the ditch. One can walk round the rampart except for one small sector where the village has broken it down and encroached. The singular thing about this bank is that the ditch is on the inside and not the outside, which suggests that it was not constructed for any defensive purpose. Why was this vast monument raised with such immense labour, for all the digging must have been done with ox-shoulder blades. Three thousand five hundred years ago this task was completed. Here in North Wiltshire, in the dim prehistoric age, was created a religious or ritual centre to which people came from all parts of the earth.

There is much we shall never know concerning this vast circle of stones, the whole shut in by a gigantic bank and ditch, and approached by a long double avenue of stones. This phenomenon belongs to the Early Bronze Age, known since certain types of pots have been discovered there. These circles of standing megaliths are connected with the lost ritual of a people who believed in spirits or gods dwelling within them. The inside ditch supports the ancient belief that, since spirits cannot pass such barriers as high banks, deep ditches, fire and water, they could be thus retained within. The belief that this was a ritual site is further borne out by the absence of any signs of domestic life, such as hut sites, pottery or cooking hearths. It is certain, however, that burials took place near these megaliths, and that they were contemporary with the erection of the stones. These immense stones were probably brought to the site on rollers and erected by means of wooden stakes and rawhide ropes, for to the Beaker people horses and wheels were unknown.

What were these people like? Certainly they were not savages. They were an agricultural race, possessing cattle and sheep, hunters of the wild ox and deer, makers of pottery and implements of stone and bone. They had nothing to do with serpent worship or Druidic rites, for they lived as long before the time of the Druids as we live after them. They have disappeared for ever with the mists of Time, taking their rites and their beliefs with them. Only the great stones, the vast earthworks with their deep ditch remain. The Saxon village that broke roads through that rampart, and nestled within for safety these twelve hundred years, is a comparative modern growth.

It is a sight of such mysterious majesty that one gazes in awe at this monument of a vanished race. One also gazes in admiration at the formidable task undertaken by Mr. Keiller. The owner of a successful marmalade business, he has devoted his wealth, time and knowledge to the salvaging of this rapidly disappearing memorial of a people dwelling here over three thousand years ago. Indifference and deliberate ruin worked havoc for generations. These stones impeded ploughing, and were therefore to be got rid of. Religious fanaticism also played its part. The Edict of Nantes, in the twelfth century, urged the faithful to pull down these pagan memorials.

In the excellent museum which Mr. Keiller has created for our delight, in the former stables of the lovely Elizabethan manor-house he inhabits at Avebury, we see the relics of a destroyer who was destroyed at his work. During the excavation of a buried stone a complete skeleton was uncovered in the narrow space between the stone and the pit being prepared for its burial. The stone had apparently fallen too soon, trapping the digger, breaking his neck and fracturing his pelvis. Now note how constructive the evidence becomes. Near the skeleton's left hip there was a discoloured patch of soil, representing the remains of a leather pouch, and upon it the pouch's contents, three coins, two silver pennies of Edward I, minted in Canterbury in 1307, and a sterling of the City of Toul. The sterling was a counterfeit coin made in the Middle Ages by a gang of counterfeiters living in France, who did a brisk business making fake coins which they traded for the genuine silver coins of the English mint.

Nor is that the end of one's knowledge of the unfortunate man. Beside the skeleton was found a pair of pointed scissors, and a small iron lancet or probe, proof that their owner practised as a surgeon-barber in Avebury around the fourteenth century! The scissors, the probe, and the coins can be seen in the museum to-day, restored to the light of day after five hundred years in the unlucky barber's tomb. The skeleton itself has been given to the safe keeping of the Royal College of Surgeons, and rests in its museum.

Among the many interesting exhibits so carefully collected in Mr. Keiller's museum, converted from the picturesque eighteenth-century stables, with delightful ornamental piers, bell tower, weather-vane, clock, and Wiltshire stone roof, there is an illuminating chart showing the history of the great megalithic monument compiled from objects discovered on the site. It runs from 2000 B.C., the Neolithic Stone Age; 1800 B.C., the Beaker Sherd Age; through the void up till A.D. 200, the Roman Age, with a sherd of Samian ware; A.D. 300, coins of Constantine; A.D. 700, a Saxon pot and stone carving in Avebury Church; A.D. 1100, south door of the church; A.D. 1500, a penny of Henry VIII; A.D. 1601, south front of the manor-house; A.D. 1850, lid of nineteenth-century pomade pot; and A.D. 1900 —found actually while excavating stone No. 14—the broken top of a Keiller's marmalade pot! Which proves in Mr. Keiller a delightful sense of humour as well as of public spirit.

We will leave our interesting and delightful host at the gateway of his lovely manor-house, with its stone gables, flagged paths, long level lawns. He must hurry away to superintend further digging. Day by day new stones are probed for, discovered, and laboriously raised. Aubrey in 1663 saw thirty-one standing in the great circle, and showed them to King Charles. Parson Stukeley in 1724 noted eighteen, Hoare in 1819 ten. The vandals had been busy. What the fanatics left the farmer quarried, splitting the stones with fire and water, and carrying them off to cowsheds, cottages and walls. Stukeley reported Farmers Green, Griffin and Tom Robinson as great sinners in this respect. "I did not lament alone, but all the neighbours (except the persons who gained the little dirty profit) were heartily grieved at it."

There were other culprits. Dr. Troope of Marlborough confessed to taking many bushels of bones found outside the rings. For what purpose? "I made a noble medicine that relieved many of my distressed neighbours," he reported to Aubrey! But to-day, proud of the fame the monument is winning, the whole village co-operates with Mr. Keiller. Of the original three hundred or so of sarsen stones which it is believed originally stood at Avebury, some sixty are now in position, and yearly their number grows. Stonehenge is celebrated, the fame of Avebury is yet to come. It fears no comparison. The circumference of the latter is 4,442 feet compared with Stonehenge's 1,107, and its diameter 1,260 compared with 300, the total area 28½ acres, compared with 1¾.

Charles II was well pleased. Even critical Mr. Pepys was astonished. He saw it on his way to Marlborough in 1668.

". . . rode all day with some trouble, for fear of our being out of our way, over the Downes (where the life of the shepherds is, in fair weather only, pretty). In the afternoon came to Abury; where seeing great stones like those of Stonehenge standing up, I stopped and took a countryman of that town, and he carried me and shewed me a place trenched in, like Old Sarum almost, with great stones pitched in it, some bigger than those at Stonehenge in figure, to my great admiration; and he told me that most people of learning, coming by, do come and view them, and that the King did so."

And having given the man a shilling, Pepys went on his way again, marvelling at the stones all around, "which makes me think less of the wonder of Stonehenge for hence they might undoubtedly supply themselves with stones." An unkind thrust at proud Stonehenge. After this reflection Pepys "did give to the poor, and menders of the highway 3s."

But we must journey on, back to the Bath Road, and in the opposite direction to the diarist. A great mound soon looms up on our right. It is Silbury Hill, at the side of the old Roman way. Like Avebury it is a mystery. No one knows when it was created nor why. It is probably the largest artificial mound in Europe, one hundred and thirty feet high and conical in shape; it's an eerie object, commanding the smooth downs, gaunt against the wide sky. Aubrey brought King Charles and his brother James to look at it: "which they had the curiosity to see, and walked up to the top of it."

How did the mound get here? One fact has been established beyond doubt. It was here when the Romans came for they deflected their road to skirt it. Repeated excavations have done nothing to solve the mystery of its origin or purpose. With no cranes or engineering apparatus, with no shovels even, for they dug with antlers and oxen shoulder-blades, our prehistoric ancestors somehow contrived to throw up an earthwork that covered five acres and is three hundred feet round at the summit. It stands now as it has stood for four thousand years, a somewhat menacing, though mute, object in the treeless landscape.

Past Silbury the road dips towards Cherhill, and as we approach this charming village the prospect towards the horizon becomes sylvan, dense woodlands rising, wave upon wave, in the folds of distant Somerset. At Beckhampton, the first village we come to, the road forks, and here the old Bath Road took a left turn, running via Devizes, but in 1745 a new road, running more direct through Chippenham, the one we shall follow, caused a disastrous setback to the inns on the old route.

For a time there was desperate competition between the coaches running on the rival routes, but the Chippenham Road triumphed, being easier and quicker.

There now appears on the skyline an obelisk, which dominates the downs at this point. At we draw near it, and look left, we find in a fold of the downs behind us an immense white horse cut out of the chalk hill-side. This is the Cherhill White Horse, one hundred and sixty feet long. It is not ancient. It is the work of ingenious Dr. Christopher Alsop, of Calne, who made it in 1780, giving it an eyeball of glass bottles. He placed flags on this green amphitheatre, outlining his horse, and directed operations with a trumpet from a hill curiously called Labour-in-vain. But that he belied its name can be seen to this day, for his horse is a noble beast, dominating the countryside.

The obelisk which keeps it company on an adjacent hill was a whimsy of a former Lord Lansdowne, who erected it to commemorate the birth of King Edward VII, who, when he saw it thirty years later, observed, "You'll be able to put a tablet on it and commemorate my death, for it'll see me out." But unless something is done this splendid stone column, one hundred and twenty-five feet high, will come toppling down. The weather and neglect have loosened the stones, which bulge ominously in places. "This monument is dangerous," says a warning notice, and two red signal lights warn Air Force pilots who delight in using it as a pivotal point. This lovely column serves no useful purpose, but our age grows distressingly short of whimsies. So grimly utilitarian have we become, in an era of economic pressure, that I should hear of its fall with sorrow. And surely Lord Lansdowne would miss his ancestor's column, so plainly seen from his seat at Bowood? So with a prayer that some public-spirited person or society would "waste" a few pounds on keeping up the obelisk, I turned and descended towards Cherhill, which nestles in a crescent of trees on the other side of the Bath Road.

Cherhill is a delightful Wiltshire village not to be missed, however much the main road speeds one on. Its yellow and white thatched cottages peer at you over the hedges of narrow lanes. It is dominated by a great tithe barn, semi-ecclesiastical with nave and aisles, a hundred and eleven feet long. Its immense stone roof rides under the sky like an ocean liner. Its timbers are massive, five hundred years old, a thousand tons of them. What junketings, what rustic revelry this cathedral-barn has witnessed when Cherhill celebrated the Harvest Home. One can hear the fiddles hard at it, and see the ground-swell of dust as lusty Jimmy Eatwell whirls round Fanny Strong Duck.

Through the churchyard gate you can read the end of the story. A tombstone marks the resting-place of James Eatwell. He preceded the Strong Ducks, who lie behind. Did a surfeit of Strong Ducks finish him off, one wonders.

Over the churchyard wall is the country retreat of one's dream, low-gabled, mullion-windowed, with smooth green lawns lined with three noble beech trees. But everything in this village tends to rustic enchantment.

The Bath Road passing Cherhill, which we now regain, once had an unenviable notoriety. Early in the eighteenth century it was infested by some highwaymen known as the Cherhill Gang. As a warning to its members, the iron-banded corpse of a highwayman used to swing from a gibbet between Beck-hampton and Cherhill. There was one rogue whose method was to strip himself naked, and then, in full moonlight, leap out upon his terrified victim. Sergeant Mereweather, returning home one night from Calne Assizes, was told to stand and deliver by the very ruffian he had got off that day!

"Last month," records a newspaper of January, 1743, "a Captain in the Army, who was journeying to Bath in a post-chaise was stopped by two highwaymen, by one of whom he was told he wanted only a guinea, which he hoped to repay. The Captain gave him a guinea, and the fellow gave the driver a shilling and told the gentleman, if stopped, to say 'Virgin Mary,' the password for the day. A little further on the Captain was stopped by four persons. On his giving the watchword they raised their hats and rode off."

In July of the same year a highwayman of these Downs, Charles Taylor, was apprehended. As he refused to plead, the ancient punishment of *peine forte et dure* was administered. Originally this meant pressing to death by weights, and was thus defined:

"That the prisoner shall be remanded to the place from which he came, and put in some low, dark room, and there laid on his back, without any manner of covering except a cloth round his middle, and that as many weights shall be laid upon him as he can bear, *and more:* and that he shall have no more sustenance than the worst bread and water, and that he shall not eat on the same day on which he drinks, nor shall he drink on the day on which he eats; and he shall so continue till he die."

But Charles Taylor suffered a milder version in the form of twisting and screwing his thumbs by whipcord. The first knot of whipcord broke from the strain put upon it; a second knot was then brought to continue the torture, but at the sight of it Taylor consented to plead. The insistence on a prisoner pleading was due to the fact that if he refused, and died under *peine forte et dure,* he could transmit his estate to his children; after pleading, if found guilty, it went to the Crown.

II

Two miles along our route from Cherhill lies Calne, in a valley amid the hills. There is so much that is pleasant in the old Wiltshire town that one is sorry to record that it is dominated in the very heart of the town by a hideous red brick factory for curing bacon. Its giant chimney is so nicely placed that it is in the centre of the picture when emerging from the main porch of the grand old church. There is no question that

Calne owes its livelihood to this factory, for when the cloth-weaving trade vanished, the curing of bacon brought prosperity to a dying town. But the factory might have been situated elsewhere, on the outskirts. The Victorian tradition of the sanctity of industry, as seen in the brick hells of the industrial North, prevailed here in Calne. There is nothing that can be done about it; bacon has the town in its grip. The shops in the ancient centre boldly proclaim their pre-eminence in bacon. The whole town is "cured."

The factory apart, Calne has every reason to be proud of the Harris brothers. They established a tradition of tireless generosity to the inhabitants. The Harrises began business in a shop in the High Street as far back as 1808. Later, in 1847, George Harris emigrated to America, where he learned to use ice as a preserving agent. When the potato famine in Ireland cut off the supplies of pigs, George Harris opened a factory in U.S.A. and sent home cured pigs. He came back to England soon after, and from that time the business expanded to its present size, so that Calne is almost synonymous for Wiltshire bacon.

But man cannot live on bacon alone, and anxious to lose sight of the factory I went to the church. Here let me confess to an act that created a local sensation. With great fore-thought the Vicar had provided for visitors a thick volume of the history of Calne. It was late afternoon when I arrived. Time pressed, and, being closing day, all shops were shut. I could sit down in a pew and read through the fat volume, but since I wanted my tea, without which the Englishman grows faint, after a little hesitation I purloined the book and bore it across to *The Lansdowne Arms,* which faces the Strand, the open space where the bacon factory confronts the Town Hall, and the river is hurried underground from one side to the other. There comfortably seated before a tea-tray, I browsed in comfort and learned all I could of Calne. Three-quarters of an hour later, on returning to the church, I encountered a very agitated verger.

"Would you believe it!" he said. "Somebody's been and stolen the History of Calne! What folks there are about!"

"There are indeed," I replied, "and I can very well believe it, for I happen to have stolen it for half an hour, and, troubled in my conscience, I've brought it back."

The poor man, dumbfounded, stared at me and then at the book. It was probably the first direct contact with a confessed kleptomaniac.

"But what if the church had been shut?" he asked.

"In that case I should have taken it to the vicar."

"He's away on holiday."

"Then I should have left it with the parlourmaid, or the gardener, or the boot-boy—or I might have bribed the page-boy at *The Lansdowne Arms* to sneak in with it to-morrow morning."

By this time the agitated verger saw I was not to be made penitent. He made a last protest.

"You know you can't do that sort of thing here."

"Can't I? But I seem to have done it!"

He laughed now. In a few minutes we were good friends. A contribution to the poor-box put us on good terms. He was glad the book had been of use.

"Don't put a chain on it," I pleaded. "Another poor scribe may want to read it at tea-time also."

There, I imagined the matter ended. But a week later, entering a stationer's shop to buy some picture-postcards, a view of the church provoked a reminiscence. A week ago, it seemed, a writer, whose name I recognized as my own, had gone into the church, and stolen the guide-book!

"He stole it!" I repeated, registering incredulity.

"Well, not exactly, sir. As it turned out, he'd only borrowed it. He wanted to read it while having his tea at *The Lansdowne*

Arms. He took it back, but it gave the verger a shock! Fancy, he's writing a book, with Calne in it."

"I'm glad to hear it—and that you've the correct version. He did take it back—which is more than most borrowers do," I said.

"Then you've heard about it?"

"Oh, yes—I happen to be the thief," I replied; and thus gave a shock to a second person in Calne.

I feel now that whenever I walk through Calne small boys will point me out as the man who stole the town's History. I can only hope the vicar has forgiven me, and he will not depart from the forethought and kindness of putting a rare volume at the disposal of visitors to his lovely church.

A beautiful, narrow, winding old street leads one to the church, which has the distinction of having provided England with an Archbishop of Canterbury. This was the saintly Edmund Rich, who declined the office at first, preferring to remain the vicar of Calne. But he was carried in triumph by the monks into the church, where, before the altar, he prostrated himself, and accepted the call, sadly. As Archbishop he threatened Henry III with excommunication unless he mended his ways, and at the command of the Pope he preached the sixth Crusade, in 1237. After a stormy period he retired to France, where he died. He was canonized seven years after his death.

Calne also had associations with another saint, a wily one if legend be true. In 978 a Witan or Council met to settle an issue relating to the celibacy of the clergy. St. Dunstan was the celibate champion and while the heated debate went on between the celibates and the anti-celibates the floor suddenly gave way, killing fifty and wounding a hundred. But the Archbishop, surrounded by his friends, was safely supported on a beam. This seemed almost like a divine pronouncement on the heated issue, but the anti-celibates were ill-natured enough to suggest that the celibates had tampered with the structure of the floor.

There are many things of note in this majestic church; a modern carved screen done in memory of a vicar by his wife, an oak chest for church funds, with three locks, the whole deeply embedded in the trunk of an oak tree so that no one can run off with it, and a war cross from the Ypres grave of the son of the fifth Marquis of Lansdowne. This cross is in turn connected with a famous letter written by Lord Lansdowne in 1917, asking that the Great War should be brought to an end before either side had been brought to the misery of complete defeat. *The Times* refused to publish the letter, the *Daily Telegraph* did, and it fell like a bombshell, heard above the roar of a world in desperate conflict. Judging from the abuse it brought down upon Lord Lansdowne, it might have been a proposal to increase the bloodshed instead of an attempt to raise the quiet voice of reason, save millions of lives, and stem an avalanche of disaster for the human race. Lord Lansdowne predicted a later necessity of adjusting the world's trade and of settling territorial claims by judgment rather than force. The Allies would win the war, doubtless, but at a cost that would create a barren victory.

Never has a letter created such a storm, coming as it did from a former Foreign Secretary. Under a deluge of abuse Lord Lansdowne sank back into a silence he maintained until his death. The war raged on. How right he was, how feasible was his proposal at that stage of the war must ever remain debatable; but of the letter's nobility and its prophetic insight there can be no doubt in this disillusioned age.

The Lansdownes from their lordly seat at Bowood dominate Calne. The Earl of Shelburne, afterwards first Marquis of Lansdowne, was a patron of art, science and letters. He and his wife entertained the great literary figures of the day. "All that makes life worth living is at lovely Bowood," said Moore, the poet. It is a mansion in the Italian style, ornamented by a grand Doric portico, with an annex three hundred feet long, the copy of a wing of Diocletian's palace at Spalato. The view is magnificent; overlooking a lake, woods, a forest and the distant downs, where can be seen the White Horse and the handsome column at Cherhill.

Some famous figures have been entertained at Bowood—Dr. Johnson, Talleyrand, Madame de Staël, Mirabeau, Benjamin Franklin, Garrick, Moore, Jeremy Bentham, and Macaulay. One evening after dinner Dr. Johnson related to the company with great gusto the story of his famous letter to Lord Chesterfield. It so delighted the company that when more guests arrived later Lord Shelburne said, "We have had something better than dinner, but Dr. Johnson will be kind enough to give it again." "That I will not," retorted the stout Doctor, "I told the story just now for my own amusement, but I will not be dragged in as a story-teller to a company." There must have been an awkward moment, but one sympathizes with the Doctor.

Macaulay, who at one time was the member of Parliament for Calne, was a frequent guest of the Lansdownes. "We had mountains of potatoes and oceans of beer. Indeed Lady Lansdowne drank her beer most heartily on the only day that she passed with us, and when I told her, laughing, that she had put me quite at ease on the point which had given me much trouble, she said that she would never allow any dandy novelist to rob her of her beer and cheese."

There was another figure at lovely Bowood, Joseph Priestley. He was appointed librarian, and for some eight years acted as literary companion to the family. He had begun life in a Yorkshire farm-house, where he was born in 1733, and later became a Nonconformist preacher. But he had a passion for science, and we remember him now because he won fame as the discoverer of oxygen. There is a tablet by the small river at Calne where he carried out his investigations, collecting gases from water bubbles. When I went to view the stream at a place now called "Doctor's Pond," running behind Mill Street, I observed a small boy fishing. "So this is where Dr. Priestley

discovered oxygen?" I asked. He retorted brightly, looking up
from his rod, "Yes—it's what makes the fish so lively." I left
him dangling a worm in the sluggish stream, hoping to catch
the oxygenated minnows.

Dr. Priestley invented a terrifying name for his discovery
of oxygen. He called it "dephlogisticated air," which he prepared in 1774 by heating red oxide of mercury with a burning-
glass. He was a tireless investigator, of native genius. He had
taught himself Chaldee, Syriac, French, German and Italian.
He was fortunate in his contact with Lord Shelburne, who
gave him £250 a year and a house, took him travelling with
him on the Continent, and when he left his service in 1780
gave him a pension of £150 for life. Some men are born lucky
even in an age of patrons.

But Joseph Priestley, a most voluminous writer, could not
resist preaching, for which he had a passion. He went to Birmingham as a Nonconformist minister, and there encountered
James Watt and Erasmus Darwin. He became such a notorious
revolutionist that when a dinner was given to celebrate the
fall of the Bastille, although Priestley did not attend it, the
mob burned his chapel and sacked his house, incensed by too
much of his dephlogisticated air. He migrated to London, but
even there he was considered "dangerous," and the Fellows of
the Royal Society, of which he was a member, shunned him.
While at Bowood he had been visited by Benjamin Franklin.
Had Franklin turned his thoughts to America as the home of
the free? To America he went in 1794, settling at Northumberland, Pennsylvania, where he lived for ten years, until his
death.

Calne, which therefore had seen Mirabeau, Talleyrand and
Madame de Staël pass through its streets in the Marquis's
coach, has known other famous literary figures. Coleridge, a
hopeless drug addict, found a refuge here in 1814–1816, in the
home of kind-hearted Mr. Morgan. This guest, who must
have been a heavy responsibility, occupied his clearer mo-

ments by writing a play, *Zopolya*, but Drury Lane rejected it. The poor man must have had bright periods when all his charm shone forth, for little Hartley Coleridge recorded that while the people were "good, comfortable and unintellectual," he "always thought S. T. Coleridge more than usually pleasant here."

Mill Street, between the church and the river, has many memories. It saw St. Edmund pass down it on his call to the primacy of the Church, it saw the grim procession of bodies that were borne along it when the plague made it a *via dolorosa*. The plague had been brought back from France by Calne men. In 1562 the Prince of Condé applied to Queen Elizabeth for assistance on behalf of the Huguenots, and offered to surrender Havre as a price. The Calne men were part of this expeditionary force.

The early prosperity of Calne as a cloth-weaving centre was largely based on Edward III's permission for one John Kempe to import a colony of weavers from Flanders. "Happy the yeoman's house which one of these Dutchmen did enter, bringing industry and wealth with them," wrote Dr. Fuller. So large was the quantity of cloth manufactured in Calne that when, according to Evelyn, the diarist, an old knight wished to move some deer from Bowood to Spye Park, a distance of more than a mile, he drove them between two walls of Calne cloth!

The cloth trade was extinct by the nineteenth century, and Calne turned from wool to bacon-curing for its livelihood. In the early days of the new industry, which now slaughters one hundred and fifty thousand pigs a year, the workers wore blue smocks and clogs, and the clatter in the streets in the early morning made Calne like a Lancashire mill town. To-day, the white overalls of the employees give it the air of a tennis tournament.

Old Calne still survives, if not in the Town Hall that stands on the site of an ancient manorial water-mill, or *The Lansdowne Arms*, with its eighteenth-century façade, then in many of the Bath freestone houses that sit snugly in the winding streets. The village green is still intact where, on its triangular site, the maypole was set up and the feast of "Robyn Whode and hys merrie menne" was held. This green was the centre of the cloth-making trade, and some of the old building mills, converted into houses, can still be seen. But what brought back to me most vividly the Calne of the Bath Road in the height of fashion were two sides of an archway leading to a yard behind *The King's Arms* in the High Street. Down each side of the archway, well preserved, though forgotten of this generation, were a list of the coaches, and their times of departure. No horse now clatters in and out of that archway, no half-frozen passengers clamber up, no ostlers bustle around, no driver gathers up the reins. Empty and silent is the place, but how bravely and freshly in its various colours of yellow, maroon, grey and red runs the bold announcement!

Gloucester
Cheltenham
Birmingham
Liverpool
Manchester
The Eclipse
Coach
from this
Office
for
London
Every morning
at ½ Past 8 o'clock
Except
Sundays.

The Hope Coach
Leaves this Office
Every Morning
Except Sunday
for
Bath and
Bristol
Where it arrives
at 11 o'clock
In Time for the
Following
Coaches
Chepstow
Tintern
Monmouth
and
Hereford
also
Taunton
and
Exeter.

It is no use our waiting for *The Hope Coach*. We have missed it, by two hours, and two hundred years. It is now lunch-time on a summer's morning, and we have nine miles to go to Bath. We will lunch at *The Lansdowne Arms,* and then take the old road for the last stage of our journey.

CHAPTER XX

Corsham, and So to Bath

AT THE TOP OF CALNE HIGH STREET we take a left turn and find ourselves on a plateau, overlooking lower ground subject to flooding. When the route to Bath via Devizes and Corsham was put out of business soon after 1743, by the new road through Calne and Chippenham, travellers were informed that coaches in summer "may keep the turf for four or five miles together," travelling on this lower ground. Our own road keeps high, particularly if we are wise enough to leave the newer Bath Road and go via Derry Hill. For by so doing we bring ourselves to the Golden Gate, the chief entrance to Bowood. Erected in 1834 by Barry, the architect of the Houses of Parliament, this noble gate and gate-house, with gilded ironwork, fronts a green from which we have a superb vista of a deep valley and wooded hills rising in terraces of foliage. The village inn, *The Lansdowne Arms,* completes this setting of rustic England. The magnificence of Bowood is seen at the end of the two-mile drive to the house, where the great Doric portico fronts the deep ravines; the wide expanses and the great trees in the park recall the forest in which James I hunted. The first marquis was a man of culture, who told Dr. Johnson that "a man of rank who looks into his own affairs may have all he ought to have, all that can be of any use, or appear to any advantage, for £5,000 a year." We smile at this, knowing he had nearly ten times that amount to lavish on his tastes. The second marquis made short work of all his father had acquired. Out went books, pictures and rare furniture. The third marquis inherited a shell, and turned it into a palace.

The property, originally bought from Sir Orlando Bridgeman, the judge who tried the regicides after the Restoration, was extended, Sir Charles Barry adding to the noble work of Robert Adam. The third marquis increased an estate of seventy acres to a thousand. He bought works of art, he cultivated the acquaintance of men of genius. Chancellor of the Exchequer at twenty-five, in the "Ministry of all the talents" he left political life to live as a great lord should live. Gardens sprang up, looking down upon a pellucid lake, and from its terraces one surveys a splendid panorama over wooded country to the clear line of the downs. The Neptune Fountain is well worthy of the Villa d'Este. A cascade, a classical temple, an island, a heronry, terraces of roses guarded by bronze stags, great lawns, clipped yews, here Diocletian himself would not have felt the splendour of his setting unworthy of a retired Emperor. The house, its treasures of art, the gardens, the private mausoleum, the woods, the whole picture is that of a nobleman expressing himself in an age of unlimited wealth, such as England will never know again.

From the Golden Gate we descend rapidly towards Chippenham, our last town on the road. Ancient, stone built, its old market was once surrounded by inns in the great coaching days. *The Angel* still exists where, as Smollett told us, Peregrine Pickle's mother was a chambermaid. *The White Hart*, a famous hostelry, no longer does business, but it can be discovered, by its beautiful façade, its bow windows and balustrade. The coaches came in the town's back way, behind the church, passing along a street of lovely Queen Anne and Georgian houses, turning into the market-place. There is still a bow window of the old inn which commands a vista either way, so that ostlers and postilions, sitting within, could see the Bath or the London-bound coaches approach.

Pursuing with my shamelessly inquisitive nose the track under the ancient inn archway, I found some ruinous stables, the old brewery of the inn, and two Romanesque pillars which once supported the open balcony round the inn yard. What a commotion of horses, grooms, travellers, and servants this now silent old yard had seen. Men of great name and fame had ridden in over its cobbles. Cromwell had lodged there, putting his men in the church. By the arch there is a greengrocer's shop. A few questions revealed the fact that the business was installed in the ancient parlour, and over crates of tomatoes, cucumbers, and bunches of scarlet gladioli, rose the great arch of the ancient fireplace where the long dead generations, just come in from the dark night and the perils of the road, thawed themselves out.

For the next half-hour I stood on a kerbstone chatting with the Mayor of a town known to King Alfred, who resided here, and whose sister married a king here. Alfred, having defeated the Danes signed the Peace of Chippenham. But it is the late Mr. Joseph Neeld who seems to dominate the old place. His bust or his portrait I encountered half a dozen times. An engraving shows him in 1850 riding in triumph through arcaded streets to open a new cheese market. Cheese and cloth have been the basis of Chippenham's prosperity, famous for their quality, but these trades have suffered an eclipse. There was a time when the tuxedos, the dress suits of the United States, derived from this Wiltshire town, if of the first quality. The fine green baize of the world's best billiard tables came off the local looms.

Leaving *The White Hart,* now split up into shops and offices, and the Mayor, in despair at the vandalism that is sweeping away the old landmarks, I wandered back down St. Mary's Street. If I had had Miss Whissitt with me I should have penetrated a dozen houses, but I did not do so badly though I lack her firm insistence in the face of rebuffs. Doors flew open hospitably. As I was seeking a pamphlet on the church, the vicar's wife invited me in. I passed, from a charming Georgian façade, through a hall and a drawing-room, to a terrace set above an exquisite garden falling to the limpid Avon, with a wooded park for a drop scene. It was so sudden, so enchanting, in its summery gaiety that it took my breath away and I felt as if I had been transported to a hillside of Fiesole where the golden sun of Italy baked the lizard-haunted walls of a Tuscan villa. This was my second vicarage opening off an old street into a green water-meadow landscape. First Marlborough and now Chippenham, and the same sad lament of a lovely house too large for a limited stipend.

Past an old house, crazy gabled, with 1693 scratched on its front, I came upon a lordly portico leading to nothing but a bungalow office in which a solicitor's clerk did his best to satisfy my questioning. He had heard that the splendid portico had been taken in lieu of rent from some backward tenant! I tried to imagine an irate gentleman storming by a gaping front door, deporticoed for debt. I went inside the country lawyer's room, complete with letter-press, musty volumes, title-deeds and leather armchairs. Through a window I looked on an astonishing garden, one of those gardens that run in a riotous strip behind houses whose fronts hold at bay the noise of the High Street, Jane Austen houses, where every kind of pride and prejudice have prevailed. It belonged to a local antique dealer. Round to the front and in I went, and purchasing *en route*, through a dark tunnel of bric-à-brac, a set of twenty-six exquisite Wedgwood classical plaques, and four old engravings, I emerged in the garden that stretched alongside the churchyard wall down to a balustrade overlooking the vicarage and the Florentine drop scene.

It was a memorable moment, intoxicated by Wedgwood and Chippenham. I was called to earth by a plea for assistance. Did I, by any chance, asked the dealer, know who was the gentleman whose marble bust stood by the geranium bed? He had been out in the rain and the sun for a year, unsaleable, lacking an habitation and a name. But by his nose I knew him, as well as by that eloquent mouth which had announced to a spell-bound House of Commons the beating of the wings of the angel of Death. "John Bright," I responded, decisively. "You should sell him to the local Liberal Club." The poor antique dealer almost wept. "And I left him out in the rain!" he wailed. I could think of many other political busts I would have willingly left out in the rain.

One of the show pieces of Chippenham is the old Town Hall. Unfortunately it is not "shown," but no one seems to object to a burglarious entrance *via* the Fire Station—very well equipped but incongruously housed in a massive timbered hall where the Elizabethan councillors held their courts. By a side-door, hidden behind a fire escape, and up a staircase loaded with discarded leather fire-buckets, I penetrated to the ancient Council Chamber, a little room, oak-timbered, where for some four hundred years Chippenham was ruled. Immediately below stairs is the ancient town lock-up, a dark hovel, so that male-factors had justice sitting upon and above them. The old chamber is dusty and discarded now, but to what heated discussions of civic policy its walls must have resounded!

The outside of this little Town Hall is the oddest sight, twin-gabled with a whitewashed turret, and stone steps mounting to a studded oak door. Do not be deceived by the date on it, 1776. For once an old place is modest about its antiquity. It was ancient in 1776, which must have been a refurbishing date. The coat-of-arms, with the motto "Charity and Liberty" shines with fresh paint. When asking for the Town Hall, which is tucked away behind the Fire Station, do not be beguiled into visiting the present Town Hall, a Victorian horror in Bath stone attempting the grandiose.

The old streets of Chippenham offer a superb medley of buildings from the sixteenth century on. The heavy stone roofs have survived many reconstructions. A bridge with twenty arches spans the Avon at the bottom of the hill where a factory transforms Wiltshire milk into Swiss milk. The medieval church, in the top part of the town, stands well, in a spacious churchyard, surrounded by a flagged walk. Its octagonal spire surmounts a tower with a balustraded parapet. Chippenham is very proud of these parapets. Its inns and houses are frequently decorated with this stone lacework.

The mud and misery of earlier days is marked by a raised causeway that leads into the town, which until 1650 had only a nine-foot pack-horse track that went over boggy ground. In the fifteenth century a local woman, Maud Heath, gave the townsfolk a causeway leading four miles across country, and thoughtfully endowed it. It is still sound, despite the atrocious verses by which the Rev. Bowles, a local vicar, snatched at his own immortality by celebrating hers. These verses are on a memorial column erected by the Marquis of Lansdowne, who had a weakness for columns.

The road to Bath leaves Chippenham by Rowden Hill, and before descending it I looked almost with envy at the picturesque Poor Law Institution, where old men sat in the sun amid flower-beds, life's worries over, and green Wiltshire all around. But doubtless there is some fly in the workhouse porridge.

Down hill we go and are soon skirting the long wall of Corsham Park. The thought of getting to Bath must not entice us from taking a left turn off the main road. This side-road by the hamlet of Cross Keys leads us straight into the seventeenth century, for we are in Corsham's High Street, the only thoroughfare of a village built in golden stone hewn from the famous quarries around. On one side of Corsham lie the church, the great Elizabethan mansion, and the lovely park.

Across the road at the end of an elm avenue leading from the Court and the church, by a corner of a road curiously named Pound Pill, we find the alms-houses of Dame Hungerford, built in 1668. I talked to an old dame, sitting in her porch, stringing beans, and found her a completely contented person. No, they had no electric light, but lamplight was soft and warm. "We're a lovely eyeful, aren't we?" asked the old lady, not alluding to herself but to the mellow gabled building behind her. I paused before the Warden's house, to envy, if not him, his beautiful porch, with Dame Hungerford's arms above it and the tablet commemorating her founding of a free-school here in 1668.

I arrived at Corsham at two o'clock intending to be in Bath in half an hour. I did not leave until five. A walk down Corsham's High Street cannot be hurried. The excitement begins by the village fountain, opposite to which there is a row of white-gabled houses, erected by Flemish Huguenot refugees in 1600. Farther along the street there is an old porch to a door, with a slit in the wall on each side, a squint from which anyone approaching, up street or down street, is seen. They were mending the roof of a cottage as I passed, and I watched them anxiously, wondering if the mossy old stone tiles would be replaced with modern machine-made ones. But all was well, and the craftsman had maintained the time-honoured tilt of a renewed gable. A grand old house made me pause. Once upon a time it had housed a magistrate, I felt certain. It was now a Maternity Home. Two windows on either side a noble door, two storeys of five mullion windows each, all beautifully balanced; it made one wish to be an expectant mother and go inside.

Round a corner, like a shy spinster, dwelt a little old stone house, and behind it rose a roof that seemed to belong to a French donjon. At the end of this curving old street, its doorsteps worn down by forgotten generations, I came to *The Methuen Arms,* standing on a corner, by the roads to Lacock and Pickwick. In the inn yard at the back there was a large coach-house with a dovecote for a hundred pigeons built in the wall, all empty. On a post by the back door of the inn there was a notice "Ostler's bell." I pulled it, and it gave the ghost of a sigh, but no ostler came to life, no stable-boy showed a bandy leg. The deserted yard had not heard the rumble of a coach or a post-chaise for over a hundred years.

I turned back through the elm avenue by the side of the great

park and came to the Court. Its noble stone gables mark a balustraded Tower, the whole edifice a paean of praise to those
Elizabethans who built it in 1582. The entrance is flanked by
a riding school, a "folly" shuts out the encroaching village, and
high yew hedges guard its privacy. Mellow in the sun, it makes
a dignified ancestral home, worthy of the ancient manor. How
ancient one cannot be certain. Edward III gave the manor to
his brother, and the tenants "enjoyed" the privilege of punishment by the gallows, stocks and pillory. Queen Elizabeth
granted Corsham to Sir Christopher Hatton in 1572, who, rumour said, was the Queen's lover. Handsome, a good dancer,
the friend of Spenser, Elizabeth called him her *mouton*. He was
made the captain of her bodyguard when he was given Corsham, but he got into difficulties and sold it to Thomas Smyth,
a local man who made a fortune by "farming" the customs of
the port of London. Smyth rebuilt the present Elizabethan
mansion and finished it in 1582.

The house passed, later, to Sir Paul Methuen, in 1742. He
had been the British Ambassador at Madrid, which resulted in
the collection of famous works now exhibited in its gallery.
This family has given a Field Marshal to England, who became
the Father of the Army and the oldest of Field Marshals. Lord
Methuen was a brave but unlucky soldier who suffered defeat
and capture in the South African War. Worn out after a long
life of soldiering, he came home at the age of sixty-eight and
lived here in country peace until he was eighty-seven, a much
beloved figure. His first wife had died fifty-three years earlier,
after a year of marriage, and was carried from the Court to the
grave near by. Her last request was that the jewels she wore at
her wedding should decorate the church chalice. So the sacred
cup bears her name, with its large pearl set in a cluster of diamonds. For over fifty years Lord Methuen, taking communion,
touched with his lips a chalice set with the jewels of his lost
bride.

The old church was so richly endowed that William the Conqueror gave its revenues to the great abbey he built at Caen, France, where he lies buried. Of Saxon origin, it has much Norman work. If St. Lawrence's, Reading, boasts the body of the perfect bachelor, then Corsham can claim a pair of perfect brothers. John and Thomas Hulbert must often have heard old Parson Paget preach, for he occupied the pulpit from the coming of the Armada to the Civil War. If his preaching resulted in the rare virtues of John and Thomas, he should have a rich reward in heaven. Thomas, a clothier, "finished his course in a powerful prayer to God," we learn, and

> *John was the eldest, a man discreet and stout,*
> *Faithful and just in all he went about.*
> *By seniority he first obtained*
> *The blessed Port that Thomas since hath gained.*

Corsham, impoverished by Thomas's death, appears to have taken pride in his son James, whose puffy face, flanked with wings, looks down on the choir. He seems to have done well for himself, for we are assured, after many glowing verses, that he was so famous that merely to mention his name is enough. But surely Sarah Jarvis outdoes them all in her claim to fame, for just before she died in 1793, at the age of a hundred and seven, she had another set of (her own) teeth!

On entering this pleasant church I took an immediate dislike to William Tasker, Gent, who announces over the porch that he chose "rather to be a doorkeeper to the house of his God than to dwell in the Tents of wickedness." This sense of humble superiority has a smug ring.

At Corsham we are almost at the end of the Bath Road, and it is singular that a patron of this church was once the Abbess of Syon, whose monastery we encountered at the beginning of the road. Happy Corsham, from whose great underground quarries has come the golden stone fashioned so beautifully by generations of anonymous masons, masters of the Tudor, Renaissance and Gothic styles.

One is scarcely out of Corsham when one enters the hamlet of Pickwick, whose name immediately recalls Dickens's immortal gentleman. Are they in any way related? In a roundabout fashion they are. The novelist's eye scarcely knows what it acquires until the moment of inspiration has declared it. In 1835 the young Dickens, a reporter for the Press, was sent by coach to Bath to report a political speech. A few months later, commissioned by a publisher, he produced the *Posthumous Papers of the Pickwick Club*. It is possible that on his way to Bath he was aware he had passed through a place called Pickwick, but it is certain he had noticed the name of Moses Pickwick, the Bath coach proprietor, for he makes Mr. Pickwick and Sam Weller comment on the similarity of name as they take their seats on the coach. "Dear me," exclaimed Mr. Pickwick, quite staggered by the coincidence. But Dickens was not staggered, since he had created it.

There is, moreover, a connection between the Pickwicks and Pickwick. Moses Pickwick, the coach proprietor, was the great-grandson of Eleazer Pickwick, who rose from the position of post-boy at *The Old Bear* to that of landlord of the celebrated *White Hart* at Bath. Eleazer Pickwick derived his name directly from the village, on the road of which he was discovered as a foundling, and so named, by guardians, after the place.

And that is all Pickwick holds of interest for us. The hamlet belongs now to Dickens through the ages.

Two more miles, down a steep hill that affords a splendid panorama of the great valley and the rising hills opposite, we come to the last village, Box, on our road to Bath. Deep down are the quarries that made Bath a city of mellow stone. Box was known to the Romans who came here for quiet from the chariot-rattling streets of Aquae Solis. It was known at a much later date to Coleridge, who lodged there at a grocer's, and was scared out of the place by finding a barrel of gunpowder under his bed. Old as Roman Bath, its ornamental lock-up still stands by the bridge.

One mile more and we enter Somerset, and, four miles more, our journey of one hundred and six miles ends in all the loveliness of Bath, set in her crescent of hills.

Epilogue

FROM THE WINDOWS of my hotel, as I looked out on the quiet crescent of houses, a glowing sunset made Bath a city of gold. I began to wonder about the many famous figures who had walked these noble pavements, whose sedan-chairs had been set down before many a stately doorway. My reverie was broken by the entrance into the dining-room of a gentleman who strode up to an adjacent table, his wife panting after him.

He was an apoplectic man, triple-chinned, with a complexion like an over-ripe peach, the more flaming because in contrast with his lack-lustre spouse. With great care he ordered dinner, then blew his nose, and pulled out a watch.

"Well, it's not so late after all. I thought we'd make it by eight o'clock," he said.

"No, we're not so late," echoed his wife.

"We've done it in just under three hours."

"Yes, dear," she answered.

"Not very interesting—but a good road."

"Yes—rather pretty at this end, but dull out of London."

"Yes," he said.

He put back his watch, and looked at the sunset.

"Fine day to-morrow."

"Yes, dear."

The soup came. One of the chins wedged a napkin. Their heads bent to it.

London to Bath in three hours! Not very interesting. And I had taken over three months!

Should I tell them——

No. I went on with my fish.

AND SO TO BATH

By CECIL ROBERTS

Author of "They Wanted *
"Victoria Four-T